Maras

Maras

Gang Violence and
Security in Central America

EDITED BY THOMAS BRUNEAU, LUCÍA DAMMERT,
AND ELIZABETH SKINNER

University of Texas Press ◆ *Austin*

Requests for permission to reproduce material from this work should be sent to:
Permissions
University of Texas Press
P.O. Box 7819
Austin, TX 78713-7819
www.utexas.edu/utpress/about/bpermission.html

♾ The paper used in this book meets the minimum requirements of ANSI/NISO Z39.48-1992 (R1997) (Permanence of Paper).

Library of Congress Cataloging-in-Publication Data
Maras : gang violence and security in Central America / edited by Thomas Bruneau, Lucía Dammert, and Elizabeth Skinner. — 1st ed.
    p.   cm.
Includes bibliographical references and index.
ISBN 978-0-292-72860-8 (cloth : alk. paper) —
ISBN 978-0-292-72928-5 (pbk. : alk. paper) — ISBN 978-0-292-73534-7 (e-book)
1. Gangs—Central America—Case studies.　2. Youth—Central America—Social conditions.　3. Juvenile delinquency—Social aspects—Central America.　4. Central America—Politics and government.　5. Central Americans—United States.
I. Bruneau, Thomas C.　II. Dammert, Lucía.　III. Skinner, Elizabeth.
HV6439.C35M367　2011
364.106′609728—dc23　　　　　　　　　　　　　　　　　　2011025249

Contents

Acknowledgments

This book grew out of my gradual awareness of the increasing virulence and importance of gang violence in Central America. Beginning in 1996 with a program in Tegucigalpa, Honduras, I visited one or more of the Central American countries of El Salvador, Guatemala, Honduras, and Nicaragua every year until the present. All of these one-week programs were under the auspices of the Center for Civil-Military Relations, which held seminars for civilian officials, police officers, military officers, and intelligence professionals. Through discussions with these officials and officers, as well as casual attention to the local news media in Central America, it became obvious to me that street gangs were perceived as an increasingly serious problem in all but Nicaragua.

Through conferences and networking with officials, experts, and scholars who study gangs, I began to publish short articles on the topic. At the suggestion of Theresa May, editor-in-chief of the University of Texas Press, with whom I conferred during a Latin American Studies Association conference in Montreal, Canada, in 2007, I realized there is a real need to at least begin to fill the huge lacuna in objective knowledge on the phenomenon. This volume, the outcome of that discussion in Montreal, is the first book on Central American street gangs to be published in English. I immediately enlisted as coeditor my colleague Lucía Dammert, a specialist on police and security issues in Latin America who has published her research for the Latin American Faculty of Social Sciences (FLACSO) project on security in Latin America.

Dr. Dammert and I then spent considerable time and effort to locate and enlist authors who had done methodologically sound research on specific aspects of the topic of Central American gangs. With the help of Naval Postgraduate School instructor Jeanne Giraldo, whose scholarship is in the general areas of organized crime, drug trafficking, and terrorism, we conducted a good deal of original research in all four Central American countries so that we could evaluate and edit the contributions from the chapter authors. Although not finally included in this book, the contribution by Ana Margarita Chávez on gangs in northern Virginia enhanced our understanding of the regional dimensions of the gangs phenomenon. I also turned to Elizabeth Skinner, a copy editor and consultant who has assisted me in several of my earlier coedited book projects. She helped coordinate and integrate the overall project so that it could finally result in this book. Her influence is found in the content of several of the chapters, including the conclusion, and in the overall construct of the book.

We are confident that the present book is the most comprehensive and objective of any works currently published in any language on this topic. It is, however, only a start, and we hope that it will be seen as just that—a scholarly literature that confronts concepts with methodologically sound data.

We could not have produced this book without the ongoing support we received from the Center for Civil-Military Relations, which not only sponsored the programs in the Central American region where we collected much of the data but also funded the book project itself. We thank the center's director, Richard Hoffman, for his unwavering enthusiasm for our work. We also appreciate the help we got from FLACSO, especially in providing funding for the translation of the chapters by José Luis Rocha and Mauricio Rubio. Dr. Dammert and I are most grateful to our contributing authors, who did original research and responded faithfully to the many requests we made as we sought to develop a scholarly and integrated volume. Finally, we would like to thank Theresa May for encouraging us to develop this book and seeing it through to publication.

Thomas Bruneau
Monterey, California
November 2010

Maras

Introduction

THOMAS BRUNEAU

A common image of Central America in the popular media, both within the region and beyond, shows tattooed young men being hauled off to prison after having murdered a similarly tattooed young man from a rival gang. This shocking depiction of the murdered and their murderers, familiar to cities in most of Central America and several in North America, is frightening not only because of the violence itself but also because of some media reports that link the most violent gangs, called *maras*, to organized crime and suggest ties to international terrorism. Government policies seeking to crush or suppress the *maras* are politically popular in most Central American countries, as are mass deportations of illegal immigrants from the United States, including alleged gang members. With an average of 53 homicides per 100,000 people, El Salvador, Guatemala, and Honduras are among the most dangerous countries in the world.[1]

This book covers the two main gangs, the Mara Salvatrucha (now commonly known as MS-13) and the 18th Street Gang (Calle Dieciocho or Barrio 18), which originated in Los Angeles and have become the most important gangs in most of Central America. It does not specifically examine the other regional and local *pandillas*, or street gangs, aside from the *pandillas* in Nicaragua, nor does it include the huge number of gangs, including Hispanic gangs, within the United States. Except as they interact with the *maras*, the book also does not address in any detail the related, but separate, theme of organized crime. This is an important point, because this distinction is too frequently overlooked in some of the popular literature, as well as in much of the political rhetoric. Having said that, it is clear that in Guatemala and Honduras the *maras* are used as an instrument, or a scapegoat, by organized crime. The differences in relationships between the *maras* and organized crime become obvious in the chapters on El Salvador, where organized crime is not even mentioned, and Guatemala, where the *maras*, while constituting a public security challenge, are basically cannon fodder for the far more powerful organized crime syndicates.

The book consists of two main sections, all of which are based on primary research. The first consists of case studies on the four major Central American countries of El Salvador, Guatemala, Honduras, and Nicaragua, plus Los Angeles, California, where the main contemporary gangs in Central America originated. The five authors utilize a variety of methodologies and diverse and rich sources in describing and analyzing the dynamics of gang formation and development in each of their cases. The second section is yet more eclectic. It includes a chapter by José Miguel Cruz that compares different gang dynamics, and in particular the response to *mano dura* policies in Central America, and another chapter, by Enrique Desmond Arias, comparing Central American experiences with gangs to experiences in the Caribbean and South America. Mauricio Rubio's chapter is focused on Central America, including Costa Rica and Panama, and describes the responses to a standardized self-reporting questionnaire. While none of the case studies nor the comparative chapters focus specifically on security, the challenges to security are a fundamental theme in all of them, and provide the rationale for policies formulated by political leaders that are severely criticized by the authors in all countries except Nicaragua. The concern with security is the basis for Clifford Gyves's chapter on the use of intelligence to combat the gangs and is the fundamental reason for U.S. interest in the topic and the region, as discussed in Cristiana Matei's chapter. Thus, while security is not explicitly examined in any of the chapters, the concern with security in fact underlies the whole book.

Before going further, it is important to answer two questions: what exactly is a *mara*, and what makes the *maras* different from other street gangs? Throughout this volume, the authors take care to distinguish between the *maras* and other types of street gangs, known in Spanish as *pandillas*. Technically, the term *"mara"* refers specifically to the gangs known as MS-13 and 18th Street, and their affiliates throughout the Western Hemisphere. As Al Valdez describes in Chapter 1, MS-13 began as a Los Angeles barrio gang called Mara Salvatrucha, made up of young Salvadoran immigrants whose parents had fled their country's brutal civil war in the 1980s. While the exact derivation of the name is unclear, *"mara"* apparently signifies a fierce, tenacious type of Central American ant, *"salva"* stands for El Salvador, while "*trucha*" is something like "reliable and alert" in Salvadoran slang.[2]

The burgeoning trade in marijuana and cocaine from Latin America, along with competition for turf, drove a spiral of escalating, unprecedented violence in the 1990s between rival gangs on the streets of Los Angeles. A major shift took place around this time, when many Mara Salvatrucha *clicas* (neighborhood groups or cells) allied with the notorious Mexican Mafia prison gang, which controlled a significant portion of the cross-border drug trade.[3] It was at this time that the number "13" was added to the initials "MS" ("M" is the thirteenth letter of the alphabet) and came to signify affiliation with these extraordinarily dangerous Southern California gangs. The U.S. policy of mass deportations of undocumented immigrants, instigated in part as a response to these developments, helped spread both MS-13 and the 18th Street Gang to Central America, where the local gang cultures quickly adapted to the California *mara* style.

The use of violence is probably the most defining characteristic of the *maras*. Indeed, their unique vocabularies emphasize brutality and criminal activity, while initiation, ascension into leadership positions, and discipline are all based on potentially fatal violence. Researchers estimate that gang members on average do not reach thirty years of age. As part of the ascension process, new members eventually have to kill a person, for no other reason than to show they can. The implication of this is that once a gang member has killed another, be he from a rival *clica* or some other group, the killer is marked and can never leave the gang. Gang initiation rites, which involve merciless beatings, can be fatal. Women are initiated either through beatings or forced sex with some or all the male members of the *clica*. The *maras* fight very frequently, not only against the authorities but also against each other, for control of turf and markets, especially to sell drugs.[4]

Street gangs typically are loosely organized and highly localized; leadership changes frequently, and activities revolve around drug sales, petty crime, and turf battles. The *maras*, unlike most other street gangs, have shown a tendency in recent years to organize in a more traditionally hierarchical manner and to coordinate their criminal activities not only across the United States but also across North and Central America. They show no restraint in their use of violence, both against rivals and within their own organizations to maintain internal order. Recent reports suggest that the *maras* are becoming involved in cross-border human and arms trafficking, as well as the entrenched drug trade, with some suggesting that factions of MS-13 are evolving to resemble an organized crime syndicate more than a street gang.[5] As José Miguel Cruz points out in Chapter 7, unlike in the United States where strong legal institutions have kept the *maras* largely in check, weak governments, narrowly punitive policy choices, and a widespread cultural tolerance of extrajudicial violence have allowed the *maras* to essentially run amok in Guatemala, El Salvador, and especially Honduras, to the point that they challenge the state's ability to govern. Although there is little evidence that the *maras* have anything to do with foreign terrorist groups, their association with drug cartels may be contributing to the uncontrolled violence in Mexico's border cities and elsewhere.[6]

This introduction first establishes the political and socioeconomic context within which the *maras* have emerged and expanded to become a major concern for security both within and beyond the Central America region. It then highlights some of the main themes regarding the *maras* and links the chapters in the book to these main themes. The primary goal of this book is to provide as complete and objective an assessment as possible of the nature and scope of the *mara* issue in Central America. The coeditors of this volume therefore sought to assemble a group of experts who could bring credible, objective research and write with authority on their assigned topic. Major differences in the nature of the threat to security among the countries of Central America, and their governments' responses, led the editors to spend a great deal of time and effort on identifying and recruiting these experts, who come from a range of disciplines and methodological backgrounds. What currently exists on gangs in the English-language media is overwhelmingly sensationalist. Some of this reporting comes through police officers and institutions that have concrete, and subjective, reasons for portraying the *maras* as even more of a security threat than they may actually be. Such reporting tends not to distinguish among the very different experiences of gang activity from one country to another or the disparate responses by state institutions to the *maras*, or to consider the implications of these responses for the *maras* and security. Scholarly literature in English on the topic unfortunately is almost nonexistent, which means that this unreliable media reporting is given far more weight than it deserves. The literature in Spanish is somewhat more balanced, but as is discussed later in this introduction, and at greater length in Mauricio Rubio's chapter on gang violence (Chapter 8), most writing on gangs has serious problems of methodology. Furthermore, virtually none of the literature, in English or Spanish, deals adequately with the very different contexts that might help explain why the situation in Nicaragua, for example, is so different from that in the other three northern Central American countries. An exception is the work of José Luis Rocha, one of our distinguished contributors, who has researched and written extensively about the consequences of these disparities.

Another fundamental problem that has become clear during the course of this project is that the ways in which governments arrive at "official estimates" of the numbers of gang members in their countries are completely arbitrary. There is no standardized, realistic basis for estimating gang membership or the total number of gang *clicas*. In El Salvador, for example, the estimate of 17,000 gang members nationwide is based solely on those who have been imprisoned at one time or another. Worse, Honduras derives its estimate somewhat bizarrely from a reading of gang graffiti multiplied by some factor or other. If these most basic numbers are not reliable, how can any analysis of gang operations and their impact offer a sound basis for policy making? Since the early 1990s, researchers have attempted to overcome the paucity of useful data from official sources by going directly to the gangs themselves and conducting both direct observation and self-report surveys of gang members. Several of these surveys are carried out on a regular basis by prestigious organizations such as the Instituto de Estudios Comparados en Ciencias Penales de Guatemala (Guatemalan Institute for Comparative Studies in Penal Sciences), Vanderbilt University, the Asociación de Investigación y Estudios Sociales (Association for Research and Social Studies), and the U.S. Agency for International Development. Not only do these anthropological methods involve serious risks for the researcher that may in themselves skew the results, but there is every reason to assume that many respondents are lying, to make themselves look good and/or to intentionally mislead authorities. This fundamental and widely recognized issue of problematic methodologies is highlighted in several of this volume's chapters, including those by Sonja Wolf, Elin Ranum, Joanna Mateo, Mauricio Rubio, and Cristiana Matei. Clifford Gyves, in his contribution on the application of U.S. intelligence techniques to gangs (Chapter 9), echoes the argument made by these authors—that government officials must make the systematic collection and analysis of information a priority in any strategy to deal with the *maras*. At a minimum, this book recommends that a different methodology, possibly a social network analysis such as EgoNet, would likely prove more promising for studying these unique organizations.

First, however, this introduction outlines some general contextual factors regarding *maras* that are roughly similar across Central America, before turning to the variations analyzed in the chapters on specific countries.

Socioeconomic Development and
Democratic Consolidation in the Region

The main countries in Central America (with the exceptions of Belize and Costa Rica) are "new democracies."[7] Until the mid-1990s they were all under some form of nondemocratic rule in which the armed forces, along with other security bodies, supported the authoritarian governments and prevented any opposition within the general population from organizing and mobilizing. Not surprisingly, various groups came into violent conflict with these repressive regimes; in the case of Nicaragua, for example, the Sandinista National Liberation Front (FSLN) took power through a revolutionary insurgency against the country's right-wing dictatorship in 1979. Throughout the 1980s, with support from the Soviet Union via Cuba, the Farabundo Martí National Liberation Front (FMLN) in El Salvador was engaged in a vicious internal conflict with the authoritarian government. Several armed opposition movements fought one another and the violently repressive, junta-led regime in Guatemala for thirty-six years, with a disastrous loss of life.[8]

With the end of the Cold War, and the separate but interrelated dynamics of conflict in each country (the defeat of the Salvadoran insurgents' "final offensive" in November 1989, the electoral defeat of Nicaragua's FSLN in 1990, and the ultimate victory in 1996 of the Guatemalan Army), relative peace became possible across all of Central America.[9] Furthermore, in all but Honduras, which did not experience the same revolutionary polarization and armed conflict as the others, the peace processes were brokered by the United Nations, with various types of support from other countries. In all cases, the negotiations included measures to establish electoral democracies.

In a recent Congressional Research Service report on economic and social indicators, all four Central American countries under consideration in this book are classified as "lower middle income." Gross national income per capita (in U.S. dollars) covers a wide range: El Salvador, $2,850; Guatemala, $2,440; Honduras, $1,600; and Nicaragua, $980. (Within the region, only Haiti is designated "low income," with an average per capita income of $560 before the January 2010 earthquake. Now

Table I.1. Population and poverty in Central American countries, 2008

	Population (2009)	Poverty rate (%)	Extreme poverty rate (%)	Unemployment rate (%)
El Salvador[a]	6,162,000	47.5	19.0	5.5
Guatemala[b]	14,030,000	54.8	14.8	
Honduras[c]	7,473,000	68.9	26.2	4.1
Nicaragua	5,749,000	61.9	20.8	8.0

Source: Unless otherwise noted, the data in this table are from United Nations, Comisión Económica para América Latina y el Caribe (CEPAL), *Anuario Estadístico de América Latina y el Caribe*, 2009 (CEPAL, 2010), http://www.eclac.org.
[a]Poverty and extreme poverty rates are for 2004; unemployment rate is for urban areas.
[b]Poverty and extreme poverty rates are for 2006; information on unemployment was not available.
[c]Poverty and extreme poverty rates are for 2007.

of course, that figure is much lower.)[10] The United Nations Human Development Reports aggregate various measures of health, education, and access to economic opportunity and then rank all countries according to how well they meet these basic needs; the lower the number, the more developed the society. Data collected in 2007 rank the four Central American countries in the "medium human development" category as follows: El Salvador, 106—a sharp decline of five places since the last report, following a slight earlier rise; Guatemala, 122—down from 121 two years before and 118 four years before; Honduras, 112—an improvement of three places after steady decline over the previous four years; and Nicaragua, 124—showing the steepest decline, from 110 and 120 in earlier reports. (For comparative purposes, the United States is number 13 and Niger is in last place at number 182. Pre-earthquake Haiti was at 149, while Panama at 60 and Costa Rica at 54 are the only two Central American countries in the "high human development" category.)[11] In short, these are lower-income countries with correspondingly inadequate levels of economic and social development. Another source highlights the low level of socioeconomic development in a different way (Table I.1).

In addition to their political and socioeconomic problems, these societies face other "vulnerabilities" that have been outlined in an influential UN report specifically focused on crime and its negative impact on development in the region.[12] The report begins by highlighting what its researchers consider the main vulnerabilities: geography; demographic, social, and economic conditions; weak criminal justice systems; the region's long history of conflict and authoritarianism; and population displacement and deportation. There is general agreement in the literature on these vulnerabilities, and they can serve as a useful way to organize or highlight problems in the region, with implications for the emergence of gangs. While based on credible and comprehensive data, however, the report nonetheless has a major, and common, flaw in that it fails to differentiate between the countries regarding the implications of these vulnerabilities. The country studies in this volume show that the challenges posed by violence and the *maras* vary in extremely important ways from country to country. The authors' analyses of the responses by governments to the *maras* problem underscore the different causes of the highly complicated *maras* phenomenon and the outcomes of government strategies toward them. What this UN report does provide for our purposes is a sketch of the background of conditions in the region, against which this volume's chapters organize and highlight specific problems, issues, and ideas.

The Problems of Geography

The UN report begins with the observation that Central America's vulnerability to crime is due to its "misfortune of being placed between drug supply and drug demand."[13] Many scholars agree that there is a direct link between drug trafficking and criminal violence. Michael Shifter, president at the Inter-American Dialogue, a widely cited think tank for Western Hemispheric studies, represents the view that drug trafficking is responsible for the region's increase in violence: "The politically motivated violence that wracked Central America in the 1980s has been replaced by burgeoning criminality at many levels, including transnational and local, much of it a product of illegal drug trafficking."[14] In addition to drug trafficking, Central America's proximity to the United States makes it a natural corridor as well for the trafficking of firearms and people. The geographical explanation hinges on the extreme disparity of wealth between the United States and Central America. The amount of money to be made in the U.S. black market, by bringing drugs and people in and sending weapons out, increases violent crime because its participants do not resolve their differences through standard nonviolent mechanisms (i.e., courts of law). Additionally, combating illicit trade diverts limited criminal justice resources from the deterrence of violent crime.

Demographic, Social, and Economic Vulnerabilities

The UN study notes demographic links to crime. According to the report, "Most street crime is committed by young men between the ages of 15 and 24, often against their peers. The higher the share this demographic group comprises of the population, the greater the number of potential perpetrators and victims in the society, all other things being equal."[15] Violent crime is often attributed to economic factors as well. The report states, "Studies of the correlates of crime have found that the distribution of wealth in a society is actually more significant than raw poverty in predicting violence levels. It has been argued that stark wealth disparities provide criminals with both a justification (addressing social injustice) and an opportunity (wealth to steal) for their activities."[16]

A Limited Capacity for Criminal Justice

The report's third reason for extremely high crime rates focuses on the Central American governments' inability to enforce compliance with the law: "The citizenry, large portions of which may have traditionally regarded the law enforcement apparatus as the enemy, also needs time to learn to trust and cooperate with those charged with protecting them. Lingering suspicions teamed with transitional hiccoughs may strain this trust relationship. Corruption can derail it altogether."[17]

The justice and morality void left by state corruption and incapacity is often filled by vigilantes, gangs, and other local power brokers. Not always content to merely lord over their respective areas, these modern-day *caudillos*, or strongmen, often push out violently into new territory, resulting in clashes with the state. Where the state tries to co-opt these actors, its legitimacy is called into question and the rule of law is reduced to an arbitrary standard of local preferences. The battles between the drug cartels, especially in Guatemala, and the "ethnic cleansing" seen in Guatemala and Honduras are widely perceived to somehow involve the sufferance of some level of the state.

Displacement and Deportation

A significant Central American diaspora of generally extremely poor refugees reached the United States (where they were not recognized as refugees in legal terms) after fleeing from the Central American civil wars of the 1980s and early 1990s. According to the UN report, "There is a widely held belief in both Central America and the Caribbean that recent crime troubles can be tied directly to criminal deportees."[18] Many policy makers in Central America claim that the deportation of large groups of illegal immigrants from the United States, many with criminal backgrounds, overwhelms their justice capacity and further destabilizes the region. (While Cris Matei specifically addresses this issue in Chapter 10, other contributing authors and the editors do not find convincing empirical support for this perception from the available data.)

A History of Conflict and Authoritarianism

The report includes psychological trauma, warlike mind-set, weak state capacity and legitimacy, and police militarization as legacies of the Central American civil wars. It suggests that "violence can become 'normalized' in communities where many people were exposed to brutality, and may be tacitly accepted as a legitimate way of settling disputes, particularly where the state continues to be viewed as incompetent, corrupt, or biased."[19] Support for this perception can be found in the research for several chapters in this book.

With data organized in the five categories outlined above, the UN report attempts to capture and explain broad aspects of the Central American crime problem, but it does not analyze cross-country variations in the manifestation of violence or the possible causes of violent crime. Rather, the result is a list of conditions that contribute to the problem of violence in general, without any attempt to account for the variations across different countries. Nevertheless, with the addition of the two factors mentioned earlier—the fragility of new democratic institutions and chronically low socioeconomic development—it is possible to begin to comprehend the context within which criminal activity, including that promoted by the *pandillas* and *maras*, takes place and, in these problematic societies, the seriousness of the challenge it poses. The main thrust of this book, however, is seek factors that can explain *variations* in the emergence and impact of the *maras* throughout Central America and the implications of those variations for security.

Emergence of Gangs in Central America

As Cruz notes in Chapter 7, one foreign researcher, Heidrun Zinecker, proposed a useful characterization of postwar Salvadoran security policies, consisting of three strategic phases.[20] The first phase was a transition period, in which new institutions of public security were established, and little or no attention was paid to issues of crime and gangs. In the second phase, criminal violence and gangs came into the spotlight of the public security institutions, and some scattered measures and reforms and counterreforms were enacted to tackle the growing problem of crime. As Zinecker argued, these measures laid the groundwork for the repressive policies to come. The third stage in the evolution of security policies was characterized by the enactment of repressive, indiscriminately applied security policies with tough-sounding names such as "zero tolerance" and "*mano dura*" (heavy hand). Cruz observes that these plans were modeled to some degree on the zero-tolerance policies of large U.S. cities like New York and encouraged by U.S. law enforcement agencies such as the FBI and the Drug Enforcement Agency, which were working with Central American governments to control crime. Although these heavy-handed security policies are regarded not only as failures but actually as counterproductive in all three of the countries where they were implemented (El Salvador, Guatemala, and Honduras), none of these countries has developed a new policy despite changes of government in both El Salvador and Honduras in 2009.

Diverse Experiences with the Gangs in Central America

Much about the variability of the gang situation in Central America is conveyed in Table I.2. For instance, there are far fewer gang members in Nicaragua than in the other three countries, and neither of the *maras*—MS-13 or 18th Street—is found in that chronically poor, conflict-ridden country. In addition, Nicaragua is seen to be significantly different from the other three countries in its homicide rate. Also clear from the table is that El Salvador's incarceration rate for gang members is extremely high relative to the rates in Guatemala and Honduras.

There is much that is disturbing, even shocking, about the *maras*. The National Civilian Police in El Salvador (known by the Spanish acronym "PNC") report that *maras* are involved in illicit drug sales, extortion, prostitution, homicide, and the illegal movement of drugs, people, and

Table I.2. Gangs and homicide rates in Central America

Country	Estimated number of gang members	MS-13 and 18th Street Gang in country?	Number of MS-13 and 18th Street members in prison	Homicide rate per 100,000 (2008)
El Salvador	17,000	Yes	7,000	55
Guatemala	32,000	Yes	400	46
Honduras	24,000	Yes	800	58
Nicaragua	4,500	No	—	13

Source: The data for this table come from several sources. The gang member numbers and presence or absence of MS-13 and 18th Street are from material provided by Dr. Humberto Posada of the Policía Nacional Civil at anti-*pandillas* conferences held in San Salvador, El Salvador, in 2007 and 2008. The numbers of prisoners are from the author's interview with Ismael Rodríguez Batres, deputy director general of prisons for El Salvador, 27 March 2009, San Salvador, and subsequent e-mail communication, 13 March 2009. The 2008 homicide rates were assembled from data from various sources provided by José Miguel Cruz.

arms across borders. In fact, these criminal activities are very similar to those described by Al Valdez in Chapter 1 on the evolution of the *maras* in Los Angeles. According to interviews with officials, extortion is the most common and regular source of funds for most of the *maras* in most of the Central American countries.[21] They increasingly arm their members with heavier weapons, including M-16s and AK-47s. Members define themselves in contrast to the rest of society and other gangs by wearing unique tattoos, using their own symbols and graffiti, and communicating through a bizarre language and hand signals. Each *mara clica* has its own elaborate internal rules as to when a gang member can fight, what the punishment will be for certain behaviors, and what is required if a fellow *clica* member is killed.

Elin Ranum, in her chapter on *maras* in Guatemala (Chapter 3), describes in convincing detail both the push and pull factors that cause young people to join a *mara*, despite the knowledge that the most likely way out is through an early death. To her more general explanation, Rubio (in Chapter 8) adds a unique and disturbing perspective regarding the attraction of the combination of power and sex that only those very close to, or involved in, the *maras* could begin to debunk with any credibility. If the causes of *mara* membership were due only to socioeconomic factors, however, Nicaragua would be at the top of the list of Central American countries in terms of *mara* membership, yet as José Luis Rocha clearly details in Chapter 5, it ranks at the bottom for very specific reasons.

Indeed, what stands out clearly in Table I.2 are the differences between Nicaragua and the other countries of this study. Nicaragua has a large number of *pandillas* but relatively little violence, and neither MS-13 nor 18th Street has gained a foothold in the country. Rocha deals specifically with the factors that make Nicaragua, despite a lower level of socioeconomic development than that of the other three countries, less vulnerable to violence and the influence of the *maras*. For instance, he notes that most Nicaraguan immigrants to the United States in the 1980s tended to be from the middle and upper classes and, instead of going to Los Angeles, went to Costa Rica and Miami, where they were embraced as refugees by the Ronald Reagan administration. Thus, their children were far less vulnerable to gang culture than their poor, undocumented Salvadoran counterparts in Los Angeles. Rocha also calls attention to Nicaragua's low population density, which meant that plenty of state-owned land could be given away to demobilized militia and insurgent fighters. This option was not available in El Salvador and Guatemala. Finally, unlike its neighbors, Nicaragua carried out an effective disarmament campaign that destroyed the large majority of weapons used in the country's civil war.

Even more important to Nicaragua's atypical experience with gangs, however, are political and security factors such as the continuing relationship between the revolutionary party—the FSLN—and Nicaragua's military and police forces after the party lost power in 1990. Rocha notes, "As a result [of this unique relationship], Nicaraguan society's relations with the state's security apparatuses are less tense and more legitimate in comparison with those in the north of Central America, where there are accusations that the military and the police are involved with drug trafficking, interfere with civil powers, and participate in bloody 'social cleansing' operations." The way the security forces later reacted to nascent gangs also was completely different from the response in the other countries, as Rocha observes: "The guerrilla origin of the National Police was a determining element in the treatment of gangs. Differing from their Central American counterparts, who have advocated stigmatizing gang activity as organized violence, the higher officials of the Nicaraguan police saw young gangsters as new rebels who were experimenting with social and generational conflict [rather than as threats to citizens' security]."

Rocha's analysis directs our attention to the role of deportation from the United States, particularly from Southern California, in both stimulating and sustaining the *mara* phenomenon in Central America. The gang problem in Los Angeles, as noted earlier, is extraordinarily pervasive and violent. The transnational reach of the *maras*, their involvement in the trafficking of contraband, and the burgeoning number of homicides due to gang violence raise very serious issues about security, not only in Central America but also in the United States. If Los Angeles, with a sound legal system and an extremely rigorous and well-funded penal system, cannot stem the tide of gang violence, how can anybody expect that a small and poor country in Central America could do any better? In their country studies for this book, Wolf, Ranum, and Mateo take a critical look at the effect of deportations on El Salvador, Guatemala, and Honduras, respectively. Although the United States still deports some 25,000 persons per year back to El Salvador and 30,000 back to Honduras,[22] none of these authors credits deportations as the key factor in the ongoing growth of Central American *maras*. The initial wave of deportations in the mid-1990s unquestionably influenced the dynamic and style of the Mara Salvatrucha and the 18th Street Gang as they emerged in the region, but those and subsequent deportations are not the reason gangs have taken such a hold on these societies.

Diverse Responses to Gangs

The different ways in which the Central American nations have responded to street gangs can best be understood by exploring how each government has chosen to define and confront challenges to public security. Rocha's analysis in Chapter 5 emphasizes the important differences in how Nicaraguan society views gang activity and makes policy to deal with it. "National security," or more precisely the security of the nation-state, refers to safeguarding the state's sovereignty over the territory and population within its borders and implies that the state should have policies to confront threats to that sovereignty. "Public security" connotes the maintenance of civil order necessary for basic societal functions (for example, commerce, transportation, and communications) and the rule of law. Finally, "citizen security" refers to the capacity of individuals and groups to exercise their political, economic, and civil rights.[23] Given the problematic level of democratic consolidation in Honduras, Guatemala, and El Salvador, the *maras* could threaten, and indeed are demonized publicly as threats to, all three levels of security. Citizens in some neighborhoods cannot go about their lives without fear of being robbed or killed. Businesses, mainly shops and transport providers, are prevented from operating unless they pay off the *maras*. Whole sections of cities, such as Guatemala City and Tegucigalpa, are under the control of *maras*, which fight each other over their turfs.[24] The resultant expansion of private security forces and vigilante and paramilitary groups further undermines the state's credibility and thus its flexibility in making policies to tackle the problem.

In Chapter 9, Clifford Gyves discusses the potential contribution that effective intelligence could make toward dealing with the *maras* threat. As noted earlier, solid knowledge about the *maras* in the scholarly and policy literature remains distressingly thin. Gyves describes in detail how a well-designed and well-implemented intelligence strategy can make a critical difference to both police and policy makers, who have seen that the strategies implemented so far in El Salvador, Guatemala, and Honduras yield ineffective and counterproductive results. Besides being very cost-effective, a properly planned and funded intelligence program that provides credible, real-time information on the *maras* could also be of tremendous value to both law enforcement and security strategists.

Since 2003 both the Salvadoran and Honduran governments have implemented *mano dura* legislation, with a very strong emphasis on law enforcement, as their primary policy to curtail the spread of gangs. El Salvador's *mano dura* policies, inaugurated in 2003 by the administration of President Francisco Flores, called for zero tolerance of gang activity, combined with the use of repressive police tactics to punish criminal behavior. Its follow-up, President Antonio Saca's 2004 Súper Mano Dura, offered more of the same, while increasing the power of the national police to make arrests without evidence of a crime. The legislation is highly subjective regarding the criteria that identify someone as a gang member, leeway that gives the Salvadoran police the authority to question and ultimately arrest young men and women without due process of law. Appearance and social background set the foundation for profiling, even though in many Central American cities, as Rubio notes in Chapter 8, crime and violence are by no means exclusive to the disadvantaged. Ultimately, however, these massive detentions have led to few actual convictions for crimes.

The Honduran government's 2003 Ley Antimaras (Anti-gang Law) mirrored much of what El Salvador already had put into practice with the original Mano Dura law: a strong emphasis on law enforcement based on a subjective interpretation of gang involvement that consequently led to indiscriminate arrests. Both countries' anti-gang legislation also stipulated extremely punitive changes in the legal processing of accused gang members, such as harsh mandatory sentencing and, in El Salvador, trials in adult court even for children as young as twelve years of age.[25] In Honduras, anti-gang legislation stiffened the maximum prison sentence for adults involved in gang activity from twelve to thirty years.[26]

Although Guatemala never formally adopted a *mano dura* approach, the authorities effectively implemented one in Plan Escoba (Operation Broom) in 2004. As Elin Ranum describes this plan in Chapter 3: "This crackdown strategy consisted merely of the massive and indiscriminate detention of thousands of youths suspected, sometimes rightly and often wrongly, to have some relations to gangs. In the absence of any specific legislation that penalized gang membership, it became common practice among prosecutors to manipulate established judicial norms in their efforts to find legal support for the detentions."

Due to the growing awareness that the *mano dura* measures were not working, and under domestic and international pressure regarding human rights abuses associated with the policies, all three countries have retreated from them. None of them, however, has to date offered any new strategies to combat the *maras*. All of the authors in this book agree that the *mano dura* policies failed to do anything substantive to curtail the *maras* and instead actually contributed to their strength by putting thousands of disaffected youths in prison alongside hardened gang members. When I interviewed senior police officials in both El Salvador and Honduras in 2008, they stated unequivocally that from the beginning they knew these policies would only make things worse. It is in this context that the chapter by José Miguel Cruz is highly relevant. He deals with the political economy of formulating and implementing countergang strategies and raises the question of whether these nascent democracies can do much beyond implement heavy-handed policies. The population, in no small part thanks to sensational media coverage, is terrorized by street violence, and it is easy for politicians to run, and win, on campaign platforms that commit them to repressive policies. Indeed, senior Salvadoran PNC officials interviewed in 2009, and a wider group of officers and officials interviewed in 2010, invariably could characterize these policies only in the context of electoral politics. Chapter 6, by Enrique Desmond Arias, takes us beyond Central America to demonstrate similarities with other Latin American and Caribbean countries. In the end, we cannot escape the conclusion that any analysis of the rise of gangs, and of organized crime for that matter, must be understood in the context of state formation and state behavior.

Going Forward

While the underlying strategy that emphasizes law enforcement over prevention in El Salvador has not changed, the government has developed a tactical institutional mechanism that enables the PNC and elements of the army to jointly combat the *maras*. Beginning in 1995, Plan Guardian combined members of the PNC with federal soldiers in joint task forces, to maintain order in rural areas where police coverage was spotty. In 2000 the plan was expanded to urban areas where the *maras* problem was perceived to be critical, under the rubric of joint anti-delinquency task forces. Among the nascent democracies of Central America, the establishment in El Salvador of a constitutional basis for the armed forces to support the police in certain circumstances is extremely important. Based on information gathered in interviews in 2008 and 2009 with military officers, police officials, and civilian prison officials, these joint units work fairly well at dissuasion and at keeping the *maras* under some degree of control.[27] After taking office in June 2009, President Mauricio Funes found himself confronted with a serious rise in gang violence, despite the supposedly positive relationship between his party, the FMLN, and the *maras*. His only policy innovation so far (as of December 2010) has been to send 10,000 troops to the streets for six months to dissuade the *maras* from violence.

In Guatemala and Honduras, there is no cooperation between the armed forces and the police, mainly because they do not trust each other and thus cannot work together. The military are sporadically sent into the streets by the presidents separately from the police. The impact of this is captured in the first line of a news report: "The government on Wednesday ordered the army to go to the streets to combat violence and the frequent multiple assassinations that have been seen recently in the main cities of Honduras."[28] In interviews with U.S. government officials and local high-level security officials in Guatemala City in July 2007 and in Tegucigalpa in August 2008, they all voiced a common theme concerning the degree of corruption in the national police forces. Indeed, the problem is so serious that PNC officials from El Salvador do not communicate with their Guatemalan counterparts before visiting Guatemala, for fear of assassination.[29]

Along with the joint task forces, El Salvador has implemented another anti-*mara* policy that helps explain the differences among the countries in the percentage of *mara* members they have incarcerated. Thanks to an arrangement in place since 2005, the Salvadoran PNC and district attorneys jointly conduct investigations of criminal activities. They have seventy-two hours to decide whether or not they are going to charge a suspect. If they go ahead with prosecution, the suspect goes before one of the eight judges in the country who specialize in gang crimes. If they decide not to prosecute, the suspect is set free. The legal system, and the process for dealing with suspected gang activity, thus are fairly sound; gang members who are convicted go to prison for an average of between ten and thirty years. This is not a solution to the *maras* problem, however, and there is widespread and growing awareness in El Salvador that no ready solution is presently available, but the combination of the new joint task forces and an improved legal system does, in the view of police and military authorities, keep it a bit more manageable than it had been previously. As one informant on this issue put it, what is different in Guatemala and Honduras is that "there is no follow-through."[30] Indeed, Guatemalan legal expert Javier Monterroso Castillo notes the total lack of effectiveness in his country's criminal proceedings, in which only 2.7 percent of criminal cases result in conviction. He concludes that the criminal investigation system has totally collapsed in Guatemala.[31] Based on interviews in Tegucigalpa in August 2008, the situation in Honduras is little different. Indeed, the data in Table I.2 illustrate this point: of 24,000 known *mara* members within Honduras, only 800 are imprisoned.[32] In one personal interview with the author, a U.S. government official stated bluntly that there is indeed competition, rather than cooperation, between the Honduran police and the district attorneys.[33]

The obstacles to combating *maras* go right to the crux of politics and violence, including that carried out by organized crime in the region and supported by corrupt officials and elites. In contrast to the situation in El Salvador, organized crime, with its de facto impunity at all levels, is the overriding issue in Guatemala and Honduras. This point was made again and again during interviews in these two countries, where *mareros* (gang members) often work as *sicarios* (hired assassins) for organized crime groups. In El Salvador there is at least a mechanism not only to capture the *mareros* but also to put them in prison and keep them there. (The Salvadoran government is planning to construct four new prisons, which will hold 6,000 inmates.) Therefore, while capturing *mareros* and putting them in prison is not a satisfactory solution to the threat of gang crime and violence, as a tactic it works better than the current awful predicament in Guatemala and Honduras.

The topic of the *maras* is regional—some suggest that it is becoming global. The phenomenon is so diverse that no single discipline or approach could begin to capture it, particularly using standard social science methodology. The editors and authors of this book thus approached this project with the stated intention of setting a standard for research and analysis that would serve as a basis for further study of the *maras* in both the United States and Central America, as well as for innovative and enlightened policy making.

PART I

CASE STUDIES

CHAPTER 1

The Origins of Southern California Latino Gangs

AL VALDEZ

Although Southern California's Latino gangs are not the oldest street gangs in the United States, they are among the most emulated and fastest-growing. The members of the first Latino street gangs in California, which formed more than a hundred years ago, were of Mexican descent.[1] It is a long distance, both in time and type, from these early, loosely structured, neighborhood groups of disaffected immigrant youths to the power and violence of today's Mexican Mafia prison gang, for instance. Research suggests that street gangs can evolve and change as they grow in size and expand their illegal business activities—for example, by becoming more organized and developing a vertical command structure.[2] Transnational criminal activities like human, arms, and drug trafficking; the theft of intellectual property; and money laundering have provided new venues for the operations of some street gangs, while the opportunity for these kinds of employment is an incentive for gang members to migrate within and between countries.[3] The growing connection between the prison community and the drug cartels operating on the street also offers plenty of employment opportunities for gang members.

Police and judicial crackdowns on gang activity in the United States and many Central American countries, notably El Salvador, Guatemala, and Honduras, have set up what is essentially a revolving door by which gang members convicted of crimes in the United States are deported to the country of their birth, only to turn around quickly and make their way back north, often through human or drug trafficking pipelines. This circular flow of criminals has spread the especially violent *maras* gangs throughout the Western Hemisphere, resulting in what may be called the globalization of violent urban gang culture.

This chapter begins with a look at the origins and evolution of the most notorious "Sureño" street gangs of Southern California, Mara Salvatrucha (from which the term *mara* became generalized) and the 18th Street Gang (also known as Calle Dieciocho, Barrio 18, or Calle 18). The chapter then examines the growing role of drugs in gang culture, both at the level of street-corner dealing, which is how most gang members are involved, and at the level of international trafficking, which has been greatly facilitated by cooperation between some gangs and Mexican drug cartels. It examines the concept of the globalization of gangs, as a consequence of both law enforcement practices and criminal enterprise, and explores the relationship between Latino street gangs and the Mexican Mafia, a gang centered primarily in California prisons that has close ties to the Mexican drug cartels. The chapter goes on to describe the various peer, societal, and legal pressures that shape contemporary gang culture and how that culture continues to evolve under these and other influences. Finally, the chapter draws some conclusions about the ways in which gang culture has changed and the directions it might take in the future.

The Origins of the 18th Street Gang and Mara Salvatrucha

Unlike their later rivals, many of the early Mexican gangs originated among youths whose families had been in the Los Angeles area for generations but had been segregated over time into impoverished barrios (neighborhoods) by the burgeoning white populations around them. Later gangs coalesced around new immigrant enclaves within the barrios, where young people, whose parents had fled rural poverty and class-based violence, felt alienated and marginalized by both the dominant urban white culture and the established Mexican American population.[4] The 18th Street Gang had been started back in the 1960s in the Rampart area, by Latino youths, primarily of Mexican origin, who had been excluded from and targeted for harassment by the established local gangs.[5] Early Mexican gangs were protective of their barrios, which tended to be culturally distinctive and exclusive, and generally preyed only on outsiders. When the newest wave of immigrant youths in the 1970s and 1980s started to form their own gangs for protection against the established Mexican street gangs, this development helped break down the barrio-based tradition and increased the conflicts between the various Latino gangs, many of which began to accept members from both Mexico and Central America. Latino street gangs began to commit crimes in their own neighborhoods, and nongang members and undocumented immigrants became a new class of prey for them. Shop owners and ordinary residents, including women and children, began to be victimized by Latino gang members within their own communities.

El Salvador's vicious and protracted civil war, which lasted from 1980 to 1992, took more than 70,000 lives.[6] The pervasive violence, a weak economy, and a lack of jobs forced the mass migration of over one million Salvadoran nationals, most of whom settled in Los Angeles and Washington, D.C., between 1984 and 1992. Some of these immigrants already had ties with La Mara, a street gang in El Salvador. Some also had ties to or were ex-members of the Farabundo Martí National Liberation Front (FMLN), a movement made up of peasants trained in community organization and guerrilla warfare to oppose right-wing death squads and the repressive, authoritarian government in San Salvador. As with every immigrant population, however, most just wanted to start a new life free of oppression and violence. To date, there are still approximately one million Salvadoran immigrants who have resettled permanently in the United States.[7]

In Los Angeles, most of the newly arrived Salvadoran immigrants, a large number of whom were undocumented, settled in the Rampart area west of downtown. Unfortunately, many of them suffered from a type of culture shock as they tried to integrate into L.A. city life. Their transition was made even harder because, although they were of Hispanic ethnicity, these often rural and poor newcomers were not fully accepted into the existing L.A. Latino culture. This outsider status encouraged some of the local gangs and even unscrupulous local business owners to view the Salvadorans as prey, knowing their victims would be afraid to report crimes to the police for fear of deportation. Of those Salvadorans who got involved in street gangs in the early days, most joined the 18th Street Gang, one of the largest and most active street gangs present in the area during this time.

In a pattern that has become familiar, the predatory and dynamic Los Angeles street environment in which immigrant Salvadoran youths found themselves became the catalyst that compelled the first Mara Salvatrucha (MS) cliques to form, between 1985 and 1988, and encouraged those few Salvadorans who had joined the 18th Street Gang to leave it. It has been reported that the founders of MS were originally members of an L.A.-based heavy-metal "stoner" group who used music and drugs as a basis for socializing, and that their gang was first known as MSS, or Mara Salvatrucha Stoners.[8] Stoner groups were popular during this period in Los

Angeles because they offered many Latino youths an alternative affiliation, particularly to the 18th Street Gang.[9]

The MSS gang later shortened its name to "MS," or "Mara Salvatrucha" (the number "13" had not yet been added to the name). When MS
was first formed, membership increased rapidly because the gang initially
provided a source of protection, assistance, associations, and connections
for newly arriving Salvadoran immigrants and for immigrants who were
having problems becoming part of the community. By the early 1990s the
Mara Salvatrucha gang was large enough to influence street gang activity
in the Los Angeles area.[10]

Also by that time some California-based Latino gang families were in
their second and third generations, and fathers and mothers were passing their gang affiliation down to their children. This period also saw
some of the traditional practices of the California-based Mexican street
gangs, which had been largely territorial and chauvinistic, all but abandoned. These long-established gangs had come to believe that the turf
they claimed was theirs by right, no matter what changes had come to
the barrio. Because of this, many uncooperative or newly arrived shop-
keepers and homeowners were targeted for crime and extortion. Some
Latino street gangs had started to take over entire communities through
fear and intimidation.[11] There were no rules, except that only the strong
survived and that the more you were feared, the more respect, control,
and power your gang would have. One way to have this power and control
was through drug trafficking (discussed in greater depth below). Within a
decade, from the early 1980s to the early 1990s, California-based Latino
street gangs had grown tremendously and were having an impact on the
quality of life of many Californians.

The Changing L.A. Gang Culture in the 1990s

The 1990s brought a lot of changes for Latino street gangs in Los Angeles. By the early part of the decade, gang violence had escalated to an
all-time high, and Los Angeles had gained a dubious reputation as the
gang capital of the United States. In 1988, Los Angeles County reported
452 gang-related murders and had approximately 50,000 gang members
in 450 different gangs.[12] In 1990 the county reported approximately 690
gangs operating within its borders. By 1991 there were estimated to be
100,000 gang members and 750 different street gangs in L.A. County.[13]

Latino gangs continued to account for a majority of the L.A. street gangs and a proportional amount of the violence.

The notoriously violent African American gangs, the Crips and the Bloods, had formed in Los Angeles in the late sixties and early seventies alongside the emerging Latino gangs and became deeply involved in the crack cocaine trade within the African American community.[14] These two prevalent ethnic gang types in Los Angeles County—Latino and African American—had coexisted for years, tolerating each other's presence for the most part. Most gang battles had been confined within each ethnic group, rather than occurring between ethnic groups, but in the 1990s things began to change.

In 1992 the Rodney King verdicts were released, and Los Angeles was torn apart by deadly race riots.[15] The media focused on the African American community's frustration with the verdicts as the source of the riots, but the street violence also had an unexpected impact on local Latino and African American street gangs. The normal tolerance between the two groups seemed to disappear, and they started to become racially polarized at the street level. Major conflicts erupted between Latino and African American gangs on the streets, as well as in local jails and state prisons.

This "black-brown" rivalry continued to develop. Exacerbating this situation was that some Latino gangs, supported by the Mexican Mafia prison gang, became the main drug distributors in Southern California and, by the latter part of 1994, had established distribution networks outside the state. Some of these Latino gangs were of mixed race and had broken the gender membership barrier as well. Many claimed the title of "Sureño" (meaning "Southerner") even though they were not directly connected or related to the Southern California–based street gangs.

The 18th Street Gang had developed a reputation for being extremely violent and ruthless by this time. Some of the gang's members had begun to migrate out of California in an effort to start up new drug enterprises under the guise of looking for work. They could easily accomplish this goal by recruiting new members from the area they were targeting. By the end of 1990 the 18th Street Gang was nationally and internationally established. Anecdotal law enforcement evidence at the time suggested that the Mexican Mafia was putting pressure on some 18th Street Gang cliques to purge their membership of non-Latinos, apparently owing to a sense that 18th Street had gotten out of control due its size and involvement in drug trafficking.[16]

The Mexican Mafia and the Sureños

The Mexican Mafia prison gang, commonly known as La Eme (the "M"), emerged in the California prison system in the 1950s, among Southern Californian street gang members of Mexican descent. Its members organized themselves and quickly took control of prison life, particularly the flourishing inside drug trade. They also managed to keep their outside drug and extortion networks operating even when they themselves were in isolation cells in such places as the Pelican Bay super-maximum-security prison in Northern California. Many became wealthy running their clandestine operations from the inside.[17] La Eme was the foundation of the Sureños, whose name was a general term for Southern California Latino gangs that includes La Eme, MS, and the 18th Street Gang. Evidence suggests the Mexican Mafia today is a midlevel distributor of drugs from the trafficking cartels to the Sureño street gangs.[18]

In 1992, La Eme sent an edict to the Southern California Latino street gangs: they were to pay a tribute, a percentage of money based on the illegal activities in which the street gang was involved. This "tax" ostensibly was to help each gang's comrades when they were sent to prison. Because of the Mexican Mafia's thorough infiltration of the drug trade, well-known reputation for violence, and high-level gang status, many gangs paid the tribute. Some Latino gangs, however, including a number of MS cliques, maintained that the drug money they earned was theirs, and they did not see why it should be shared with the Mexican Mafia. This defiance of La Eme led to conflict between MS, the Mexican Mafia, and the Latino gangs that were paying the tribute.[19] To maintain their status and control of the streets, the Mexican Mafia put the non-taxpaying gangs and gang members on a "green light" list, which simply meant that it was open season to attack or kill them. The Mexican Mafia used some street gang members as muscle to enforce its orders, and there were cases in which a gang member would kill another member of his own gang on orders from La Eme. This action was taken even though, at the time, the Mexican Mafia was publicly advocating that Latino street gangs stop the escalating violence between them.[20]

The opposition to paying the Mexican Mafia tax nevertheless grew to the point that some Latino gangs started calling themselves "green lighters." They were proud that they were tax-free and would advertise it, even to the point of getting tattoos that included the words "tax-free" and "green light." Occasionally the gang graffiti would include the words "tax-free neighborhood."[21]

About this same time, Joe Morgan, a prominent leader of the Mexican Mafia, announced what became known as the Eme Edict—street orders to the Sureño gangs to stop drive-by shootings and other gang violence, a development the media helpfully publicized. This edict, according to several Mexican Mafia members and associates, was announced as a community service to decrease Latino street gang violence and resulted in a "gang truce" between Latino street gangs in Southern California. At least, it was presented and appeared that way to outsiders.[22]

It has become clear from testimony by gang defectors that despite the do-good publicity, the real motive for the so-called truce, or Eme Edict, was to allow La Eme to infiltrate every street gang and put a representative in place to enforce the collection of its taxes. Furthermore, as one such defector noted, "we already had it planned out that California would be carved up . . . into slices, with each member receiving an organizational turf."[23] The Mexican Mafia sought to extend its control over the Southern California Latino street gangs and to control drug trafficking in Los Angeles and surrounding counties, in part by monopolizing the use of violence.[24] The edict's motive at the time, however, was successfully hidden behind the public outcry to stop the gang violence.

The edict, whatever its motivation, clearly did not take effect right away, because the county still experienced 803 gang-related homicides in 1992, up from 771 the year before, and the majority of the murders still involved Latino street gangs.[25] Nor, in the end, did the falloff in gang violence in East L.A. last long. Nevertheless, to illustrate how powerful and influential the Mexican Mafia was, between April and September of 1992, after the edict was announced, there were no drive-by shootings in the East Los Angeles area, a part of L.A. that was traditionally very active with gang violence and notoriously deadly.[26]

By 1993 the Mara Salvatrucha gang was reportedly involved in the trafficking of illegal drugs, extortion, robbery, and murder. Once the tribute issue was finally settled, MS aligned itself with other Southern California street gangs and the Mexican Mafia, and MS cliques started using the number "13" along with their gang name to signify this Sureño alliance. The thirteenth letter of the alphabet is "M," so use of this number implies that the gang or individual is aligned with the Mexican Mafia. Probation and law enforcement officers began to encounter MS and MS-13 tattoos and graffiti a short time after the alliance was made. Because of the Southern California alignment, MS-13, like other Latino street gangs, might also use the common *sur* or "Sureño" tattoo or graffiti to further emphasize the gangs' ties. If these terms are used, they are referring to a general alliance with the Mexican Mafia and the Sureño style of gangsterism encountered in Southern California.[27]

According to a 2008 Rocky Mountain Information Network report, there are three types of Sureño gangs: Latino gangs that are from California, Latino gangs that form and operate outside the state of California, and immigrants from Central America and Mexico who claim Sureño status.[28] Thus "Sureño" might be better understood as an umbrella term that describes a set of behaviors common among Latino street and prison gangs globally, rather than an indication of the geographical origin of the gang's members.[29] These behaviors also help those who study the gang phenomenon diagnose whether a gang actually is or only claims to be from Southern California—for instance, identification with the number "13," as mentioned above.

What makes the MS gang and others like it unique is that some members maintain active ties with their gang factions in Central America and Mexico. Like 18th Street, Mara Salvatrucha has become an internationally known street gang. Some East Coast MS members also have family ties to West Coast cliques. Some anecdotal evidence from law enforcement sources suggests that many MS gang members who maintain contact with one another within the United States and in El Salvador do so because they have a business-type relationship with other criminal organizations in Central America to establish illegal firearm, drug, and human smuggling networks.[30] By some definitions, these ties put MS-13 into the category of a transnational gang and indicate that at least some of its elements may be evolving toward an organized crime operation.[31]

The U.S. Immigration and Naturalization Service (the predecessor to U.S. Immigration and Customs Enforcement, or ICE) began a crackdown on street gangs in the early 1990s, which led to an identifiable migration mechanism for the Southern California gangs. At the peak of the program in the mid-1990s, 40,000 criminal illegal immigrants—some of whom were experienced, U.S.-"trained" MS-13 and 18th Street Gang members—were being sent back to Central America each year. As the deportation process continued, Central American countries experienced an unprecedented growth of street gangs and violence. It has been estimated that up to 70 percent of the Central American youths who join a gang claim affiliation with either MS-13 or 18th Street.[32]

Shifts in Gang Relations after 1995

By late 1995 the concept of respect among gang members had changed completely. Respect was based no longer on age, experience, and knowledge but, as mentioned before, on the presumption that the more one was feared, the more one was respected. The concept had been changing subtly for years, due to many factors: a lack of self-control among younger gang members; the development of gun violence as the preferred way to settle disputes; the rapid growth in the number and size of gangs; and the increase of drug use and trafficking within the gang populations. Methamphetamine was becoming more readily available and popular within the fourteen- to twenty-four-year-old age group, which included many Latino gang members. Some users became so brazen that assaults on law enforcement officials also began to rise, and gun battles between gang members and the police became increasingly common. By now, the gang ethic of the 1950s and 1960s, which held the gang's barrio, community members, and local law enforcement officers to be off-limits for gang crime and violence, was completely absent in many cliques, and gang psychology had permanently changed. The new ethos that took its place meant essentially that, for many gang members, there simply were no rules.

The short-lived Eme Edict aside, statistics for Los Angeles County in early 1995 made clear that gang violence was still increasing. Between 1993 and 1994 there had been a reported 1,507 gang-related murders in the county. At that time, there were approximately 140,000 gang members in some 1,100 different street gangs, with the majority still being Latino.[33] For L.A. County, 1995 turned out to be a peak year for gang-related murders, with a total of 807 deaths. Specialized corrections, law enforcement, and judicial units were working overtime to curb the gang violence. Gang populations reached an all-time high that year as well, with some estimates indicating that there were more than 1,500 different street gangs within the county of Los Angeles alone.[34] The 18th Street Gang, which had become the largest Latino gang in California with an estimated 20,000-plus members, was actively recruiting "taggers" (young, entry-level vandals). At the time, anecdotal evidence indicated that there were at least 30,000 members in the 18th Street Gang nationally.[35]

Some Latino gang members at this time started to conceal their gang membership or affiliation from the police, which might have been due to increased awareness of recent California anti-gang legislation that provided for additional prison time upon conviction of a violent crime that was related to gang activity.[36] It nevertheless was apparent that Latino gangs were developing criminal specialties: some became expert at car thefts or drug sales, while others specialized in counterfeit identification and extortion. Some Latino street gangs even became experienced at committing home invasions and takeover-style robberies.

It was also in the mid-1990s that innovative Latino gangs developed the concept of the "gang gun." Often this would be some type of handgun that could easily be concealed in a place known only to members. Any member of the gang could use the weapon and then return it to the location where it was hidden. Gangs used machine guns like the AK-47 when these weapons were accessible, while assault rifles were popular because of their superior firepower, but of course such large weapons were harder to hide. Some Latino gang members were involved in arson and bombings during this highly violent period. Thanks to the Internet, which provided instructions and plans on how to build improvised explosive devices, pipe bombs and Molotov cocktails were the most commonly used explosive devices. A few gang members specialized in arsons and would fire-bomb rival gang members' homes and cars in lieu of a drive-by shooting.

In contrast to the extreme levels of gang violence Southern California experienced in 1995, however, 1996 and 1997 saw successive decreases in gang-related murders, a trend that was reflected across the state. Los Angeles County had 452 gang-related deaths in 1997, a little more than half of the 1995 peak.[37] While violence between Latino gangs reflected that decrease, the California Norteño-Sureño regional rivalry continued to be a major cause of violence between Latino gangs throughout the country. (Norteños, or Northerners, are an informal coalition of prison and street gangs in Northern California, originally affiliated with the notorious Nuestra Familia gang, and are traditional bitter rivals of the Mexican Mafia and the Sureños.)

Although gang membership in general in Los Angeles County also decreased slightly in the latter part of the decade, female membership bucked the trend. In some Latino street gangs, the gender barrier was broken: not only could girls and women become members in formerly all-male gangs, but there was a slight increase in the number of all-female gangs. In some cases, girls or women even became co-leaders of their gang. Female Latina gang members were involved in drive-by shootings, robberies, carjackings, and murders, and in some cases they shared equal responsibility with their male cohorts for the protection of gang turf and fellow gang members.

By 1998, street gangs were reported in every U.S. state and on Native

American lands, while Latino gangs could be found in forty-eight states. Originally an urban-suburban phenomenon, gangs also had established a hold in rural America and in small to midsize towns across the country.[38] Latino and African American gangs continued to draw the majority of new gang members nationwide, but it was the Latino street gangs, many of which now had a mixed-race membership, that by 1999 were the fastest-growing type of gang in the country. The 18th Street Gang was reported to have cliques in seventeen states and Canada, while some members had developed strong ties with Mexican drug traffickers who operated in the Tijuana area of Mexico.[39] Latino gangs, including MS-13 and 18th Street, generally continued to be loosely structured, operating in cliques or small subsets of the gang with which they claimed affiliation. As 1999 came to an end, there were still Latino gangs that continued to pay the Eme tribute, which perpetuated the Mexican Mafia's influence on Southern California–based Latino street gangs.[40]

In 1996, Mara Salvatrucha gang members had been identified in fourteen states, but by 2002 the gang's presence was reported in twenty-eight states and was widespread in Central America. Besides their presence in California, MS cliques were also reported in Oregon, Washington State, Alaska, Hawaii, Mexico, and Canada. The large numbers of Salvadoran refugees and immigrants who had settled in Washington, D.C., and New York were also vectors for the growth of Mara Salvatrucha. In 2008 the gang was reported in forty-eight states, leaving only South Dakota and West Virginia reportedly free of MS-13.[41] The 2009 *National Gang Threat Assessment* put the total number of national and regional gangs in the United States as of September 2008 at about 20,000, comprising more than a million members nationwide. (The numbers of strictly local gangs are considered too numerous to count.)[42]

Traditional Latino turf-oriented gangs could still be found across the country, but the concept of turf for some Latino gangs had become fluid, so that any place they were in could become their temporary turf. Thus these gangs might claim an entire city, not just one neighborhood of it. Since there were no turf boundaries to identify, these gangs also might not have used graffiti, or "tags," in the manner of traditional Latino gangs.

By the late 1990s, as gangs became more diffuse and less territorially identified, some Latino members of the same gang were living in cities or even counties away from their clique's "home turf" and became something like part-time gang members. They would occasionally travel back home to meet with their peers, a not-uncommon pattern among Latino gangs. When not with the gang, these individuals might have a fairly normal lifestyle as full-time students, hardworking employees, even the married parents of small children. When visiting their gang, however, they would revert back to the gang psychology.

By late 1999 another unique phenomenon was seen among Latino street gangs. Some gang members and associates were able to get and hold down jobs as court clerks, police cadets, police officers, state and county employees, and employees in prominent corporations. There were gang members even among enlisted military personnel; they continue to pose a particular concern because of the danger that they will come home and train other gang members in military skills and tactics.[43] Many of these part-time gang members never did and still do not display gang-type tattoos or clothes. Immigrant gang members also may be legitimately employed in the United States, while at the same time maintaining the obligations of gang membership and in some cases keeping in contact with peer members from their country of origin. Like his or her American-born counterparts, this type of Latino gang member can straddle two worlds successfully, a choice that is more common than most people would think. While traditional Latino gang members remained loyal to the same gang no matter where they moved or whether or not they were incarcerated, in 1999 this was becoming less true for the new type of gang member, who might belong to one gang in his city of residence, another where he socialized, and, if he or she was in prison, even a third.[44]

The Evolving Gang Ethos

By the time Mara Salvatrucha emerged as a threat to the streets in the 1980s, it was clear that gangs had chosen guns as their favorite tool. Guns were used to incite fear and to intimidate not only rival gang members but peers as well, not to mention the community at large. The number of juvenile gang murders was increasing nationally, while assaults on innocent bystanders, law enforcement officers, and corrections officials also increased. Juveniles in gangs became involved in an unprecedented number of gun assaults as the numbers of gang members and street gangs grew across the country. Many people within the California Latino community are reluctant to assist law enforcement with gang-related investigations because they fear retaliation from gang members. This is a real and constant danger for those who live in gang-controlled neighborhoods, such as several areas of Los Angeles County where Latino street gangs have established a stronghold. Furthermore, undocumented immigrants often believe that they might be deported if they cooperate with law enforcement.

The most criminally active and the most prone to violence apparently tend to assume gang leadership in an informal manner. This cadre of "shot callers" (slang for street or prison gang elites), who in some parts of the country are as young as fifteen or sixteen years old, can exert a strong influence over the subordinate gang members and have a major impact on the gang's activities. Latino gang violence can be brutal. Gang shootings have occurred in churches, aboard public buses, at movie theaters, and on or near school campuses. Younger Latino gang members in particular have tended to be very violent. Even when socializing or "kicking back," they typically are armed and may travel in small groups, always prepared for a chance encounter with rivals. Latino gang members have repeatedly stated they are not afraid to go to jail, and some have even been willing to attack police officers rather than be arrested. The gang mantra has become, "The more you fear me, the more you respect me."[45]

Besides being "jumped" into a gang—an initiation ritual that involves fighting with or simply getting beaten up by one or more established gang members—West Coast Latinas have the option of being "sexed" in. The first sexing-in rituals dictated that a roll of dice would determine the number of sexual partners the prospective female gang member must accept in order to formalize membership. Currently, sexing-in can involve any number of male gang members.

In the United States, many Latino gangs still guard and patrol the turf, or barrio, that "belongs" to their gang. This reactive need to protect territory has long been and continues to be a source of violence between Latino gangs. In the Latino street gang culture, losing a life in defense of the neighborhood is considered an honor both to the gang and to the individual gang member who has paid the highest price. The gang member's sacrifice will become a perpetual casus belli, and his surrogate family, his gang, will avenge his death.

A gang member's death is often memorialized in a well-attended funeral, at which peer gang members will dress in special clothing. At the burial site itself, gang members will typically lay their gang's colors, in the form of bandanas, down on the coffin, as a last gesture of respect. Some gang members say farewell by pledging to avenge the death, as if the deceased had become a martyr for "the cause." The feelings accompanying such pledges intensify the rivalry between gangs. A gang funeral can be a highly emotional and potentially volatile situation.[46] Getting even for the loss of a comrade is called payback or retaliation. For all gangs, especially Latino street gangs, there is a tendency for a payback or retaliation to escalate; thus the payback for one death could be a multiple counter-killing. This concept of revenge through violence is often found in gangs that engage in drug sales.[47]

Motives for gang-related homicides have been as simple as the crossing out of gang graffiti by a rival gang. Gang members have been killed for a "mad dog" stare or for seemingly no reason at all. In the highly emotional gang culture, an insult, no matter how small, never goes unanswered. In the case of even a perceived insult, the entire rival gang and every individual in it is held responsible. No matter how minor the transgression was, it will be answered in an escalated, likely violent way.

More tragically, innocent people, including small children, are dying because of this attitude. It is estimated that as many as 50 percent of the victims of deadly gang violence are simply bystanders. In yet another disturbing trend, Latino street gang members have been involved in the intimidation and murder of witnesses, ambushes of on- and off-duty police officers, and rapes. Some Latino gangs have earned such a reputation for retaliation and violence that jurors in criminal trials involving gang members have expressed fear of being attacked themselves. Because there is no longer a gang ethic that tempers the most impulsive behavior, and gang psychology mandates the use of violence, innocent victims are often dismissed as collateral damage. Gang members typically do not feel responsible for the results of their lifestyle.[48]

Transnational Gangs, Transnational Crime

Researchers classify gangs as first-, second-, or third-generation, according to their level of organization and types of activity. The early Mexican-based gangs of Los Angeles, including 18th Street, exemplified the first generation: turf-oriented, localized, loosely organized, engaging in "unsophisticated criminal activities." The second generation is organized in a more businesslike way and focuses more on markets—typically for drugs—rather than turf. Leadership roles are stronger within these gangs. Most urban gangs fall into one of these two categories. Third-generation gangs, by contrast, are highly structured and center on the acquisition of money and power through sophisticated criminal activity. They operate across borders and can come to resemble crime syndicates more than street gangs.[49] Some researchers believe there are MS-13 cliques in Latin America that can be classified as third-generation, and that MS-13 in the United States is evolving toward a third-generation structure as it deepens its level of organization across the country.[50]

Despite some similarities to the Mafia, however, most street gangs lack the hierarchical organization, structure, or capital of a real crime syndicate. They may engage in the same types of crimes, such as drug trafficking or even human smuggling, but they operate at a much lower level and are usually more opportunistic and far less businesslike. The varied motivations that bring youths into gangs also tends to encourage anarchic attitudes and prevent the group from focusing on a narrow set of goals, such as a criminal enterprise would require.[51]

Anecdotal law enforcement evidence suggests that gangs similar to Mara Salvatrucha have established cliques in Canada, Mexico, Honduras, Guatemala, El Salvador, and Spain. The 18th Street Gang is reported to have cliques in Canada, Mexico, Honduras, Guatemala, El Salvador, Australia, Germany, France, England, Lebanon, and Peru. The Latin Kings have been reported in Mexico, Canada, El Salvador, France, and Spain. The Black P Stone gang has been reported as far north as Canada. Blood "sets" (cliques) have been encountered in Honduras, England, Haiti, and Bermuda. Crip sets have been reported in Canada, England, Bermuda, and the Netherlands. The Chicago-based Gangster Disciples have been reported in Canada, Panama, and South Korea. Jamaican gangs have established themselves in Great Britain and the United States. It is also well known that many of the U.S.-based outlaw motorcycle gangs have chapters in Canada, Australia, and Europe.[52]

This is by no means a complete list of global gangs; it does, however, demonstrate that some gangs have established cliques in other countries and are to some extent transnational. What is at issue here is how such data can be interpreted, because having cliques in other countries does not necessarily imply that an entire gang is involved in criminal activities, nor that it necessarily maintain ties with its counterparts in the United States.

Nevertheless, once a gang clique in another country is found to be involved in crime, this often is interpreted by the media and law enforcement to mean that all members and cliques of the gang are involved in crime. This conclusion simply is not accurate. No more than a few members of the gang might actually be involved, and they might not have any contact with the parent gang. Their gang identification alone should not qualify the entire gang as transnational or globalized. To make such a connection, both the nature of the criminal activity and the clique's actual ties to the gang in its country of origin should be examined.[53] The U.S.

Federal Bureau of Investigation (FBI) created the MS-13 National Gang Task Force in December 2004 to coordinate law enforcement efforts at all levels across the United States and disseminate information among agencies. It also established the Central American Fingerprint Exploitation initiative as a means to merge criminal databases of U.S. and Central American law enforcement agencies.[54]

Having said that, internationally deployed gang members and newly formed cliques can and sometimes do facilitate illegal drug trafficking operations for the parent gang. Often these gang members speak a second language and are familiar with the geographic area in which they operate, unhindered by the local rules and international trade regulations that legitimate businesses have to abide by. Gangs that have established themselves in the drug trade also have relatively unlimited financial resources. It therefore becomes very easy to expand operations and draw in more gang members to work the business.

Academic research suggests that the main reason for migration by gang members is employment.[55] In this case, the Mexican drug cartels use Latino gang members to assist them in their drug trafficking operations.[56] Some street gang members have been trained to help with gang hits and money collection and to carry out extortion. There is recent evidence that Latino gang members have even helped with the smuggling of undocumented Mexicans into California.[57]

If U.S. authorities positively identify a suspect who has fled abroad, then to apprehend the suspect, they must work through the law enforcement structures of the country in which they locate him or her. This is especially true if the suspect gang member is under eighteen years of age. Most countries (including Mexico) do not have a death penalty, a circumstance that makes suspects eligible for the death penalty in the United States nonextraditable.

A recent report from the Center for Immigration Studies found that between 2005 and 2007 the U.S. Immigration and Customs Enforcement agency had deported well over 8,000 gang members back to their countries of origin.[58] The research showed that 59 percent were deported to Mexico and 17 percent to El Salvador, totaling 76 percent of the deported gang members.[59] Yet because of intense anti-gang suppression programs in several Central American countries, the deported gang members frequently return to the United States in what is being called a boomerang effect.[60] Sometimes this reentry is fueled and paid for by the illegal drug, arms, and human trafficking businesses. The connection between street and prison gangs and foreign drug trafficking organizations is strong and will continue to afford the opportunity for employment. Latino gangs will likely continue to evolve and change as illegal markets expand.

During the 1980s, MS and its main rival, the 18th Street Gang, battled for control of the lucrative drug trafficking business in the Rampart district of West L.A., a struggle that saw violence between these two gangs and the surrounding neighborhoods escalate and began to draw in other Latino gangs. By 1992, although there was no clear winner, MS-13 had gained control of at least some of the Rampart drug turf area.

Several other Latino gangs, such as 38th Street and Big Hazard, had also become heavily involved in drug sales during the 1980s, and trafficking became a specialty crime that some gang members perfected. During this period Latino prison and street gang members also began to form relationships with drug suppliers in Mexico. Drug trafficking in the United States is dependent on the importation of most of the drugs that are consumed. Only methamphetamine and marijuana are manufactured or grown in any real quantity within the United States itself. U.S. Drug Enforcement Agency research shows that the majority of drugs that are sold and consumed illegally in the United States are imported from foreign countries via Canada and Mexico, which have been portals for illegal drugs for many years. New observations show that some street and prison gangs are becoming more involved in this international business.[61]

In their efforts to escape law enforcement and supply the growing American drug appetite, and benefiting from increasingly sophisticated communications technology, some gang members began traveling regularly across the U.S.-Mexican border and down into Central America. In doing so, these Americanized gang members not only introduced the American gang lifestyle into the countries of Central America but also seized the opportunity to develop and maintain connections to criminal elements in these same countries as they developed their sources and transit routes to bring drugs and other illegal products into the U.S. market. At the same time, they continued to communicate with and maintain connections to their gang in the United States. In essence, some California-based Latino gangs had become international. Thus, gang "globalization" was at least in part an outgrowth of the need for drug traffickers to network with foreign suppliers.

In the context of the spread of the California gangs, globalization should be understood as a process that increases communication, travel, and the scope of business. Some California-based Latino gangs have been very active in these areas, following the developmental stages suggested by researcher John Sullivan.[62] According to the United Nations *World Drug*

Report, drug trafficking in 2007 was a $341 billion a year global business, accounting for about 8 percent of the world's economy.[63] Mexican and Central American street gangs have cornered a considerable share of this lucrative market.

Cocaine brought in from South America became a very popular—and profitable—recreational drug across the United States during the 1980s, while addiction to the less expensive crack formulation of cocaine ravaged U.S. inner cities. During this period drug use once again became prevalent among the young population, especially gang members, after a period of decline in the 1970s, and many of them started to get involved in drug trafficking. In the first decade of the twenty-first century, according to data from the High Intensity Drug Trafficking Areas program, methamphetamine and cocaine were the two most abused drugs in the western half of the United States, after marijuana.[64]

Given Americans' prodigious drug appetite, it is no surprise to find that some street and prison gangs have become deeply involved in drug trafficking. The National Alliance of Gang Investigators' Associations (NAGIA), in conjunction with the FBI, the National Drug Intelligence Center, and the Bureau of Alcohol, Tobacco, and Firearms, issued a report in 2005 about gang activity in the United States. The executive summary states that, according to the most current data, the primary source of income for America's street gangs is drug trafficking.[65] Further research indicates, however, that most gang members who sell drugs at the street level do so independently and are not directly connected to any of the large, organized national and transnational gangs that are involved in drug sales.

A typical street dealer might be a nineteen-year-old male child of Latino immigrant parents, living in any major U.S. city. He wears the uniform of his gang, has never traveled outside his city, and makes money by standing on the corner near his apartment complex selling $10 bags of crack. He might pull in $100 of profit a day, a little more than he would make at McDonald's for far less work.[66] By the time the crack he sells hits the city streets, it has most likely been touched by more than a dozen people as it passed through at least three countries, but the young street dealer isn't likely to have an interest in the global supply chain of the drug he sells.

This profile is typical of many U.S. gang members who engage in drug dealing. There is some anecdotal evidence from law enforcement agencies that suggests this is the same way many gang members in other countries deal drugs. It has been reported that in some areas of Central America, street gangs are used by narcotics trafficking organizations to help with "street muscle" or security. These gang members are then paid in drugs rather than money.[67] This implies that the Central American street gang members who sell illegal drugs are also part of the global drug market, and yet, like the young U.S. dealer, they cannot see and do not care about their role in the big picture.

Latino members of both street and prison gangs have now established themselves in foreign countries to facilitate supplier connections and importation routes for foreign drug trafficking organizations. In this manner, the drug market compels some gangs to globalize and organize so that they can continue to expand their drug business. Nevertheless, very few gangs overall are directly involved in the globalized drug trafficking process. This is consistent with research data collected by NAGIA for its 2005 report. As described above, most gang members who are involved in drug dealing operate locally and part-time, or in small groups of individual dealers.

Conclusion

The Mara Salvatrucha and 18th Street gangs are the most notorious of the international Latino street gangs to originate in the racially diverse, economically stratified, and violent environment of Los Angeles in the 1980s and 1990s. From their beginnings as a refuge for typically poor, unassimilated immigrant youths, these *maras* have proven highly adaptive, transforming themselves into widespread, loosely organized criminal enterprises that move enormous amounts of drugs, guns, cash, other contraband, and undocumented human beings across borders, in league with the drug cartels of Latin America and the prison gangs nurtured in the U.S. penal system.

The culture of the *maras* rewards extreme violence and ruthlessness. The early gang ethos of respect for one's own neighborhood and avoiding engagement with police has long since broken down. Easy access to weapons and money, coupled with widespread drug use and the revolving-door prison system, brought gangs into virtually open warfare in the streets of Los Angeles and other major cities in the 1990s, although there is some evidence that the cartels and organized crime are attempting to impose at least a degree of discipline at the street level, if only because drugged-up operatives and misdirected violence attract the attention of authorities and cut into profits.

So far, solutions have been hard to come by. Deportations from the United States to Central America continue to facilitate the spread of gang culture, while Americans' failure to deal effectively with their demand for illegal drugs lures gang members back into the country and pumps money into their operations. As more and more countries come to regard the international *maras* as a threat to national security, leaders will need to address the full set of both causes and effects of gang culture across the Western Hemisphere if they are to find solutions.

CHAPTER 2

Street Gangs of El Salvador

SONJA WOLF

El Salvador's gang landscape, dominated by Mara Salvatrucha (MS) and Calle Dieciocho (the 18th Street Gang, or simply "18th Street"), has grown increasingly complex in recent years. The authorities have tended to depict these groups as part of a larger transnational gang structure that spans the United States, Central America, and Mexico and has mutated into a new form of organized crime.[1] According to El Salvador's Policía Nacional Civil (National Civilian Police, or PNC), the gangs are heavily armed and have developed a sophisticated structure of organized cells that specialize in areas such as logistics, recruitment, attack, and murder.[2] More controversially, they have been linked to Colombian rebels and Mexican drug cartels, and they have been accused of participation in extortion, *sicariato* (contract killing), and the trafficking of drugs, weapons, and humans.[3]

The local gang problem, some have argued, is largely fed by gang members deported from the United States, who connect with their peers in El Salvador and escalate the domestic crime rate.[4] Lately, the gangs have allegedly resorted to mutilating and decapitating their victims as a way of initiating newcomers and terrorizing society.[5] Generally, gangs are held responsible for at least 60 percent of all homicides committed in El Salvador. One senior prosecutor even went so far as to claim that murders could be almost entirely eradicated if only all gang members were detained.[6] The mass media have generally echoed these statements through sensationalist and uncritical coverage. The reality, however, contrasts with the official view on a number of points, notably the gangs' historical roots as well as the volume and nature of their criminal involvement.

The First Gang Study in El Salvador—1991

El Salvador's street gangs are not a recent development—indeed, they first surfaced as early as 1963—but little information exists on the early stages of the phenomenon. The most comprehensive research on this period was conducted in 1991 for a bachelor's degree thesis project and entailed structured interviews with 116 members of twenty-five different gangs in Greater San Salvador.[7] These barrio groups, going under names such as Morazán, Gallo, AC/DC, Poison, Furia, Lacra, and Magia Negra, were mainly based in the marginal communities of the capital and the municipalities of Soyapango, Apopa, Ilopango, Ciudad Delgado, and Mejicanos. Gang members ranged in age between seven and thirty-one years, but most were between fifteen and twenty-two years old. Males accounted for 76.7 percent of the membership, and 23.3 percent were female; some gangs did not admit any girls. All of these youths came from lower-class or lower middle-class backgrounds, and 66.6 percent of them had grown up in dysfunctional families. Marginal housing conditions were the norm, and educational levels were generally low. The majority of members were engaged in some kind of remunerated work—generally jobs that paid poorly—and those with a criminal record were struggling to secure decent employment. By and large these were youths who felt rejected or ignored by family and society and had turned to a gang in search of support, understanding, and fun.

Although the gangs had developed initiation rites, members could abandon the group when they started a family or formal work. Baggy clothing and long, unkempt hairstyles were preferred but optional, and any tattoos tended to contain religious or diabolical symbols or the names of girlfriends and rock bands. Designated leaders did not exist, and influential youths took decisions only after consulting with the rest of the group; indeed, the interviewees stated that they often acted without the knowledge of the so-called shot caller. In line with their skills, individuals assumed specific functions: some trained their peers in weapons use and theft while others stole wallets or necklaces, burgled cars, looked out for the police, or distracted the police during a chase. Gangs differed on the adoption of written rules, but all expected their members to show unconditional loyalty and solidarity and not to snitch on the group. Funds were raised to support the families of detained or deceased youths, and informants were severely punished.

Gang members spent much of their time hanging out, partying and taking drugs, fighting their rivals, and committing robberies. Drug consumption prevailed over sales and, like crime incidence, had reached critical levels. Of the survey's participants, 87.9 percent affirmed they were taking drugs frequently or occasionally, primarily low-cost substances such as alcohol, paint thinner, glue, and marijuana, a practice that partly served to overcome hunger and cold. Violence was common in gang confrontations, which were conducted for fun or territorial control, and 96.6 percent of these youths admitted to using weapons, especially knives. Moreover, 77.5 percent of interviewees had reportedly inflicted injuries on others, committed murders, and carried out small robberies, the latter as a survival strategy to overcome discrimination and their inability to succeed in the job market.

Recent Trends

At the time the study was conducted, Mara Salvatrucha and the 18th Street Gang had already established a foothold in El Salvador and were exhibiting notable dissimilarities with these traditional groups. Their gang garb had identification value, organizational levels were greater, internal norms were stricter and more violent, and adult responsibilities did not affect gang membership. More importantly, these youths had more sophisticated weapons (especially sawed-off shotguns and explosives), consumed costlier drugs (crack, heroin, and powder cocaine), sold more illicit substances, and carried out large-scale robberies.[8] Subsequent to the establishment of MS and 18th Street in El Salvador, gang patterns appeared to change rapidly. In 1993 the Fiscalía General de la República (Attorney General's Office, or FGR) identified 236 gangs nationwide (185 specifically in the capital city), whereas in 1996 the PNC detected a mere 54 *clicas*, all of which claimed affiliation with MS, 18th Street, or the *pandilla* Mao Mao and were located in Greater San Salvador.[9] These developments foreshadowed some of the changes that the gang phenomenon would undergo in the years to come.

Today, MS and 18th Street are El Salvador's main street gangs. Other groups, such as Máquina and Mao Mao, exist, but they have neither the public profile nor the security impact that characterize their U.S.-inspired counterparts. Given the difficulty of defining and counting gang members, reliable information is hard to obtain. Official figures include only youths who have come into contact with law enforcement, and it is unclear to what extent these records are updated to reflect dropouts, deaths, and new affiliations. In any case, the actual number of gang youths is likely

Table 2.1. *Clicas* **and gang membership in El Salvador departments, 2004**

Department	MS-13	18th Street	Other gangs	Total	Total number of gang members
		Number of clicas			
San Salvador	51	35	11	97	3,337
Usulután	20	18	2	40	231
San Miguel	21	1	10	32	483
Cuscatlán	16	11	2	29	300
La Paz	0	8	9	17	590
Sonsonate	8	5	0	13	—
Chalatenango	8	1	2	11	100
Santa Ana	7	4	3	14	1,450
La Unión	5	4	1	10	168
Ahuachapán	5	2	2	9	624
Cabañas	5	3	1	9	—
La Libertad	0	7	1	8	1,285
San Vicente	1	1	2	4	120
Morazán	3	1	0	4	26
Total	150	101	46	297	8,714

Source: Data from "PNC tiene en la mira a 309 clicas de las maras," *El Diario de Hoy*, 2 September 2004, http://www.elsalvador.com/noticias/2004/09/02/nacional/nac8.asp.

to exceed available estimates. Over the years, figures for El Salvador have oscillated anywhere between 10,000 and 30,000 gang members. In 2004 the PNC published its hitherto most detailed data set, revealing the presence of 10,200 gang members and 309 *clicas* in the country's fourteen departments, or administrative districts (Table 2.1).[10]

The number that generally circulated as the total of gang members during the implementation of Mano Dura (Strong Hand) policies, which began in 2003, was 10,500.[11] The PNC has not, however, indicated how this picture has changed following the apparent dissolution of some *clicas* and the growth of others. For example, the Consejo Nacional de Seguridad Pública (National Council of Public Security, or CNSP) suggested that in early 2007 some 1,600 youths had joined a gang, but it failed to explain how this information was obtained.[12] In 2006 the police announced that 9,300 gang members had been registered, and in 2009 this figure was revised upward, to 16,000.[13] Variations notwithstanding, these numbers have always included current and former gang members in detention. In fact, their share of the overall prison population has expanded drastically, climbing from 3,310 of 16,762 inmates (about 20 percent) in 2005 to 7,258 of 20,906 detainees (nearly 35 percent) in mid-2009.[14]

Despite a generally greater geographical dispersion, gangs continue to be concentrated in the marginal communities of the capital and the municipalities of Apopa, Soyapango, Ilopango, and Mejicanos.[15] Gang youths in these areas are predominantly male and come from low-income, dysfunctional families. The average entry age is between eleven and fifteen years, but members are now largely young adults rather than adolescents. Most have only intermediate levels of education and left school just prior to or after joining the gang.[16] Unsurprisingly, a 2006 survey among 316 imprisoned gang members found that 83.5 percent of interviewees had been low-wage workers before their arrest.[17] Reasons for gang affiliation vary and have not substantially changed over the years. Key motivations remain *el vacil* (the lifestyle—a whole range of licit and illicit pursuits that promise fun and excitement in a gang), family problems, a desire for support and respect, and peer pressure. An unusual finding was that 6.3 percent of male participants in the survey said they joined a gang in order to settle scores with rivals. Interestingly, the same study showed that while friendship was perceived to be an important benefit of gang membership by 27.8 percent of youths, and 8.2 percent perceived respect to be a benefit, 46.8 percent thought that gang affiliation brought no benefits at all, and only 0.6 percent stated it afforded them access to money—presumably because funds derived from unlawful activities go to the group rather than its individual members.[18]

In other ambits, however, these groups have undergone important transformations, some more apparent than others. Youths are rejecting highly visible tattoos and adopting a more conventional dress code and hairstyle, ostensibly to avoid police detection.[19] Entry requirements have been toughened such that new recruits are now subjected to riskier initiation tests, including even the killing of opposing gang members. Additionally, some researchers suggest that the gangs have cultivated a more hierarchical leadership and specific internal roles.[20] It is clear that they effectively control certain penitentiaries and conduct criminal activities from their cells, at times with the complicity of prison guards.[21] For security reasons, the gangs have also restricted drug use among their members mostly to alcohol and marijuana and have prohibited the consumption of harder drugs, such as cocaine.[22]

Contrary to their earlier preference for knives and homemade weapons, gang members have come to rely more heavily on commercial firearms, including military weapons, and thus to perpetrate more lethal violence.[23] Equally striking is their growing participation in more serious crimes, particularly homicides, robberies, extortions, and drug sales, as well as the illegal possession and carrying of firearms. What is more, violence is no longer used exclusively against rivals but is also used in internal paybacks and attacks against prison guards, as well as on civilians suspected of collaborating with the police—developments that have led some analysts to conclude that these entities have evolved into a new form of organized crime.[24] Yet despite their increased criminal involvement, the gangs lack group aims and exist only because marginalized youths see in them the means to find the fun, respect, and social status they are otherwise unable to obtain. This chapter argues that El Salvador's gang problem has worsened largely due to the tardy and ideological responses of a state run by the elite class. It traces gang transformations prior to Mano Dura, situating them in the broader context of crime and violence in El Salvador, before examining the government's anti-gang policies. The chapter then considers more recent changes in gang patterns and concludes with a brief assessment of the public security threat they imply.

An Anatomy of Violence

Mara Salvatrucha and the 18th Street Gang gained ascendancy in the early postwar period (El Salvador's civil war lasted from 1980 to 1992). Some of the territorial gangs, tapped by the anti-junta guerrillas as guides during their 1989 offensive, subsequently joined the combatants' demobilization and reinsertion process after the war ended.[25] Others dissolved over time, but many would be largely absorbed by the gangs that U.S. deportees brought into the country with them. The armed conflict had prompted an estimated one million Salvadorans to flee their country and seek shelter in the United States, particularly in the already impoverished, overcrowded, and gang-affected neighborhoods of East and South Central Los Angeles. The idiosyncratic nature of the asylum policy of President Ronald Reagan (1981–1989) meant that the Salvadorans were generally denied refugee status. Forced to live clandestine lives, these families not only experienced a host of socioeconomic problems that rendered their children susceptible to gang enticements, but were also exposed to deportation.[26] The end of the Salvadoran civil war, combined with a surge in anti-immigrant feeling, spurred U.S. authorities to target offending noncitizens more aggressively for repatriation. The Illegal Immigration

Reform and Immigrant Responsibility Act of 1996, which expanded the definition of deportable aggravated felonies to include a range of lesser offenses, further facilitated this process.[27] Soon El Salvador began to receive scores of deportees, some of whom brought the U.S. gang culture and lifestyle with them.

Returning youths often felt disoriented in a country they had few memories of, and they felt alienated by the humble surroundings they encountered.[28] Although many of them hoped to make a fresh start, weak family ties and continued marginalization prompted some to carry on with the gang life they knew best.[29] Their comparatively smarter dress, money, and romanticized tales of gang life held a fascination that local adolescents found hard to resist.[30] Gradually the latter adopted the identities of MS or 18th Street and, with them, the hostility between the two gangs. By 1996 a survey found that 86 percent of participants were affiliated with one of these groups and only 14 percent belonged to other gangs.[31] Thus two distinct phenomena had merged, not because of active recruitment or violent takeovers but because El Salvador constituted fertile terrain for gang development.

In recent years, the growing number of deportations coincided with the country's deteriorating crime situation. Salvadoran officials were quick to attribute the rise in delinquency rates to criminal deportees from the United States, especially gang members.[32] While it cannot be discounted that some returnees turn to gang or criminal activities in their home country, this does not, however, appear to be the dominant trend. According to a 1996 study, the gangs comprised mainly local youths; only 11 percent of interviewees had chosen membership while they lived in the United States.[33] Furthermore, of the 36,698 repatriates the country received in 2004, mostly from the United States and Mexico, 94.4 percent had no criminal record.[34] Only 20 individuals (0.97 percent) among those who had committed offenses had been expelled for gang membership.[35] This suggests that most deportees are not offenders but merely undocumented migrants. In light of these figures, there is reason to doubt that deportees, be they gang members or not, are the prime culprits in the crimes that cause most alarm in El Salvador. Nevertheless, before reaching conclusions about the causes of El Salvador's increasing crime problems, more research is needed into the extent to which deportees actually participate in gangs or delinquency upon their return.

Once MS and 18th Street had established themselves as the dominant gangs in El Salvador, they began to experience a series of important qualitative changes. Early studies had indicated that youths primarily joined a gang in search of emotional support, belonging, identity, respect, and social status. Few youths considered access to money and drugs to be a benefit of gang membership.[36] In one 1996 survey, 66.6 percent of respondents had been incarcerated, mostly for robbery and fights rather than drug possession or homicide. Gang violence was found to be fairly high: 63.8 percent of interviewees had been injured in the last six months, mostly by the rival gang and with blades rather than firearms. The same research put regular drug use at 71.9 percent, the most popular substances being marijuana, cocaine, or a combination of the two.[37]

A follow-up survey conducted in 2000 showed that the gang problem had significantly worsened.[38] Habitual drug consumption had reached alarming levels, and the use of crack in particular had intensified. Interestingly, 12.2 percent of youths admitted to daily drug dealing, suggesting that this activity had become a source of income for many gang members. The study further suggested that drug use correlated with their involvement in criminal violence, as both victims and perpetrators. More youths had served time in prison; the use of pistols, explosives, and rifles had notably increased; and 23 percent of respondents owned up to a murder. The researchers concluded that although solidarity, friendship, and identity remained important reasons for gang membership, what had formerly been secondary incentives, such as power, social visibility, and access to money and drugs, now assumed greater significance and denoted an apparent shift toward motivations that favored the exercise of criminal violence.[39] These developments were fueled by a number of factors, but before exploring them, gang activity first needs to be situated within the broader crime problem.

The Faces of Violent Crime

Crime and violence rank among El Salvador's most serious problems. Homicides, though amounting to only a small proportion of all recorded criminal offenses, have long been of particular concern. In the early 1970s the country already was experiencing a murder rate of 30 per 100,000 inhabitants, at the time the highest rate in the entire Latin American continent. Homicide levels remained high through the civil war period but exploded in the early postwar years.[40] After peaking at 138 killings per 100,000 inhabitants in 1994, the rate declined but resumed its ascent in 2003.[41] By 2006 an average of eleven people a day suffered a violent death, and the Instituto de Medicina Legal (Forensic Institute, or

IML) registered a homicide rate of 68 per 100,000 inhabitants, the highest in the Western Hemisphere.[42] The magnitude of the situation has even prompted the Organization of American States to assert that El Salvador is experiencing an undeclared civil war.[43]

Between 70 and 80 percent of homicides are committed with firearms, and the victims are mostly males aged fifteen to twenty-nine.[44] Although crime and violence create generalized feelings of insecurity throughout the population, it is the urban poor who are disproportionately affected by it. In Greater San Salvador, one of the areas with the highest incidence of murders, marginal zones see much greater levels of violence than the more affluent areas.[45] Since the wealthier and more influential sectors of the population remain largely unaffected, the Alianza Republicana Nacionalista (Nationalist Republican Alliance, or ARENA), which held power from 1989 until the election of March 2009, lacked the incentive to tackle this social problem.

Government and law enforcement officials have tended to associate the upward trend in homicides with gangs, attributing the rising casualties to disputes over territories, leadership, or drug sales; attempts by members to withdraw from the gang; and refusals to meet extortion demands.[46] Yet, although gang members perpetrate a significant number of violent crimes, establishing their level of responsibility for the mounting homicide rate has proved difficult. A cursory comparison between the territorial clustering of gangs and murders indicates that the two phenomena are not necessarily related. Four of the country's five departments with the highest homicide levels (Santa Ana, La Libertad, La Paz, and San Salvador) also exhibit the highest gang density, but in Ahuachapán, where the gang presence is equally strong, the murder rate remains below the national average. Similarly, while four of the five departments with the lowest homicide levels (La Unión, Usulután, Chalatenango, and Morazán) also have the least gang exposure, the fifth, San Miguel, has a greater gang presence than the other four but a lower murder rate than La Unión.[47] Although these data offer no definite conclusions about the gangs-homicide nexus, they suggest that the nature and prevalence of violent crime can be better understood by accurately mapping the spatial incidence of homicides, gangs, and other delinquent activities such as drug trafficking.

IML figures, based on an initial review of the crime statistics, certainly paint a more complex picture of murder trends than might be expected. Forensic data, covering homicide motive categories such as gang violence, common crime, and unknown motive, consistently show that gang involvement in killings has been considerably lower than is habitually claimed by the authorities. Although the PNC attributes the majority of murders to these groups, IML reports indicate that gang members have actually committed between 3.3 percent (in 1999) and 25.2 percent (in 2007) of homicides nationwide. Clearly, although this fraction has grown over the years, it remains well below figures put forth by law enforcement. Interestingly, between 30.3 percent (in 1999) and 11.8 percent (in 2006) of homicides are caused by common crime, while those with unknown motive and perpetrator range between 54.6 percent (in 1999) and 72.1 percent (in 2007).[48] According to forensic experts, the characteristics displayed by some of the latter cases points to executions by organized crime groups.[49] Presciently, a United Nations investigation conducted in the early 1990s warned that the old right-wing death squads of the civil war period had metamorphosed into organized crime networks but could be reactivated to commit politically motivated assassinations.[50]

Studies into extrajudicial executions have revealed that the victims, often unidentified, include gang members as well as social and political activists. Between 2001 and 2005, at least 622 corpses were discovered, mostly in isolated sites, either shot through the back of the head, with hands and feet tied, or tortured, dismembered, and burned.[51] As might be anticipated, the police have often described these as gang killings, contending that the youths were using mutilated bodies to intimidate society and rivals alike.[52] While gang involvement in some of these instances cannot be dismissed, the clandestine mutilation of victims is not a traditional hallmark of gang homicides, which tend to occur in broad daylight and to involve firearms and male gang members.[53] Instead, research found that while some of these murders were perpetrated for no apparent reason, the features and frequency of others indicated motives of "social cleansing" or collective terror.[54] The intensification of this phenomenon in the months prior to the 2003 elections also suggests political objectives behind the killings.[55]

Extralegal executions tend to remain uninvestigated, and past administrations have rejected allegations that extermination groups may be operating from anywhere within state institutions.[56] In recent years, however, the Procuraduría para la Defensa de los Derechos Humanos (Ombudsperson for the Defense of Human Rights, or PDDH) has identified a growing number of cases in which police-run "social cleansing" units tortured and subsequently eliminated their targets, including gang youths.[57] Ultimately, only reliable investigations can shed light on the thousands of annual homicides and the extent of gang involvement in them, but police and prosecutorial weaknesses mean that at present fewer than 4 percent of the murder cases that are probed result in a conviction.[58] These circumstances necessarily cast doubt on official claims that gangs are to blame for most murders.

The Politics of Crime Control

Over time, four factors have helped exacerbate El Salvador's crime and gang situation. One of these is a culture of violence: a system of norms, values, and attitudes that facilitates, promotes, and legitimizes the use of violence in interpersonal relations.[59] Given El Salvador's long history of social repression, this culture of violence clearly developed over many decades, but the country's intense and protracted civil war aggravated it in important ways. The armed conflict not only universalized access to weapons and taught the skills required for their handling but also normalized violence as an instrument for dispute resolution.[60] This normative system is reproduced in homes, schools, and society at large, such that successive generations of children have been raised in an environment that favors aggression over dialogue and fosters a social permissiveness, if not approval, toward the carrying and use of firearms.[61]

A victimization survey found that more than 38.7 percent of all Salvadorans and 42.6 percent of youths aged eighteen to twenty-five would like to obtain a firearm to counteract their prevailing sense of insecurity.[62] El Salvador's firearms legislation, widely considered too lax, contains no restriction on the number of weapons a citizen may own and even permits civilian use of assault rifles such as the M-16 or AK-47.[63] An estimated 450,000 firearms, more than 60 percent of them unregistered, are currently in the hands of civilians. In other words, one in four adult males owns a weapon—an elevated figure relative to gun ownership rates in other societies in Latin America and elsewhere.[64] This gun proliferation is partly fed by the remnants of the war arsenals, since many ex-combatants did not surrender the rifles and explosives under their control, despite agreements to do so.[65] Despite the apparent success of some attempts at tighter gun regulation, such measures have never been widely applied.[66] Ironically, a number of officials retain a stake in private security companies and gun imports and sales, business pursuits that apparently preclude them from endorsing stricter regulations.[67] Inevitably, this hands-off attitude toward the arms sector makes violence—by gang members or others—more lethal.

While the norms, attitudes, and values anchored in the culture of violence may mold gang activity, their influence on the gang phenomenon should not be overstressed. Decades of authoritarianism and the subsequent civil war normalized the use of aggression among large parts of society, not just among gang members. The persistence of a culture of violence helps explain a widespread preference for tough anticrime measures, including military participation in public security tasks, but it does not seem to elucidate the particular dynamics of MS and 18th Street. Above all, the argument loses much of its weight in view of the experiences of other isthmian countries. Honduras has been experiencing levels of gang membership and gang violence similar to those in El Salvador, even though its history of authoritarianism and political violence varies considerably from that of its next-door neighbor. Not only did Honduras suffer no civil war, but its military governments exercised relative restraint in stifling the population. Even when the repression increased, the victim rate paled in comparison with the staggering tolls reached in Guatemala, El Salvador, and Nicaragua.[68] This last nation, on the other hand, had lived through the brutal four-decade-long Somoza dynasty before riding out a revolutionary struggle and the U.S.-financed counter-revolutionary Contra war. Yet, although gang violence has increased of late, Nicaragua lacks the scale of gang affiliation and hostilities (let alone the MS–18th Street enmity) that marks El Salvador.

The gradual growth in the volume and brutality of gang violence may instead have other roots. One such source lies in internal group dynamics. Gang violence is often confined to bragging, and youths are not equally capable of or committed to it. However, violence constitutes a key element of a gang's mythology and identity, serving to unify its members and to distinguish the group from others.[69] In El Salvador there have been cases in which clique members resorted to collective violence such as gang rapes in order to foster group cohesion. Given the closed and secretive nature of these groups, this practice is underexplored and will likely remain so for the foreseeable future. If these processes could eventually be investigated, however, they could shed much-needed light on more hidden mechanisms of violence promotion.

Another aspect of internal group dynamics concerns environmental influences on gang behavior. The Mano Dura policies intensified gang members' criminal involvement, prompting them to step up extortions and violently enforce extortion demands in order to support their imprisoned peers. The impact of other violent actors, however, has been largely ignored. The presence of drug trafficking organizations or other armed groups can radically alter the shape of a traditional street gang, often by bending them to the needs of the more professional entities.[70] The characteristics of this transformation hold particular relevance for Central America, where Mexican drug trafficking organizations have strengthened their presence (more on this below). The drug trade's effects on the gang world have been tentatively explored in Nicaragua. Longitudinal research showed that over the last decade or so the gangs have evolved from traditional street gangs into more predatory groups dedicated to protecting local drug markets through the imposition of fear and arbitrary violence.[71] That the persistent lack of opportunity drove gang members further into the underground economy should guide future gang policies in Central America. In El Salvador similar developments have yet to be documented empirically at the community level. Doing so may well show that much of what is currently being labeled as gang violence is in fact drug-related violence.

A second factor concerns the combined impact of postwar demobilization programs and police reforms. Reintegration measures were ill-conceived and insufficient to meet ex-combatants' needs. Severance pay reached—with considerable delay—only 11,000 of an estimated 42,000 former soldiers and guerrillas, and land distribution, which for many held little interest in the first place, was equally slow to materialize.[72] More importantly, these initiatives privileged technical training over job reinsertion and therefore left a large number of disgruntled fighters with little choice but to rely on illicit activities for their livelihood. In the most notorious of these cases, uniformed members of the soon-to-be-dissolved Policía Nacional (National Police) committed a bank robbery, an incident that was recorded on video and later broadcast on television.[73] The situation was not helped by a weakened and corrupt justice system. Before and during the armed conflict, El Salvador's three militarized police corps had maintained order through intimidation and lacked specialized investigative skills, engaging instead in torture to extract confessions.[74] In addition to their death squad involvement, these law enforcement bodies had also been complicit in crime, including arms and drug trafficking.[75]

The 1992 Peace Accords eliminated the old security forces and in their place created the PNC, with a doctrine stressing the civilian, apolitical, and professional nature of the corps. Because its deployment did not keep pace with the dissolution of the National Police, however, substantial parts of the country had no police presence for almost a year, and the PNC was ill-prepared and under-resourced for tackling the resultant crime wave.[76] These limitations were no coincidence. The Alfredo Cristiani administration (1989–1994) had agreed to police reforms to achieve the parallel disarmament of the guerrilla Frente Farabundo Martí para la Liberación Nacional (Farabundo Martí National Liberation Front, or FMLN), but it was less committed to building a professional and democratic institution.[77] Furthermore, the government appears to have been concerned about losing its influence over a key instrument of political control and social order maintenance. Deliberate attempts were made to perpetuate authoritarian policing structures, notably by placing a disproportionate number of former military personnel in the command structure.[78] Since its early days, the PNC has thus lacked meaningful investigative capacities and has been plagued by abuse and corruption.[79] The recently elected FMLN government of Mauricio Funes has expressed its commitment to address this institutional crisis, but only time will tell to what extent its efforts will succeed.

The third factor is the illegal drug trade, which remains vastly under-researched and has yet to yield studies that illuminate its impact on violent crime in El Salvador. Central America is located between the world's primary cocaine suppliers and its main consumers. Drug trafficking spread through the isthmus during the region's civil wars as an important source of revenue for both insurgent and state armies. Corruption and limited law enforcement capacity have since ensured the viability of established smuggling channels; currently the subregion is believed to be the transit zone for an estimated 88 percent of U.S.-bound cocaine.[80] The drug trade can lead to high murder rates in the affected areas, and although the quantitative results are uncertain, the connection itself is not. In some areas, illicit substance use has driven up robberies, thefts, rapes, and homicides to such an extent that traffickers have even threatened to kill offending buyers to deter unwanted police attention. Among sellers and distributors, territorial disputes, outstanding payments, and suspected reporting to the police can trigger fierce clashes and murders. And yet, although the amount of drug-related violence is arguably substantial, precise figures are unavailable.[81]

According to a recent intelligence report, Mexican cartels have begun to redouble their operations in El Salvador. Their presence in this country goes back to the 1990s, when local traffickers offered the cartels their services to move drugs and money across Salvadoran national territory.[82] Stung by concerted crackdowns at home in recent years, however, the

Mexican organizations have progressively moved south, and the violence that characterizes their business has moved with them.[83] Tracking drug movements will therefore be crucial to establishing the trade's contribution to homicide levels. Trafficking routes seem to have varied over time, but the nature of these changes is not entirely clear. A UN publication states that shipments are no longer airborne but largely travel on maritime routes since the Mexican cartels relieved their Colombian counterparts of control of the regional drug trade.[84] Yet another report claims that stepped-up monitoring and interdiction of airborne and maritime deliveries crossing Central America have compelled Mexican traffickers to rely increasingly on land-based smuggling, a method that also encompasses littoral maritime and short-range aerial trafficking.[85]

The fourth factor concerns the long-standing absence of a coherent anti-gang strategy. The street gangs grew in marginal communities, places marked by overcrowding, a weak public infrastructure, nonexistent or deficient basic services, inadequate recreational facilities, and weak social capital.[86] The neoliberal economic policies the government adhered to during the last two decades permitted the elite to consolidate its wealth while exacerbating poverty and inequality.[87] Out-migration and remittances have gone some way toward raising human development standards, but past governments made no serious effort to create meaningful education and employment opportunities or to improve gang-affected communities.[88]

If the authorities showed no discernible interest in broader measures that could have inhibited gang formation and recruitment, they attached even less importance to gang-specific programs. The official response to the phenomenon consisted of sporadic suppressive measures and attempts to toughen juvenile and criminal laws so that youths under the age of eighteen, blamed for many of the homicides, could be tried as adults. No consistent gang prevention or rehabilitation programs were put in place.[89] The situation in the penitentiary system was allowed to become particularly dire. Neither the youth detention centers nor the adult prisons offered any genuine rehabilitation.[90] Instead, the penal complexes maintained degrading conditions and now operate at more than 200 percent of their capacity.[91] Inmates could hone their criminal skills, and riots ending in injuries and deaths were (and still are) all too common.[92] As a result of this lack of official involvement, the gang problem continued to grow throughout the 1990s and had become difficult to control by the time the first gang policy was announced.

From Mano Dura to Súper Mano Dura

In a 1993 survey of Salvadorans, nearly half of the interviewees (47 percent) identified a gang presence in their neighborhood.[93] Despite early signs that the problem was assuming more serious proportions, it did not receive the official attention it warranted. This vacuum was partly filled by nongovernmental organizations (NGOs), which—equipped with good intentions but short on resources and expertise—offered limited prevention and rehabilitation services to potential and actual gang members.[94] On 23 July 2003 the then president Francisco Flores descended on one of the capital's most notorious gang communities to launch his government's new policy, Mano Dura.[95] Since the gangs had been blamed by leaders and the press for the majority of homicides, the implication was that the plan would both dismantle these groups and cut down on violent crime.[96] In the ensuing months, the authorities embarked on graffiti removal, joint police-military anti-gang squads patrolled the streets, and police carried out massive area sweeps to detain suspected gang members.[97] The sensationalist media, which played a critical role in demonizing these youths and framing Mano Dura as an effective strategy, supplied abundant coverage of these spectacular crackdowns.[98]

The criminal prosecution of arrested gang members was meant to be facilitated by a temporary Anti-gang Act (Ley Antimaras, or LAM), ratified in October 2003. The six-month bill, aimed at individuals above the age of twelve, proposed to make gang membership a crime punishable by two to five years in prison.[99] These provisions breached a number of constitutional guarantees and international human rights norms, including lowering the age of legal responsibility and requiring no evidence that an offense had been committed. Instead, the police could simply detain everyone they deemed to be gang members by virtue of physical features, such as tattoos, or manner of dress.[100] The measure prompted immediate resistance among human rights defenders, judges, and opposition politicians, who not only objected to the terms of the proposed law but also insisted there was no need for special legislation at all and called for greater emphasis on prevention and rehabilitation.[101] The government, for its part, was faced with an unexpected dilemma, because most recently detained gang members were released for lack of evidence, and the legislature initially failed to enact the LAM.[102] Once ratified, the decree was challenged on constitutional grounds, and many judges opted not to apply it because of the human rights violations it allowed.[103]

The Supreme Court of Justice eventually determined the law to be unconstitutional, but the ruling came only days before the LAM was due to expire and helped the ARENA party save face prior to the March 2004 presidential elections.[104] Furthermore, on the day the verdict was delivered, the Legislative Assembly passed a similar three-month anti-gang act, which increased the prison sentence for gang membership to between three and six years.[105] In June 2004, domestic critics found support again when the United Nations Committee on the Rights of the Child requested the abrogation of the LAM, but by then President Antonio Saca had entered office and was about to introduce his own gang policy.[106] The suppression activities certainly enabled the police to identify and register many of El Salvador's gang members, but they also squandered scarce resources and were downright ineffective in securing convictions or controlling crime. During the first year of the plan, 19,275 gang-related detentions were made (including repeat arrests), but more than 95 percent of cases were dismissed.[107] More importantly, the homicide rate rose from 2,172 murders in 2003 (a daily average of six) to 2,762 in 2004 (a daily average of seven).[108] Despite its ineffectiveness and abusive nature, however, Mano Dura instantly appealed to a population that lived in constant fear of victimization, and this public attractiveness was critical to the adoption of the policy.

The Electoral Context

Given that El Salvador had experienced no recent spike in gang violence, and homicide figures had declined in previous years, the sudden need for gang control in 2003 might seem surprising. Mano Dura, however, can best be understood as a populist policy whose primary purpose was not to curb street gang activity but to improve the ARENA party's electoral advantage in the eight-month run-up to the 2004 presidential elections.[109] Although ARENA had successfully defended the presidency since 1989 and dominated the Legislative Assembly together with other right-wing parties, growing disenchantment with the country's economic direction benefited the FMLN, which steadily augmented its share in parliamentary seats and municipalities. The first significant swing occurred when the Left regained control of the San Salvador mayor's office in 1997, a trend that deepened with the elections of 2000 and 2003, in which the FMLN overtook ARENA in the Legislative Assembly.[110] Although victory would again go to the Right in 2004, in the preceding months it was widely felt that the FMLN's recent gains had strengthened prospects for a shift in the formal power structure.[111]

Past surveys have shown that Salvadorans' perception of the main national problem influences their political preferences. In other words, citizens will favor one of the two largest parties over the other depending on whether they are preoccupied with economic issues or crime.[112] For much of 2003, public opinion had identified the economy as the overriding problem, and this assessment had adversely affected ARENA's levels of support.[113] In an October poll, however, almost half the population indicated that security was most important to them, and for the first time as many as 21 percent of respondents identified gangs as the key national topic.[114] The same survey revealed that 88 percent of interviewees supported Mano Dura, and a majority believed the plan would help lower crime.[115] Furthermore, in the space of a few months ARENA had managed to displace the FMLN in polls on voting intentions.[116]

One factor behind this shift was the greater popularity of ARENA's presidential candidate, thirty-eight-year-old Elias Antonio Saca, but another was clearly the introduction of Mano Dura.[117] Although one might argue that the ruling party's good showing was merely an unintended effect of the plan rather than its purpose, both the timing and the inconsistent nature of the gang policy suggest that the strategy indeed aimed less to reduce gang violence than to win votes. This inference was confirmed by a leaked ARENA executive committee memo, which acknowledged that Mano Dura and its backing by the majority of voters gave ARENA an immediate opportunity to associate itself with a winning theme and present itself as the party that was toughest on crime.[118] As it became apparent that gang control would afford ARENA substantial political benefits, that issue became a central campaign theme and was ultimately one of the reasons for the Right's presidential victory.[119] Nevertheless, widespread criticism of suppressive crackdowns, the judges' lack of cooperation, and the expiry of the LAM required President Saca to adopt a revised gang policy.

The Rhetoric of Gang Prevention and Rehabilitation

The Saca administration's strategic plan recognized that crime and violence remained challenges for the country and pledged that a special effort would be made to address the gang problem through prevention, law enforcement, and rehabilitation/reinsertion.[120] Announced in late August 2004, Súper Mano Dura initially centered on additional legal reforms, police raids, and anti-gang squad deployments.[121] While the authorities made gang suppression a priority, the much-lauded prevention and rehabilitation programs were introduced only after a considerable delay. Mano Amiga (Friendly Hand) was aimed at preventing at-risk youths from joining gangs, while Mano Extendida (Extended Hand) sought to help gang members reintegrate into society. The institutions tasked with the implementation of these initiatives were the Secretaría de la Juventud (Youth Secretariat, or SJ) and the CNSP.

The SJ was established in 2004 as an agency of the president's office, to execute JóvenES, a program aimed at promoting the development of young people.[122] In pursuit of this objective, the SJ developed the Plan Nacional de Juventud 2005–2015 (National Youth Plan 2005–2015), which incorporated no coherent gang strategy and instead proposed a series of activities structured around five main pillars.[123] One of these concerned "Vulnerable Groups" and comprised Mano Amiga and Mano Extendida. Although Mano Amiga had been announced as a gang prevention program, in the plan it was presented as a much broader form of early intervention to assist youths at risk for crime, gangs, drug addiction, and teenage pregnancy. Similarly, Mano Extendida was described as an initiative that sought the rehabilitation and reinsertion of gang members, juvenile offenders, drug addicts, and street children aged fifteen to twenty-four years. Specifically, it aspired to teach values, offer spiritual assistance, education, job training, health services, tattoo removal, cultural activities, and sports activities and to facilitate the search for employment.[124]

The programs focused on the twenty most crime-ridden communities and were made operational by a multiagency system in which the SJ was meant to act as the national coordinator of existing gang control efforts, manage resources, and monitor and evaluate the various projects.[125] During its lifetime—the secretariat was abolished by President Mauricio Funes in June 2009—it spent vast amounts of public money on promotion.[126] However, most of its technical staff lacked the necessary expertise and were simply young ARENA supporters who received generous salaries while being groomed as a future party cadre.[127] Overall, the SJ appeared to be a fundamentally weak and politicized institution that was created to demonstrate the Saca government's commitment to prevention and rehabilitation, but displayed neither a vision of comprehensive gang control nor a real interest in it.

Unlike the secretariat, the CNSP has been actively engaged in gang prevention and rehabilitation, though with few tangible results. Originally founded to advise the head of state in public security matters, the council was later assigned a role in crime prevention and, more recently, in gang rehabilitation. Its gang prevention work has largely revolved around ProJóvenes, a five-year European Union–sponsored project that pursued community and municipal organizing, strengthening of families, education, vocational training and employment, and, lately, rehabilitation and reinsertion.[128] Targeting youths aged ten to twenty-five in Greater San Salvador, the initiative rotated among the most severely homicide-affected (rather than gang-affected) communities, but it left out those communities where lack of security and weak organizing were deemed to preclude successful interventions. The program not only appeared insufficiently gang-specific and excluded areas that should have been prioritized for gang control efforts, but also, curiously, privileged sports and social infrastructure over other activities. The initial ProJóvenes program terminated in 2008, but it has now entered a second five-year phase.[129]

At the heart of the council's gang rehabilitation program lay the *granja-escuela*, a rehabilitation center located in the department of Sonsonate. Opened in 2005, the *granja* had each year housed a group of former gang members aged sixteen to twenty-five. Over a period of some six months, the youths were offered spiritual and psychological assistance, health services, tattoo removal, sports, education, and vocational training in areas such as rose growing, chicken farming, bakery skills, and cosmetics. These practical skills were supplemented with a short course in business administration to facilitate self-employment and thus offset the lack of domestic job opportunities. The *granja*, however, faced a series of significant limitations, including severe budget constraints; few boarders, whose stay was too brief to be effective; and the scarcity of meaningful job opportunities (which was not sufficiently counterbalanced by the self-employment option). Moreover, that some of the "graduates" were subsequently placed in a private rehabilitation center testified to the weakness of the project.

While Súper Mano Dura was being enforced, gang arrest figures continued to climb, but so did the homicide rate, suggesting that the real perpetrators remained at large and the plan had been a resounding failure. Claims as to the plan's efficacy began to lose their credibility, and in a 2005 end-of-year survey, 45.4 percent of Salvadorans thought the measure had helped little or not at all in lowering crime.[130] By mid-2006, Súper Mano Dura had become a political liability and was quietly withdrawn. A new plan, Maestro de Seguridad, shifted the law enforcement focus from area sweeps and mass detentions to the investigation of individual gang "leaders" and gangs as organized criminal structures.[131] This preference was accompanied by a discursive emphasis on the gangs' alleged mutation into transnational criminal organizations and on greater participation by authorities in transnational anti-gang cooperation, measures chiefly aimed at sharing information and establishing strategies to counter regional gang expansion.[132] Clearly, suppression remained the preferred strategy, and this had adverse effects on the gang problem.

The Legacy of Mano Dura

Following the implementation of Mano Dura, the gangs underwent a number of important transformations that were partly the unintended but, in some ways, inevitable consequences of a deeply flawed ideological plan. Both Mara Salvatrucha and the 18th Street Gang toughened their entry requirements and made their selection process more rigorous to reduce the possibility of enemy infiltration and ensure greater control over their members. New recruits are now more carefully screened and assigned riskier initiation rites that may range from the commission of fairly banal criminal offenses to the killing of a rival gang member.[133] MS, for its part, has stopped admitting females, considering them too weak and unreliable to be trusted with gang-related matters.[134] Drug use, which was long one of the chief attractions of gang life, has been restricted, although the consumption of alcohol and marijuana continues to be allowed and indeed is frequent. Harder drugs such as cocaine, however, have been prohibited altogether as they impair the alertness of many youths, whose resultant deaths ultimately weaken the gangs.[135] While these changes appear to have been prompted by pragmatic considerations rather than external threats to group integrity, others evidently occurred in direct response to Mano Dura.

By indiscriminately suppressing gang members and concentrating them in special prisons, the plan encouraged more clandestine behavior and increased gang cohesion and criminality. The youths abandoned highly visible tattoos, chose more conventional clothing and hairstyles, and began hanging out in private places to minimize police persecution.[136] The crackdowns certainly strengthened gang identity and loyalty, but doubts remain about the extent to which they provoked structural and leadership changes. According to some analysts, the gangs adopted a more formal, hierarchical structure in which members assume specific roles, such as the *palabrero* (leader), the *tesorero* (administrator and treasurer), or the *soldado* (one who executes the missions that the group or leader assigns). Similarly, these researchers claim that the gangs long recognized only informal leaders, but since the time of Mano Dura have created formal leaders, including leaders at regional and national levels, who are accepted both inside and outside the prisons.[137] These studies, however, seem to uncritically echo official descriptions of the gangs and contradict not only the established literature in the field but also other research on El Salvador's gangs. Those findings suggest that while specific roles and organizational capacity exist to a certain degree, the gangs continue to have a more horizontal structure and only local "leaders," who are consulted by other members but do not have the final word.[138]

More importantly, gang members have been increasingly implicated in robberies, the illegal possession of firearms, and especially homicides and extortions.[139] Yet, because much of the available data is based on arrest figures, the true extent and nature of gang crime remain ambiguous. Certainly, the gangs heavily extort the country's transportation sector to purchase weapons and pay the defense lawyers of their detained peers. By 2004 the police attributed 50 percent of all extortions to the gangs; by 2009 this number had increased to 70 percent.[140] Arrest numbers also suggest that gang homicides increased by 55 percent between 2004 and 2005, leading one analyst to conclude that gang violence worsened during the Mano Dura years.[141] While IML data point to a similar upward trend, higher arrest and incarceration figures may actually misrepresent the reality of gang crime.

One difficulty relates to the definition of a gang homicide, which may be gang-related or gang-motivated. The first describes cases in which the offender or the victim is a gang member, while the second refers to crimes committed because of a gang objective, such as retaliation, witness intimidation, or offenses serving as initiation rites.[142] Evidently, the use of the "gang-related" definition yields a greater number of gang homicides and, by implication, a very different picture of the gang problem. The Salvadoran police appear to use this classification, but for illustrative purposes it is interesting to break down the PNC statistics into both categories. Of the 229 murders carried out between 1 and 24 January 2005, 92 (40 percent) were gang-related, but a gang member was the perpetrator in only 77 killings (33.4 percent), and in 35 of them (15.3 percent) both the offender and the victim were gang members.[143] While the motives in all of these cases were not specified, the example shows that better investigations and more accurate definitions could provide a clearer picture of gang crime. The second difficulty is that a number of gang members have been sent to prison on trumped-up charges. Weak investigative work by police has compelled the FGR to routinely rely on either police agents or *testigos criteriados* (offenders who are offered a sentence reduction in exchange for giving witness testimony in a different case) to achieve a guilty verdict. Fabricated statements by some of these witnesses have, however, led to false convictions.[144] Indeed, judges have discovered that certain prosecutors have attempted to use the same witness in up to fifty different cases.[145] Gang members themselves reported that the PNC and the FGR have linked gang youths to crimes they did not commit and had them sentenced to many years in prison.[146] While the true magnitude of this practice is unknown, its occurrence distorts gang information and ensures impunity for the real perpetrators.

Transnational Criminal Organizations?

The nature of other perceived transformations is more contentious. First, given the regional presence and communication links of MS and 18th Street, the Salvadoran authorities have described the two groups as transnational entities. The existence of such cross-border ties is unsurprising, especially since some gang members are deportees. The fact that youths in different countries claim affiliation with the same gang, however, does not necessarily point to the proliferation of transnational gang networks that each answer to a single chain of command. In a 1996 gang survey, 15.5 percent of respondents acknowledged maintaining regular contact with their peers in the United States (other nations were not covered by the study). Interestingly, the affirmative answer was higher among MS members (19 percent) than 18th Street members (14.4 percent).[147] This information might guide future research into the density of transnational gang connections, specifically the idea — defended by some observers — that MS has a tighter grip over its affiliates than its rival.[148]

Nonetheless, a 2006 survey among imprisoned gang members reported similar results: 28.2 percent of interviewees (data not broken down by gang) admitted sustaining at least sporadic connections with their counterparts in other nations, notably the United States (37.2 percent), Mexico (19.9 percent), Guatemala (15.3 percent), and Honduras (15.3 percent).[149] This coordination was pursued for a variety of purposes, especially to exchange intelligence (42.9 percent); to give and receive orders, codes of conduct, and action plans (23.1 percent); to send money and weapons (17.6 percent); and to help gang members leave the country (3.3 percent). The study found no evidence, however, of systematic and institutionalized links between the gang structures in North and Central America, let alone the existence of cross-border gang networks.[150] Since both surveys were self-report studies, some respondents may have preferred to withhold information about the breadth and density of transnational gang ties. Nevertheless, the available data suggest that these bonds are not as structured and extensive as is officially asserted. For the time being, it appears that MS and 18th Street are better understood as networks of autonomous groups that share a symbolic, identificatory, and normative affiliation.[151] The transnational gang discourse, however, has important repercussions: it diverts attention from the local conditions that spawn the gangs, and by depicting the problem as a shared one, it becomes no one's responsibility.

Second, the Salvadoran police have likened the street gangs to organized crime, arguably because they form solely for criminal objectives, possess a hierarchical transnational structure, use weapons and communications technology (such as radios and cell phones), and traffic in drugs.[152] Some analysts have accepted the view that the gangs have, or are about to, become a new form of organized crime whose basic aim is to participate in the shadow economy.[153] But even though illegal pursuits are part of street gang identity, this orientation to delinquency is insufficient to classify them as organized criminal groups. The latter are constituted exclusively for illicit gain and act collectively rather than as subsets.[154] They require mature, professional members with organizational skills, well-defined leadership and specialized group roles, codes of conduct with clearly understood sanctions, and locations for profits to be used for group purposes. Typically, organized crime groups develop relationships with legitimate businesses as well as political and legal institutions.[155] If they collaborate with gang youths, they hire them only for specific activities.[156] Street gangs, by contrast, are generally incapable of behaving as these more professional actors do. Typically, the gangs have younger members, a shifting leadership, intermediate levels of organization, frequently broken codes of honor, and versatile and independent criminal behaviors.[157]

In El Salvador's gangs, too, leaders enjoy considerable influence, but they can be replaced if deemed unsuited to the task or even "corrupt." For example, Carlos Ernesto Mojica Lechuga ("el Viejo Lin") was long portrayed as the national 18th Street leader, even though his peers discharged him and sentenced him to death for pilfering gang funds.[158] A gang survey in 2006 adduced further evidence that the gangs fundamentally differ from organized crime groups. The study revealed that the average age at which youths join a gang remains at fifteen years.[159] The reasons for joining have not substantially varied either: the principal motives continue to be the lifestyle (36.7 percent), followed by family problems (15.5 percent), peer influence (9.2 percent), and protection and respect (8.9

percent). Similarly, as mentioned earlier, the perceived benefits of gang membership were seen to be none (46.8 percent); solidarity, friendship, and support (27.8 percent); respect and protection (8.2 percent); freedom (2.2 percent); and money (0.6 percent). As these findings indicate, El Salvador's street gangs are unlikely candidates for organized crime. Youths join these groups to fulfill a range of individual social needs, and crime is a by-product of gang affiliation, not its goal. Indeed, the respondents declared that some gang members and *clicas* act as foot soldiers for organized crime (mainly for targeted killings, weapons smuggling, car theft, and drug distribution), but not the gangs as such. NGO staff and justice sector workers corroborated this information.[160] The implication is that, despite their increasing criminal involvement, the gangs remain a social problem that needs to be addressed as such. Depicting them as organized crime is analytically unhelpful and only invites inappropriate policy responses.

Third, Salvadoran authorities have asserted that the gangs consider drug trafficking a key source of income and that 18th Street even plans to take over the drug trade.[161] There is reason, however, to question the extent of the gangs' involvement in this business. Drug gangs require a clear, hierarchical leadership, strong group cohesiveness, a code of loyalty, a narrow focus on drug sales, and avoidance of non-sales-related criminal involvement.[162] Street gangs, by contrast, tend to lack the capital, knowledge, and power to rival professional organizations. Instead, drug dealing is more often associated with individual gang members or subsets of them.[163] In Central America, the bulk of cocaine trafficking occurs in large shipments controlled by Colombian and Mexican cartels. Some gang members provide minor logistical or security support, but MS and 18th Street are unlikely to manage the drug trade.[164] Indeed, "el Viejo Lin" conceded that the gangs are interested in playing a more extensive role in drug trafficking, but their financial capacity is insufficient to meet the cartels' demands.[165] Moreover, El Salvador's drug market is too small to be a major source of income. A 2006 national drug use survey conducted in urban areas found cocaine and crack use to be below 0.5 percent. Shipments appear to transit the country intact, rather than being repacked and sold.[166] Former gang member and MS founder Ernesto Miranda ("Smokey") disclosed that cocaine sales in Los Angeles had earned him some US$3,000 a day, while his subsequent crack deals in San Salvador yielded no more than US$100 a day.[167]

As regards the ties between the street gangs and higher-level drug dealers, a local study distinguished between *banderos*, *transeros*, and gang youths. The *banderos* are members of organized crime groups who traffic drugs, weapons, or cars and may participate in kidnapping rings. *Transeros* (drug dealers) sell drugs to gang members for retail on the streets and, along with the *banderos*, are said to enjoy protection as a result of their connections with corrupt police officers. Gang members interviewed for the same study reported that some youths or *clicas*, but not the gangs as such, were associated with drug sales.[168] PNC elements, for their part, acknowledged that gang members are merely employed by more powerful traffickers, but that these latter are rarely arrested.[169] A notable exception concerns the *narcodiputado* (literally, "narco-deputy") Eliú Martínez, who had transported sizeable cocaine shipments for a Guatemalan associate of the Gulf Cartel and is currently imprisoned in the United States.[170] In sum, evidence indicates that the street gangs are minor players in the drug trade. Overemphasizing their role deflects attention from more influential actors who need to be identified and prosecuted if drug trafficking and its associated violence are to be curbed.

Conclusion: Reassessing the Gang Threat

There is no doubt that the gang problem has grown more serious and complex over the years: the youths use heavier weapons, the nature of the crimes they engage in has changed, and the volume of crimes has increased. Yet, while the gangs now pose a different and more critical public security threat from that of past years, they remain largely a local security issue. At the same time, official sources give us a biased and inconsistent picture of gang activity, and research has not kept pace with recent developments. Although our knowledge of these groups remains sketchy, and their impact on violent crime is not fully known, this impact should not be exaggerated. El Salvador clearly has a multifaceted urban crime crisis that needs to be addressed in its entirety. An exclusive focus on the gangs will not substantially improve this situation.

The contemporary gang threat in El Salvador cannot be understood in isolation from public institutions, notably the police and the media. Past administrations either ignored the gangs or preferred to suppress them. The groups' negative evolution might have been forestalled had governments reacted sooner and with a policy that blended prevention, rights-respecting law enforcement, and rehabilitation. Indeed, one might argue that it is the failure to create both a comprehensive anticrime strategy and professional, well-resourced institutions that jeopardizes people's lives.

Moreover, widespread police corruption has exacerbated the gang problem. Rather than enforcing the law, many agents become accomplices not only by accepting bribes, leaking information, and engaging in cover-ups but also by supplying gang members with drugs and weapons or charging them "taxes."[171] The mass media, too, have played their part in inflating the gang threat. Studies have shown that public perceptions of insecurity often exceed the actual threat of crime and violence. Paradoxically, for example, a victimization survey conducted in 2004 revealed that 68.6 percent of Salvadorans felt the gangs were little or no trouble in their community, but 91 percent of the population considered them to be a national problem. Respondents who felt intimidated by the gangs had evidently been influenced by the media.[172] Thus, while the gang threat should not be downplayed, it clearly exists in the mind as much as on the streets.

El Salvador's street gangs are unlikely to turn into organized crime groups, but they are destined to stay and grow in the continued absence of a full-fledged, well-reasoned gang policy. In some communities, a second generation of gang members is already being raised, largely oblivious to any other way of life and less receptive to gang intervention programs than their parents. The Funes government certainly expressed its commitment to an alternative gang strategy. Apart from taking specific steps, such as the closure of the Youth Secretariat and staff changes in both the CNSP and the PNC, the administration pledged to emphasize prevention, prison-based rehabilitation, and investigative policing.[173] A tangible anti-gang strategy nevertheless has yet to materialize. The challenges are many: elite resistance to structural changes, weak social capital, and a lack of resources and expertise. Unless El Salvador takes a different approach to gangs, however, it will have to live with them for many more years to come.

CHAPTER 3

Street Gangs of Guatemala

ELIN CECILIE RANUM

Youth gangs are far from a new phenomenon in Guatemala: observers have reported gangs there since the 1950s.[1] It is the gangs that appeared in some areas of the capital in the 1980s, however, that are commonly accepted to be the origins of the gangs that operate in the country today.[2] The youth gangs that emerged in the 1980s developed and operated within specific territories or barrios, without making any noticeable efforts to expand their activities or spread to other areas of the city or country. Violence was generally limited to gang rivalry, along with some petty crime in public areas. Today the story is quite different. Youth gangs are associated with high levels of crime and violence. Their structure appears to be better defined and more hierarchical than it was two decades ago. Yet even though today's gangs appear to be different from the earlier barrio gangs, Guatemalan youth gangs still preserve some of the old characteristics. Any effort to address the phenomenon of gang behavior should consider its highly complex nature and the many differences that exist in individual behavior within a gang and behavior between the gangs. As is discussed in this chapter, gangs should be treated as a serious part of Guatemala's crime problem, but not as the cause of it. Gang violence must be understood in the context of other forms of violence resulting from institutional weaknesses and other features of the Guatemalan state and society. The government's delayed and inadequate response to the problem has only contributed to the country's escalating gang rivalry and violence.

This chapter briefly discusses the emergence and evolution of the gang problem since the 1980s and situates it within a highly complex environment where institutional weakness, inequality, and an uncertain separation between the legal and illegal spheres are important features. It also assesses the current situation, with special attention to gangs' participation in violence and gang members' dual identity as both perpetrators and victims.

Gangs in Names and Numbers

As in neighboring El Salvador and Honduras, two "international" gangs,[3] Mara Salvatrucha (MS) and the 18th Street Gang (Calle 18 in Spanish), dominate the youth gang universe in Guatemala. According to a U.S. Agency for International Development (USAID) assessment, these two gangs constituted 95 percent of all gang membership in Guatemala in 2006.[4] Other gangs of more local origin still exist, such as the Latin Kings, the Breakeros, the Cholos, and the Wifers. Although they represent a marginal portion of the youths who are involved in gangs, their existence illustrates the diversity of the gang phenomenon in the country.

Guatemala's National Civilian Police (known by the Spanish acronym PNC) estimated that the country had some 8,000 to 10,000 gang members in 2006.[5] Other estimates for the same year went as high as 14,000.[6] The discrepancy is due to the many difficulties any effort to quantify a phenomenon of this kind faces. Among them, first, is that gang activity has become increasingly clandestine in recent years. Second, "outsiders" find it hard to determine whether a person is a gang member or not. A third factor is that many of those who once were noted on a police register probably have been killed, others may have retired from gang activities, some may have migrated, and new youths, unfamiliar to authorities, have come in.[7]

What seems to be clear, however, is that gangs have sprung up throughout Guatemala. What was once a phenomenon primarily of the capital city is today considered a national problem. Nevertheless, there are important geographical differences in the levels of gang presence. According to police registers, the capital area reported the highest concentration of gangs in 2004, followed in decreasing order by the southwestern, northwestern, and central areas. In contrast, the eastern part of the country had little gang presence.[8] These geographical variations are particularly interesting when considering the highly marked cultural and demographic differences between these areas. With the exception of the capital area, gang presence appears to be stronger in regions that are characterized by high proportions of indigenous groups, whereas in the eastern areas the population is predominantly ladino (of mixed European and Amerindian blood; called mestizo in other parts of Latin America).[9]

Institutional Weakness and Gang Proliferation

Although today's dominant gangs in Guatemala—Mara Salvatrucha and the 18th Street Gang—originated among Latin American immigrants in Los Angeles, California, in the 1980s, the origins of most currently active Guatemalan youth gangs trace back to the local gangs that appeared in the country in the 1980s. In Guatemala and other Central American countries—particularly El Salvador and Honduras, where gangs have demonstrated a similar pattern of indigenous development[10]—scholars emphasize the local origins and traditions of youth gangs, arguing that their existence permitted the relatively rapid expansion of the MS and the 18th Street Gang in the region.[11] Furthermore, Guatemala and Honduras were, and still are, very fertile ground for gang proliferation.

In the mid-1980s, gangs started to emerge in schools and in specific parts of Guatemala City, and their names reflected their origin.[12] Juan Merino associated some of these new gangs with emerging youth-focused social protest groups, basing his argument on a groundbreaking 1988 study of gangs in Central America published by the Guatemalan Association for the Advancement of Social Sciences (AVANCSO).[13] Although this association may be valid in some cases, the gangs that gave rise to the current phenomenon emerged in neighborhoods in the capital and had few, if any, characteristics of movements with a political aim. As in El Salvador, these gangs fulfilled social needs for youths in these areas. Over time, these gangs established territories, and the defense of their territories soon fueled rivalry with other gangs. By the end of the 1980s, Mara Salvatrucha and the 18th Street Gang had also established a considerable presence in the country. This increase in gang presence led Guatemalan officials to accuse gangs of being responsible for most of the criminal activity in the country.[14] Nevertheless, Guatemalan youth gangs had been associated with relatively low levels of violence until the end of the 1990s, at least in comparison with their Salvadoran counterparts.[15]

At the same time, as Merino observed, police persecution and repression also provoked violence among some gang members.[16] This suggests that there are multifaceted reasons for the increase in gang violence and that gangs have evolved and transformed within the Guatemalan environment. The contemporary gang phenomenon must be explored within this context, rather than simply as a consequence of the arrival of the Californian gangs.[17]

The Spread of California Gang Culture

Deportations of convicted criminal gang members from the United States beginning in the early 1990s were important in the transformation of gang culture in Guatemala. As with the case of El Salvador, the impact of deportations needs to be carefully analyzed along with other issues creating a context conducive to gang proliferation in Guatemala. While the appearance of Mara Salvatrucha and the 18th Street Gang in Guatemala as well as other Central American countries is closely associated with the deportation of gang members from the United States, this factor alone is not sufficient to understand the gang phenomenon in Guatemala. As emphasized above, local youth gangs already existed before deportations started to take place, and any effort to explain the rapid growth and expansion of gangs should consider a number of domestic social, political, cultural, and individual factors.[18]

Once the Californian gang culture was imported to Central America through deportations, it came to dominate the gang scene in Guatemala within a few years. How did the Californians establish themselves and expand within the country? The lack of information and hard data about this process makes it difficult to establish a clear picture of how it took place, but what information is available suggests that in some cases MS and 18th Street absorbed many of the existing local gangs, while in other cases deported gang members formed gangs in their new neighborhoods.[19] This indicates that many of the deported MS and 18th Street members continued their gang activity after they returned to their native country.[20] The rivalry between MS and 18th Street was also transferred to Guatemala. Nevertheless, although experienced gang members from the United States enjoyed certain levels of respect at least in the first years, locals in Guatemala soon gained leading positions within their gangs. While the local gang culture was influenced by the Californian gang style, the *clicas* (independent local subgroups or cells of a gang) that emerged throughout the country responded to local dynamics. In the case of both California groups, local *clicas* constituted the larger gangs, but little is known of any coordination and contact between the *clicas* themselves at this time. As is discussed further below, the deportation of gang members from the United States appears to be less important today, at least in Guatemala, than it was in the 1990s. It is necessary to consider other factors in order to understand why gangs have been able to expand.

The Guatemalan Environment

The environmental model proposed by the Pan American Health Organization is a useful tool for understanding why gangs emerge and spread in some countries of the Central American region. This model emphasizes factors such as social exclusion; a culture of violence; rapid and uncontrolled urban growth; migration; communitarian disorganization; drugs; the dynamics of violence; dysfunctional families; the influence of friends already involved in gangs; and the need of youths to construct personal identities. The significance of these factors varies with each case, but in general they help explain why gangs have emerged and proliferated in some communities.[21]

As mentioned above, gangs started to emerge in the 1980s, during a time of civil war and authoritarian rule. Guatemala's armed conflict was rooted in historical inequality, discrimination, and exclusion. Political and economic power had been concentrated in the hands of a small, entrenched elite that governed with support from the powerful armed forces almost without interruption since the country gained its independence from Spain in 1821.[22] Guatemala's internal conflict was the longest (1960–1996) and one of the most brutal and bloody conflicts in Latin America. Approximately 200,000 people were killed during those thirty-six years, and some 1.5 million were forced to flee their homes. Although the highlands were most directly affected by the war's atrocities, decades of brutal violations of human rights inflicted deep injuries on the entire society. The social fabric was seriously damaged, fear was widespread in the population, and the culture of violence was reinforced.[23] This historical legacy posed enormous obstacles to recovery in the postwar period that are yet to be overcome.

Guatemala still lags behind most of the region in terms of human development. The United Nations Development Programme ranks the country as the second poorest in Latin America.[24] Approximately half of the population is living in poverty.[25] Income distribution is squeezed: the poorest quintile receives 2.9 percent of total income, in sharp contrast with the 59.5 percent of total income that goes to the richest quintile.[26] Public investment in health and education remains low, 30 percent of the adult population is considered illiterate, and only one in three children is enrolled in secondary education. These social conditions become even more critical for the indigenous population, which constitutes 38.4 percent of the total population.[27] This group has been the principal victim of the social exclusion and ethnic discrimination that still characterize the country.

A chronic inability to deal with social issues is only one of many signs of the Guatemalan state's weakness and fragility. More than a decade after the signing of the peace accords that ended the country's civil war, international observers continue to express concern over the weakness of state institutions, particularly in terms of security and human rights.[28] Although this is far from a new problem, it has become more evident in recent years, particularly with regard to Guatemala's public security institutions.

The division between legal and criminal at every level of society is tenuous in today's Guatemala. Many politicians, public functionaries, businessmen, and members of the military are involved in both kinds of activities. Any doubt about the infiltration of criminal structures into the state apparatus was dismissed after the 2007 assassination of three Salvadoran deputies in Guatemala.[29] Links from drugs traffickers, organized crime, and "social cleansing" groups to the higher levels of the National Civilian Police and the Ministry of Internal Affairs (Ministerio de Gobernación) were discovered in the aftermath of the scandal, and this was just one among several cases of politicians and public functionaries who were detained for illegal activities.[30] Nor are relations between the state and organized crime a new story. During the civil war, the Guatemalan army managed to secure important financial resources through a sophisticated balance between legal and illegal activities.[31] This access to nonstate funding converted the army into a powerful economic actor and thus an even stronger political power. Unfortunately, some of these corporations remain intact today, and in some cases they have developed into shadow parallel power structures.[32] Their presence not only weakens the state but also fosters an environment of impunity that favors illegality.

These and other powerful sectors have been reluctant to give up their privileged position. The construction of the National Civilian Police force has suffered from this resistance. Reforms that could have corrected the shortcomings of the peace accords, such as their failure to establish public security as a strictly civilian domain, have not been implemented.[33] Instead, the continued integration of members from the armed forces has been the most common response to the National Civilian Police's inability to combat crime. This, together with insufficient mechanisms of internal control, has impeded the development of an efficient, democratic, and civilian police force.

Political institutions such as the political parties and Congress also are

Table 3.1. Homicides in Guatemala, 2000–2006

	2000	2001	2002	2003	2004	2005	2006
Number of homicides	2,904	3,230	3,631	4,237	4,507	5,338	5,885
Homicides per 100,000 persons	28	30	32	37	38	44	47

Source: Programa de las Naciones Unidas para el Desarrollo (PNUD), *Informe estadístico de la violencia en Guatemala* (Guatemala City: Programa de Seguridad Ciudadana y Prevención de la Violencia del PNUD Guatemala, 2007). This report is based on numbers obtained from the National Civilian Police.

weak, and this has delayed the development of legislation and a framework for public policies.[34] The incomplete transition to functional democracy and rule of law means that the state remains absent in many areas of the country. This situation, illustrated by what Guillermo O'Donnell terms "brown areas," has created vacuums of power that favor the persistence or emergence of nonstate actors, many of them acting illegally.[35] In this specific context, parallel power structures and other criminal actors have been able to increase their presence and constantly challenge the integrity of the state.[36]

It is therefore not surprising that crime and violence have increased sharply in the postconflict period. Even though homicides dropped considerably in the first years after the conflict ended, from 43 homicides per 100,000 habitants in 1997 to 29 per 100,000 in 1999, this reduction was not sustained. On the contrary, homicide levels have increased constantly since 1999, reaching a rate of 47 homicides per 100,000 habitants in 2006. This characterizes the country as one of the most violent in the hemisphere (Table 3.1).

Victimization surveys also suggest an increase in crime in recent years. In a 2006 study, 19.2 percent of the population reported having been the victim of a crime during the previous twelve months. This represents an increase from 2004, when 12.8 percent of the surveyed confirmed that they had been the victim of a crime.[37]

Guatemala is an important transit point for the drug trade. While drug cartels formerly preferred the Caribbean corridor, today approximately 88 percent of the cocaine traded from South America to the United States goes through Central America and Mexico.[38] It is difficult to understand the intensified rivalry between drug cartels and the increased visibility of drug-related crimes as separate phenomena from the increase in drug trafficking in the region. Most of the drugs passing through Guatemala are destined for the United States, but a share of them remains in the country for local consumption. Although drug consumption levels in the region are relatively low, it is likely that the growth of a domestic market has both provoked a struggle among rivals to dominate it and attracted new actors to this lucrative business.[39]

In this context, where illegality has benefited from impunity, where opportunities are scarce and a high proportion of the population is living in marginal urban or semiurban areas, gangs have appeared as a tempting alternative for many youths in their search for identity and possibilities for the future. Previous studies in El Salvador described a duality of "push and pull" factors behind young people's entrance into gangs.[40] Gangs may appear attractive to many youths, both for the gang lifestyle (*el vacil*) itself and as a source of friendship, brotherhood, solidarity, respect, and power. As suggested by Maria L. Santacruz Giralt and Alberto Concha-Eastman, on the one hand the *vacil* reflects the gangs' function as a supplier of power and respect, attributes many youths are looking for.[41] On the other hand, complex social, familial, cultural, communal, and individual conditions are factors that may push young people into gang activities.

A "Transnational Youth Gangs" survey in 2006 of gang members in Guatemala shows that the motivations for entering a gang do not differ much from those found in earlier studies in El Salvador.[42] In the Guatemalan case, family problems are the main reason that youth enter gangs (accounting for 40 percent of those surveyed). For 33.8 percent of the surveyed, the *vacil* appeared to be the main reason for joining. Influence from friends was cited by 7.7 percent as their reason for entering, and 4.6 percent had joined out of a desire for protection and respect. Only 1.5 percent mentioned economic reasons for entering the gang. The reasons why youths enter gangs appear to be the same today as they were five years ago. My personal interviews with gang members confirm dual motivations that led them to gangs: the attractive aspects of gang life, such as the clothing, power, and special slang; and the problems that young people experience growing up in marginalized areas. Most gang members enter the gang at an early age. According to the survey, the average age of entrance was 14.7 years. Interviews with gang members show that, in many cases, contact with gangs is established between the ages of seven and eleven. Nevertheless, entering the gang is not necessarily the result of a real decision-making process. Many potential gang members have grown up in areas with a gang presence and have friends who are gang members. To them, entering the gang may seem like a natural path. Some are the brothers, sisters, sons, or daughters of gang members, many of whom have been assassinated or detained in prisons, and rancor and the search for revenge are important motivating factors for this generation of gang members.

The State's Response to the Problem

Before the turn of the present century, Guatemalan authorities paid little attention to the gang problem, at least in terms of public policies and programs to address it. As in neighboring El Salvador and Honduras, a punitive attitude dominated whatever state programs existed. In contrast to those two countries, where reforms of the penal codes institutionalized the criminalization of gang membership, Guatemalan crackdown programs were not backed by legal reforms.[43] The lack of a legal foundation appeared to be no hindrance for the police in their implementation of zero-tolerance policies.

The most important and most famous of these plans, Plan Escoba (Operation Broom), dominated all efforts to control gangs in 2003 and 2004. This crackdown strategy consisted merely of the massive and indiscriminate detention of thousands of youths suspected, sometimes rightly and often wrongly, to have some relation to gangs. In the absence of any specific legislation that penalized gang membership, it became common practice among prosecutors to manipulate established judicial norms in their efforts to find legal support for the detentions. Drug possession was the most common charge, and thousands of youths were brought into the judicial system accused of that crime. A study conducted by the Instituto de Estudios Comparados de Ciencias Penales de Guatemala demonstrates that the large majority of these detentions were illegal.[44] In only 1.1 percent of more than 5,000 detentions examined by the institute did the judge find legal grounds to justify a formal charge against the suspect.

Although only a minimal number of the cases ended in a formal sentence, the charge of drug possession was quite useful in terms of holding gang members in prison. The Guatemalan penal code permits provisional detention for drug-related crimes until the case is closed or a sentence is pronounced. In 2003 and 2004, several thousand detentions saturated a judicial system already suffering from serious deficiencies, and any process could be delayed several months before it was dismissed or closed.[45] Consequently, thousands of young people illegally detained and accused of that particular crime had to spend months in overcrowded jails and prisons. Moreover, the manipulation of procedure and the law seriously weakened the youths' legal and individual rights. This practice also had a serious impact on the gang phenomenon (discussed further below). More recent reforms of procedural norms, particularly in the case of minors, to some extent reduced this arbitrary practice, as reflected in a reduction in the detentions of minors.[46] Nevertheless, representatives from the judicial system have recognized that law enforcement officers continue to manipulate procedural norms, despite efforts to improve legal guarantees.[47]

When detentions do not depend on the support of prior investigations and evidence that may prove the suspect's participation in the crime, but instead rest on a law enforcement agent's subjective assessment, detentions are easily repeated. Of the gang members who participated in the 2006 "Transnational Youth Gangs" survey, 44.7 percent confirmed that they had been arrested six times or more. In the most extreme case, the participant reported thirty-five detentions. These results show that gang members enter and exit the judicial system quite frequently, further exposing the inefficiency and weakness of the judicial and police systems. This inefficiency is also reflected in the duration of provisional detentions. Approximately half of those surveyed were still waiting for a resolution of their case. The average time in prison was ten months among those with provisional detentions, while the gang members who had already received a sentence had spent nineteen months in jail on average.

No other high-profile crackdown strategy has been launched in Guatemala since Plan Escoba.[48] Representatives from the police institutions maintain that the PNC operates with a much more preventive vision than some of its Central American neighbors.[49] It is, however, difficult to find any clearly established police strategy that supports this claim. There have also been few indications of prevention programs in a wider sense. The government-created CONAPREPI (National Council for Violence Prevention and the Promotion of Values and Coexistence) never got to play the role it was intended to have,[50] and the proposed violence prevention strategy has yet to be transformed into public policies.

Guatemalan authorities have not managed to institutionalize a legal framework for either repression or prevention of violent crime, which shows Guatemala's institutional weakness. The result is a large gap between discourse and practice and, even more seriously, a weakening of both individual rights and the judicial system.

Evolution after Anti-gang Programs

Increasing homicide rates and a rise in violence in general, and gang violence in particular, clearly indicate the failure of crackdown policies to combat gangs and reduce violence in Guatemala. Moreover, government policies, or in this case practices, have had an opposite and unwanted impact on the gang problem. Although gangs are a dynamic phenomenon that constantly evolves and transforms, the sharp increase in gang activity and intensifying levels of violence associated with gangs in recent years cannot be analyzed without considering the possible counterproductive effects of government practices.

Various sources agree that the principal result of the crackdown policies was the strengthening of the gangs.[51] This strengthening is reflected in closer gang cohesion, stronger internal organization, and more powerful leaders. The repression also forced the gangs to adopt more sophisticated methods, to increase their use of violence, and to engage in new activities that generate more income. While they were in the prisons and juvenile detention centers, the gang members strengthened their relations within the gang and with other criminal actors.[52] In many cases, young people with few or weak ties to the gang were arrested, and then established new and stronger ties with the gangs while in prison. The imprisonment of gang members encouraged the gangs to develop new organizational structures. New leadership emerged within the prisons; crimes were in many cases planned within the prisons and in the barrios, while gang members outside the prisons received and executed the orders that came from the inside.

Gang rivalry transferred from the streets to the prisons. It also intensified. The serious inability of authorities within the Guatemalan prison system to maintain control generated a semianarchical situation within the prisons, where de facto power lay in the hands of certain inmates rather than with officials. Prison uprisings, aggression between rival gang members, and massacres have been frequent in Guatemalan prisons. In August 2005 at least thirty-five gang members were assassinated in a series of gang confrontations in several prisons. These incidents provoked the rupture of a nonaggression pact between the two principal gangs within the prisons and is considered to have been a catalyst for subsequent escalations of gang rivalry both in the prisons and on the streets.[53] As one gang member put it, "We've had losses. They've killed some seven 18s [members of the 18th Street Gang] recently. . . . After that, I do anyone. . . . I do anyone of the others. . . . Now we just want to see how we can kill the others."[54]

Although gangs today have a more complex and more hierarchical structure than a decade ago, the levels of organization will vary with each *clica*. By 2006 there was no indication of a national leader among either of two dominant youth gangs.[55] No one doubts the existence of communication and some level of coordination between the *clicas*, but it is not clear what constitutes this communication. Gang members themselves describe their communications as informal and merely a question of friendship, brotherhood, support, and information exchange. Of the gang members who participated in the 2006 "Transnational Youth Gangs" survey, 55.4 percent admitted that their *clica* had communication with other *clicas*, and 24.3 percent indicated a more formal level of communications that included cooperation and the planning of activities. Each *clica* has a certain level of autonomy within the gang, which is reflected in the varying levels of violence associated with each group. While some *clicas* may be well organized and have access to resources (obtained through illegal activities), others have a much looser structure. There are also important variations in each gang member's participation.

The anti-gang programs are probably not the only factors that have influenced the recent transformations of the gangs, but they are without doubt an important one. And indeed these effects are not very surprising. Research on gangs in the United States has repeatedly indicated that indiscriminate crackdown policies may have perverse effects on gangs.[56] In particular, prisons have been singled out as a key factor in understanding gang transformations.[57] At the same time, researchers need to analyze factors such as the dynamics of crime and interactions with other criminal actors, as well as the particular and changing character of gangs, in more detail. While migration was, as discussed above, important for the transformation of gang culture in the 1990s, deportation and migration seem to play less of a role today. Despite an increase of deportees back to Central America in recent years, the large majority of gang members in Guatemala have never been outside the country. Gang members deported from the United States do not automatically receive privileges within the gang but have to gain its confidence. This may vary, however, according to the position and record the person has in the gang.[58] Although the international movement of gang members obviously has some kind of influence on the gang phenomenon, this correlation should be treated carefully to avoid any misleading conclusion.

Few, if any, observers will dispute that youth gangs today represent a challenge to public security in Guatemala. One could, however, question the validity of contentions that gangs bear the main responsibility for Guatemala's skyrocketing crime levels.[59] Crime statistics give little information on perpetrators and the motivations behind criminal activities. Yet a review of crime levels in the different regions of the country shows that, with the exception of the capital area of Guatemala City, homicide rates are considerably higher in regions where little or no gang activity is reported. This suggests that other actors besides gang members are involved in a large part of the lethal violence that affects the nation. Homicide levels are particularly high in the eastern part of the country, an area that traditionally has been characterized by drug trafficking and organized crime.[60]

Other findings may support this hypothesis. A report by the United Nations Office on Drugs and Crime refers to a police study that attributed 14 percent of all homicides taking place in January 2006 to gang activity (58 of 427 murders).[61] The UN Development Programme conducted surveys in Guatemala City that show a considerable reduction in the public's perception of gang members as the main actors in crime. In the 2004 survey 45.9 percent of respondents believed that gang members were the main ones responsible for the crime activity in their neighborhood. In 2007 this percentage dropped to 24 percent; on the other hand, citizens tended to perceive that common delinquents had become the principal criminal actors.[62]

The above-mentioned survey results should not be interpreted as an effort to ignore or underestimate the participation of gang members in criminal activities. Rather, they emphasize that there are several actors involved in Guatemala's criminal universe, and although gang members must take their share of the responsibility, one should not ignore the existence of other actors.

What types of crimes are most gang members involved in? In 2004, police registers show that drug-related crimes, robberies, fights or quarrels, and the possession of weapons were the principal reasons for detention of gang members. That year, only 1.8 percent of the arrested gang members were accused of homicides. The high frequency of drug-related crimes is probably associated with the police detention strategy discussed above. This does not exclude the likelihood that some gang members accused of this type of crime were actually involved in drug-related activities. Neither does the low percentage of gang members arrested for homicides necessarily mean that gang-related violence rarely involved as-sassinations, as the low figure may reflect the poor capacity of the police to carry out homicide investigations. It has not been possible to access police records since 2004, and this impedes any attempt to compare over time the causes for which gang members have been detained. Neverthe-less, the gang survey conducted in prisons suggests that police tactics may have changed in recent years. Of those surveyed, 41.5 percent were ac-cused of homicides. Robberies and drug distribution were the second and third most frequently mentioned crimes. These figures may indicate an increasing involvement of gangs in more serious crimes and a growth in gang-committed homicides in recent years. They may, however, also in-dicate a shift in police strategies and plans, in which drug-related crimes are no longer a preferred excuse for arresting gang members.

The Rise of Vigilantism

Gang-related violence is not only a story of gang members as perpetra-tors. In recent years, the victimization of gang members has increased, and extrajudicial killings have reached alarming levels. Youths in general are the main victims of homicide violence in Guatemala. According to figures from the National Civilian Police, 37 percent of all homicide vic-tims in 2004 were young men between the ages of sixteen and twenty-five, for a total of 1,661 young men murdered that year.[63] Men between twenty-six and thirty-five years old were the second most affected group, at 25 percent of all homicide victims. Although there are no statistics that identify victims according to gang association, the dynamic of violence makes it likely that gang members constitute a significant portion of the victims in these two age groups.

There seems to be a general consensus that the number of assassina-tions of gang members has been increasing in recent years.[64] Although a part of this increase is probably due to intensified gang rivalry, some has been attributed to a growth in what is being called social cleansing, along with the accompanying formation of vigilante groups that carry out this function. In 2004 the Human Rights Ombudsman's Office (Procurador de los Derechos Humanos) of Guatemala concluded that 16.5 percent of a sample of murders of youths aged twenty-five or younger had the char-acteristics of extrajudicial and arbitrary killings, which are the third cause of death among Guatemalan youths.[65] In 2006 the United Nations sent

Philip Alston—its special rapporteur on extrajudicial, summary, and arbitrary executions—on an official mission to assess the situation in Guatemala. In his report, he emphasizes that gang members and other "undesirables" are often the victims of acts of social cleansing, which in some cases are committed by police personnel.[66]

Sources from the judicial system, academic institutions, and nongovernmental organizations expressed the same concern and singled out police agents as one group of actors behind the increasing number of gang member assassinations and incidents of social cleansing in Guatemala. This increase in gang member deaths occurred at the same time that detention of gang members became less frequent, leading some sources to suspect that there may be a correlation. Furthermore, during the period when gang members were being detained en masse, the police established registers of those being detained, and some now fear that social cleansing groups have used this information to target victims.

Gang members themselves also identify police agents as the principal actors behind the increasing number of assassinations of gang members. More than half of the gang members who participated in the 2006 "Transnational Youth Gang" survey (52.3 percent) stated that the police were the main ones responsible for the murder of gang members. Of the remaining survey respondents, 23.1 percent accused a rival gang of the attacks, 7.7 percent stated that social cleansing groups were behind the increasing murders, 6.2 percent mentioned ordinary people, and 3.1 percent referred to their own gang. An additional 4.6 percent referred to other actors, and 3.1 percent said that they did not know.

The participation of police agents, together with businessmen, drug traffickers, organized crime groups, and common citizens in the extrajudicial execution of gang members does not necessarily indicate that social cleansing is a state policy, nor that authorities know about this practice and accept it. In the case of Guatemala, however, connections between social cleansing groups and both state institutions and high officials came to light under the Óscar Berger Perdomo administration (2004–2008).[67] It is nevertheless important to point out that common citizens also take part in acts of social cleansing. The overall environment of insecurity, a general lack of confidence in the justice system and the state, and in many cases the absence of the state, along with traditions of collective action, have led citizens to take justice into their own hands, including the carrying out of lynchings, a practice that is relatively frequent in Guatemala.[68]

Some Final Reflections

There is no doubt that, in recent years, the Guatemalan youth gangs have adopted new characteristics and evolved into a somewhat different phenomenon from the gangs that emerged in the 1980s. Law enforcement representatives have repeatedly characterized the gangs as organized crime, and some have even called them a threat to national security.[69] Such assertions should be treated extremely carefully, and a thorough examination of gang dynamics is needed before reaching such conclusions. Indeed, one of the main challenges when dealing with gangs is merely to treat the phenomenon for what it is, and not as something larger and more menacing. Youth gangs are highly complex, and the phenomenon should not be overestimated nor underestimated. Although gangs are important actors in Guatemala's inflated crime levels, they are far from the only ones. Gang members are also among the principal victims of violence; they are constantly suffering abuses not only in terms of physical violence but also from the criminal justice system that is supposed to protect them. The absence of a comprehensive governmental response to gangs has intensified the problem. The causes of the problem have not changed, however, and within a context of institutional weakness and inequality, gangs remain attractive to many youths in their search for identity and opportunities.

CHAPTER 4

Street Gangs of Honduras

JOANNA MATEO

Honduras has some of the highest poverty rates in the Western Hemisphere. Of its estimated 7.5 million inhabitants, more than 50 percent live on an income below the poverty line. In recent years, however, Honduras has made some progress in boosting its economy to reduce such dire numbers. It has enjoyed positive economic growth, in part due to trade agreements such as the Central America–Dominican Republic–United States Free Trade Agreement, and its gross domestic product continued to improve, from 4.7 percent in 2004–2005 to 6.3 percent in 2007.[1] Yet simultaneously the country is facing an increasingly challenging crime situation, brought on in large part by the growing influence of the *maras*. These gangs, in particular Mara Salvatrucha (MS-13) and the 18th Street Gang, threaten to hamper the economic growth and foreign direct investment Honduras needs to address its high levels of poverty and unemployment. To date, numerous articles and studies have attempted to understand this ever-growing, complex problem facing the region and to propose solutions. Although frequently viewed by the media and academia as a regional problem—even the U.S. Department of State has proposed a regional strategy to address the *mara* problem—each country in the region suffering from high levels of *mara* activity has its own unique story.

Much of the attention in the United States and international media on the rise of youth gangs and their associated violence has focused on El Salvador, leaving the impression at times that Honduras is the forgotten nation among those facing the challenge of the *maras*. While sharing commonalities with its neighbors, such as high urban poverty rates, weak institutions, and a society mired by corruption, no single explanation of why a country suffers from *mara* activity suffices. *Mara* activity in Honduras can be traced back more than two decades, yet the situation in the late 1980s barely resembles what the country faces today. As in other countries in the region, the impetus to join *maras* (the most violent gangs) or *pandillas* (street gangs) in Honduras had its origins in a need for self-protection, and members observed a certain moral code. Members were predominantly young males—disaffected youths for the most part, from broken homes, with few employment prospects. The criminal activity carried out by *pandillas* was considered little more than a nuisance for public order. Yet, by 1999, Honduran police forces estimated that some 400 different gangs existed in the country, and the number of gang members swelled into the tens of thousands.[2]

Originally contained within Honduras's borders, gang members today find shelter in other countries and are increasingly mobile. There is a persistent back-and-forth migratory flow of *mareros* (members of *maras*) between Honduras and neighboring countries such as El Salvador and Guatemala, and even to and from Mexico and the United States, which makes it even more difficult to estimate the number of *mareros* within a country's borders at any given time. Where once the *pandilla* youth gangs were concentrated primarily in urban areas, engaging in petty crime and other "menacing" behavior, the situation has now transformed into a security epidemic. Today the violence attributed to youth gangs has broadened and become more vicious. From terrorizing local businesses with demands for protection "taxes" and threats of violence to intragang warfare, hired hits, and robberies and assaults on public transport, the two predominant *maras*, MS-13 and 18th Street, simply outman security forces in Honduras. Both a symptom and a cause of a deteriorating security environment, *maras* are overwhelming the already weak, cash-strapped, and ill-equipped justice and security systems in the region, and Honduras is no exception. The *maras'* presence threatens the economic future of the country, repelling foreign direct investment and sucking resources from a state that in many ways is unable to meet the basic needs of its society.

Gang Central?

Of all the countries in Central America, Honduras is frequently cited as being home to the largest number of gang members. Reliable data and statistics, however, are difficult to come by on many issues related to the *maras* in Honduras, including gang membership. Reported numbers widely vary, from as few as 4,000 to as many as 36,000;[3] by way of comparison, membership is estimated at 14,000 in Guatemala and 10,000 in El Salvador. Today the Community Police of Honduras, part of the Gang Prevention Division of the Ministry of Security, estimate that there are some 10,000 to 15,000 active gang members in the country. This much lower number, in their view, distinguishes the active, at-large *mareros* from those who are currently incarcerated or have escaped to the country's interior regions and remain in hiding ("inactive" status) until they can migrate to another country or believe it is safe to reemerge and re-engage with their gang.

Some studies refute official police estimates of gang membership in Honduras and argue not only that membership is decreasing but that it was never as high as official sources claimed. A study by Tomás Andino Mencía for the Washington Office on Latin America, for example, concludes that gang membership in Honduras in 2006 stood at only 4,621—thousands fewer than the numbers cited by official police sources.[4] Andino rightly points out that official calculations of gang numbers are flawed because they use a subjective definition of a *marero* determined by the police forces themselves. Moreover, police officials in most cases arrived at their estimates by using the highly imperfect method of observing the amount of graffiti to calculate the number of *clicas* (independent local subgroups or cells of a gang) in a neighborhood. They would then multiply that figure by the number of *mareros* they estimated to be in a *clica* to calculate total membership. While the methodology that underlies official statistics is clearly deficient, Andino's conclusion that some 4,000 gang members exist in Honduras is also greatly dependent on assumptions that he himself admits are subject to a large margin of error, such as the percentage of deportees from the United States that eventually joined a gang. Ultimately, the wide variance in numbers of *mareros* cited by different sources highlights the flawed nature of calculating such statistics. The varying definitions of what constitutes a *marero*, and perhaps the difficulty today of distinguishing between violence committed by gangs and violence committed by organized crime and drug trafficking cartels, complicate the ability to arrive at reliable numbers.

History of the Rise of the *Maras*

Despite perennial disagreements on the number of *mareros* in Honduras, there is little disagreement that the phenomenon has exploded in the last two decades. The dramatic growth of gangs in Honduras can be traced to a number of factors in the country's turbulent modern history, and it is nearly impossible to conclude which might be the dominant one. Honduras did not endure the bloody civil conflicts that devastated its neighbors El Salvador, Nicaragua, and Guatemala and exposed their societies to a culture of political violence and brutal authoritarianism. Yet Honduras's pivotal role in the United States' Central America policy throughout the 1980s—centered on the "rollback" of communism—and the subsequent flawed transition from military to civilian rule, coupled with the ultimate failure of neoliberal economic policies in the 1990s, among other factors, led to poor economic performance and a host of societal ills that still weigh on the country today.

During the early 1980s the Central American countries were entangled in a process of political change, wrestling with military dictatorships and with Washington's meddling in civil conflicts. In the eyes of Cold War strategists, Honduras held the geopolitical importance of a country on the road to democratization in a region haunted by the threat of communism. The United States maintained a strong military presence in the country as a means to support the Contra insurgents in Nicaragua and the El Salvadoran military in their fight against the then revolutionary guerrilla organization Farabundo Martí National Liberation Front (FMLN). At the time, the United States naively and narrowly defined a democracy as a country that held "free and fair" elections, and Honduras was viewed by the United States as a potential rising democratic star among countries in a war-torn region. Military dictatorship in Honduras ended in 1981 with the election of Roberto Suazo Córdova, and the country started on a path toward civilian rule.

The initial return to civilian rule unfortunately did not translate into a secondary role for the military in political life. On the contrary, President Suazo deferred to an ever-strengthening military. The use of death squads, torture, and other "dirty war" tactics aimed at rooting out communism and alleged sympathizers of El Salvadoran guerrillas, or infiltrating labor and peasant groups, became acceptable means in the name of protecting national security.[5] Combine this with a massive increase in U.S. military aid (from $3.9 million in 1980 to $77.5 million in 1984 and $81.1 million in 1986), and Honduras became what some scholars termed a *democradura*: a nominally democratic government that is really under military rule. Due to Honduras's unique role in Washington's Central America policy throughout the 1980s, its armed forces increased in strength, numbers, and control precisely when the country was attempting to leave its history of military rule behind. As a consequence, adequate measures toward strengthening civilian-controlled institutions and the imposition of a checks-and-balances system in government, in particular as it relates to the military, did not transpire. The military held veto power over cabinet positions and engaged in illegal activities, such as the drug trade; the lines between police and military forces were blurred, and military personnel enjoyed de facto immunity from prosecution.[6]

With the end of the Cold War, Honduras's importance for U.S. policy in Central America abruptly diminished. U.S. military aid declined, but the state lacked the power to rein in a once-powerful military accustomed to evading accountability. The end of the civil conflicts in the region ushered in international support to reform the states' judiciaries and police forces in an effort to reduce military influence. In Honduras, efforts to purge military authority from the civilian police forces included the removal of senior police officials who had once served in the military, as well as incorporating the use of small sidearms, rather than automatic weapons, by police officers. By 1998, Honduras had completed the transition from its National Police to a newly created, civilian-led Security Ministry. But as some scholars point out, removing formal military traits from policing is frequently easier than actually creating a sustainable model of civilian policing.[7] While some programs may have succeeded in purging overt militarization in newly created civilian police institutions, they were perhaps less successful in instituting effective police and judicial practices. For example, a 1997 assessment by the U.S. Justice Department found that the majority of instructors in police academies in Honduras had served under the prior militarized system. While the transition to civilian rule in Honduras, specifically in regard to public security, may have done away with the obviously negative aspects of a militarized society, it did not replace it with effective and accountable policies and practices. Moreover, although more stringent selection standards for police officers were implemented, salaries remained abysmally low, in particular for lower-level police agents, thus creating an atmosphere conducive to corruption.[8]

As a slow and difficult transition from a militarized society took place in Honduras, the region as a whole, devastated economically by the civil conflicts, was in dire need of an economic jumpstart. The United States soon turned its sights away from fighting communism to reviving the economically embattled region. The so-called Washington Consensus of the 1990s—trade liberalization, privatization, and the implementation of strict monetary and fiscal policies—became the antidote for macro-economic instability, hyperinflation, and deepening poverty in Latin America.

An economic stabilization plan was initiated in Honduras in 1990, and although poverty rates did decline somewhat, Honduras continued to struggle with high rates of poverty throughout the decade. In 1992 some 50 percent of households were living in poverty and 30 percent in extreme poverty, with the majority of the poor population living in rural areas. By 1993 the overall poverty number began to improve slightly, but urban poor populations, whose numbers were 18 percent higher than they had been in 1989, suffered the most from the economic stabilization plan, according to a World Bank report.[9] Research has indicated an association between rising inequality and higher levels of violence within a society, and the urban poor are more likely to suffer from—and be held responsible for—increasing violence.[10]

While the civil conflicts in both El Salvador and Guatemala may have created a culture of violence and brutality that helped nurture a phenomenon like the *maras*, Honduras did not experience civil conflict. Nor can the imperfect transition from military dictatorship to civilian rule be implicated as the predominant reason why Honduras has suffered from such high levels of gang membership and activity. Yet it does shed light on why initial reactions by the government to a security threat like the *maras* were repressive. It is likely a confluence of factors, rather than one in particular, that better explains the reality of Honduras today. Indeed, countries that suffer from high levels of gang activity in the region all share certain realities: weak institutions, high levels of poverty, and the breakdown of family units due to economic hardship. Other factors, such as the illegal drug trade, further squeeze already weak, underpaid, and poorly equipped security forces in countries like Honduras, and they provide the *maras* with additional illicit and lucrative activities in which to engage.

Moreover, the neoliberal economic policies pushed by the United States in the wake of the civil conflicts did not foster the much-needed economic growth that was anticipated, as demonstrated by the increase in the percentage of urban poor three years after the introduction of an economic stabilization plan. This dire economic situation sent a wave of Hondurans to neighboring countries and the United States in search of a better life. Unlike in El Salvador, where many residents fled for reasons related to the civil conflict and political violence, Hondurans saw immigration to the United States as a means to improve their economic reality.[11]

Tenuous economic conditions were greatly aggravated by the devastating effects of Hurricane Mitch in October 1998, causing a further emigration of Hondurans. The storm left some 5,000 dead, displaced hundreds of thousands of people, and caused an estimated $3 billion in damage. According to statistics cited in Andino's study, 61.4 percent of all Hondurans living outside the country in 2006 had left between 1998 and 2005. Moreover, in the aftermath of the hurricane, the number of child laborers shot up 42 percent, highlighting the calamitous effects the storm had on the poor and middle classes. The severe economic impacts of the hurricane, coupled with a subsequent influx of undocumented and criminal deportees from the United States, may have been the catalyst for the surge in gang membership as youths turned to gangs for survival.[12]

A U.S. Cultural Export

In 2005 the U.S. Department of Justice estimated that some 30,000 gangs with 800,000 members existed in 2,500 communities throughout the United States, most of them concentrated in Los Angeles, northern Virginia, and New York City.[13] The 18th Street Gang and MS-13 originated in Los Angeles and greatly influenced and recruited from Central American immigrants and their children. Linked to Los Angeles's 18th Street, the 18th Street Gang now present in Honduras was originally started in the United States by Mexican immigrants in the 1960s. Its members began recruiting Central American immigrants. The MS-13 was started by the children of refugees of the civil conflict in El Salvador, mainly as a support network but also to defend themselves against other U.S. gangs. (For a detailed look at the rise of Latin American gangs in the United States, see Chapter 1 in this volume.) It is understandable why immigrants and their children were particularly susceptible to joining the violent gangs if one views gang culture as a social phenomenon—a means of securing acceptance and belonging. Many Honduran immigrants to the United States also found themselves suffering the same poverty in Los Angeles that they did back home. Lacking English-language skills and a means to obtain even the basic necessities of life, many of them—sometimes out of fear, sometimes out of a need to belong—saw gang membership as a means of survival. Unlike in Honduras, however, in the United States they found a relatively organized and violent gang culture.[14]

The United States is frequently blamed for exporting gangs to Central America, when in reality the U.S. export was a new gang culture that existing *maras* in the region adopted. Gangs were not a new phenomenon to Honduras. According to the Honduran Community Police, MS-13 and 18th Street first appeared in Honduras in the 1990s. Other youth gangs such as the Rockeros and Los Cholos also emerged in the 1990s, partly in reaction to the move away from an authoritarian government, but they bore little resemblance to the Los Angeles–based gangs. Two decades ago *maras* were loosely organized and used weapons such as knives to commit crimes. Gang activity in Honduras at the time was predominantly focused on defending territory, and gang members were not particularly mobile. They limited their activities to petty crimes such as vandalism and spray-painting graffiti. Yet dire economic conditions and an atmosphere of violence led some of these gangs to turn to more serious criminal activities as a means to survive. The dynamics and culture of gang activity in the region further changed when these youth gangs were met with a massive influx of deportees from the United States, including returnees who had been members of or exposed to the culture of the more violent and organized U.S.-based gangs.[15] What cities such as Los Angeles, New York, and the suburbs of Washington, D.C., suffered from in terms of violent gang activity would soon be replicated in Honduras, bolstered in part by a rigorous new U.S. immigration policy.

In the 1990s, the United States began to take an increasingly hard-line approach to immigration issues. By the mid-1990s, some 40,000 illegal immigrants with a wide variety of criminal backgrounds were returned to the Central American region.[16] In 1996 the United States passed the Illegal Immigration Reform and Immigrant Responsibility Act, which targeted noncitizens with criminal records for deportation.[17] Between 1997 and 2007, more than 100,000 Hondurans were deported from the United States, with the largest increases in the number of deportees occurring after 2005. In 2004 the United States deported 8,752 Hondurans back to their country. In 2005, more than 15,000 Hondurans were deported, and the number continued to rise in following years.[18] Thus grew the exportation of one of the United States' biggest crime threats to one of the poorest corners of the world. Honduras, a country crippled economically and barely able to meet the basic needs of its citizens, now found itself facing head-on a criminal phenomenon and security threat that even the superpower United States was struggling to contain.

Not all of the deportees were criminals. Some deportees had immigrated with their families when they were children, and they were sent back merely for being in the United States without documentation. These younger deportees barely spoke Spanish, and upon their return to Honduras, their only means of reintegrating into society was through their gang connections. As deportations continued, the pool of recruits, particularly of youths, became larger. Intrigued by the new arrivals, some of whom displayed characteristics of U.S. gang culture—such as tattoos, a distinctive language, and the use of hand signals to communicate—the smaller, less organized gangs indigenous to Honduras adopted the U.S.-based rules and style of gangs, and many were incorporated into the larger MS-13 and 18th Street gangs of U.S. origin. The better organized and disciplined MS-13 and 18th Street, some of whose members likely received support from and maintained communication with members outside Honduras's borders, were successful, through their organizational skill and fearlessness of violence, in rapidly absorbing the smaller local gangs.[19] Older gang members would require junior members or new recruits to engage in petty theft and other crimes as a means of initiation. More seasoned gang members engaged in more sophisticated criminal activity, including the already established drug trafficking networks operating in and around the region. In time the rules of membership for *mareros* became stringent. Members were required to live by certain codes to demonstrate not only their membership in a particular gang but their loyalty as well. Rites of initiation—including being subjected to beatings by fellow gang members or carrying out an execution—were a means for gang leaders to demand a high level of loyalty from their new recruits. For both 18th Street and MS-13, the most important strictures were loyalty to the gang and respect for the rules.[20] Leaving a gang became almost impossible—only death or religious conversion were plausible routes out—and the Honduras groups adopted the "live or die by the gang" mentality of U.S. gangs. Acting as a surrogate family for disenfranchised youths living in a country mired in poverty and lack of economic prospects, gangs grew in size and became better organized than the government that tried to rein them in.

Whether occurring as a coincidence or a consequence, the spread of more highly organized and violent gangs that mirrored their U.S. counterparts was matched by an increase in drug trafficking in the Central American region. Although it is difficult to determine the direct influence the drug trade has had on the rise of *mara* activity in Honduras, the shift in patterns of cocaine trafficking beginning in the 1990s from the Caribbean corridor to the Central American transit corridor cannot be ignored. Whether it was because the *maras* took advantage of a judicial and security environment incapable of confronting complex issues such as the illicit drug industry, or because eventual *mara* involvement in the industry helped strengthen their control, reach, and organization, the youth gangs continued to thrive alongside an increase in illicit drug movement through the region. With the *mareros* working as musclemen for drug traffickers or accepting payments in illegal drugs, their involvement in the massive drug trade along the transit zone further complicated an already overwhelming problem for the Honduran government. As with most statistics and data related to gangs in Honduras, there is little hard evidence to back up claims of *marero* involvement in the drug trade and other forms of organized crime. Yet anecdotal evidence suggests *mareros* are hired by organized crime leaders to commit crimes such as car theft, kidnappings, and drug trafficking.[21]

Between 1999 and 2001, the homicide rate in Honduras soared, from 41.2 murders per 100,000 inhabitants to 53.7, a level higher than that of any other country in the region.[22] (El Salvador, the country with the second-highest murder rate in the region, saw homicide rates decrease slightly in this same period, from 36.2 murders per 100,000 inhabitants in 1999 to 34.6 in 2001, but its rate later increased again; see table 7.2.) Although it is difficult to determine the degree to which gangs were involved in the increase in murder rates, particularly in light of the simultaneous increase in drug activity in the region, in the eyes of the Honduran government the increase in violent activity was almost unilaterally attributable to the *maras*.

It is in this context that the *maras*, as they exist and operate today in Honduras, first emerged and flourished and found themselves the focus of a repressive, hard-line response from the Honduran government.

Governmental Responses to the Rise of *Maras*

In the early 1990s, prior to the emergence of U.S.-style gang culture in Honduras, the government did not have a consistent or definitive response to *mara* activity. Despite the presence of indigenous gangs such as the Rockeros and Los Cholos, which carried out petty crime and some violent acts, *pandillas* were not, in the perception of the public, affecting its well-being or safety. By the mid-to-late 1990s, however, as gang violence soared, a debate ensued in Honduras over recent government policies that the public believed had led to the increase in violence: the abolition of mandatory military service, and the passage of a penal code for youths (Código de la Niñez y la Adolescencia).[23] The institutions charged with overseeing crimes committed by minors, the police forces, and the judiciary were all ill-prepared to handle such a large influx of children and adolescents into the criminal justice system, and *mara* activity and membership exploded at the end of the 1990s. While the then president Carlos Flores resorted to some repressive measures to combat *mara* activity—measures that were the precursors to the policies known as Cero Tolerancia and Libertad Azul (Zero Tolerance and Blue Liberty) in the following administration—he did so sparingly and with caution, given the attention human rights groups were placing on the recently passed youth penal code.[24]

In a context of rising murder rates and gang activity within Honduras's borders, coupled with an increasingly active drug trade, Ricardo Maduro campaigned for president in 2001 on a platform of zero tolerance for the *maras*. By this time, Honduran society attributed much of the violence to gangs. Poor neighborhoods in some areas had been overtaken by gangs, who imposed "war taxes" (extortion for protection) to allow residents to move from one neighborhood to another. *Mareros* became better armed, moved into middle-class neighborhoods, and attacked businesses and residential properties. The increase in murders and violent crime produced an enormous amount of media attention, particularly focusing on gang involvement. Some scholars argue that the amount of media attention on gang-related activity was disproportionate to the actual levels of crime that could be attributed to the *maras*, and thus exacerbated fears and the perception of insecurity among the public. As *mareros* became the scapegoats for the rise of crime and violence—both in the media and in political discourse—the public became more amenable to the adoption of repressive tactics to combat the problem.[25]

Once in office, Maduro became the pioneer in Central America of *mano dura* (strong arm) policies against gangs, born out of the belief that the *maras* were the primary perpetrators of the violent crime afflicting the country. Instituting *mano dura* strategies required reforms to the Honduran Penal Code ten times between 2003 and 2006 to redefine certain crimes and increase penalties and sentences.[26] In particular, reforms to Article 332 of the Penal Code became known as the Ley Antimaras (Antigang Law).[27] Along with setting fines of anywhere from US$5,000 to US$15,000 (87,500 to 262,500 Honduran lempiras) or up to thirty years in prison for "gang leaders, gangs or other groups that associate with the standing purpose of executing any act constituting a crime," Article 332 prohibited "illicit association" and specified that activities such as displaying tattoos, associating with suspected gang members, or even dressing a particular way were sufficient evidence for detainment. With his policy known as Libertad Azul, Maduro again erased the lines between military and police responsibilities, a division that had tenuously been demarcated only a few years earlier. Joint military-police units would conduct raids in neighborhoods where gang activity was suspected, in some cases arresting youths for little more than dressing as a gang member or having tattoos.

The severe zero-tolerance policies Maduro enacted did little to stem the tide of violence in Honduras or deter gang activity in the long term. Initially there was a decrease in the murder rate (from 55.9 murders per 100,000 inhabitants in 2002 to 33.6 in 2003, with a further decline to 31.9 in 2004). Yet murder rates began to steadily climb again beginning in 2005.[28] While murder rates may have subsided temporarily, the population of the country's jails swelled with suspected gang members, and prisons became the new training and organizing grounds for detained gang members. Detention centers also became centers of violence: deadly riots have broken out in Honduran prisons, during which hundreds of suspected *mareros* died. While violence escalated in a prison system incapable of dealing with so many detainees, links between gangs apparently became stronger, gang activities more violent, and smaller gangs continued to be incorporated into the now-dominant MS-13 and 18th Street.

As Maduro's *mano dura* policies gained attention—and emulation—in neighboring countries, human rights groups and activists for youths began to raise international awareness of the excesses of the hard-line strategies adopted to combat the gangs. In particular, they decried what they believed was evidence of "social cleansing" of youths: murders and assassinations that in many cases were disregarded and went unpunished by civil authorities. Although not all murders could be attributed directly to the police or their hard-line tactics, the level of impunity that came with such repressive measures was suspected to have led to an overall increase in violence against youths. Between 1998 and February 2006, Casa Alianza, a nongovernmental organization (NGO) that works with street children, reported that a total of 3,091 children and youths had been murdered in Honduras.[29] Hundreds of street children were allegedly the victims of *mano dura* strategies, believed to have been the targets of rogue police officers or hired gunmen for businesses taking the law into their own hands. Others were victims of gang violence. The majority, however, were murders with no known motive or perpetrator. In 2000, Casa Alianza brought a case before the Inter-American Commission on Human Rights (IACHR), accusing police forces of the illegal detention and murder of three underage boys and an adult male in 1995.[30] The case, known as the Four Cardinal Points (Cuatro Puntos Cardinales), gained international attention, and in 2004 the Honduran government accepted responsibility for the detentions and killings. In 2006 the IACHR condemned the government for its connection to the deaths. The courts in Honduras, however, have yet to proceed against those suspected of the crime.[31]

Post–*mano dura*: The Current State of Affairs

Although popular at the time, particularly with a citizenry terrorized by the proliferation of gangs throughout the country and media inclined to sensationalize the *maras* phenomenon, the hard-line approach to fighting gangs not only failed miserably in Honduras but backfired. A purely law-enforcement approach to fighting the *maras* ignored many of the realities that helped create an atmosphere where youth gangs grow and flourish: abject poverty, lack of economic opportunities, and wholly inadequate judicial and law enforcement systems. Moreover, it caused *mareros*—who frequently have no other option than to remain in a gang—to adapt to the hard-line tactics. They became more mobile (i.e., transnational), changed their modus operandi, and tightened rules of membership. According to some Honduran police officials, they also responded by becoming even more violent, organizing and operating underground, and changing their appearance to make themselves less identifiable as gang members.[32] They stopped congregating in public, and many no longer followed the traditional rules that identified them as gang members, such as particular forms of dress, the use of hand signals to communicate, and the display of tattoos. Although there are no reliable data to substantiate the extent of these claims, *mareros* in the past have adapted easily to changes in law enforcement tactics, which is demonstrated by their continued activity and presence throughout the region.

In reaction to *mano dura* policies and the official assault on civil liberties, Honduras gained international attention from human rights groups, as evidenced by the Casa Alianza case. Moreover, after homicide rates again began to climb steadily in 2005, the zero-tolerance policies instituted by President Maduro no longer appeared to be having the desired effect. The number of *mareros* arrested under Article 332 also began to decline (from 277 detained *mareros* per month at the end of 2003 to only 15 per month at the end of 2004), thanks to the adaptive changes the *mareros* made.[33] In 2006 the public's perception of insecurity, already high by regional standards, continued to rise: some 35 percent of the population believed that crime was the primary threat facing the country (up 18 percent from 2004), and a substantial majority (84 percent) believed it threatened the country's future.[34]

The election of Liberal Party candidate Manuel Zelaya in 2005 ultimately led to a shift in how the Honduran government proposed to address the *mara* phenomenon. Running on a platform to combat corruption, fight poverty, and make government more transparent, Zelaya eventually also advocated a new approach to the fight against the *maras*. He claimed to favor rehabilitation for gang members, indicating a more comprehensive approach to public security and gangs. Zelaya managed to defeat the ruling-party candidate Porfirio Lobo, who had worked with President Maduro in Congress to reform the penal code that criminalized gang membership. Zelaya touted what he saw as a great achievement in the fight against the *maras*: abandoning the *mano dura* approach and replacing it with policies focused on prevention, which was led by the Community Police of the Gang Prevention Division. A bloodless military coup removed Zelaya from office in June 2009 and replaced him with a civilian rival, Roberto Micheletti, after Zelaya tried to float a referendum to revise the constitution.

Indicating a move toward a more preventative approach to the *maras* problem, the Honduran Community Police have developed five gang prevention programs, each aimed at a different sector of society. According to officers involved in them, these programs were designed by the police forces themselves and were specifically tailored to the realities that Honduran society faces in dealing with the *maras*. The program EREM (Educación para Resistir y Evitar las Maras, or Education to Resist and Avoid Gangs) is aimed at children in the fifth and sixth grades. Topics covered include understanding the impact *maras* have on society, how to recognize a *marero*, the negative effects of drug use, and techniques *mareros* use to attract recruits. Another program, COBAMA (Conocimientos Básicos en Maras, or Basic Facts on Gangs), which is sponsored by the European Union, is designed to educate judges, prosecutors, teachers, and other members of society on issues such as the strategies used by the *maras* in their illegal activities. The other programs include one specifically for parents on how to keep their children from joining gangs, one similar to EREM but aimed at adolescents, and one for training police agents to become instructors in the various prevention programs. Apparently due to enormous overhead and administrative costs, however, the programs have limited reach and little money to properly administer and maintain them.[35]

Internationally, the *maras* phenomenon has caught the eye of the EU. Any role the United States may be playing in combating the *maras* in Honduras, which today is a limited one,[36] has been eclipsed by actions of the Europeans. (For more details, see Chapter 10 in this volume). The EU is quietly pouring its euros into the region, not just for combating the *maras* but for a wide variety of social and economic development programs. Honduras is the second-largest recipient of EU assistance (after Nicaragua), which currently stands at approximately €338 million (US$488 million).[37] The specific reforms proposed by the EU to improve public security are closely tied to a variety of prevention/rehabilitation programs targeted at the gang population, and offer evidence of an international consensus that a purely law-enforcement approach to the *maras* phenomenon is inadequate. The necessary police and judicial reforms (some undertaken with EU assistance) include strengthening the investigative police unit — specifically, the unit charged with investigating the deaths of young people. The number of police officers (144 per 100,000 residents) is one of the lowest in the region, and prosecutors far outnumber public defenders. Budgets for the judicial system are abysmally low (just over US$8 on a per capita basis) and have not increased nearly enough to handle such a surge in criminal activity. The prison system is also crumbling — incarceration rates (164 per 100,000) and prison overcrowding are extremely high for the region.[38] Human rights and due process training are essential for security forces, particularly in the aftermath of *mano dura* and the tenuous transition from a militarized to a civilian police force. Support for witness protection and reinsertion programs is also critical, to allow *mareros* to leave gang life with some level of protection by the state from retribution by other gang members. Decentralizing and extending the community policing programs and involving civil society organizations, such as NGOs and church groups already working on prevention programs, are necessary to assure coordination among the various sectors and to minimize overlap in the face of limited budgets.

Although there was a policy shift from *mano dura* to gang prevention, that message appears not to have reached members of the NGO community, who blame the government for inaction. This may be due to the poor funding — and thus limited reach — of many of the Community Police prevention programs. Yet it is likely also due to the suspicion and mistrust that have developed between civil society organizations and government — a sentiment that was deepened by the repressive policies of the Maduro administration. In some cases, civil society leaders and NGOs have strongly criticized the government's efforts to deal with the *maras*. NGOs working in the country see the *maras* as a consequence of much larger, more difficult-to-tackle issues plaguing society—widespread poverty, crumbling public institutions, lack of economic progress and opportunities—that cannot be solved with law enforcement and security measures. Labeling a problem as a "gang" problem, or a policy as "anti-gang," is not the correct approach in their view, as youth gangs are a consequence of the social and economic problems characteristic of a weak state. Prevention programs will ultimately fail if the country's socioeconomic problems are not properly addressed.

Numerous small NGOs and church organizations in Honduras have run prevention and rehabilitation programs for the gang population. Yet many of the programs have been halted altogether for lack of funds. More discouraging, however, is that there appears to be little coordination among the NGO community and its wide mix of gang prevention programs; coordination between NGOs and state programs is even worse, if it exists at all. With so many small, localized programs, duplication is likely widespread. Although many NGO and other civil society leaders believe that prevention efforts—as opposed to a purely law-enforcement approach—are what will ultimately lead to some level of success, it is difficult to ascertain what that success entails. Little, if any, information is available on factors such as recidivism rates, overlap with other NGO or government programs, and how law enforcement policies and activities interact with civil society programs.

Conclusion

Historically one of the region's poorest countries, Honduras has also emerged as one of the most violent in Latin America. The complex phenomenon of the *maras* took root in Honduras due to a confluence of factors. The country's history in the 1980s, although less violent than that of Guatemala and El Salvador, sheds light on why certain variables, such as poor economic conditions and a less-than-perfect transition to civilian rule, helped foment an atmosphere that allowed youth gangs to flourish. It also helps explain why the populace was so accepting of extreme hardline policies to combat the *maras*, and why a relatively young and weak culture of democracy remains threatened by spiraling levels of violence.

Faced with some of the highest murder rates in the region, due in part to *mara* activity, Honduras, like many struggling democracies and economies, was ill-prepared to handle such threats as MS-13 and 18th Street.

Added to the mix was an aggressive U.S. deportation policy, which unintentionally exported a vicious gang culture that disaffected Honduran youths adopted. The fallout from *mano dura* policies bitterly exposed Honduras's weaknesses in fighting crime and maintaining security within a democratic framework. Fragile public institutions, already poorly funded and improperly run, crumbled under the pressure of a swelling security epidemic.

The shift from a hard-line approach toward fighting gangs to programs focused on prevention and rehabilitation is a welcome step, yet it could very well be short-lived. The abrupt removal of President Zelaya by military forces in June 2009 glaringly demonstrated just how tenuous democracy, along with civil liberty protections and rule of law, are in Honduras today. Moreover, the shift is viewed in some circles as cover for inaction by a state unwilling—or worse, unable—to grasp the complexity of the problem, given that funding of such programs has been wholly inadequate. Honduras is in need of more comprehensive civil reforms and democratic consolidation to assure security improvements. It is unlikely the country will find itself free of *maras* at any time in the foreseeable future. European assistance, while commendable, remains uncoordinated and will not suffice. Broad international support and expertise, coupled with strong domestic political will, are required if there is to be any hope of properly controlling such a dangerous and complicated phenomenon.

CHAPTER 5

Street Gangs of Nicaragua

JOSÉ LUIS ROCHA
TRANSLATED FROM THE SPANISH BY MICHAEL SOLIS

The presence of gangs in Nicaragua is not a new or unique phenomenon. Groups of adolescents involved in activities tied to delinquency can be traced back to at least the 1970s and perhaps even farther. In that decade, the gang led by the famous gangster Charrasca (a pseudonym) took part in insurrectional battles led by the Sandinista Front to overthrow the dictatorial Somoza dynasty. The officers of the National Guard stationed in the city of León trembled before Charrasca and his fighters, who liked to capture the soldiers most detested by the population and roll them up in barbed wire.[1] This and other gang formations of the time, however, were ephemeral. There was another surge in gangs in the 1980s, due to the diminished capacity of the revolutionary state to offer jobs, provide social investment, and implement youth-friendly sociopolitical policies.

Despite their fleeting nature, these gangs from the 1980s inspired those that emerged at the beginning of the following decade. The Barilochis, the Pitufos, and the Mau-Maus were legendary gangs in the 1990s and pioneers of a rare type of gang in Nicaragua: the institutionalized gang, one that persists in time and conserves its name, symbols, tattoos, territorial control, and ethical code. Having surged early in the 1990s, the gangs known as the Rampleros, the Cancheros, the Power Rangers, and the Plotts have now been operating for nearly two decades.[2] Instead of creating new groups, successive generations of youths from the Reparto Schick area of Managua have integrated into these gangs, renewing the cannon fodder but also maintaining the traditions, a characteristic that these groups share with the famed gangs of Chicago, Cape Town, and Rio de Janeiro.[3]

The institutionalization of gangs nevertheless has not been an obstacle to their transformation. During the 1990s the gangs of Managua maintained characteristics similar to those attributed by Deborah Levenson to Guatemalan gangs at the end of the 1980s: territorial control, a source of identity, primary socialization on the streets, and the quest for a "family" in the gang.[4] The first Nicaraguan gangs had done their patriotic military service and wanted to revive the adrenaline, spirit of camaraderie, and social activism that they experimented with in the 1980s.[5] Generations of gangs in the following years also thirsted for the fame, respect, power, and material goods that proclaimed social status and made that status very visible in their brand-name choices of clothing.[6] The inhabitants of their home neighborhoods viewed these cohorts of gang members as their defenders, because they confronted the invasions of rival gangs. The gang, whose principal activities consisted of often bloody and deadly fights, the consumption of marijuana, and petty assaults, thus functioned as a mechanism of cohesion for youths amidst a context of social atomization.[7]

Initially the National Police did not bother to track the gangs. In the turmoil of the 1980s they were more interested in problems pertaining to national security than those related to citizen security, a subject that acquired relevance only in the post–civil war 1990s. The first inventory of data was gathered in 1995 and showed that there were 47 gangs with approximately 4,500 members nationwide.[8] In 1999, Nicaraguan gangs peaked at 110 groups with 8,250 members in Managua alone, where 58 percent of Nicaragua's gangs were concentrated.[9] The gangs in other cities had a much lower profile and density: after Managua came Masaya (14 percent), Chinandega (11 percent), Estelí (8 percent), Jinotega (5 percent), Granada (3 percent), and Matagalpa (2 percent).[10] In 1999 a police operation profiled the great majority of these gangs as part of an ambitious national plan that aimed to capture and imprison gang leaders, as one component of an integral strategy for the social rehabilitation of "at-risk" youths, in which the media, churches, businesses, and nongovernmental organizations (NGOs) would have defined and meaningful roles.[11]

In the beginning of the twenty-first century, drugs acted as a catalyst for gang activity. A change in the route for South American cocaine going into the United States made Nicaragua an important trafficking zone. Many Nicaraguan cities became centers for the growing commerce and residual addiction to drugs.[12] The National Police registered an increase from 857 to 1,289 drug *expedios* (illegal outlets) in the country between 1999 and 2002.[13] The *pandilleros* (members of street gangs known as *pandillas*) went from throwing stones during street fights to smoking "stones" of crack on the street corners of the neighborhood, and they assaulted their neighbors to get the money to sustain their consumption. Their relations with neighbors deteriorated as a consequence of the erosion of their ethical code.

Surprisingly, several gangs were deactivated partly because of police pacification operations and the work of evangelical churches and NGOs. In recent years, however, the police registers of gangs have been inconsistent and incomplete. The most credible of these showed that there were 268 gangs and 4,500 *pandilleros*, slightly more than half the peak numbers.[14] The most recent report from the Nicaraguan police claimed 2,707 members in 183 groups in 2007, of which only 20 groups were categorized as *pandillas*.[15] The predominant age range among gang members fell from 18–25 to 15–18 years, and the average number of members per gang fell from 75 to 17. The last survey of geographic distribution (in 2003) found that only 33.2 percent of the country's gangs were concentrated in Managua, down from 58 percent in 1999.[16] The concentration in Managua of both police forces and NGOs was apparently responsible for this effect. John Hagedorn's observation that gangs evolved and adapted to different contexts applies directly to the Nicaraguan case study: the Charrasca gang participated in anti-Somoza skirmishes in an atmosphere of insurrectional fighting back in the 1980s, and now the current gangs — thanks to the redirected cocaine route through Nicaragua — are involved in the trafficking and consumption of drugs.[17] In the following sections, the contextual factors and outside forces that have molded the gangs into their present form are examined.

The Importance of Context

The evolution of Nicaraguan gangs toward pacification and atomization goes against the evolution of gangs in the rest of Central American, where they have tended toward consolidation into two main *mara* conglomerates and higher levels of violence. The extremely violent and criminal transnational gangs, the 18th Street Gang and Mara Salvatrucha (or MS-13), predominate in most other Central American countries, having essentially absorbed other gangs. One of the biggest mysteries for investigators, police, and NGO workers dedicated to juvenile rehabilitation is the contrasting course of gang development in Nicaragua. For the sake of analysis, it is important to start with two distinct questions: First, why are *maras* not in Nicaragua? And second, why are Nicaraguan gangs less violent than those in the rest of Central America? Context provides some answers.

In 1988, Levenson found in Guatemala a type of gang with characteristics similar to those of the rest of Central America at that time: small
groups in each neighborhood or on each street, who shared an intense
feeling of camaraderie and a culture of identity associated with the control of territory.[18] A follow-up study of gangs in the region, done in El
Salvador in 1992, focused on the *maras*,[19] which were then in an embry-
onic state but by 1996 had achieved their current notoriety.[20] The 18th
Street Gang, formed in the 1960s in Los Angeles, had a varied national
and racial composition, which was unusual for gangs at the time. According to Levenson and Francisco Escobar, the 18th Street Gang took
root in Guatemala, Honduras, and El Salvador. MS-13 was formed in Los
Angeles in the 1980s by immigrants of Salvadoran origin and currently
has members from most U.S. states.[21] (For more on the origins of these
two gangs, see Chapter 1 in this volume.) Both absorbed almost all of
the gangs in the northern part of Central America by consolidating local
gangs.

The deportations of gang members from the United States starting
in the 1990s played a key role in the expansion of the *maras* into Central America—and in their failure to infiltrate Nicaragua. Between 1993
and 2005, 22,512 Salvadorans, 16,714 Hondurans, and 13,550 Guatemalans
who had spent time in jail were deported from the United States; some
of them were members of the *maras*. By contrast, only 2,991 Nicaraguans
were deported during that period.[22] In general the Nicaraguans have been
less affected by deportations from the United States than other nationali-
ties: of the 310,884 Central Americans deported between 1992 and 2007,
only 3 percent (9,619) were Nicaraguan.[23] In addition, gang activists were
less likely to be among the relatively few deported Nicaraguans, since the
pattern of Nicaraguan settlement in the United States has been different
from that of other Central American immigrants. The *maras* had their
origin in the city of Los Angeles, where 368,416 Salvadorans were living in
2004.[24] Nicaraguans as a national group have, since their first migratory
waves in the 1980s, preferred the city of Miami, where 79,896 had settled
according to the last U.S. census, as opposed to only 29,919 registered in
Los Angeles.

The reason for the lower levels of deportations of Nicaraguans is significant. In absolute terms, the explanation is that the principal migratory destination of Nicaraguans is Costa Rica: fewer immigrants to the
United States means fewer deportations. But Nicaraguans are also less
affected in relative terms, a finding that has its roots in the particular
experience of most Nicaraguans entering U.S. society. Alejandro Portes

and Alex Stepick note that the Cuban residents of Miami, largely exiles of the Cuban Revolution, felt political affinity with the relatively prosperous Nicaraguans who fled the leftist Sandinista revolution in the 1980s; Cuban leaders in Miami contacted Republican Party senators to ask them to respond to the plight of the recently arrived Nicaraguans.[25] Thus many Nicaraguans were taken in as political refugees who had fled from a Communist regime, rather than being denied legal status as most of their poorer Central American counterparts were. The procedures for naturalization and residence were inordinately smooth for the Nicaraguans. Because they have not only been less subject to deportation but also have had a less traumatic transition into U.S. society, Nicaraguans have had less motivation to turn to gangs for assimilation.

Of gang members interviewed by the Instituto Universitario de Opinión Pública (IUDOP)—a part of the Universidad Centroamericana (Central American University) in San Salvador—approximately 17 percent had been deported from or returned from the United States.[26] In the city of El Progreso, Honduras, Jorge González found *pandilleros* from Los Angeles who had arrived in Honduras as messengers with instructions from gang leaders or as the carriers of funds to purchase weapons.[27] The dynamic of the gang "is seen as based on the orders that arrive from the United States," according to interviewee José Membreño. "The majority of homies noted a preferred taste for the lifestyle [rather] than feeling like they had another job to do. There was something that 'fascinated' them and made them feel even stronger: knowing they were backed by other homies in other cities and countries."[28] In contrast to this evidence, in Nicaragua no links have been detected between the dynamics of gangs and gang migration, on the one hand, and locals who are dissatisfied with their situation, on the other. In both of these cases, migratory patterns seem to have been decisive in shaping either the intensity or the absence of those correlations.

Democratization and Demilitarization

That the *mareros* (*mara* members) feel strengthened by a sense of belonging to a transnational force is linked to the belligerent character of their structure and activities. Though not a complete explanation for the spread of gangs in countries that are in a postconflict phase, it is reasonable to perceive the foundations of current violence in the only partially successful attempts at democratization and demilitarization that Central

American countries have made since the 1990s. The armed conflicts that rocked the Central American region in the 1970s and 1980s were products of the region's poverty and economic inequalities, the explosion of long-postponed demands for justice and opportunity, and the violent repression by authoritarian military states.[29] That period left damage that still haunts the countries of the region. Military officials and their institutions, although displaced, continue flexing their power to make Central American societies "democracies of low intensity."[30] In Guatemala, for example, a legacy of this period was the economic strengthening of the military, whose retired officers in the 1990s were recycled as ministers and deputies in capital cities overrun by drug trafficking, until they themselves were corrupted into an "arm of the hidden powers."[31]

The democratic transition, where it occurred with any success, still created obstacles that have yet to be overcome. The devastation of the Nicaraguan civil war (1978–1990) led to an unstable transition to democratic civilian rule. Studies have shown that there were 1,560 violent incidents involving arms and 1,248 victims between 1991 and 1994.[32] Because the signing of peace agreements between the revolutionary Sandinista government and the Contra counterrevolutionaries was almost simultaneous with the 1990 electoral defeat of the Sandinista National Liberation Front (FSLN) party by the National Opposition Union (UNO), pressure from the United States to demilitarize Nicaragua as part of Washington's anti-Sandinista strategy was successful, as were its efforts to strengthen the judicial infrastructure to meet international norms.[33] In its first 100 days, the new government abolished mandatory military service and reduced to 36,000 soldiers an army that had once had well over 120,000.[34] Military reductions continued during the UNO government (1990–1997), until the Nicaraguan military had become the smallest of Central America, with 14,000 soldiers in 1995; that number had dropped to 12,187 in 2002, setting the record for military demobilization in Latin America. Additionally, the military budget decreased sharply from $182 million to $31 million between 1989 and 1995.[35]

With a low population density—42 inhabitants per square kilometer—and a relatively large amount of state-owned territory, the government had the option of giving away land in negotiations to disarm the remaining demobilized groups of fighters from both sides. The first disarmament protocol assigned 25,000 hectares of cultivatable land on the southern border of Nicaragua to demobilized counterrevolutionaries,[36] an unimaginable concession in El Salvador and Guatemala, countries with 332 and 120 inhabitants per square kilometer, respectively, and densely concentrated areas of farmland. Between 1990 and 2004 the Salvadoran army shrank from 63,175 to 13,000 soldiers, and the Guatemalan army from 46,900 to 27,000.[37] Demilitarization concerns not just the reduction of soldiers, however, but also the political and socioeconomic reintegration of the demobilized personnel. In Nicaragua both sides maintained a strategy of political activism and were rewarded with substantial parcels of land. The numbers of those demobilized increased to 100,000, many of whom desired a return to civilian life. This was true both for those who had fulfilled their mandatory military service and for those members of the Contra resistance who wanted to go back to previously held occupations independently of the state's offers.

In El Salvador, Honduras, and Guatemala, although some demobilized men had the good fortune to be absorbed by emerging private security companies, others became involved with organized crime. There are indications that demilitarization is an unresolved topic throughout the region and that it has left a bitter aftertaste. Skirmishes involving the remnants of the paramilitary Civil Self-Defense Patrols in Guatemala, and the execution of children and youths at the hands of paramilitary groups in El Salvador and Honduras, are symptomatic of how deeply rooted violence is and how poorly concealed authoritarianism remains in the region. The gravitation of former military and paramilitary members to organized crime groups is symptomatic of a deficient and incomplete demilitarization process that never met the expectations of those involved and did not offer them a viable means to shed their military identity.

Another side to the violence is the relationship between society and the military apparatus. In this sense the quantitative reduction in numbers of personnel does not matter as much as the qualitative reconversion to civilian status. In El Salvador, Honduras, and Guatemala there has been a continuum of military control, domestic repression, and interference in other state institutions, despite efforts to demilitarize police forces and move toward autonomy of the state and an end to military oversight.[38] The anemia of the civilian democratic sectors in Central American states is accentuated by the intervention of military officials in other institutions. The delegitimization of judicial power is a common denominator. In Nicaragua, however, this weakness does not present the same risks that it does in Guatemala, where judicial power is ostensibly independent but ends up being neutralized by the intimidation of judges and lawyers by current and former military officials. From 1997 to 2000 there were 337 attacks aimed at the judicial process in Guatemala, undermining the establishment of rule of law in that country.[39] This situation is exacerbated by links between the state and organized crime in Guatemala, Honduras, and El Salvador, a pathology that results in what sociologist Peter Waldmann labeled an "anomic," or lawless, state and the Washington Office for Latin America now calls a "captive state," where the state structures responsible for governance are themselves implicated in crime and violence.[40]

In contrast to this situation, Nicaragua's FSLN-controlled police and army, as part of a strategy of corporate survival under pressure from the U.S. government and political forces that did not favor the FSLN, opted toward professionalism. Security officials designed plans that, although not entirely free of controversy, sought to reduce the military's size, worked to integrate the disadvantaged into Nicaragua's socioeconomic and political life, and institutionalized the police and military structures, thus ending FSLN control over them.[41] As a result, Nicaraguan society's relations with the state's security apparatuses are less tense and more legitimate than those in the north of Central America, where there are accusations that the military and the police are involved with drug trafficking, interfere with civil powers, and participate in bloody "social cleansing" operations against their own citizens.

Weapons and Homicides

Another aspect of the democratization-demilitarization process that has a direct effect on violence in general and on youth violence in particular is the destruction of the ample arsenal of weapons distributed during the civil wars. In Nicaragua, pressures to reduce the armed forces also led to the widespread destruction of weapons. In September 1990, in a ritual that came to be a custom during patriotic festivals, 15,000 weapons of all types were destroyed.[42] Between 1992 and 1994 the special units for the disarmament of the armed forces collected 53,475 firearms, 23,473 grenades, 7,072 mines, 165,405 kilograms of explosives, and 10 million rounds of ammunition for various weapons.[43] Other sources claim that 142,000 weapons were destroyed between 1991 and 1993, placing Nicaragua's among the twenty largest programs for weapon destruction in the world from 1991 to 2006 and, without a doubt, in first place in the ratio of small arms destroyed per capita.[44] This work continues year after year. In 2008, in compliance with the Special Law for the Control of Arms and Regulation of Firearms, Munitions, Explosives, and Other Related Materials, the National Police melted down a total of 12,994 firearms that had been either confiscated or handed in voluntarily by the population.[45] The 2007

Small Arms Survey found that in Nicaragua there were 7.7 weapons for every 100 people, far fewer than the 13.1 in Guatemala but higher than the 6.2 and 5.8 in Honduras and El Salvador, respectively.[46] The availability of arms, however, is not the only indicator of demilitarization, as the very peaceful Costa Rica has a ratio of 9.9. What is important is the meaning of weapons in the political and cultural context. The weapon destruction operations in Nicaragua not only reduce the availability of weapons but also are public rituals that stigmatize their unlawful use. The use and the socialization of weapons—thus-far-unmeasured indicators of societal violence—are variables that need to be better understood in order to establish a link with homicide rates, the clearest indicator of the daily impact of easily available weapons.

In 2006, Nicaragua had a rate of 12.46 homicides per 100,000 inhabitants, very close to the rate of 11.3 in Panama, a country without previous military conflicts, and considerably less than the 55.3, 45.2, and 42.9 of El Salvador, Guatemala, and Honduras, respectively.[47] In a once-peaceful region, homicides have been the most commonly used indicator to illustrate the failures of the new models for fair and democratic societies. In El Salvador and Guatemala, homicide rates increased from 36.2 to 55.3 and from 23.7 to 45.2, respectively, between 1999 and 2006.[48] The countries whose governments received the most military help from the U.S. government in the 1980s are those that in the postconflict phase have seen the highest homicide rates. The repressive methods that sustained authoritarian and undemocratic regimes have bred a more aggressive and increasing type of juvenile violence.

Evolution of Gangs in Nicaragua and Other Environmental Factors

The *pandillas* and *maras* of Central America should not be examined apart from the histories described above. The evolution of gangs in Nicaragua has not followed the same course as that of its regional counterparts, due to differing contextual and political conditions. Nicaraguan gangs initially were characterized by strong territorial identity, support from the neighborhood, occasional robberies, frequent fights with other gangs, and a well-defined honor code. In the early 2000s, however, a series of changes transformed the character of the gangs: the average age decreased, confrontations between gangs declined, *pandilleros* lost interest in the defense of the neighborhood and began to prey on their neighbors, the honor code was relaxed, and gang identity and cohesion began to dissolve. Gang members became increasingly preoccupied with consuming, manufacturing, and trafficking drugs and less interested in fighting other gangs.

Drugs have been the greatest catalysts for recent gang activity, with a significant increase in trafficking and prosecution. The total of those detained for the possession of drugs increased from 628 to 1,746 between 2000 and 2004.[49] But drugs are not the only force for change in Nicaragua's gang culture. The decrease in gang violence has occurred in a climate of relative restraint in police operations and proactive civil policies in various communities where gangs tend to operate. NGOs and their network of advocates have offered a range of opportunities in such neighborhoods: regular employment, paid labor, and involvement at the micro level in local politics. Frictions between international organizations and the government of President Arnoldo Alemán (1997–2001) created an exceptional situation in Nicaragua: the country saw an increase in external aid channeled through NGOs, which then extended their activities throughout the country. Although the majority of the NGOs do not have a mandate to work with gangs, it seems reasonable to assume that their interventions have had direct and indirect effects on the level of gang violence. On one side, they have expanded offers for local employment and opportunities for political activity. On the other, their advocates have exercised a type of informal social control that is not coercive in nature.

In addition to these conditions, as described earlier, the flows of Nicaraguan migrants were significantly different from general Central American migratory patterns and thus made the absorption of Nicaraguan gangs by the *maras* that had originated in Los Angeles more difficult. The combination of demilitarization that included land grants, the release of soldiers who saw their military service as temporary, the massive destruction of arms, low instances of organized crime, the noninterference of the military in other aspects of the state, and intensive NGO activities that reinforced community networks created the necessary conditions for a type of gang in Nicaragua that was less violent and more susceptible to pacification.

Governmental Responses

During the 1980s, Nicaragua's National Police paid scant attention to juvenile gangs. They did not even register the numbers or delinquent activities of such groups. The revolutionary government had to focus on threats to national security that came from counterrevolutionary groups.

In Guatemala and El Salvador as well, rebel guerrillas, rather than gangs— although they did exist—continued to be the principal focus of attention for the police and army. Worries about citizen security in Nicaragua and the identification of gangs that threatened security grew throughout the 1990s until it became a chief mission for the Ministerio de Gobernación (Ministry of Internal Affairs) in the Alemán administration. In this period, many countries experienced a weakening of the central state, along with the shrinking of social services and the widening of police powers and incarceration.[50] Nicaragua suffered this wave of fear for "citizen security" at a time when the revolutionary police force was in the process of institutionalization, the state government was highly dependent on external sources of aid, and the political realm was deeply polarized.

The guerrilla origin of the National Police was a determining element in the treatment of gangs. Differing from their Central American counterparts, who have advocated stigmatizing gang activity as organized violence, the higher officials of the Nicaraguan police saw young gangsters as new rebels who were experimenting with social and generational conflict. This vision was reflected in the police's first diagnosis of and plan for gangs, a strategic document that proposed to combine police work with the activities of churches, NGOs, and schools.[51] Its application coincided with another strategy—to imprison the most notorious *pandilleros* and carry out disarmament programs in District II of Managua. In that district the gangs signed peace treaties that they presented before their mothers in special ceremonies. The National Police also, however, retained certain aspects of their citizen security policies, to the satisfaction of their superiors in the Ministerio de Gobernación, decreeing the gangs to be "delinquent associations" and continuing to apply repressive policies, though these were much less intense than in other parts of the region.

Each aspect of the strategy was led by one of the forces that vied to gain control of the police. The group of police commissioners close to the Sandinista Front, for instance, promoted disarmament as part of a populist FSLN strategy to maintain gangs as proven allies in support of student and transportation strikes. The police commissioners closest to the traditional elites counted on a corporate survival strategy, yielding to pressure for more repressive measures from civilian superiors alarmed by juvenile delinquency. Both camps discovered their joint interests when Nicaragua began to figure in international forums as an exceptional country regarding the government response to gangs. President Enrique Bolaños (2002–2006), in an effort to attract foreign investment, tirelessly reiterated the idea that Nicaragua was the most secure country in Central America.[52] The funds for preventive community action began to flow, and preventive strategies were incorporated into official police policy, as evidenced by the naming of Police Commissioner Hamyn Gurdián, who had advocated the disarming of District II, as the new head of the recently created Office of Juvenile Issues. Nicaraguan gangs were reclassified into two categories: criminal gangs like those in the rest of Central America, and "innocuous" juvenile groups. There were reported to be 62 criminal gangs and 255 innocuous ones in 2003.[53]

The creation of the Office of Juvenile Issues and its adoption as a preventive model have been enormously beneficial for legitimization and the generation of funds: the Inter-American Development Bank gave Nicaragua a loan of US$7.2 million for a program of citizenship security that focuses on violence and juvenile delinquency.[54] This reinforced the conciliatory discourse and propaganda on the exceptional character of the Nicaraguan police. Gurdián argued that the Nicaraguan police had overcome repressive penal models and sought to understand and put the issue in context: "The police have functions that are legally exclusive and reflect the legal concept that says 'rob those who rob others.' . . . But here [in Nicaragua] we transcend the penal process. We embody a sociological, criminological, and anthropological focus for the future. We have an ecological focus that implies viewing the individual from a societal point of view."[55] The prevention model is presented as a proactive one that tries to influence children, adolescents, and youths before "they cross the line between risk and delinquency." Likewise, it presents a model that "also tries to rescue those youths who have committed crimes[,] to give them an opportunity in life and so they feel valued as youths."[56] The application of this model had very sound elements: young *pandilleros* could participate in social events and work on beaches as lifeguards, for example, and ongoing armistices included clearing the gang members' records to remove the stigma of labeling them as criminals.

Another dynamic was intertwined with and ran parallel to the one described above. The country's political polarization resulted in corruption charges being brought—justifiably—against officials of the Alemán administration. The international community made bitter accusations about the manner in which the Alemán government had managed the international aid that arrived in response to Hurricane Mitch, which devastated Central America at the end of October 1998. In an attempt to stem the deterioration of these relations, government officials accelerated the ap-

proval of largely stagnant legal projects directed at youths. They calculated that passage would present a counterstep to the questionable management of President Alemán, an action that would appear to be more
socially responsible and consonant with the globalization of legal norms.
During Alemán's administration, the legislature approved the Code of
Childhood and Adolescence (1998), the Law for the Promotion of the Integral Development of Nicaraguan Youth (2001), and the National Plan
for the Integral Development of Youth (2001). The emphasis placed on
the legitimacy of these laws led to the creation of new state entities: the
special Ombudsman for the Child and Adolescent (2000) and the Secretary of Youth (2002). This entire institutional evolution marked a sharp
contrast between the attitudes of the Alemán and Bolaños administrations in Nicaragua and those of President Ricardo Maduro in Honduras,
the ruling ARENA party in El Salvador, and the Guatemalan government
during this period, which began to apply repressive *mano dura* (strong
arm) anti-gang policies and, at least in Guatemala, countenanced extrajudicial executions of suspected *mareros*.

Pandillas were never considered the principal threat to citizen security
in Nicaragua, as they were elsewhere. Preventive policies and the operation of community police were, however, seen as successful and led to
points of programmatic harmony between the police and the directors of
the newly coined entities, the Ombudsman and the Secretary of Youth.
Given the realities of the terrain—the streets of principal cities—the preventive model and institutional harmony were not, however, as impec-
cable as suggested by the rhetoric and the legal theories of the imple-
menters of the codes. The Code of Childhood and Adolescence (hereafter
"the Code") was soon perceived by police squads and many citizens as an
instrument that essentially guaranteed impunity to delinquent youths.[57]
The decrease in the average age of gang members is due, in part, to the incentives within the Code, which define special penal treatment for minors
under eighteen years old. Police squads thus began enforcing extrajudicial
punishment more often, as a means to evade the strictures of the Code,
by beating detainees and later setting them free, a very efficient method
for avoiding tiresome procedures and the costs that are supposed to be
covered as stipulated by the new legislation. Above all, such tactics served
as counterweights to legislation that still lacks social acceptance. Some of
these beatings have resulted in the death of victims.[58]

The two-faced police policy—beatings and the application of the preventive model—has sustained an effective ambivalence among *pandilleros*

and friction with other institutions that compete with the police for external financial resources. The substantial dependence on external funds, the strategy of satisfying donors, and the competition for resources in general have opened the subject of juvenile violence in Nicaragua to debate by numerous voices of variable and unequal power.

Neither the Strong Arm nor the Benevolent Hand

One year after the approval of the Code, the implementation of Police Plan 1999 put more than 400 adolescents in prison without legal guarantees, the majority of them younger than fifteen years of age; this was in blatant violation of Article 95 of the Code.[59] Such abuses of power, the arbitrary seizure of delinquent adolescents, and the failure of the police to comply with the Code were attributed to prejudices against the Code held by many police officers despite the official position of the National Police's leadership, and were denounced by the Ombudsman and certain NGOs. These arrests obviously were not presented by the National Police as policy, but they nevertheless had the effect of atomizing gangs by weakening them and depriving them of their most experienced members. With time, the police placed more emphasis on the preventive model, and the application of the Code won ground, reducing the imprisonment of minors and, in turn, *pandilleros*. The number of adolescents deprived of freedom dropped from 449 in 1998 to 36 in 2003.[60] What remains unclear, however, is the degree to which, as a reaction to this decline, the extrajudicial punishments frequently seen in the news media have multiplied.

The official policy of the police, judging by their statistics, has borne much fruit: the rehabilitation of at-risk youths; the sponsorship of sports tournaments to get youngsters off the street; the creation of 2,064 Committees for the Social Prevention of Crime (Comités de Prevención Social del Delito), with 20,000 volunteers; and the establishment of a varying number—relatively trivial on the national scale—of scholarships and permanent jobs for youths. Before the appearance of these preventive programs, the National Police did not worry about separately tracking gang crimes, which saw a notable reduction between 2002 and 2007, from 17 to 6 homicides, 122 to 17 injuries, and 32 to 26 penal violations.[61] In the same period, the police continued to reintegrate 3,979 youths into society.[62] These data, however, should be handled with caution. A survey of the news media and recent fieldwork in neighborhoods of the capital have found a decrease in gangs,[63] but one that is not as pronounced as that registered by the police, whose statistics reflect an official interest in promoting the exceptionality of the Nicaraguan case. The police's optimism tends to exaggerate results, and has reached the extreme of attributing the absence of *maras* in the country to its work, a perception that many state officials and some international organizations share, perpetuating the illusion that public policies are a decisive factor for determining trends of this type. Little attention is given to the historical trajectories and structural elements that are of far more importance. Still, there is no doubt that the police's attitudes and policies have been crucial elements, especially regarding their turn toward preventive programs.

It is necessary, nevertheless, to take a measured view of the actions and merits of this one actor. In fact, Nicaraguan society as a whole has moved toward forms of conflict resolution that reflect tolerance and are based on policies that do not permit a *mano dura* response. At the same time, such policies also do not reflect a laissez-faire attitude or a benevolent hand.

The present situation may eventually change. The return to power of the FSLN in 2007 has been accompanied by a resurgence in gang activity, including groups that had been inactive for some time. Military officials of the FSLN seek to use the apparently random activities of these gang members as a clandestine means to implement governmental repression and reportedly have orchestrated this reemergence. Analysts and social workers have voiced their alarm and condemnation of the near-term consequences that these developments could have if they reverse the decrease in violence by and rehabilitation of gang members that have been achieved only with great effort.[64] Until now, Nicaragua has had a very different experience with *pandillas* from its Central American neighbors, but it will be up to Nicaraguan society as a whole to see that politics do not undermine its achievements.

Conclusion

While focusing mainly on Nicaragua, the analysis in this chapter seeks to explain the currently unique situation of gang formation and behavior in this country as contrasted with the situation in three Central American neighbors where the *maras* are a very serious problem. The answer lies not only in geography (having ample land to distribute to demobilized counterrevolutionaries) and immigration/deportation patterns but also in the nature of the security forces and the NGO community and how they have dealt with at-risk youths and criminal activity. The analysis here highlights that state behavior is indeed a critical variable in explaining why *pandillas* have yet to transmute into *maras* in Nicaragua. In the current political environment, however, there is a risk that this undesired transformation could occur.

PART II

RESPONSES TO GANG VIOLENCE

CHAPTER 6

State Power and Central American *Maras:*
A Cross-national Comparison

ENRIQUE DESMOND ARIAS

Countries across Latin America face growing crime rates and substantial levels of fear among their citizens, both of which lead governments to impose harsh policing policies and cause citizens to turn to private security firms, vigilantism, or even lynch mobs in efforts to more effectively protect their loved ones and their property.[1] Conversations about crime, fear, and gangs in the region often begin and end with the idea that states are too weak to adequately provide protection to the population, and that the rights inherent to the democratic systems that today govern almost every country in the region are somehow antithetical to security. This common discourse, however, represents a very limited way of looking at the challenges facing the region. Evidence from around the globe suggests that organized crime often thrives *in collusion* with the state rather than in opposition to it, and effective law enforcement is more often associated with open and transparent preventive and investigative policing activities than with harsh and abusive security strategies.[2]

Every country, however, is different: within each country, different types of criminal groups and sectors of the population have dissimilar relationships with security officials and political leaders. The types of state-criminal relations that foster organized crime in southern Europe, for example, are different from the types of relationships that foster violence and drug trafficking in Colombia. As with other elements of national social and political life, the structure of criminal activities and its impact on the wider life of the citizenry are integrally linked to particular local histories, social structure, and government policies. Understanding large-scale criminal activity and social disorder such as exist in much of Latin America today necessitates understanding complex local political and social histories and institutions.

As other chapters in this book make clear, these ideas apply to the case of the youth gangs (*pandillas* and *maras*) of Central America. Building on original research I conducted on gangs and criminal activity in other parts of Latin America and the Caribbean, as well as a study of recent works on Guatemala and Nicaragua, this chapter examines the historical, political, and social factors that have given rise to *maras*. It looks closely at the ways these gangs differ from those observed in other countries, and particularly at what appear to be rather weak relations between these groups and state officials.

The State and Criminal Structures in Latin America

In their classic book *Shaping the Political Arena*, Ruth Berins Collier and David Collier argue that the efforts of Latin American states to incorporate and provide basic rights to their working class were an essential element in determining the political structure of the region in the twentieth century.[3] The particular nature of this process shaped both the polities themselves and the crises those polities would eventually face as the century moved forward. The book concludes with the wave of authoritarianism that swept the region in the 1960s and 1970s, but the authors' core insight applies to the problems of regional violence today. How states attempted to integrate large portions of the population into political life determined many of the challenges that those states have faced in the period after the end of the authoritarian regimes.

Latin American states today face challenges from criminal organizations based on the particular nature of these incorporative policies and the ways they failed in the 1970s and 1980s. Thus, for example, in Brazil the limited incorporation of the urban working class through corporatist structures created conditions in which large numbers of working Brazilians fell outside these structures. Those who were left out had to find ways to protect and govern their own neighborhoods, from which emerged various forms of armed groups that ran the neighborhoods, each having a different type of relationship to the wider polity. In Colombia, by contrast, integrative policies collapsed into civil war in the 1950s. This civil war then gave rise to a series of armed groups, including paramilitaries and guerrillas, which continue to play a substantial role in Colombian politics. As a final example, in Jamaica, incorporation occurred through the efforts of political parties to win elections by arming supporters in the 1950s and 1960s. The gang-state relationship that developed there prevailed through the 1980s, changing in response to the retreat of certain types of clientelist activity during austerity programs. That relationship continues to affect the structure of crime and disorder in downtown Kingston.[4]

Unlike in many other Latin American countries, in Nicaragua and Guatemala the integration of the working class into the wider political system was substantially limited by the extent of local poverty, the tight control that authoritarian regimes maintained over the local population, and extended civil war. This pattern is most stark in Nicaragua, where the Anastasio Somoza dictatorship reigned by force for over forty years, with little effort to integrate the poor and working class into the political system. Lower-class incorporation first arrived in Nicaragua with the Marxist Sandinista revolution that overthrew Somoza in 1979, approximately fifty years after such incorporation in the rest of the region. The post-1979 revolutionary government built a series of mechanisms to maintain working-class support but became mired in long-term low-intensity conflict with the United States–funded Contra (counterrevolutionary) rebels. The expenses of this conflict, as well as state mismanagement, undermined wider political efforts by the government to transform the national polity and "consolidate control." In 1990 the ruling Sandinista National Liberation Front (FSLN) lost power in free elections to an opposition coalition, but Sandinista agitation, combined with continued pressure from only partially demobilized Contras, led to ongoing rural conflict that slowly crept into the cities.[5]

The *pandillas* that now operate in Managua emerged out of the series of civil conflicts that began in the aftermath of a major earthquake in Nicaragua in 1971 and that did not subside until the 1990s. During the entire period from the beginning of the FSLN uprising in the 1970s to the present, Nicaragua has had fairly high levels of youth violence. As José Luis Rocha points out (in Chapter 5 of this volume), however, during the country's extended civil war much of this violence was legitimized through connections with official institutions. The youth who today might participate in a *pandilla* would have been a member of pro-government or rebel military forces in those years. The initial explosion of organized *pandillas* in Nicaragua occurred in 1990 with the end of the civil conflict, when many teenagers were demobilized from the army and, with years of combat training but little work available for them to do, turned to street crime and violence to survive. This situation was exacerbated by the difficult economic situation that the country found itself in, which provided little opportunity for employment and few effective ways for the state to integrate the working-class population into national political life. To make matters worse, in the 1980s the FSLN government had distributed arms to popular militias that were organized to fight the Contras. The government never recovered all of the weapons after the fighting ended, and many remained in the hands of the population. Over the long term, this laid the ground for a rise in youth violence in Nicaragua and, as a result of the export of these unregistered arms, in other countries in Central America as well.

Guatemala presents a different story. As was the case with Nicaragua, the aspirations of working-class Guatemalans for economic integration were bound up in an extended revolutionary struggle that has defined the conditions of crime in that country over the last decade. Where Nicaragua languished under the boot of the Somoza regime for forty years, however, Guatemala achieved a political opening in the 1940s and 1950s that was similar to what was occurring in other parts of Latin America. From 1945 through 1954, under Presidents Juan José Arévalo and Jacobo Arbenz Gúzman, Guatemala progressively worked to integrate the poorer population into the polity and to provide explicit rights to the large indigenous population in the country.[6] In 1954, however, a military coup d'état led to dictatorship and triggered a large-scale popular uprising, which brought together Marxist and indigenous groups that fought against the government though 1996. This thirty-six-year civil war reached its most brutal period in the mid-1980s, when a genocidal military campaign killed between 50,000 and 75,000 indigenous citizens.[7] The years since the end of the conflict have been characterized by substantial economic stresses that have forced many citizens to go abroad, and a fear of crime that has led to a large number of lynchings by vigilante groups.[8]

Elin Ranum's chapter on Guatemala (Chapter 3 in this volume) indicates that Guatemala's *maras* emerged out of this conflict for two reasons. On the one hand, the country had a problem similar to that in Nicaragua, where large numbers of young men who had served in the military or rebel groups were demobilized and, in the context of World Bank–imposed economic austerity programs in the 1990s, found few economic opportunities as civilians. Many of these individuals turned to crime. On the other hand, large numbers of poor Guatemalans migrated to other parts of Guatemala and the southwestern United States as a result of the war and the lack of opportunities at home. Those young people who had migrated to the United States often felt compelled to join the local gangs (such as Mara Salvatrucha and the 18th Street Gang) to protect themselves in dangerous urban neighborhoods. The implementation of harsh anti-immigrant legislation in 1996 led to the deportation of many of these young people, who arrived back in Guatemala with little more than their gang ties and their criminal experience to help them survive, thus furthering the development of *maras* in Guatemala. Internal migration fed the problem because it broke down traditional social and communal ties, causing some young people to join *maras* in their new towns in an effort to find community.

The immigration question operates very differently in Nicaragua. While the generally poor Guatemalan immigrants for the most part moved to Southern California, which at the time suffered from serious gang problems, Nicaraguans principally moved to Miami, a city with a more limited gang presence. These largely middle- and upper-class Nicaraguans in Miami were given status as refugees from a socialist revolution and so received a greater degree of support from both the administration of President Ronald Reagan and Miami's anti-Marxist Cuban-American community than Guatemalans received from either the state or society in California. As a result, fewer Nicaraguans were deported, and those who returned to Nicaragua rarely had had experience with dangerous gangs.

These two histories reveal broad trends that help us understand the relationship between state power and criminal activity. The popular experience of politics in both Nicaragua and Guatemala has been defined by civil war. Unsuccessful demobilization contributed in each case to the problems of criminal violence after these wars. On this level, both countries have much in common with Colombia but less with others such as Mexico, Brazil, and Jamaica. In Guatemala, on the one hand, a brutal civil war lasted thirty-six years and culminated in genocidal acts against indigenous groups. In this extremely violent context, large numbers of Guatemalans were forced to emigrate, while substantial internal instability compelled large populations of displaced people to move to cities. These migratory movements and the fear engendered by the war created the basis for a stunning upswing in gang violence in the 1990s. In Nicaragua, by contrast, the FSLN attempted to integrate the population into the political system, and the war itself was much shorter and never became as brutal, which helped minimize migration. These factors, plus the relative welcome Nicaraguan immigrants received in the United States, have restrained the growth of both *maras* and overall levels of societal violence, even though Nicaragua experienced economic dislocations similar to, if not worse than, those in Guatemala in the 1990s. In this sense, the nature of the struggle for working-class incorporation helped shape the criminal problems both countries face.

Corruption and Gang Activities

The impact of state power on criminal activities is not limited to historical forces. Connections with public officials, including the police, are essential to the ongoing activities of organized crime. The contemporary shape of criminal groups is very much influenced by the nature of state corruption and how that is inserted into illegal marketplaces. Beyond the Central American cases we are examining here, the effects of official corruption can be seen in a variety of Latin American countries.

Perhaps the best-known example of this today is Mexico, where extensive problems within the Mexican state have provided ample space for the expansion of criminal networks that many believe are having a politically destabilizing effect. Under PRI (Institutional Revolutionary Party) rule in the 1980s and into the 1990s, powerful political figures took substantial bribes from large-scale drug dealers in exchange for protection from prosecution. This process began at relatively low levels, with criminals paying off low-ranking state police officers to facilitate the criminals' rise to prominence. The more significant the illicit activities, the higher-ranking the police and state officials who became involved in the racket until, in the case of the most powerful drug dealers, state governors and high-level national political officials were directly on the take.[9] In the most celebrated case of this kind, the general in charge of Mexico's drug enforcement administration took money from one of the major drug cartels. During his administration, arrests of drug traffickers had gone up, but investigators found that this official had made good on his arrangement with the underworld by arresting members of a competing cartel.[10] All of this corruption existed in parallel with a tightly bound hierarchical extortion scheme within the police force, in which low-level officers had to extort money from criminals and other citizens to pass onto their immediate superiors, who were in turn obligated to pass a portion ever higher, until funds reached the police chiefs.[11]

This structure of corruption, in its hierarchy and in its federated centralism, reflected the structure of the Mexican state at the time. High-level political appointees held power, and those lower in the political structure owed them support in exchange for patronage. This political system was centralized in Mexico City, and all power emanated from the presidency, the top of this patronage pyramid. This contrasts substantially with the case of Brazil, for example, where the federal government is much weaker and where most police power lies directly in the hands of independently elected state governors. The result, in contrast with Mexico's situation, is that criminal activities and corruption schemes vary substantially by state, with different police forces and state-level political structures having vastly different systems of venality. Thus Rio de Janeiro, São Paulo, and Minas Gerais, three wealthy neighboring states, each have had different experiences with corruption over the past ten years.

Chapter 3 on Guatemala and Chapter 5 on Nicaragua in this volume provide similar insights into the question of official corruption in their own particular contexts. In Nicaragua, as in Rio de Janeiro, the drug trade is a basic survival strategy, not just for poor individuals but for whole communities that are unable to meet basic needs. In these conditions, those who control the drug trade provide critical support to families and communities that have limited access to opportunities for business investment and social support. The police that operate within particular communities simply become part of these larger local-level drug machines by looking the other way when they see drug deals, by taking bribes, and by smoothing relations between the drug traffickers they know and other police officers. At the same time, Rocha makes clear in Chapter 5 that in Nicaragua there is a gap between the *pandillas*, which are only intermittently involved with drugs, and local drug capos and politically connected "big fish." While local drug dealers work with the police and occasionally are subject to police pressure, large-scale drug dealers and organized crime groups are better connected to the state; they have the protection of networks of "narco-police" and members of the judiciary who are reluctant to pursue action against them. Indeed, in such a highly unequal and politically networked context, *pandillas* appear to play a low-level function in the drug trade by providing occasional street labor to dealers and, through their visible presence and criminal activities, a distraction for the police from more powerful traffickers. The police willingly direct their actions against the *pandilleros*, who are only marginally involved in organized crime, rather than focus on more serious—and more dangerous—criminals. The police apparently have even on occasion provided weapons to well-connected gang members. The Nicaraguan state, despite its shift to ostensible democracy, is highly corrupt, with extensive crooked political "gangs" that control a substantial amount of state power. All of this reinforces a sense of impunity in the country, at least for those with power, that makes it very difficult to control organized crime effectively.

The issue of corruption should also be considered in the wider context of political contestation in postrevolutionary Nicaragua. A large portion of the police leadership is made up of old FSLN cadres who are closely linked to the political efforts of President Daniel Ortega and the party leadership. These police leaders maintain links with *pandilla* members because of the latter's usefulness in promoting demonstrations and other political activities. This presumably provides some protection to these groups, but it also exposes them to pressure from those police factions not allied with the FSLN.

Guatemala also suffers serious problems with official corruption that have impacts on the activities of local *maras*, as Ranum notes in Chapter 3. There have been close connections between the Guatemalan state and organized crime since the 1970s, when government officials began looking to criminal activities to fund their side in the civil war. Indeed, extensive corruption within the police prevents serious law enforcement efforts that do anything more than attract press attention to repressive tactics. Police take bribes from *mareros* in return for impunity, thus undermining popular confidence in the state. Perhaps the greatest problem with official corruption and impunity in Guatemala is the participation of the police in vigilante "social cleansing" groups and lynch mobs that target undesirable elements of the population, in many cases members of *maras*. Police participation in these activities further undermines trust in state institutions.

The stories of police corruption and impunity in both of these cases reflect the history of each country, and the specific nature of each state has a considerable effect on the activities of the *pandillas* and *maras* within them. Both countries are highly stratified and corrupt. Powerful and politically connected criminals have access to substantial political protection in exchange for the services they provide to state officials. In a reflection of the inequalities in both countries, *pandillas* are cut off from this high-level protection; the same is true for drug gangs in Rio de Janeiro, but its situation stands in contrast to that of Colombia and Mexico. The differences among these cases are a result of the political culture of centralization in both Mexico and Colombia and the integrated and hierarchical nature of crime in those countries. At the same time, the quality of police impunity and corruption in each country is defined by its history. While some Nicaraguan police leaders, who are part of a politically contested police force in that country, work with *pandillas* to promote local political efforts, in Guatemala the history of mass violence against the poor has led the police to become involved in death squads that target *maras*.

The State and Policy Choices in Propagating *Maras*

In addition to the history and nature of official corruption, actual policy choices also contribute to the strength of criminal gangs. In Jamaica, for example, politicians removed shantytowns from downtown Kingston in the 1960s and 1970s and built public housing in their stead. These same politicians, however, used access to the public housing to build safe political bases in particular constituencies. The result was that while the better quality of housing improved life for many poor Kingston residents, criminal gangs gained control of those areas and used them to take over parts of Jamaica's drug trade. Similarly, in Medellín, Colombia, today national government efforts to reduce paramilitary violence have met with substantial success when measured by homicide rates, which have declined from more than 200 per 100,000 inhabitants to around 30 per 100,000 inhabitants in the first decade of this century. A close observation of conditions on the ground, however, reveals that the state has partially achieved this decline in violence by handing power over some neighborhoods in the city to paramilitary groups that had been only nominally demobilized. The result is increasing paramilitary control over these neighborhoods. Since 2007 the national and municipal governments have engaged in a concerted effort to bring some powerful paramilitary leaders to justice. These efforts, however, have contributed to escalating violence as some criminals resist such efforts and as disorganization has grown in the criminal world.[12] There is some evidence that, in Rio de Janeiro, social investment by government agencies and nongovernmental organizations often is co-opted by drug traffickers, who may end up controlling how those funds are spent. As a result, state spending to reduce crime actually can strengthen criminal groups.[13] What these cases have in common are active policies by the state that lay the groundwork for the organization of criminal groups. Evidence from Central America similarly suggests that the poorly conceived dispersal of government resources also tends to strengthen criminal groups there.

In Nicaragua a considerable number of elaborate and seemingly progressive policies that are in place appear to have little effect on the overall existence of *pandillas* or actually strengthen these groups. At the heart of the problems emanating from Nicaraguan policy are the contradictory tensions between the Procudaduría (National Prosecutor's Office), Sandinista and non-Sandinista police elites, and the street-level police force. While the Procudaduría defends a relatively sophisticated set of laws designed to provide protections to adolescent gang members, the different segments of the police remain divided on strategy. On the one hand, police leaders with links to centrist and rightist political elites promote the idea that Nicaragua has relatively low levels of violence. On the other hand, Sandinista police leaders promote policies to build contacts with youths in order to achieve political ends. Finally, the street-level police implement brutal anti-gang policies that reinforce fear and social discrimination. In the end, large amounts of money are expended on contradictory policies that augment fear and do not provide basic protection to the population, results that undermine the people's trust in the state.

Guatemala's anti-*mara* strategy is focused almost exclusively on repression. Although the Guatemalan legislature has not passed specific anti-*mara* laws, the police have adopted highly repressive strategies such as 2003's Plan Escoba (Operation Broom). This plan, as Ranum observes in Chapter 3, was brutally repressive and based on the massive detention of suspected *mareros* on legally tenuous grounds. Thus, of more than 5,000 detentions between July 2003 and July 2004, only 1.1 percent of detainees were formally accused, and of those only half were convicted. Even these efforts, however, were counterproductive: they did not decrease levels of violence on the street, but they did increase tensions between gangs and promoted cohesion within gangs. In general, because time in prison limits opportunities for the young people who are incarcerated to seek employment, go to school, or take advantage of other formal-sector opportunities, it serves only to deepen relations among gang members.[14] At the same time, under intense police pressure, conflict increased between the different *maras*, leading to greater overall levels of violence in Guatemalan society.

On the whole, events related to gangs in Guatemala and Nicaragua are similar to experiences in other counties in Latin America. Policing policies have tended to reinforce and shape these groups. As one keen observer of violence in Rio has noted, the unpredictability of repressive police actions drives the residents of poor communities into the hands of gangs, who take on the role of protectors, and thus facilitates criminal activity.[15] Guatemala and Nicaragua also show, however, that particular national experiences and local government practices help shape local gangs. In Nicaragua a divided police force has developed contradictory strategies to deal with *pandillas* that appear at times to have given support to them and at other times tried to repress them in ways that enhanced group cohesion. Guatemala, without a populist influence such as the former FSLN cadres within the Nicaraguan police, adopted a much more repressive strategy that has had the effect of strengthening the country's *maras*. Over the long run, deep divisions and corruption in Nicaragua's political system have been reflected in anti-gang strategies that have deepened divisions in Nicaraguan society. Guatemala, for its part, has developed a militarized response to gangs that has served mostly to weaken state legitimacy and restrict democratic rights in a futile effort to repress the violent youth gangs. Over time, this is creating serious problems for political order in Guatemala and diminishes overall support for the wider democratization effort there.

Popular Fear, State Power, and Crime in Central America

An odd paradox exists in many of the cases mentioned in this chapter, which is particularly noticeable in the context of Central America. The population at large and the media treat gangs as a major threat to social order. The popular image is of readily identifiable wayward youths who impede the rights and security of other segments of the population and who force law-abiding citizens to seek private protection, demand state intervention, and cower in fear behind the walls of their homes.[16] But almost without exception, the mostly poor young people who are held out as scapegoats for much of the violence that affects the societies they live in are among the most disempowered members of those societies, and they are the group most readily subject to all manner of state and social repression and disenfranchisement. In Brazil the adolescent, mostly black youths who populate the city's drug gangs have no more than an elementary school education and have relatively little political power. Their ability to remain active and avoid arrest is a testament in part to their own wits but, more often, to the connections they and the more wealthy criminals behind them have to the police and other state officials. At the same time, the ones cowering in fear in their fortified condominiums are more often than not quite powerful and well connected, both economically and politically.

A close look at criminal activities in Nicaragua, Guatemala, and Rio de Janeiro suggests that while street gangs maintain some links with the police and in fact are often exploited by police officers who demand bribes to supplement their meager incomes, these gangs have much weaker connections within the political system than the capos who run major organized crime operations. Indeed, the chapters in this book on Guatemala and Nicaragua suggest that the fear provoked by these youthful drug gangs serves as a convenient distraction from the much more serious challenges posed by organized crime groups that can fund major state operations and influence political outcomes.

The treatment given by the media to these problems reinforces this disparity. While the press focuses on the powerful images of poverty and identifiably different youths with tattoos and, in the Brazilian case, large weapons, it often avoids doing the very difficult reporting on large-scale extortion rackets and official corruption that would be necessary to bring an end to those activities.[17] While reporting on low-level drug trafficking can put a reporter in danger, the risks posed by that type of journalism are much more limited than the risks of investigative reporting on police corruption, for example. A drug dealer may get the opportunity to hurt or kill a reporter who is visiting the dealer's neighborhood, but the substantial lack of reach of street drug dealers means that even relatively powerful dealers have very little ability to travel publicly between neighborhoods or lash out at reporters in other parts of the city. Major organized crime figures, by contrast, rarely face these types of challenges, because their powerful connections provide them protection. Investigating someone high up in organized crime or a police corruption operation puts reporters at risk for being pursued more widely within their country or even internationally. In some cases, a good reporter may have nowhere to hide and few good images for the eleven o'clock news.

A comparison of Brazil, Mexico, Jamaica, Colombia, Guatemala, and Nicaragua is revealing. In some cases there is a clear public link between the high-level international criminals and the low-level gangs that do much of their work. In other cases there is more distance and a less clear link. The more that effective and powerful criminals can obscure or limit their ties to street gangs, the less likely it seems that governments are forced to actively move against these kingpins. Even when there are substantial rumors of official collusion with organized crime, governments seem compelled to act against the most powerful criminals only when their connections with other criminals or the state are revealed. Thus in Brazil, Nicaragua, and Guatemala, on the one hand, there are few apparent contacts between powerful criminals and street gangs. As a result, state officials rarely move against these criminals but regularly put pressure on gangs. On the other hand, in Mexico, Jamaica, and Colombia, revelations of clear relationships between powerful crime bosses, politicians, and street-level criminals have led to major national scandals, forcing the governments to make efforts to bring the more powerful criminals to justice, even at a major cost to individual officials and, some argue, political order.[18] The starker the relations between high-level organized crime and street gangs, the more likely it is that the state will move against both the powerful criminals and the poor urban gangs that are usually the target of police actions.

Part of the reason for this is the dangers politicians face in pursuing powerful members of organized crime. While it is easy for the press to attract attention to street gangs, and the idea of the danger posed by a street gang resonates with popular conceptions of crime, it is harder to draw attention to large-scale organized crime, which often looks as mundane as any legitimate business. Politicians thus have little reason to go after organized crime figures and, as described earlier, may in some cases take bribes from these criminals. Street gangs, by contrast, usually do not have the reach to actually threaten the types of politicians who make decisions about policing and security strategy. All of this makes it much easier for politicians to avoid dealing with the high-level crime problem until the world of elite organized crime is linked to the direct threat that residents encounter on the streets. In the case of Mexico and Colombia, these links appear to have become prominent simply because organized crime operations became extremely large and drew in many other criminal activities. In the case of Jamaica, such attention arose as a result of the historic and prominent links between Jamaican politicians and gangs that later became involved in the international cocaine trade.

Facing the difficulty of dealing with powerful criminals, states often exploit the fear generated by media coverage of gangs by pursuing public and highly repressive policies or by simply not reining in street-level police actions, as occurs in both Guatemala and Nicaragua. This gives political leaders the ability to appear "tough on crime" without actually incurring the risks associated with targeting more powerful criminals, who may have political protection. In addition, this strategy allows political leaders to exploit the fears of the population about the crime problem and give the state and the police a freer hand to pursue a variety of possibly extralegal or undemocratic policies.

Conclusion

The foregoing analysis has described the importance of state power in supporting criminal activity in Central America. Building on comparisons with other Latin American countries and the Caribbean, the chapter has provided a detailed analysis of how the state system and historical structures contribute not just to the existence of criminal gangs but also to the particular shape they take within different political systems. The evidence suggests that the existence of gangs and more powerful criminal organizations does not simply reflect a failure of the state but is in many ways a function of history, the structure of the state, and particular policies. This discussion has revealed some significant similarities between the Central American *pandillas* and *maras* and the drug gangs in Rio de Janeiro, as well as some differences between these groups and the organizations operating in Jamaica, Colombia, and Mexico. At the heart of these patterns, however, are the activities and structures of state power, as well as the history of conflict in each police organization. Indeed, contemporary criminal gangs in Latin America appear at times to be forms of governance and civil conflict by noninstitutionalized and illegal means.

CHAPTER 7

Government Responses and the Dark Side of Gang Suppression in Central America

JOSÉ MIGUEL CRUZ

Why have Central American *maras* become so violent and organized? How did youth gangs in El Salvador, Guatemala, and Honduras turn into a major threat to security in North America, while in Nicaragua they still remain street bands? What is the key difference in the evolution of the gang phenomena in these Central American countries?

Most of the studies on *maras* in the region have focused on the factors that supposedly lie behind their emergence, such as migration, poverty, social exclusion, a culture of violence, and family disintegration.[1] Although some of these explanations help us understand the early development of Central American street gangs, they have failed to elucidate why organizations such as Mara Salvatrucha (MS-13) and the 18th Street Gang have not taken root within the impoverished and troubled society of Nicaragua. More importantly, those hypotheses also fail to explain why *maras* have institutionalized and developed into powerful, armed groups.

Some authors have pointed out that states themselves have been major players in the growth of *maras* because governments have not always enacted the right policies and strategies to curb the *maras* phenomenon. In most of the literature about gangs, and about Central American *maras* in particular, there is an assumption that the role of the state in the development of gangs is just a matter of successful or failed institutional policies: gangs appear and expand in those countries in which the government fails to enact the appropriate policies and enforce the law. In societies where intelligent policies and strategies effectively enforce the law, the conventional wisdom says, gangs are contained and deactivated. So the task of creating public policies regarding youth crime and gangs is often reduced to attempting to hit on the "right formula" to tackle gangs.

In several cases, these assumptions can be deemed correct. A sound policy and an effective law enforcement strategy are indeed conducive to the control of gangs or, at least, to the reduction of their felonies and violence. But this prescription presupposes that the state and its formal institutions of security are in full control of the forces that carry out the rules, plans, and strategies to curb gangs and their violence; it also presupposes that institutions of security operate only within the limits established by the law. In other words, the notion that the problem of gang reproduction and expansion has to do exclusively with the types of implemented policies and the effectiveness of law enforcement implies that the state is represented only by formal institutions that practice law-abiding behavior.

This chapter will refute such notions, based on an examination of the *maras* phenomenon in Central America. The main argument is that in order to understand why youth gangs have evolved into criminal organizations in El Salvador, Guatemala, and Honduras but not in Nicaragua, we should study the degree to which government attempts to curb gangs involved a significant share of informal measures. Such measures have entailed state actors operating on their own, as well as the use of illegal activities, to suppress and control gang violence. This is not to say that government responses in Central America, particularly in the gang-ridden countries of Honduras, Guatemala, and El Salvador, were all illegal or that top government officials deliberately sought to break the law in their battle against *maras*. It means that in the institutionally weak and unstable states of Central America, every policy to tackle *maras* has been accompanied by a significant amount of informal activity that transformed gang behavior in unexpected ways.

Behind this proposition lie three theoretical premises and one factual point about gangs in northern Central America. First, gangs in general, and particularly Central American *maras*, have never been a static phenomenon, and as Joan Moore has pointed out regarding Los Angeles gangs, they have never been allowed to evolve by themselves.[2] Therefore it is impossible to understand the current character of Central American gangs without addressing the particular contexts within which they have developed. Second, gangs respond to threats of violence or attacks by increasing group cohesion and strengthening their organization.[3] And third, as gangs grow stronger, they integrate what have been called "networks of criminal governance," which contribute to the overall levels of violence.[4] As for the reality of gangs, research shows that current *maras* in Guatemala, El Salvador, and Honduras have become a new expression of organized crime in Central America.[5]

In this chapter, I argue that the steep transformation of street gangs into *maras* in Guatemala, El Salvador, and Honduras but not in Nicaragua is largely due to the types of responses wielded by the states, to the extent that these responses allowed or even encouraged actions that reinforced what Elin Ranum calls illegal spheres.[6] Gangs transformed themselves in order to deal with the conditions created by state and government policies, and they took advantage of the spaces of illegality and informality opened by those policies. Gangs in Central America ended up more violent and more organized because government responses compelled them to strengthen, as well as provided the opportunities and resources to do it through the areas of illegality and the networks of crime broadened by such policies.

The preceding statement does not mean that other factors, in particular the considerable influx of returned migrants and deportees from the United States, have not contributed to the transformation of gangs in Central America, but the impact of migration and deportation has been frequently oversold, and it has diverted attention away from research on the impact of domestic factors, such as state policies and the political economy of violent armed groups. The central subject of this chapter, then, is state responses against gangs and how they have contributed to the transformation of Central American *maras*. That is why the comparison between Nicaragua and northern Central America is illuminating. Although Nicaragua also has street gangs, they never developed into the power protection rackets they are today in Guatemala, El Salvador, and Honduras.[7]

This chapter is divided in three sections. The first section briefly describes the policies, laws, and strategies the four Central American governments implemented to tackle the *maras*. The second part addresses the political economy of the responses: how governments decided on the policies; the political forces that prevailed in the formulation of the responses; and the discourses used to frame the responses. The third part explores the outcomes of the governments' policies, particularly with regard to their effectiveness in curbing gang crime and gang development, the consequences (intended and unintended) that government policies yielded, and how they created conditions that strengthened or weakened gangs.

Characterization of the Responses

Youth gangs have been prowling Central America's capitals for some decades now. They were brought to light, however, when the end of the region's internal conflicts exposed the problems of public insecurity, poverty, and exclusion that still lingered in these societies. As reported by several pioneer studies, street gangs used to be groups of teenagers in small bands that operated in various areas of Central America's metropolises and controlled them through the use of violence.[8] During the civil wars and social conflicts that prevailed in the region in the 1980s, these gangs were contained through the same mechanisms of intense, often violent repression that the authoritarian regimes then in power used to suppress political dissent and disorder. Besides this, the extreme militarization of these societies made it very difficult for young city dwellers to form large groups or to engage in such violent actions as to draw the attention of the authorities. Youth street gangs certainly existed, and some of them were considered violent,[9] but they drew little concern from these authoritarian regimes.

The end of political strife brought some public attention to the problem, and local scholars and the media began to note the proliferation of these bands in Central American cities. In an early survey on crime in El Salvador, conducted in 1993, nearly 50 percent of the urban population said there were street gangs in their neighborhoods.[10] Nevertheless, the governments did not acknowledge gangs as a pressing issue, at least for a while. Heidrun Zinecker has proposed a characterization of postwar Salvadoran security policies that consists of three strategic phases.[11] The first phase was a transition period, in which new institutions of public security were established, and little or no attention was paid to issues of crime and gangs.[12] In the second phase, criminal violence and gangs came into the spotlight of the public security institutions, and some scattered measures and reforms and counterreforms were enacted to tackle the growing problem of crime. As described by Zinecker, these measures laid the groundwork for the repressive policies to come. The third stage in the evolution of security policies was clearly characterized by the enactment of repressive security policies that were wielded indiscriminately in broad brushstrokes[13] and bore powerful names such as "zero tolerance" and "*mano dura*" (strong arm).

Despite some differences, it is possible to make some generalizations about these periods with regard to the official public security responses, at least in the northern countries of Central America (Guatemala, El Salvador, and Honduras). Also, a fourth phase, unfolding as this chapter is being written, can be added to the list. This phase consists of the official abandonment of the "broad brushstroke" for a more discrete set of policies that combines focused strategies of suppression with some preventive and reintegrative measures. Nonetheless, this does not mean that crackdowns on *maras* have ended; rather, the magnitude of and the publicity given to this type of government action against gangs have been somewhat reduced.

This evolution of public security policies in northern Central America represents a major contrast to the development of government responses in *mara*-less Nicaragua, where the policy changes have been marked less by the intensity of repression than by the magnitude of police involvement in preventive strategies, and the support that such policies have won from the Nicaraguan public. Rocha notes that, despite the often inconsistent approaches to tackling gangs and an aborted program of repression in the late 1990s, Nicaragua did not experience the intensive crackdowns seen in the northern countries.[14] As stated above, the purpose of this chapter is to compare the government responses that triggered the particular development of Central American *maras*. Hence, more important than tracing the complex evolution of government policies in each Central American country is to identify the types of policies that differentiated the relationships between the actors involved in tackling the gangs, and how those policies affected levels of violence.

The key feature that distinguishes the mixture of government responses in Central America is whether or not they have applied the broad brushstroke in the form of *mano dura* crackdowns. Broadly put, two types of government response against the *maras* have taken place in Central America: one dominated by zero-tolerance and *mano dura* policies, aimed directly at gangs and youths suspected of being involved in violence (as in Guatemala, El Salvador, and Honduras, with some important differences between them),[15] and the other characterized by the development and implementation of government-sponsored preventive programs for youths (as in Nicaragua). The broad-brushstroke policies, on the one hand, consisted of police programs — or even congressional acts — that labeled the *maras* and the youths associated with them as the main source of domestic crime and a major threat for regional security.[16] From this standpoint, gangs had to be suppressed by all means. The preventive plans, on the other hand, included programs that — for the political reasons outlined by Rocha in Chapter 5 of this volume — took into account the complexities of juvenile crime and made an effort to categorize the different youth groups, from vulnerable populations to organized crime gangs. The government then enacted different programs according to the characteristics of the groups.[17] Suppression was not ruled out, but neither was it the only or even a dominant strategy for tackling Nicaragua's gangs.

This is not to say that the governments with *mano dura* gang policies did not have specific prevention, rehabilitation, and reinsertion programs. Neither does it mean that the Nicaraguan government and some of its institutions never repressed *pandilleros*. It means, rather, that in northern Central America the emphasis has been on repression, while Nicaragua has favored a more integrative approach. In the repressive model, the most important indicator of success or failure is the number of gang members who have been removed from public spaces. With the Nicaraguan model, the most important indicator is the number of young people enrolled in preventive programs created by the police and the Nicaraguan Youth Institute (Instituto Nicaragüense de la Juventud).[18]

Three aspects characterize the implementation of *mano dura* policies in northern Central America. First, the repressive plans were, at least in discursive terms, inspired by the zero-tolerance policy—oriented more toward penalizing wrongdoing than preventing it—that had been implemented in several North American cities, especially in New York City. It was selected as a model because of its apparent success in reducing levels of criminality, but also because U.S. agencies such as the Federal Bureau of Investigation, the Drug Enforcement Agency, and police departments from several U.S. cities cooperated extensively with Central American governments in the area of public security.[19] In contrast, the Nicaraguan approach was rooted more in a communitarian-based deterrence strategy, described by the then deputy police director Francisco Bautista as a "social accord" (*concertación social*).[20] Furthermore, Rocha describes how the Nicaraguan police pondered over the different approaches taken in American cities in the fight against gangs.[21] According to Rocha (based on a paper written by Francisco Bautista in 2003), the Nicaraguan police noted in particular that whereas "zero-tolerant" New York reduced crime to the same extent as "community-oriented" San Diego, the latter managed to accomplish that with significantly fewer arrests and even reduced the number of complaints against the police for human rights abuses.

Second, the indiscriminate policies used in Honduras and El Salvador entailed the enactment of special laws, executive acts, and the rewriting of criminal codes to allow the police and assorted law enforcement agencies to round up, incarcerate, and prosecute gang members and any youths remotely suspected of criminal activities. In 2003 the administration of Honduran president Ricardo Maduro reformed Article 332 of the Penal Code, which opened gang members to prosecution for membership in a criminal organization regardless of whether they or their group had actually been convicted of any crime. In El Salvador, where the *mano dura* type of policy reached its highest level of sophistication, an anti-gang law was enacted in July 2003 under the administration of Francisco Flores. This act, known as Ley Antimaras, also aimed to facilitate the detention and prosecution of suspected gang members based on the newly classified felony of illicit association (*asociación ilícita*) and gang membership. In both cases, the new rulings gave complete authority to the police—and in some cases to military personnel—to carry out arrests based on arbitrary decisions and thin evidence. In El Salvador, the police could use tattoos, hand signals, dress codes, and physical appearance as evidence of gang membership. Although this specific directive was not included in the Honduran reform, the Honduran police acted on the basis of similar criteria, jailing even children who happened to be dressed like gang members.[22]

In Guatemala, even though legal measures were not passed to support the anti-gang crackdowns, the police implemented suppression plans based on arbitrary interpretations of the existing laws. For example, as reported by Ranum in Chapter 3, police jailed youths they suspected of gang membership by indicting them for possession of drugs, even though most of those detentions were carried out illegally. In sum, public security institutions in northern Central America were in effect given a license to hunt gangs and youths based on very weak legal constraints.

Third, these broad-brushstroke policies were essentially plans for full suppressive police intervention in civilian life. As we have seen, Honduras and El Salvador approved laws or legal reforms allowing security forces to pursue and capture youths suspected of belonging to a gang without evidence or due process.[23] In these countries, as well as in Guatemala, the governments used such plans as linchpins in larger government agendas; all moved to reclaim the use of national armies in operations against gangs; and all developed operations that allowed for the capture and mass incarceration of gang members, thus saturating and overpopulating their penitentiary systems. For example, a 2005 report by the National Civil Police in El Salvador details how, between 23 July 2003 and 8 July 2005, the police captured 30,934 gang members. Although the majority of these arrests represent multiple captures of the same person (gang members were arrested, freed after forty-eight hours, and then arrested again), the figure reflects the volume of gang-related police activity that took place in a relatively short period of time.[24] In Honduras, operations aimed at incarcerating gang members resulted in a much smaller number of gang members in prison. According to Tomás Andino, approximately 2,000 persons accused of membership in "illegal associations" were incarcerated between August 2003 and December 2004.[25] More than half of these people, some 277 per month on average, were arrested in the first five months (between August and December 2003). The intensity of operations in Honduras, whose legal system permitted longer prison sentences for gang members, reduced the number of gang members on the streets during the first months and, along with them, the number of later arrests. Between July 2003 and July 2004 in Guatemala, 10,527 persons were detained for drug possession, and an additional 11,708 were detained for petty crimes in "preventive" centers set up in the Department (district) of Guatemala, which contains the capital, Guatemala City.[26] These arrests represented 49.3 percent of all incarcerations made in that one department. Only 1.1 percent of the arrests for drug possession, however, were later formally indicted by the courts. In most of the cases, the judge either did not find sufficient evidence or determined that the evidence was collected illegally, meaning that the detention was illegal. Even so, at the beginning of the police campaigns, the judicial system acquiesced in those illegal detentions to give the police some time to collect evidence.

In sharp contrast, Nicaraguan police created Committees for the Social Prevention of Crime (Comités de Prevención Social del Delito) in a number of impoverished neighborhoods of Managua, under a pilot project to prevent the spread of gangs. Between 1999 and 2003, this project awarded scholarship grants to more than 400 former gang members, while arresting more than 900 other gang members, 72 of whom were later indicted. This project gave way to a Dirección de Asuntos Juveniles (Office of Juvenile Issues) within the National Police force. This office started its activities based on an assessment of the gang situation in Nicaragua, using more than 800 gang members as research subjects. These subjects were later used to expand social prevention programs to more communities and to collaborate with the police on community strategies. Most of these programs entailed a close working relationship between police officers and teenagers, whether they were gang members or not. In direct contrast to what was happening in the countries of the north, a new Procedural Criminal Code (Código Procesal Penal) was passed in December 2002. This code provided a more *garantista* (committed or reliable) framework in the security and justice systems, and one of its main objectives was to reduce the rate of incarceration in Nicaraguan prisons.[27]

In a critical stance, however, Rocha has also argued that police operations on the ground are more sympathetic to gangs because an important sector of the Nicaraguan police force consists of Sandinista-leaning officers. This police leadership would be able to use gang groups associated with the party during periods of turmoil in order to advance partisan political agendas.[28] This analysis, nevertheless, does not negate that Nicaraguan police have used a completely different approach when dealing with gangs, and that they have been less prone to tolerate extralegal and criminal activities from their own members in the fight against gangs.

Preventive plans and programs also existed in the northern part of Central America. In fact, in El Salvador, along with the relaunching of the *mano dura* plan in 2004, called Súper Mano Dura, came the launch of the Mano Amiga (Friendly Hand) and Mano Extendida (Extended Hand) plans, designed to thwart gang membership and rehabilitate gang members. In addition, institutions such as the National Council of Public Security (Consejo Nacional de Seguridad Pública) and the National Secretary of Youth (Secretaría Nacional de la Juventud) were also committed to developing prevention programs within those plans. In Guatemala a president's commission called CONAPREPI enacted the National Policy of Youth Violence Prevention (Política Nacional de Prevención de la Violencia Juvenil), which was aimed at "strengthening state capacity to prevent youth violence" and improving the quality of life for Guatemalan youths.[29] In addition, the Interior Ministry and the Presidential Commission for Human Rights developed several local prevention programs in communities with high levels of crime. In Honduras, shortly before the launching of the zero-tolerance programs, the Congress passed an act regarding the prevention of youth gangs (the act was called Ley de Prevención, Rehabilitación, and Reinserción de Personas Vinculadas a Pandillas), but it took around four years to be implemented by the government.[30] Even today the law has had minimal impact.

It is important to note that, despite their apparently good intentions, most of these preventive-approach laws and plans were weakly implemented. The official effort to confront gangs in the years 2001–2006 was oriented toward their suppression, and this policy dominated the political life of Central American societies while it was in force.

The Political Economy of the Response

To assess the full impact of the zero-tolerance plans in Central America, it is crucial to consider the political context in which they were implemented. Three points are important to understanding the impact of the anti-gang programs in Central America. First, besides fighting *maras*, the zero-tolerance plans were designed by the incumbent administrations to win political support among the population. In most cases, this support was intended to be translated into electoral ballots. Second, those plans involved the articulation of a public discourse that put street gangs at the center of public security problems while downplaying human rights, rule of law, and the mechanisms of political liability. And third, as these plans gained internal and external political support, segments within the institutions, as well as civil society organizations, found themselves powerless to modify the terms of the plans.

Mano dura policies were created not only to fight the crime generated by *maras* but also as a political ploy to win votes in elections and to help the governments gain legitimacy among populations disenchanted with their poor performance. The first case of this political manipulation is found in Guatemala during Alfonso Portillo's 1999 presidential campaign and in the postelection implementation of his Plan Escoba (Operation Broom) in 2000, which was aimed at controlling gangs. In Honduras, President Ricardo Maduro put in place zero-tolerance plans (first called Libertad Azul, or Blue Liberty), which included wide-reaching operations conducted by police and military forces to pursue and incarcerate gang members. Zero-tolerance programs were also used as part of the electoral platform of the "officialist candidate" (candidate of the party in power) in the Honduran elections of 2005. It was in El Salvador, however, where *mano dura* policies aimed at the *maras* had the most obvious electoral aims. The government presented its first *mano dura* policy only nine months prior to the 2004 presidential elections.[31] Thirteen months later, following the party's reelection, the new government pushed the Súper Mano Dura plan, which was deemed a continuation of the preceding plan. In this context, the Mano Amiga and Mano Extendida plans were launched to ameliorate public criticism raised by the previous plan. They were also launched in the context of another electoral campaign, this time for deputies in the Legislative Assembly and mayors in El Salvador's cities, which were hotly contested by the ARENA and FMLN political parties in particular.

The overtly political nature of these plans required not only intense publicity for the anti-gang strategy but also a media campaign promoting a particular point of view about the crime problem and the best way to tackle it. Yet again, the Salvadoran case is illustrative. The Mano Dura plan was launched at a nationally broadcast live press conference by President Flores, of the ARENA Party, using a wall full of graffiti as a backdrop. As the president talked, flanked by the army chief and the police director, the broadcast intermittently flashed the tattooed faces of gang members. Later, during the implementation of the Mano Dura and the Súper Mano Dura, the police carried out their commando-like operations in front of cameras, for later broadcast on prime-time television. Besides this, the government spent thousands of dollars to publicize the numbers of police raids and arrests of gang members in the national media.[32] Honduran president Maduro and his public security minister, Oscar Alvarez, even participated in the public staging of zero-tolerance raids. Escorted by a troop of journalists and media technicians, the president and/or the minister would personally supervise the police raids as they descended over the impoverished neighborhoods of Tegucigalpa and San Pedro Sula in their official helicopters.

Only in Guatemala, where the administration of Óscar Berger Perdomo (2004–2008) kept a distance from the media-hype style of the preceding—and disgraced—Portillo administration, did the government not seem to be interested in publicly promoting the crackdowns as the favored response for solving the gang problem. But Guatemala is an interesting case for revealing the conflictive relationships within the government when dealing with crime and gangs. Top officials in the Berger administration, including the president and his social and economic cabinet, were inclined to a less repressive approach to the gangs while developing preventive programs. It is within this climate that the National Policy of Youth Violence Prevention was enacted, and this is the reason why a zero-tolerance law was never actually passed in Guatemala. Nevertheless, law enforcement officials, including the minister of the interior and the chief of police, promoted a harsher approach to the gang problems.[33] Supported by public opinion and a lingering authoritarian political culture, the police continued cracking down on *maras*, but with less fanfare, using the existing laws and modifying only some police procedures.

There were disagreements between factions within the governments of other Central American countries as well. But while the hawkish approach had more leverage in Honduras and El Salvador because it was being promoted from the very top levels of the government, it failed in Nicaragua because the police—which promoted a softer approach—had a significant amount of political power within the Nicaraguan administration.[34]

Perhaps the most important ingredient of the media campaign that complemented the raids in the streets was the promotion of an official viewpoint that labeled gangs as the main threat to public security and at the same time downplayed the observance of human rights. Official statements and speeches announcing the anti-gang programs emphasized the need for all-out war on gangs and delinquent youths, while criticizing legislative respect for and observance of the rights of suspects. The first element of the public campaign was the promotion of the idea that a good deal of the criminal violence was perpetrated by street gangs and youths. When President Flores launched the first Mano Dura plan in El Salvador, he justified it by saying that 40 percent of homicides were committed by gang members; one year later, when newly elected President Antonio Saca launched the Súper Mano Dura plan, he insisted that gangs were mainly responsible for violence in El Salvador. Police chiefs and government officials repeated this message while the broad-brushstroke plans were in force. For example, police authorities claimed that 75 percent of all violent crimes in Honduras were committed by gangs.[35] These assertions were also echoed by Central American media. Newspapers and television newscasts promoted the notion that gangs were the major perpetrators of violence in Central America.[36] Despite official statements that gangs are to blame for much of society's violence, however, there has been some contention about the actual percentage of crimes committed by them. For example, reports from the Salvadoran Forensic Institute (Instituto de Medicina Legal) show that street gangs perpetrated 10 percent of the homicides committed in El Salvador during 2004 and 13.4 percent during 2005.[37] In Honduras the United Nations Development Programme's *Human Development Report* for 2006 questions the official figures on the percentage of felonies committed by the gangs, but it does not provide alternative data.[38]

The second element of the public discourse in favor of the crackdown was an often open contempt for the human rights of youths and gang members, as well as sharp criticism for the observance of due process in the judiciary. Generally speaking, the message was that human rights and the rule of law were obstacles to combating gangs. A statement by President Maduro of Honduras sums up this position:

> Given the 6 million Hondurans with their hands tied in the face of gang violence, whose human rights are more important? Those of the innocent citizens representing the vast majority of the population, or those of the criminals violating the rights of others? As soon as the Anti-*maras* Law goes into effect we'll storm the streets to do what the Honduran people have demanded: freedom from the yoke that *maras* have placed on them.[39]

This attitude was repeatedly conveyed by executive officials, while police authorities frequently accused judges and existing laws of protecting gang members. As observed by a German researcher, supporters of the Mano Dura plans often complained about a *sistema (ultra) garantista* (guarantee of civil rights) for the benefit of the criminal.[40]

The public discourse also offered a justification for the Mano Dura policies by invoking popular demands for security. Political leaders sought to validate the broad-brushstroke policies against *maras* by claiming that most of the people wanted the government to enact severe policies against gangs. Heidrun Zinecker reports that when former Salvadoran president Alfredo Cristiani was asked about the Mano Dura plans, he responded, "This was what the population wanted: the *maras* were to be stamped out, even if this meant killing the *mareros*."[41] In fact, in the first year of implementation of the policies in El Salvador, around 80 percent of the population did support the Mano Dura programs;[42] in addition, more than 60 percent of the public believed the plan was effective for fighting gangs.[43] This level of support bolstered the legitimacy of the government and helped the ARENA candidate, Tony Saca, make political inroads in the 2004 presidential election. Although no survey data about the public support for this kind of program in Guatemala and Honduras are available, it can be argued that at least some segments of the population supported equally harsh measures in those countries. A public opinion poll conducted at the end of Maduro's term showed that most Hondurans believed he had done a good job of fighting gangs and improving public security.[44]

Crackdowns against gangs provided political capital to the governments that implemented them. As shown in Table 7.1, the police and the national governments of Honduras and El Salvador received some of the highest levels of citizens' trust while the anti-*mara* plans were in force (2003–2006). In 2008, when the plans had long since been removed from the public eye in Honduras and El Salvador, trust in the government and in the police had generally decreased. In Nicaragua and Guatemala, by contrast, such levels remained relatively stable.

The levels of apparent public support for the gang crackdowns made it difficult for civil society groups and some sectors within the administrations to oppose the broad-brushstroke policies. In Honduras, for example, there was a national discussion for a time, between 2001 and 2002, regarding proposed legislation for minors that would have integrated comprehensive research, concepts, and measures to address the problem of youth violence. A wide range of institutions contributed to this debate. The implementation of zero-tolerance policies, however, along with the changes to the Honduran Penal Code, undid these efforts. After that

Table 7.1. Public trust in Central American governmental institutions (on a 0-to-100 Scale), 2004–2008

	Trust in central government			Trust in police		
	2004	2006	2008	2004	2006	2008
Guatemala	49.4	43.9	50.1	39.6	42.4	40.3
El Salvador	60.6	52.3	46.9	64.6	52.3	48.6
Honduras	43.7	52.1	42.8	56.7	50.4	44.0
Nicaragua	39.8	37.4	38.1	54.2	52.3	53.8

Sources: Dinorah Azpuru, *Political Culture of Democracy in Guatemala, 2008: The Impact of Governance* (Nashville, TN: Latin American Public Opinion Project [LAPOP], Vanderbilt University, November 2008); Kenneth M. Coleman and José René Argueta, *Political Culture, Governance, and Democracy in Honduras, 2008: The Impact of Governance* (Tegucigalpa, Honduras: LAPOP, 2008); Ricardo Córdova Macías, José Miguel Cruz, and Mitchell A. Seligson, *Political Culture of Democracy in El Salvador, 2008: The Impact of Governance* (San Salvador, El Salvador: LAPOP, August 2008); Orlando J. Pérez, *Political Culture of Democracy in Nicaragua, 2008: The Impact of Governance* (Nashville, TN: LAPOP, Vanderbilt University, October 2008).

happened, several organizations accused the Honduran government of hampering the efforts to reduce youth violence, but they were not able to stop the crackdowns in the short term.[45] In El Salvador the massive informal support these anti-gang policies received from large segments of the population, along with the political polarization of Salvadoran society (divided between the rightist party ARENA and the leftist party FMLN) prevented civic organizations from becoming legitimate spokespersons to the government. The crackdowns, however, gave rise to some alliances and networks that dealt with children and attempted to generate a watchdog system to protect minors. These groups also presented a series of reports whose internal impact eventually led to the withdrawal of the Mano Dura plans.[46]

In sum, the broad-brushstroke policies encompassed not only a strategy to tackle the gang problem but also a political crusade intended to restore public trust, regime legitimacy, and electoral support. Their implementation entailed an official discourse that targeted gangs and marginalized youths with the full force of the state's security apparatus. This discourse also minimized the importance of the human rights of gang members and evoked significant support from the population. These elements would play a fundamental role in reshaping the relationships between the police, gangs, and the population. Such transformations would reinforce the *maras* and would contribute, to some extent, to the later deterioration of public security in northern Central America.

The Effectiveness of the Response and Its Dark Side

Paradoxically, the zero-tolerance plans in Guatemala, El Salvador, and Honduras did not eradicate the *maras*, nor have they significantly reduced the levels of criminal violence that rip apart Central American societies. In fact, quite the opposite occurred. By 2006, levels of violence had increased in nearly all Central American countries (see Table 7.2). Only in the case of Honduras were homicide rates lower by a few points in 2006 than in 2002 (the year previous to the launch of its zero-tolerance plan), but this reduction did not represent a major change in the overall prevalence of crime. In Guatemala and particularly El Salvador, crime steeply escalated during the implementation of the crackdowns.

Furthermore, the *mara* problems did not recede, nor did gangs stop generating violence. According to most of the independent research that has been conducted in recent years in Central America, gangs came out of the crackdown period stronger, more organized, and less visible than they had been before.[47] Although police officials say that gang recruitment has been reduced because of the crackdowns and that much of the problem has moved into the jails — now ridden with anarchy and violence[48] — I have argued that, during the first few years after 2000, Central America's gangs evolved from street gangs into something like transnational prison

Table 7.2. Homicide rates per 100,000 inhabitants in Central America, 2000–2006

Country	2000	2001	2002	2003	2004	2005	2006
Guatemala	26	29	32	36	38	44	47
El Salvador	43	37	36	37	43	51	56
Honduras	49	52	48	46	47	45	43
Nicaragua	9	10	11	12	11	13	13

Sources: UNODC, *Crime and Development in Central America: Caught in the Crossfire* (Mexico City: UNODC, 2007); Heidrun Zinecker, *Violence in a Homeostatic System: The Case of Honduras*, PRIF Reports, no. 83 (Frankfurt: Peace Research Institute Frankfurt, 2008).

gangs, and they have converted prisons into nodes for regional criminal activities.[49] In any case, by the end of the decade, several cliques in El Salvador, Guatemala, and Honduras were engaged in organized crime networks, drug trafficking, and widespread extortion. *Maras* are still a threat to public and hemispheric security, and violence is still rampant in northern Central America.

The key element of *mara* activities nowadays is what is called *la renta*— namely, extortions. According to various sources, Central American gangs collect most of their money by extorting the population. Guatemalan gangs, for instance, collect around US$4 million every year just in the suburb of Villanueva in Guatemala City.[50] In El Salvador, according to the police, 70 percent of the extortions are committed by gangs, who tax transport unions, convenience stores, and informal businesses on the streets.[51]

If we understand organized crime along the lines of Charles Tilly's notion that "protection rackets represent organized crime at its smoothest,"[52] Central American gangs fit very well into the category of organized crime and represent a clear illustration of how youth gangs can end up as organized crime groups. *Maras* in El Salvador, Guatemala, and Honduras have been able to develop economies in which the members of the gang demand money from someone who wishes to receive protection against threats or to avoid any harm perpetrated by the same members of the group. Central American gangs are organized crime not because they are involved in street drug–trafficking activities—some of them certainly are—but first and foremost because they have been able to develop complex networks of protection rackets that allow their survival as groups.

In contrast, gangs in Nicaragua have not seemed to experience such a transformation. According to a gang assessment by the U.S. Agency for International Development, based on figures from the Nicaraguan National Police, gang membership and activity have decreased in recent years. Gangs still preserve a sort of disruptive youth profile in which the most common activities are mugging, picking pockets, and attacking rival gangs.[53] Although some authors have talked about a new generation of Nicaraguan gangs that are more interested in drug trafficking and racketeering, these groups are far less violent and threatening than their northern peers.[54]

How can these divergent paths in gang evolution be explained, considering that Nicaragua's social environment is very similar to that of Guatemala, El Salvador, and Honduras? This chapter contends that the nature of the various government responses is largely responsible for these differences in the evolution of Central American gangs. This is not to say that patterns of international migration have not played a role in reshaping gangs in the northern countries, but, as will be discussed in the remainder of this chapter, it is impossible to understand the current *mara* situation while ignoring the lateral consequences of the broad-brushstroke policies. These unforeseen consequences can be summed up in three interrelated types of events. First, the Mano Dura policies exacerbated extralegal violence against the gangs, perpetrated by state actors such as the police and the military. Second, Mano Dura encouraged the participation of other armed actors such as vigilante groups and "social cleansing" squads in actions against the gangs; it also hampered the activities of actors and institutions devoted to preventing violence and stimulated the escalation of violence by involving many other armed actors. And third, the policies led to the incarceration of massive numbers of gang members across the region. In line with the theoretical explanation provided by Scott Decker and others about the processes of gang organization,[55] the extralegal violence and vigilante attacks increased the levels of threat for gang members, forcing them to tighten their bonds and become more violent in response. The massive incarceration of gang members, by the same token, opened the opportunity for them to regroup, organize, and respond to the threats.

The heavy-handed policies in northern Central America only exacerbated the illegal use of state force. Extralegal violence by police officers and the military did not appear with the zero-tolerance plans—it already existed. Some state agents simply took this opportunity to increase their illegal activities under cover of the all-out war against gangs, enabled, for the most part, by the institutional weakness that characterized most of the police institutions in the region. Although many reforms had been implemented to strengthen and institutionalize public security in Guatemala, El Salvador, and Honduras, including the creation of new police forces, nonetheless these institutions preserved several corrupt elements that perpetuated extralegal practices.[56] Not only did these actors actively participate in the maelstrom of violence unleashed against the *maras* as part of the Mano Dura policies, but they also jumped into the criminal networks of which the gangs were part. A 2007 multicountry research project that included gang members and police officers in Central America revealed that gang members regularly had to pay the officers for protection.[57] Furthermore, a public opinion poll conducted among

Table 7.3. Police corruption in Central America

	Guatemala	El Salvador	Honduras	Nicaragua
Percentage of former gang members who say the police extort gang members[a]	88	65	88	38
Percentage of the population that believe the police are involved in crime[b]	65.9	48.8	47.2	25.1

[a]Data are from UNODC, *Crime and Development in Central America: Caught in the Crossfire* (Mexico City: UNODC, 2007); and Heidrun Zinecker, *Violence in a Homeostatic System: The Case of Honduras*, PRIF Reports, no. 83 (Frankfurt: Peace Research Institute Frankfurt, 2008).
[b]Data are from Americas Barometer database (LAPOP, Vanderbilt University), http://lapop.ccp.ucr.ac.cr/.

the population in the region revealed that most Guatemalans and almost half of Salvadorans and Hondurans believe the police to be involved with crime (Table 7.3).

In other words, anti-gang crackdowns were conducted by institutions riddled with corruption, which not only exacerbated the illegitimate use of force but also contributed to the establishment of underground criminal networks originating from the very top of the institutions.[58] This was possible because the state security institutions slackened their systems of internal control and supervision. In Honduras, for example, the government was indifferent to how zero-tolerance policies were implemented and was disinclined to control abuses perpetrated by its own agents or to prevent the involvement of external actors in "social cleansing" operations. A U.S. State Department report on human rights in Honduras in 2005 cited extralegal assassinations and the summary execution of those suspected of belonging to gangs, committed by members of the police and security forces.[59] There have also been massacres inside Honduran prisons, probably committed with the participation of the authorities; in one year more than 170 incarcerated gang members were murdered.[60] Other reports on human rights have published similar findings for Guatemala[61] and, to a lesser degree, for El Salvador.[62] But in all of these countries, extralegal violence from state agents against gang members seemed to have increased during the harshest anti-gang crackdowns and, in some cases, melded with the gang violence.

The policies also indirectly allowed actors other than those linked to state apparatuses to participate in the war on gangs. This included financing by businesspeople for the illegal vigilante groups, the participation of civilians who sought retribution in the form of "social cleansing," and the development of an economy of crime wherein assassins were contracted to confront enemies. Violence generated by other members of society was attributed to the youth gangs, which became scapegoats for all forms of crime prevailing in these countries at the time of the Mano Dura policies.[63]

All this was possible, in part, because the official rhetoric used to promote and justify official anti-gang policies created a climate in Central American society that certain sectors interpreted as ripe for "social cleansing" activities aimed at gang members. The call for a war on gangs became a kind of license to exterminate young people associated with gangs and to take advantage of opportunities to join the networks of vigilantism and crime.

Yet the mechanism that perhaps most facilitated gang organization and recruitment within the Mano Dura plans was the simultaneous incarceration of thousands of youth gang members and wannabes. Within the prisons, the *maras* began to organize themselves in a more extended and more structured fashion. It was there that dozens of members from widespread regional *clicas* of the same gang first established contact with each other, recognized that their gangs consisted of a myriad of uncoordinated groups, and developed a more structured organization. Incarceration enabled gang members to function as a sort of standing assembly in which they could debate, make pacts, and decide on structures, strategies, and ways to operate that had to be observed by the members of all the *clicas*. This was made possible, in part, by the decision of the authorities to separate prisoners in detention centers according to their gang affiliation, to cut down on intergang violence within the prisons.[64] These conditions enabled the gangs to set up their networks on the inside and to create organizational structures that extended both inside and outside the jail walls, similar to what some had experienced in U.S. jails with gangs like the Mexican Mafia. The broad brushstroke, by sweeping up foreign gang members, also facilitated communications and connections at the international level among gang members. Prison is where the present gang leadership in three countries of Central America was established.

Massive incarceration also helped the gangs establish links with organized crime and drug-trafficking networks that already operated from the jails, in some cases with the assistance of prison guards. These contacts ultimately provided money, guns, and resources to the *maras*. They also afforded *mareros* the opportunity to wield some power within the criminal networks that operated from the prisons. This power was exerted not only over other gang members and *clicas* but also over criminal networks that involved other violent actors such as organized crime. In the end, incarcerating thousands of *mareros* provided the conditions for the gangs to institutionalize and organize, reshaped and strengthened the criminal networks already operating in these countries, and reinforced the bonds between the violent actors inside and outside state institutions.

Conclusion

Maras initially responded to Mano Dura policies by increasing their cohesion, hierarchical organization, and resolve to use violence. These reactions in large part mirrored the violent measures taken by the states and their security institutions. Gangs responded to the use of extralegal force by state actors with further extreme violence, while massive incarceration in effect provided the strategic space, the resources, and the connections with other violent actors and criminal networks for gangs to wage war against the state and society. As one 18th Street Gang leader told a couple of journalists while in prison:

> Before this [the Mano Dura plan] began, it was different. We hadn't gotten to seeing things collectively. The system has united us more because there is something there; we could call it solidarity. . . . And, like it or not, we cannot look at things individually, because they haven't treated us individually, nor have they pursued or locked us up individually.[65]

Gangs did not evolve the same way in Nicaragua, in part because the spaces and the control of violence were never yielded by the state in its fight against crime, but that was not because Nicaraguan institutions were by any means perfect. While Nicaragua has its share of extralegal activities and criminal elements lurking from within institutions,[66] its institutional mechanisms of accountability and control have been more effective at deterring illegal practices than have those of the northern states of Central America.[67] These differences relate to broader issues in Central

America—namely, the distinctive processes of state formation, the monopoly over the legitimate use of force, and the utilization of informal groups in the management of security and order. But these issues go beyond the scope of this chapter, and they have been treated elsewhere.[68]

In sum, the experiences of Honduras, El Salvador, and Guatemala make clear that it is a mistake to limit the discussion about government responses toward gangs and crime to an either-or dichotomy between prevention and repression. The state must in fact always be ready to meet the demands for security with both kinds of policies. The critical dilemma is, rather, whether state institutions and their operators are strong enough and accountable enough to fulfill their tasks without violating the rule of law. The main challenge in the fight against crime in Central America still lies in its institutions.

CHAPTER 8

Elite Membership and Sexualized Violence among Central American Gangs

MAURICIO RUBIO

TRANSLATED FROM THE SPANISH BY MICHAEL SOLIS

Evaluations of juvenile violence in Central America, and the prevention programs based upon them, face three types of limitations. The first is relatively easy to overcome and has to do with the manner in which evidence is gathered. In technical jargon, most studies suffer from a type of sampling bias: the majority of gang-related research is based on fieldwork carried out exclusively in the marginal neighborhoods of cities or in rehabilitation centers, with young people from poor backgrounds. Because this method has excluded violence committed by the children of elites from the overall analysis, it has established a narrow association between juvenile violence and economic scarcity that has dominated both the diagnosis and the formulation of preventive policies.

The second limitation, linked to the first, concerns the difficulties in detecting, analyzing, and explaining the differences in gang activity between countries, regions, or cities. As the investigations have a marked local component and are not representative of the entire youth population of a country, it has not been easy to compare the studies in a systematic manner. Thus any conclusion regarding the elements that the studies may have in common, and those elements that contrast the different types of gangs (e.g., the *maras* and *pandillas*) and the distinct local manifestations of juvenile violence, is tenuous.

The third restriction, perhaps the most deeply rooted and difficult to overcome, is the persistence of assumptions that are based more on ideology and politics than on analysis of the available evidence. One side sees the *maras* as an extension of transnational organized crime—including fundamentalist terrorism—and therefore a threat to regional security, which must be met with war. On the other extreme, we are told we should regard these gangs as a rebellious and emancipating movement protesting for a radical change of social structures. In both cases, one of the most notorious peculiarities of the Central American *pandilleros* and *mareros* has remained absent from the analysis: sexualized violence exercised against other youths, gang members or not, around them.

This chapter begins with arguments for promoting the utilization of self-reported surveys on youth behavior as the most suitable mechanism, perhaps the only one, to diagnose a range of juvenile problems, such as delinquency, gang affiliation, substance abuse, and adolescent prostitution. It then devotes specific sections to three aspects of gang behavior that have been relatively ignored in the current diagnosis of juvenile violence in Central America. Based on the results of self-reported surveys, the chapter calls attention to the great variety of juvenile violence in the region, explores violence committed by the children of the middle and upper classes, and insists on the incorporation of a key element into the diagnosis: violence exercised not by the legal system or by foreign mafias but by youths against their own neighbors, friends, romantic companions, and enemies.[1] The chapter closes with reflections on the risks of delegitimizing judicial response in the face of youth violence.

History of Self-reported Surveys

Early empirical studies about delinquency were based on official sources.[2] With this information, criminologists constructed geographic maps of crime and, in certain cases, identified economic, social, and demographic characteristics of the aggressors. In the United States, these exercises indicated that crime was concentrated disproportionately in the poorest and most marginalized city sectors and that those condemned by the judicial system were people from the working class and ethnic minorities.

Beginning in the 1930s, it became apparent that this type of information was not the most adequate for the diagnosis of crime, since it did not give an idea about types of hidden delinquency, which constituted what was known as the *cifra negra* (unknown data) of criminality. Sofía Robinson calculated that the number of juvenile delinquents doubled when those passing through unofficial agencies and courts other than juvenile courts were taken into account. She further discovered that the choice of the facility where the offenders were sent for correction depended to a great extent on their social background. Robinson thus concluded that judicial information was not only insufficient but also misleading.

Edwin Sutherland provided the initial push for what would later become the methodology of self-reported surveys. His pioneering work on white-collar crime was a great challenge to the generalized notion that members of the favored social strata were less likely to break the law. In the 1940s, Austin Porterfield published *Youth in Trouble*, which constituted the first work based on a self-reported survey. The author analyzed the judicial sentences of just over 2,000 delinquents in Texas and carried out a parallel survey among more than 300 youths from Texan universities. He found that each one of the university students was responsible for at least one of a number of specific infractions and that these were as serious as some of the infractions of the delinquents. Very few of the students, however, had to pay a visit to the courts.

In the 1950s, J. F. Short and F. I. Nye, studying high schools in various U.S. cities, found that among youths with differing social and economic backgrounds, there were no significant discrepancies in their reporting of infractions. The results of this study stimulated a good number of projects that found that, of the majority of young people committing crimes, only a small number were committing serious crimes in a repetitive manner. The relationship between social status and the reporting of infractions was weak and did not reflect the findings of studies based on official statistics. Travis Hirschi's *Causes of Delinquency*, published in 1969, was perhaps the first important effort to question assumed relationships between social status and criminal activity by utilizing self-reported surveys. This book became one of the most influential in the history of criminology. A large part of the efforts to contradict crime theories in the last three decades has been based on this type of methodology.

At the end of the 1970s, given the persistence of the problem of incoherence between self-reported surveys and official statistics of delinquency, some researchers began to examine the source of these inconsistencies. They raised the possibility that self-reported surveys were revealing a distinct collection of misconducts that the other sources did not capture. It was subsequently observed that the root of at least part of the problem was that a small proportion of young people commit a disproportionately high number of felonies. In the general surveys these "intensive delinquents" would be underrepresented.

These developments in the methodology of gathering information coincided with a new criminological emphasis in the 1980s on the ethnology of the aggressors. The focus on the few intensive aggressors brought about a trend in research on chronic delinquents. In 1988, experts from fifteen countries met in the Netherlands and agreed to launch an ambitious comparative project based on relatively homogenous self-reported surveys. The results tended to confirm the principal finding of a scant association between the socioeconomic status of youths and their reporting of infractions.[3] In Latin America, outside of the surveys summarized in this chapter and the pioneering projects carried out by Christopher Birbeck in Venezuela and other work in Colombia,[4] there has been a shortage until recently of applications of this methodology of collecting empirical data.

Incidence of Gangs, Insecurity, and Delinquency

A finding worth highlighting from the Central American self-reported surveys is the increased presence of gangs in the region.[5] It is useful to clarify that in this chapter what is understood as a "gang" (*pandilla* in Spanish) was identified by the youths in the self-reported surveys. The youths were not supplied with a definition or previous clarification of the term. In countries where the term *"mara"* is common, this was the word used in the form; in the other countries, the term *"pandilla"* was used instead. The structure of questions eliminated the possibility of confusion between a gang and a group of companions or friends.

More than half (57 percent) of the educated youths—a random and representative sample of the population—reported living in a neighborhood where there were active gangs, and 4 in 10 noted having a friend in a gang (Figure 8.1). Regarding these statistics, there were important geographic differences. In Managua, Nicaragua, 81 percent of the students indicated that gangs were active in their neighborhoods; in Panama, approximately half of the students (49 percent) reported personally knowing a gang member; and in the Metropolitan Zone of the Sula Valley (ZMVS), Honduras, 33 percent reported gang activity and 24 percent knew gang members. Additionally, the rankings among the locations depended on the indicator being examined.

The proportions of students who reported having belonged to a gang were much lower, averaging less than 3 percent (Figure 8.2). The incidence of gangs within the educational system also presented large discrepancies between regions. The largest proportion of students who were gang members was observed in Panama (5.5 percent), followed by Managua (3.4 percent), the rest of Nicaragua (3.0 percent), Tegucigalpa, Honduras (1.8 percent), and the ZMVS (0.7 percent). The maximum and minimum incidences differed by an order of nearly eight to one.

These findings highlight that in places where the *maras* dominate—

PERCENTAGE OF POSITIVE RESPONSES AMONG STUDENTS

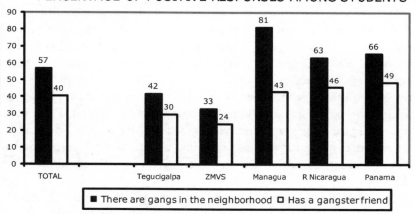

Figure 8.1. Self-reported incidence of gangs by region. *ZMVS* = Metropolitan Zone of the Sula Valley, Honduras; *R Nicaragua* = the rest of Nicaragua (not counting Managua).

PERCENTAGE OF POSITIVE RESPONSES AMONG STUDENTS

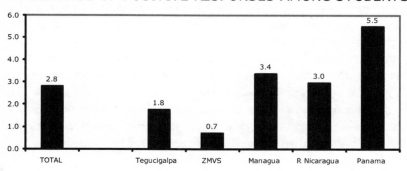

Figure 8.2. Self-reported gang membership by region, in response to the question "Have you ever been the member of a gang?" *ZMVS* = Metropolitan Zone of the Sula Valley, Honduras; *R Nicaragua* = the rest of Nicaragua.

Tegucigalpa and San Pedro Sula (ZMVS)—the incidence of association, regardless of whatever indicator is used, is lower. The presence of gangs in neighborhoods, as well as reports of personally knowing a gang member and association with one of these groups among students, was lower in the surveys carried out in Honduras, where *maras* operate, than in countries with youth *pandilla* gangs.

Thus the results of these surveys suggest that the *maras* are a less generalized phenomenon among youths than the *pandillas*. It is not overly venturous to view the former as more organized, and at a later phase in their development, than the latter. Transnational associations such as the 18th Street Gang are, in effect, *maras*. In countries like Nicaragua, where the term *"mara"* is not used, it is frequently explained that "the *maras* have not yet arrived here." As one Nicaraguan official put it, "There are two distinct realities; the members of the Mara Salvatrucha make pledges of fidelity through rituals and pacts for those who want to join. Thus, how one enters the gang's society is very serious. In Nicaragua, by contrast, youths enter gangs for reasons pertaining to fun, unemployment, and a lack of alternatives, having nothing to do with the idea of commitment [to the gang]."[6]

Paradoxically, *maras* can be considered less impulsive, better organized, and more instrumental in the use of violence than the *pandillas*. In the *mara*, violence tends to connote more closely with that typically associated with war rather than with quarreling. Incidents such as the massacre of twenty-eight people who were traveling on a bus in San Pedro Sula at the end of 2004, attributed to the Mara Salvatrucha in response to the Honduran government's political crackdown against juvenile delinquency, tend to corroborate this observation. Other results from the surveys are in the same vein.

An important fact to note is that, with the notorious exception of Managua, the perception of neighborhood security among students is relatively more favorable in places where gangs appear to be a more generalized phenomenon. It can be observed that the proportion of youths who express feeling either very secure or very insecure is more negatively affected by *maras* than by *pandillas* (Figure 8.3). The exception, as indicated, is Managua.

The perception of security may depend not only on the presence of gangs but also on other factors, such as common delinquency. A question worth resolving concerns the association between the presence of gangs in neighborhoods and the probability of falling victim to an attack, whether by a gang member or a nongang member. According to the survey, when a student reports that there are gangs in his or her neighborhood, the probability he or she will also report having fallen victim to a criminal attack increases by 66 percent. This statistic varies considerably among regions, with a much larger impact in Panama (165 percent) than in the ZMVS (103 percent), Managua (88 percent), Tegucigalpa (82 percent), and the rest of Nicaragua (38 percent). In all of the surveys, this

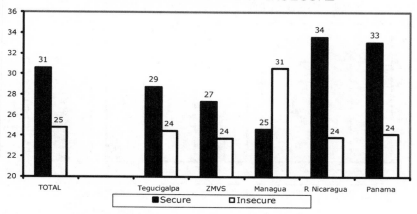

Figure 8.3. Self-reported feeling of security by region, in response to the question "How safe do you feel in the neighborhood streets?" *ZMVS* = Metropolitan Zone of the Sula Valley, Honduras; *R Nicaragua* = the rest of Nicaragua.

coefficient is statistically significant, but it is far from being the only element that explains variations in the rate of victimization. In addition, the share of petty crime for which gangs are responsible varies considerably from place to place.

One thing that can be observed in all of the locations where the survey was administered is that the presence of gangs was an important factor in the insecurity felt among the youth population; this impact was greater than that of having been the victim of street delinquency and, in this dimension, the regional differences seemed to be less important (Figure 8.4). In effect, calculating which of these two phenomena — the presence of gangs in the neighborhood and being victimized — had a greater repercussion on youths' perception of security reveals that the impact of the former was greater and more statistically significant.

Amid these results, the impact of gangs on students' perceptions of insecurity in Panama is noteworthy, as it was close to half that observed on average in the other regions (see Figure 8.4). It should be noted that a good indicator of the incidence of gangs is the degree to which students reported the presence of gangs in their neighborhoods. This is strongly linked to students' perceptions of insecurity and fear. Thus the next logical step for future research will be to compare and contrast information

CHANGE (%) IN THE PROBABILITY OF FEELING VERY INSECURE
DUE TO THE PRESENCE OF GANGS IN THE NEIGHBORHOOD
OR HAVING BEEN A VICTIM OF THEIR ACTIONS

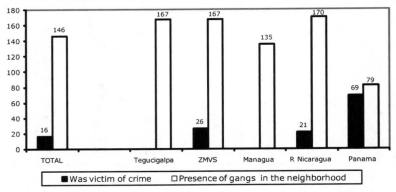

Figure 8.4. The effects of neighborhood gang presence and of having been the victim of a crime on youths' perception of their own insecurity. The results for Tegucigalpa and Managua for "Was victim of crime" were not positive or significant. *ZMVS* = Metropolitan Zone of the Sula Valley, Honduras; *R Nicaragua* = the rest of Nicaragua.

about the influence of gangs that has been gathered by police authorities or nongovernmental organizations with polls carried out among a representative sample of the student population.

On the other hand, in places where the presence of gangs appears more generalized, these groups seem to have less effective power over the life of the neighborhood. This observation supports the idea that the incidence of gangs—the number of members in the neighborhood—does not always correspond to the intensity of their activity. With respect to the self-reporting of infractions, an analysis of the discrepancies between gang members and youths within the school system supports the impression of basic differences between the *pandilla* and the *mara*. It would seem that, again with the exception of Managua, in the places where the *maras* operate there is a larger difference between the numbers of infractions committed by gang members and the numbers committed by students. In other words, the findings suggest that the *maras* tend to commit more infractions than the *pandillas*. Whereas in Tegucigalpa and San Pedro Sula gang territories the number of gang offenders exceeds that of student offenders by about 80 percent, in Panama the difference between the two groups is reduced to 50 percent.

Wealth Is Not a Vaccine for Violence

"The true poor of this world suffer from the rich and destroy one another, but they do not cause massacres between us. They attack only those who yearn for supremacy, not those who suffer marginalization."[7] This observation by Fernando Savater challenges what have been called "poignantly bourgeois" explanations—such as poverty, injustice, and the violations of war—for terrorism by Islamic extremists. Similar explanations have also been applied to the phenomenon of the *pandillas* and the *maras*, with economic scarcity commonly cited as a determining factor for violent youth behavior. In conjunction with this hypothesis, poverty would be a *necessary* condition linked to gangs, for the hypothesis proposes, sometimes with no extenuating details, that all gang members are poor. It further insists that there are no bands of aggressors who come from comfortable or well-off families. In this view, wealth is a type of vaccine against crime and violence.

According to one observer, "In *all* of the cases, gang members are poor people, youths from marginalized neighborhoods, the majority living in an urban environment, many expelled from schools, unemployed, abused, minorities in search of social or collective identity; as is more commonly said, street people."[8] What is missing from the assertion that gang members are of humble origin is that, almost always, the design of the studies from which this observation is derived makes such a result inevitable, since the youths interviewed are not randomly selected to represent the general population but are chosen from only the poorer, working-class neighborhoods.

The results of the self-reported surveys, by contrast, do not affirm that all gang members come from meager backgrounds or that they have been expelled from school. In all of the locations where the survey was carried out, there were reports of connections between gangs and students. And among *mareros* and *pandilleros*, there was no shortage of youths who reported belonging to the middle and upper classes. With the possible exception of the survey carried out in San Pedro Sula, Honduras, where being part of the upper class appears to nearly eliminate the possibility of being linked to the *maras*, in the other places where the survey was carried out, between 5 percent and 16 percent of the youths from the upper class reported links to *pandillas* or *maras* (Figure 8.5).

Among gang members who responded to the poll, nearly half were situated in the lower class. Twenty-six percent reported belonging to the lower middle class, 18 percent in the middle class, and 10.4 percent in

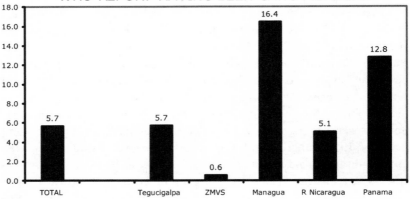

Figure 8.5. Self-reported gang membership among upper-class youths by region. *ZMVS* = Metropolitan Zone of the Sula Valley, Honduras; *R Nicaragua* = the rest of Nicaragua.

the upper class. There are notable regional differences in these averages. Panama has the lowest fraction of gang members (3.5 percent) who reported belonging to the elite. In Tegucigalpa, in contrast, an impressive 42.5 percent of the *mareros* said they belong to the upper class (Figure 8.6). Another consideration is that among the lower-class youths surveyed, 95 percent had never belonged to a gang; neither had a majority (73 percent) of non-students (Figure 8.7).

There is not sufficient information in the surveys to know the path that youths who describe belonging to the elite took to become gang members. Are these young men members of the elite who chose to become gang members, or were they young gang members who ascended socially due to their gang membership? From the perspective of public policy and prevention programs for juvenile violence, both scenarios are pertinent to the general diagnosis.

If we consider the first scenario, this group of young male gang members is of great analytical interest because understanding them would advance a more sophisticated diagnosis of gang violence. That gang membership includes youths to whom the common discourse of poverty or misery does not apply—that is, people who have resources, such as access to ball fields or private swimming pools, for occupying their spare time in harmless ways—is a challenge to the implicit idea that good economic opportunities constitute a type of vaccine against juvenile violence. Gen-

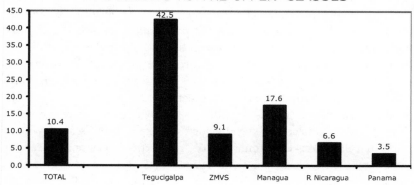

Figure 8.6. Proportion of gang members who reported that they were in the upper class, by region. *ZMVS* = Metropolitan Zone of the Sula Valley, Honduras; *R Nicaragua* = the rest of Nicaragua.

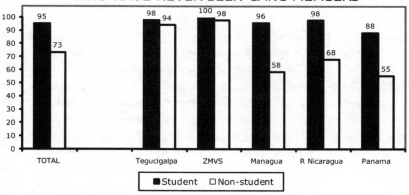

Figure 8.7. Self-reported proportion of lower-class students and non-students who had never belonged to a gang, by region. *ZMVS* = Metropolitan Zone of the Sula Valley, Honduras; *R Nicaragua* = the rest of Nicaragua.

erally, it can be said, however, that gang members from good social positions are less vulnerable to the letter of the law. This is a recurring observation from self-reported polls carried out in different parts of the world.

Violent adolescents from good social positions constitute a prime source of recruits for paramilitary organizations, security organizations, and the poorly named "social cleansing" groups that now contribute to spirals of violence with retaliations and private vendettas, thus undermining state institutions and limiting the impact of prevention programs. Furthermore, if we consider youths who can bring in resources for acquiring arms and can support the gang with business aptitudes, the ability to purchase their impunity from law enforcement, the capacity to lead or subcontract "dirty work," and contacts in the security organs, their impact on violent organizations can be great.

In the second scenario, regarding young gang members who rise through the organization's social ladder, the explanation is not less pertinent but illustrates the limitations of "reinsertion" programs based on the learning of modest trades and suggests that, from an economic perspective, the gang would not be a simple plank for survival but rather an alternative pathway for becoming wealthy in an expedited manner.

The Colombian experience is rich in examples of youths from good social positions who became involved with armed organizations or established their own groups. The leaders of the Cali Cartel began with the kidnapping of a university classmate who was involved in the drug trade. Ricardo Palmera, a high-level banking executive, was linked with the FARC (Revolutionary Armed Forces of Colombia) and offered his knowledge of victims' finances to aid with kidnappings in the region. The leadership of the ELN (National Liberation Army, another Colombian leftist insurgency) originally comprised elite university students in the 1970s. The leaders of the paramilitary groups never had financial difficulties. There are also several examples of huge fortunes amassed in just a few years by intrepid youths in criminal organizations. It remains clear from the few available testimonials of gang members from the upper class that their setting for doing business is not on the streets but rather inside condominiums or private clubs.[9] By operating in such exclusive territories, the wealthier gangs are less visible, and it is less probable that they will take part in the types of studies or interviews that are frequently used to infer that economic scarcity is endemic to the violent.

Bands of privileged youths are not peculiar to Colombia alone. In a focus group about gangs, a young Guatemalan noted that "there are gangs in his neighborhood, not poor people, but rather the upper class."[10] In Brazilian cities like Brasília, Rio de Janeiro, and São Paulo, juvenile gangs have also been detected among the upper classes.[11] A journalist coined the term "silver-spoon gangs" to describe the wealthy youths in Brazil who attack or assault others.[12] In Trinidad and Tobago the "posh gangs" recruit their members from the middle and upper classes. In some cases, their involvement in drug trafficking is complemented by additional, legal employment.[13]

In the 1990s there was a scholarly interest in the Central American *maras* that operated in high schools, but currently they receive little attention. Those who were interested included researchers who emphasized poverty as a condition for gangs, which prevented them from understanding the existence of more "comfortable" gangs that deserve increased discussion. Among those who are discussing this latter type of gang is Manfred Liebel, who speaks of *la vida loca* (the crazy life) of the *maras* and defines it as "the sensation that gangs fight with rival gangs from other neighborhoods, with other bourgeois youths who think they know more than them."[14] The central point of a work entitled "Middle Classes: Violent and Organized" is the high incidence of crime committed by wealthy youths.[15] Further challenging the misleading poverty theory are research centers that study the phenomenon of bullying, in the form of both verbal and physical aggression; this behavior has not received adequate attention in several countries, but it shows up in surveys carried out in Central America.[16] Also important for questioning the association between violence and poverty are examples of criminal organizations that recruit people with education and good contacts—specifically from the upper class.[17]

The limited attention given to the violent wealthy is due in part to their small numbers and lower public visibility, but this explanation alone is insufficient. Some ideological factors have perpetuated the assumption of an automatic association between poverty and violence. The first, which is not worth detailing too deeply, is the categorization of juvenile violence as a form of rebellion against an unjust society: the young poor person is violent because he or she is protesting and therefore is contributing to the transformation of society. A second, more diffuse influence was literature from the beginning of the industrialization era. In effect, characters like Charles Dickens's Oliver Twist, Gavroche of Victor Hugo's *Les Misérables*, and Mark Twain's Huck Finn encapsulate the contemporary gangster figure who, without any alternatives, resorts to crime in order to survive. This romantic aura consequently generates sentimentality, empathy, and acceptance of their infractions and mischievous demeanors. A notable study of Central American gangs explicitly establishes this parallel and calls Finn the "wanderer" of literature, whose creator famously said, "Don't let schooling interfere with your education," in response to criticism. According to the study's author, "Twain blessed the position occupied by the rebel: the capacity to whip the established order, ridicule the commonplace, and undermine the apparently solid foundations of institutions."[18]

Some literary references challenge this naive idealization of contemporary gang members who are more violent—especially regarding women—than the mischievous characters of fiction. *La mara*, a novel that is essentially a report of activity in the border region between Guatemala and Mexico, describes in detail the hunting of women by gang members, who pose a threat to emigrants detained for passport and visa control by the authorities.[19]

These observations do not seek to substitute a hypothesis of elite violence for the one relating to economic scarcity. The condition of being wealthy, just as that of being poor, is a weak indicator of the tendency toward aggression. This has been shown clearly through the results of the self-reported surveys in Central America.

Additionally, the spectrum of infractions and crimes committed by privileged boys from the upper class is similar to that of gang members from working-class neighborhoods, and the elites contribute to the gang in whatever ways they can.[20] This has included arranging for drug traffickers to financially support a presidential candidate's electoral campaign with a portion of their drug profits. The distinguishing factor can perhaps be best understood by the phrase used in Colombia: "Justice is for those from the *ruana* [the poor]."[21] This means, essentially, that privileged boys are able to avoid police investigations, which makes it even easier for them to evade academic and sociological investigations. Perhaps this is the reason why so little regarding the young, violent class of privileged boys appears in works that influence public policies on gang and juvenile delinquency prevention.

Silence Regarding Gang Rape

A recurring type of aggression perpetrated by the sons of elites that is impossible to incorporate into the theory of economic scarcity is that of sexualized violence. In this type of crime the victimizer frequently enjoys a more favored social position than the victim.

There have been few trials for the so-called feminicides that have occurred in Ciudad Juárez on the Mexico-U.S. border, where more than 400 young women, the majority of whom were modest factory workers, had been killed as of early 2008, and another 400 have "disappeared." One of the convicted, Abdel Latif Sharif, tells the story of Alejandro, "a Mexican in his twenties, white, rich, and arrogant who fell in love in 1990 with a poor, adolescent girl named Silvia, dark-skinned, thin, and with long hair." According to Sharif, "That girl wanted to stop seeing him, and during the middle of that year he killed her out of spite. The case was never investigated, nor was he detained for the crime: Alejandro's family had paid the authorities to prevent that from happening."[22]

Contemporary versions of the so-called droit du seigneur ("the noble's privilege" or the "right of the first night") persist in the rural sector of various Latin American countries.[23] Equally difficult to incorporate into the traditional assumption that violence is generated by poverty are cases of sexual abuse by the rich and powerful against those less powerful, which can trigger a variety of psychological and social problems among youths, including affiliation to gangs.[24]

The findings of the surveys also suggest that the pattern appears to be generalized for sexualized violence as well: wealthy victimizers, poor victims. Although there is no direct information regarding the relative social positions of those involved in the incidences of rape, survey data support this conjecture. On the one hand, the number of youths from the lower class who report having been raped is double that reported by youths from the upper class; this is true for students—a representative and random sample—as well as the uneducated. Among the perpetrators, on the other hand, the number of upper-class youths who acknowledge having participated in a rape is double that of lower-class youths, regardless of affiliation with a gang.

Once again, the gang's role as a catalyst of sexualized violence is evident, and it is worth noting that these results are statistically significant. For the female victims, the improvement of social class, passing from lower to middle or from middle to upper, reduced by 17 percent the probability that she would report being raped. Being linked to an educational system lowered that chance by 44 percent, and living in a neighborhood with an active gang presence increased the risk by 73 percent.[25] For male perpetrators, on the contrary, belonging to the upper social stratum increased by 37 percent the chance of having participated in a rape; if they belonged to a gang, the likelihood increased dramatically. The perception that the gang was a leading influence in the neighborhood increased these chances by 65 percent.[26] For males, neither age nor linkage to an educational system had a significant effect on the probability that they had committed sexual violence. These findings corroborate the idea that the presence of *pandillas* or *maras* in the neighborhoods significantly increases the risk of sexual violence against local women. Additionally, various testimonials offered representative accounts of a particular type of sexual attack: gang rape.

The following are excerpts from witnesses and perpetrators of gang rapes in various communities.

> Rapes have become a common occurrence in Las Lomas. They began as isolated incidents, and later they became a way of life. Some thought that this ritual had begun with outsiders, not people from Las Lomas. Others said that they started with some crazy guy, but the others followed the example, because the attacks gave them a *false sense of power*.[27]

> We were well armed; we attacked the cars that came in for selling [i.e., so that we could sell them]. We went through the houses and robbed everything good they had and it didn't matter that we killed six who were inside. With no regrets. We also raped the girls and older women. Even on the street. If someone said anything, we made them pay. . . .
> It was then that I decided that everyone from my gang would take her by force. One day I invited her to school when it was empty, and I invited my brothers, and about 25 of them came. And I cut her hair with scissors. I usually don't rape girls, but that girl was tight.[28]

> The drugged ones, they go out circling for women they wanted to rape. It happens here: there are so many guys on the streets who like to do it. That is their hobby. . . . And if you walk with your girlfriend, they shoot her, just like that. They left and they were never punished. It's because everyone's afraid: if you report them, they are going to kill you.[29]

> [Wendy] was stopped in the square in the Lusiana district of San Pedro Sula when she was taken by force by the MS gang, who carried her to a house in the same district. There one of the gang members sexually abused her, while they tried to drug her by force, and as she resisted, they began to beat her and threatened to kill her. When everyone had satiated their beastlike instincts, the guys decided to make a deal with her, saying they would charge fifty lempiras per person who wanted to have sex with her. . . . Wendy could identify the gang members but decided not to report them because she is convinced that nothing will happen to them anyway.[30]

Gang rape is ritualized through the practice of *trencito*, which consists of making a young woman offer herself sexually to the men as an initiation for entering the gang. This practice of *trencito* is quite widespread and, under the same name, has been confirmed as a hazing ritual for women in the *ñetas*, a gang of Puerto Ricans, Dominicans, and Ecuadorians with branches in Spain.[31]

There is no lack of Central American observers monitoring sexual relations within gangs who view the *trencito* as a model of emancipation for women. These researchers manage to see in these rituals "signs of equity with the women" or to devise euphemized and innocuous descriptions for gang rape, such as "giving love."

> In the case of women, the ritual of admission has several variations. They ask them to fight each other, but there also exists the practice of "*el trencito*," or "giving love." One girl recounts: "One day I was walking around so happy, and then four guys from the clique told me to let my hair down. I told them no, and for that they assaulted me, and one of them told me, look, crazy girl, if you don't give up we are going to eliminate you, it's better for you to be good. And well, me so drugged up, what could I do? Nothing. They touched me, four of them going into me."
> After this ritual, the girl admitted to other similar attacks. Above all, the women, as well as the men, are expected to fight against other gangs and the police, or "have fun." The boys' disrespectful treatment of the girls opens a space for discussion. Not all gangs practice the forms described above. There are *maras* that completely prohibit the discriminatory roles that normally affect women in society; the women assume positions equal to men, and may even have an influential voice in the gang. This equality also applies to homosexuality. While in Central American societies homosexuality is generally considered to be abnormal, like a sickness, in many Central American gangs members engage sexually and openly, women with women and men with men, without any type of discrimination. In the AVANCSO study, half of the women acknowledged having lesbian relations, which does not exclude having had relations with men.[32]

It is easy to presume, based on the evidence, that the prospect of sex is an efficient hook for recruiting adolescents charged by hormones into gangs.[33] A useful case study to illustrate this tendency, since it also challenges the question of economic scarcity, is that of the gangs of Latino immigrants in Spain. In 1999, five Latin Kings who had been "crowned" in Ecuador arrived in Galapagar, a small town of the Community of Madrid. Soon after, they moved to the capital itself. Their first task as a group was to begin recruiting girls of their nationality.

> [The gang] King Ñatín and the others had started in the bars frequented by Latin American women. Their girlfriends had already joined the gang and had certain rules for behavior. The most significant was perhaps the prohibition of associating with men who were not dubbed "Latin Kings," or the obligation to mourn for six months if they broke up with anyone in the gang. Violating these rules had consequences. Eric [the leader] was given great importance. The gang reserved various queens for his disposition, since they didn't have a rule regarding the matter, and they kept the girls by recruiting new, older members to form part of the rappers' "crazy life." . . . They also had an immense waiting list of hopefuls from the various Latin American districts in Madrid. . . . Two had arrived in the neighborhood, and two hours later, they were surrounded by girls who wanted to be girlfriends of the worst one in the neighborhood. After a few days, various high school boys wanted to be like them; or worse, they wanted to be full members of the gang. . . . Between 2000 and 2001 tens of young women had taken the bait of the supposed crazy life of sex and violence and were accepted into the gang. The organization grew with the same speed of Eric's musculature or the number of tattoos on his skin.[34]

A Latin Queen corroborated with her testimonial the explicit strategy of monopolizing women in the gang:

> You can't smoke until you are 18, and you can only have relations with Latin Kings. If later you break up with one, you have to mourn for six months and during that time you can't be with anyone else. . . . [As punishment for breaking the rules,] you would have to remain still while a queen hit you for 30 seconds, or 60, or three minutes: she would punch your body and smack you in the face.[35]

Gang fights have been known to result from partner disputes or jealousy. It therefore is not farfetched to believe that these kinds of altercations are probable catalysts for at least some of the innumerable arguments, fights, battles, and all-out wars that Central American gangsters engage in throughout the regions where they operate.

The Need to Depoliticize Gang Violence

At the heart of the political debate regarding what communities should do in the face of juvenile violence in Central America are the roles of the police and the judiciary. Recommendations for putting the priority on prevention in the educational system or on police crackdowns[36] should not ignore the importance of having the work of the police and judiciary complement one another. An ideological vision of the gang problem as a regional security threat results in excessively naive and inconsistent approaches, such as police repression. On the other hand, the interpretation of the continuity of violence as rebellion—from the days of Spanish conquest to the dictatorships backed by "Uncle Sam," and now to countryside massacres, indigenous genocide, and the arrival of the *maras*—would postulate a type of emancipation from the chains of oppression. This interpretation has been offered as a means to delegitimize any form of official repression, but it is not based on facts, testimonials, or common sense.

The systematic denunciation of any judicial response by the state to serious crimes, even though such responses are routine in any consolidated democracy, contributes little to the solution of juvenile violence. The reason is simple. If the state and its judicial institutions do not offer a swift and adequate response to criminal behavior such as homicide, in accordance with the law, it is probable that the victim's family, people close to the victim, or those who feel vulnerable to being victimized in the future will retaliate on their own in a more damaging and bloody manner than would any contemporary penal code.

Academic arguments about the treatment of marginalized youths who are looking to "form their identities" are insufficient responses for anyone who has suffered violence at the hands of the *mareros*. Furthermore, an adequate judicial response to extreme violence is the only way to defend the victimizers themselves from private vengeance, which is always bloody and out of official control. It is one thing to say, as has already been generally accepted, that the judicial response to gang violence should follow precise and strict procedures that respect the human rights of the aggressors. It is another thing entirely to delegitimize that response by asserting that all suppression is not only useless but is also an integral part of the problem.

It is clear that when one tries to take one or two incidents that can readily be associated with gangs, such as gang rape, and apply them to a desexualized and overpoliticized context, not much will be done to advance understanding of the dynamics of juvenile violence or how to prevent it. According to numerous testimonials, during the thirty-six-year internal insurgency in Guatemala, indigenous women were subjected to rape and torture before being killed by the military in an almost routine fashion.[37] But the supposed continuity between this type of aggression on the part of soldiers against rural, indigenous women in the middle of armed conflict, and the modern feminicides, which are urban and for the most part committed against women by gangsters with scant political ties, is unconvincing. One of the existing links between the two situations, the general impunity of the aggressors, is not sufficient to sustain a charge of conspiracy against the ruling classes, and it contributes little to finding a judicial solution to such incidents, since it inherently dismisses the notion of responsibility for such violent actors.[38]

The hypothesis that suggests the rapes and murders of women are orchestrated by organized crime is not supported by serious analysis. Another argument sees a continuity of violence from the era of the insurgency to the days of the Mara Salvatrucha, highlighting the gang members' lawless spirit and desire to terrorize. A poster used by a nongovernmental organization, for example, reinforces accusations concerning the responsibility of security forces in the incidents of "feminicide" and theories of continuity between current and past violence, by depicting various murdered women, among them an indigenous woman being shot by a military officer. To complicate the already confused panorama even more, the poster is captioned, "Women are tired of the *mano dura*," an apparent reference to Mano Dura (strong arm) anti-gang policies.

In terms of the relationship between aggressors and victims, there is a clear discontinuity between the reasons for sexual violence during armed conflict and those that can be attributable to the gang members, for the latter use sexual violence against their own women, the ones from their own neighborhood, including against those who become members of their own gangs. The historical persistence of violence against women is an element that not only clouds the diagnosis but also impedes efforts to control the violence.[39] Although a considerable number of Mexican women have been murdered in Ciudad Juárez, which is a known hub for extremely violent youth gangs with possible connections to Mara Salvatrucha, an extensive Amnesty International report does not mention even once the terms *pandilla* or *mara* but seems instead to focus on the patriarchal, domineering nature of male-female relations. "Everything seems to indicate that the young women are selected by their victimizers because they are without any type of power in society."[40] This suggests that it is "the system" that violates and kills the women. Until a serious investigation takes place and the actual perpetrators are reliably identified and brought to justice, such facile explanations will do nothing to stop the violence or make up for the abdication of the Mexican judicial system.

Conclusion

Contrary to common assumptions about the youths who become members of street gangs and *maras*, this chapter draws on a large set of data to demonstrate that gangs are able to attract members from all walks of life, not only from the poor and uneducated. Some *mareros* have even been able to use the wealth they acquire from their illegal activities in the gang to ascend to the middle or upper classes of society, where they lead a virtual double life as a gainfully employed citizen while retaining their ties and loyalty to the gang. These "white-collar" gang members bring job skills such as accounting or fund-raising to gang activities; young people in trusted positions in government or society may be targeted for recruitment by the *maras* specifically for such skills, to help run the gang's criminal operations.

These findings fly in the face of accepted wisdom about gangs, since almost all studies until recently began from the premise that gang members virtually without exception come from the impoverished sectors of society. This assumption itself arises from a flawed research methodology that pulls data from an unrealistically narrow portion of society and thus underreports the levels of crime perpetrated by middle- and upper-income youths. To the contrary, recent primary-source surveys that provide the data for this chapter find that in societies where the *maras* are present, well-to-do youths self-report levels of participation in crime and gang activities that belie previous assumptions about the power of wealth and status to inoculate youths against gang membership.

Finally, the chapter highlights a typically neglected theme of gang life, which is the sexual brutalization of women, including violent rape, both inside and outside the gang. Flawed research and mistaken assumptions about the causes and composition of gangs mean that policies intended to solve problems like recruitment and endemic sexual violence will be less likely to reach their intended goals or to make a difference in the lives of those who have been the victims of gang crime.

CHAPTER 9

The Use of Intelligence to Combat *Maras*

CLIFFORD GYVES

Societies, communities, police, and governments wrestling with the *maras* may find their countergang efforts more effective when they are built on accurate and comprehensive knowledge about the problem. Information on the *maras* themselves, the environment in which they reside and operate, how they behave, and the communities they affect can assist all of society's stakeholders—public and private sector alike—in evaluating the *mara* problem, predicting the *maras'* evolution, and forecasting both the potential effects of the gangs and the results of future countergang strategies. In a word, *intelligence* can underpin a successful countergang campaign.

Intelligence, most commonly associated with statecraft and military operations, enables countries to gain leverage in international diplomacy, secure advantage in conflict, and address issues that affect their national interests. But intelligence is an indispensable tool in many other ventures outside of statecraft. Police, for example, use law enforcement intelligence to fight crime, while corporations gather business intelligence to evaluate markets, develop products, assess consumer interest, and predict economic trends. Intelligence has a rightful place in strategies to tackle the *maras* and mitigate their impact on society and its citizens. Yet, while government has a presiding interest in protecting society from the *maras*, a countergang intelligence program nevertheless cannot limit itself to government circles. A countergang campaign's numerous stakeholders, both inside and outside government, demand roles for a varied set of players, and each of them has a part in gathering or using intelligence.

Government, the police, civil services, schools, hospitals, utility companies, realtors, religious groups, and ordinary citizens all hold a stake in controlling gang activity, and all can contribute to the value of intelligence based on their unique perspective on the *maras*, the gang environment, and *maras'* effects on society. But the various stakeholders do not merely provide information; they also need the intelligence the analysts produce, so they can, at a minimum, protect themselves from the *maras* and, in a more active sense, play a specific role in combating the problem.

Having such a diverse collection of stakeholders can present some challenges. Working together in the intelligence arena requires sharing both raw data and the refined intelligence published by analysts. But sharing intelligence can be touchy. "Intelligence" is thought to be the traditional domain of government departments and ministries, officials, law enforcement offices, and "spy" agencies. Sharing it with private sector and citizen groups, nongovernmental organizations (NGOs), and foreign partners goes against the inherent trend toward secrecy that characterizes the traditional intelligence world.

How can a society overcome this inertia? One method is to use "tearlines"—distilled intelligence tailored for the individual customers. Tearline reports extract relevant information from a more extensive or detailed report for use by a specific audience, while redacting more sensitive data that the specific audience has no need to know. Police may need information about upcoming drug deals or the locations of *mara* safe houses and the homes of key gang leaders, without necessarily knowing how an intelligence agency acquired the information—for example, from human informants or wiretaps. Missionaries may need to know which gang is operating in their neighborhood and what crimes it commits, but need not know the locations of safe houses, cell leaders, or the specifics about their smuggling routes and black market connections.

Tearlines provide a decent work-around for sharing relevant intelligence between agencies or across sectors of society. Ultimately, though, a successful multisector countergang campaign will require a cultural shift from one of intelligence secrecy to one of information sharing and collaboration. Only then can intelligence be used to its full potential to stem a full-spectrum problem like the *maras*.

Intelligence helps resolve an issue by first allowing stakeholders to define and understand the problem. The *mara clica* represents more than a mere collection of criminals or a smattering of isolated crimes. A *mara clica* can best be examined as a *system*. Once stakeholders in society grasp how the system functions, they can devise plans to impede that function and shrink the gang problem.

The *Maras* as a System

Defining the *mara* as a system provides a useful paradigm against which authorities and community leaders can evaluate the gang and its activities and develop appropriate intervention and suppression mechanisms. A *mara clica* system incorporates identifiable inputs, processes, and outputs. Inputs can enable the criminal enterprise to function as well as sustain the organization itself. Drugs, precursor chemicals used to make narcotics, weapons, money, stolen goods, and trafficked people constitute inputs to the system's processes and thus allow it to function. Inputs that sustain the *mara clica* itself include new members and money. The *mara*'s processes are simply the means by which the gang converts inputs into outputs; that is, they are the criminal activities in which the gang engages, such as narcotics production and distribution, material and human smuggling, theft, protection rackets and "rent" collection, kidnapping and extortion, intimidation, assault, murder, and membership recruitment. The processes generate both intended outputs and unintended by-products.

Intended outputs are those goods and services the *mara* generates as part of its profit-making enterprise. These are normally illicit products and services, like drugs, prostitution, the smuggling of goods and people, territorial "protection" services, and murder for hire, but may also include some legitimate business ventures, such as stock market investment. Other intended outputs consist of visible power-projection activities the *clica* engages in to identify its presence and turf, intimidate or eliminate rivals, and otherwise protect its interests. Examples include marking members with distinctive tattoos, tagging turf with graffiti, and murdering rivals and transgressors in a brutal, ritualistic fashion as a public message.

A *clica*, like any enterprise, will also generate unintentional outputs—a sort of waste or by-product of its presence and activities that gives the organization a unique signature it does not consciously publicize. These incidental outputs, together with the ones the *mara* intentionally broadcasts, serve as indicators that can enable authorities to develop an intelligence strategy for gang suppression. Much as a wake indicates the nearby presence of a boat, where it has been, and where it is headed, incidental outputs are telltale "ripples" that can reveal the *clica*'s inputs and processes. Such indicators may include an increase in theft rates; a rise in the quantity or a shift in the type of drug use on the street; smuggling of contraband (base chemicals, weapons, or illegal goods) into the area; or a spike (or sudden drop) in citizen complaints to police. The list of indicators can be extensive and represents a key component in the development and application of gang-related intelligence.

There can be general support for the use of intelligence, as gang problems affect many sectors in a society. Gangs in general, and *maras* in particular, bring higher crime rates into a community, levying a greater burden on the citizens and the police. Schools become recruiting grounds and marketplaces for drugs and other contraband, and they provide a stage for intergang rivalries and demonstrations of violence. Hospitals and clinics treat the victims of gang violence (both innocents and gang members alike), while ambulance services may encounter difficulties responding to emergency calls in neighborhoods that the *maras* control. A gang presence will affect the local real estate market, and a community's demographic makeup will shift as certain ethnic groups find a niche in *mara* territory while others take flight. Because the problem is community-based, it requires solutions across the full spectrum of society. The police, government officials, community leaders, church leaders, real estate agents, school administrators, hospital staff, firefighters, and utility workers all become embroiled in the problem and thus must participate in finding a solution. They need good information about the problem in order to make educated choices in devising potential countergang strategies: they need intelligence.[1]

Intelligence is information that has been processed, analyzed, and placed into a form that can be used to achieve a predefined goal. Intelligence producers provide decision makers with information the latter can apply to strategies or policies that deal with a particular problem. The applications for military intelligence are rather straightforward: military commanders develop strategies and tactics based on information about the enemy's intentions, battle plans, and military capabilities and weaknesses; geographic information and weather data; and poststrike battle-damage assessments.

The Intelligence Process

Those people who require intelligence—government officials, police, health professionals, economists, educators, corrections officials, and community members—are *intelligence consumers*. Before consumers can have useful intelligence, *collectors* must first gather disparate pieces of relevant data and pass them to *analysts*, who in turn assemble them like a puzzle and figure out what they mean; analysts answer the "So what?"

question that comes from the jumble of raw data. The lines between the collector, analyst, and consumer roles often get blurred, as people and organizations may fill overlapping functions. The police, for instance, have their own internal intelligence operation, which includes collecting field data about criminal problems like gangs and carrying out analysis either by trained analysts in a larger department's gang division or by ordinary detectives in a smaller department. Those in the operations division, as consumers, apply the analyzed intelligence to devise enforcement operations.

The law enforcement consumer base, however, is broader than this example would imply. A large police department with a dedicated gang unit might have some officers gathering the raw field data, others analyzing the data, and still others using the intelligence to direct ongoing investigations or execute enforcement and suppression actions, like serving warrants or mobilizing special patrols. The consumer function, however, is not limited to a distinct end user, as the process above would imply. Intelligence production relies on an iterative process, whereby collectors, analysts, and consumers collaborate to assess the value of the raw data gathered and the relevance of the finished intelligence that comes out. This interaction turns the collectors into consumers, as each division then uses what it learns to refine its own processes. Collectors readjust their collection plan based on intelligence outputs. The analysts identify pieces of information they lack—that is, they identify what they don't know about the *maras*—and then they task, or *levy*, the collectors to gather data in that vein. The finished intelligence the analysts produce tells the collectors what their raw data mean and what value the data have, and then helps direct the collectors as to where to focus future collections, gather additional data, and fill the *intelligence gaps*.[2]

Feedback permeates the intelligence process. Decision makers, as consumers, tell the analysts whether the finished intelligence products provide useful, "actionable" information for them. The analysts advise the collectors as to the value of the raw data inputs they are providing. The U.S. intelligence community encapsulates this iterative intelligence process in what it calls the *intelligence cycle*.[3]

The cycle begins in the planning and direction phase, when the consumers define their intelligence needs—the information they need to make decisions and develop strategic plans or operations. Intelligence collection managers then distill those needs into requirements for the field collectors, who gather the information during the collection phase in accordance with the intelligence "shopping list" the consumers have passed to them. These raw data must be collated and organized during the processing phase into a form the analysts can use. In some cases, audio intercepts and wiretap recordings will have to be transcribed; in others, the information may have to be translated from a foreign language. In the analysis and production phase, analysts apply their craft to identify patterns and trends in the data, forecast future developments (predictive analysis), and ascribe meaning to the mosaic of raw data. Once they have completed their work, the analysts publish their findings in a finished intelligence product, which is distributed to consumers in the dissemination phase and used by them to craft their decisions and plans. The cycle begins again as the consumers reassess their information needs — what intelligence they still lack, or what new questions have emerged from the information they have just received — and build new collection requirements.

Defining Strategic Intelligence Goals

The initial step in the intelligence cycle requires the end users of intelligence on gangs to define broad goals for the intelligence producers. As the key decision makers, the end users must determine whether they want to concentrate on curbing the *maras'* criminal activity or disbanding the *clicas* themselves (or both). How they plan to use the information will dictate what types of intelligence they need, which in turn will guide the work of the collectors and analysts.

Collection

Intelligence analysts have direct access to a myriad of information sources from which to draw data about *maras*. An analyst can glean some useful information that can be shared with other law enforcement agencies from public sector databases, court records, real estate documents, social service files, public health records, demographic surveys, open-source media publications and broadcasts, or even utility records. By contrast, law enforcement information, such as investigative case files, confidential informant reports, or wiretap transcripts, is derived from collection activities the police conduct.

The police must shape their collection approach — particularly any sourcing strategy involving informants — around the targeted *mara*'s status in society or its respective subset of society. If, on the one hand, the *mara* operates brazenly and openly on turf that it effectively controls, and it holds the local residents in fear of retaliation, the police will need to take a subtle tack on gathering field intelligence. They will have to emplace more undercover officers rather than rely on overt beat patrols, and they should employ confidential informants in lieu of open contacts with neighborhood residents. Authorities must emphasize operational security and covert source-handling tradecraft to protect their informants and their collection operations. If, on the other hand, the *mara* is forced underground or on the run under pressure from authorities, the police can more readily interview citizens on the street or openly contact neighborhood residents; they can also make more direct and overt observations of the environment through routine patrols.

Analysis

Analysis provides the key to turning raw field data into useful information. Analysts sift through the raw data and, using a combination of tools and personal experience (learned intuition), decipher patterns across the spectrum of disparate data and ascribe meaning to them. This meaning may place a gang's current activities and attributes into a historical context. Other analysis will attempt to extrapolate how a gang might look or behave in the future, based on historical trends. Yet another type of analysis will seek to explain the motivations, causes, strengths, and vulnerabilities of a gang, which will enable policy makers to formulate enforcement operations, suppression options, or prevention strategies.

Gang analysis takes two distinct forms. Counteractivity analysis (CAA) illuminates trends in the timing, types, and location of gang activity, looking for ways to curb the gang's criminal enterprise. The analyst will attempt to isolate the system inputs that feed the criminal process and the system outputs, both intended and unintended, those criminal activities generate. The analyst can enumerate indicators for the police, giving them a list of what to watch out for on the streets that will help them identify criminal gang activity. Further analysis should highlight pressure points the police can manipulate to curtail the gang's processes.

Countergroup analysis (CGA) seeks to inform prevention and suppression strategies that target the organization itself in an effort to shrink it, impede its growth, or prevent a gang from taking root in a given locale. CGA zeroes in on those factors that allow the organization to exist and stay healthy. This analysis may identify trends in the growth, evolution, or migration of the *clica*. It may identify environmental conditions and factors that invite a *clica* to move into a neighborhood, establish predomi-

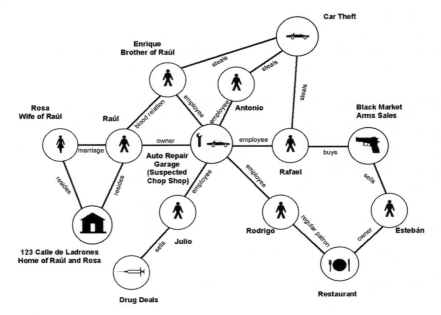

Figure 9.1. A *mara clica* mapped as a network.

nant control over geographic turf or a particular criminal enterprise, or simply to flourish as an organization. Countergroup analysis is somewhat broader than counteractivity analysis, in that CAA can contribute to overall CGA. Incorporating CAA into the equation should reduce a gang's viability, insofar as mitigating a gang's ability to operate undercuts its ability to sustain itself.

CAA-driven enforcement operations can tease out additional information about the organization itself to feed the CGA process. Analysts will attempt to map out a *clica*'s organizational structure using social network analysis, wherein they chart group members, assets, and activities (called network *nodes*) and the relationships between them (called network *links*). Figure 9.1 depicts a *clica* network, in which the nodes—activities, places, and people—are depicted as circles and the relationships, or links, are shown as lines.

An underground organization such as a criminal gang is difficult to map, and analysts normally develop only an incomplete picture of the organization's full membership and activities. Authorities can, however, use known nodes and links to identify previously unknown nodes. Certain nodes in the *clica* network might serve as enforcement pressure points:

isolating or eliminating a known node (a person or transaction), for instance, will force the organization (the network) to adapt and compensate. Such compensation can in turn generate incidental outputs, often in the form of new transactions that will illuminate new relationships or even new nodes. For example, if the police interdict a shipment of contraband (system inputs), the *clica* will have to go to "plan B" and contact the supplier to send another. If the police apprehend the supplier, effectively removing him or her from the network, the *clica* will have to contact an alternate source. By monitoring these communications (surveillance of known nodes), the police can identify other nodes connected to the network (e.g., the backup suppliers activated by plan B).[4] In other words, the police have interdicted inputs in order to activate dormant or unknown lines of communication and identify previously unknown nodes.

Countergroup analysis can identify neighborhoods in advance that might be at risk for infiltration by a *mara*, and thus it can enable authorities and community leaders to get ahead of growth patterns and implement social intervention and gang prevention programs. For example, a CGA research group selected Napa, California, as one of three cities to study based on statistical reports of gang migrations into the area during 1992. Researchers hoped to ascertain the underlying causes for the spread of gangs in that area, which were suspected to be more complex than simple crime-related stimuli. The study found that Mexican immigrant laborers moving up to the Napa Valley in Northern California to find work encountered strong prejudice and hostility from resident Hispanic Americans. A gang known as the Norteños (Northerners), composed of third- and fourth-generation Hispanic Americans, maintained a rivalry with the Southern California Sureños (Southerners), who hailed from more recent immigrant stock, generally first- or second-generation immigrants from Mexico and Central America who had settled in the south of the state (see chapter 1 in this volume for more on the origins of the Sureños). The recent Mexican arrivals in the Napa Valley found themselves immediately categorized as Sureños, though they may have come with no gang affiliations at all. Ultimately, many of the immigrant youths, faced with violent harassment by the Norteños, sought refuge in the company of the Sureños, increasing the size of this gang and expanding the intergang conflict.[5] Unfortunately, this case study was conducted after Napa had already developed a gang problem, so its findings could not help prevent or mitigate gang infiltration there. Its results suggest, however, that a similar methodology, if applied early enough, might enable countergang campaigns to identify the real factors that stimulate gang activity and expansion, and thus avoid the kinds of generic assumptions about causes that are frequently embraced by the media and law enforcement and too often lead to equally generic and ineffective countermeasures.[6]

This approach to law enforcement intelligence analysis constitutes the lynchpin of effective crime prevention strategies and countergroup campaigns. Counteractivity analysis tends to support crime-oriented policing (COP) and generally focuses on incident-based statistical data concerning types of crime and the times and locations at which crimes occur.[7] (This tactical assessment is sometimes called crime analysis.) The end users of crime analysis in a COP program are the police investigators and patrol officers who endeavor to locate and apprehend perpetrators for prosecution. Meanwhile, a countergroup approach incorporates information from multiple sources to contextualize criminal activity within a social, economic, and geographic milieu, examining the problem from a strategic perspective.[8] This strengthens the countergang campaign by adding preventive strategies to the reactive tool set of investigation, apprehension, and prosecution. While police leverage intelligence to chisel away at a gang's membership and operations through suppression measures, public administrators, civil servants, social support agencies, and citizens can use the analytical products of CGA to work together to render the local environment a less hospitable place for gangs to flourish.

An assessment of socioeconomic data across Central America by José Miguel Cruz, who is the author of chapter 7, identified conditions that either fostered gang development in some neighborhoods or inoculated others against the *maras*. Seemingly disparate factors, upon closer analysis, contributed to a decisive determinant of the *mara* presence and influence: "social capital." The *maras* thrived in an environment with low social capital—that is, in neighborhoods where the sense of community was weak or where interpersonal relations were marked by distrust and suspicion.[9] In neighborhoods where the inhabitants harbored a distrust of their municipal government, perhaps fostered by corruption and real or perceived neglect amidst a lack of government services or infrastructure, the community was less likely to band together to curb the *maras'* encroachment and less likely to work with the government to address the gang problem.[10] Housing conditions in El Salvador made a good predictor of gang prevalence, for example, but not merely as a reflection of inhabitants' income. Rather, the predominance of renters, as opposed to homeowners, in a given neighborhood suggested that the inhabitants were more mobile, transient, and less likely to establish roots, reducing the strength of social bonds within the community.[11] A heavy presence of socially "unhealthy" establishments, like bars or brothels, also reduced a neighborhood's social capital, inviting gang presence and activity. Conversely, barrios that offered safe public gathering places, like meeting halls or parks, enjoyed stronger community ties and proved more resistant to the *maras'* incursion.[12]

Thus CGA, as a strategic discipline, digests more than pure law enforcement information and crime data. A careful review of multiple information sources, from census data (official or unofficial), citizen interviews, social services files, and demographic trend data, can highlight the conditions that lead to gang development or expansion, and can identify flashpoints for gang violence. The key is for the intelligence players to gather and analyze information from a myriad of sources, many of which may not normally be associated with traditional intelligence or police work.

Intelligence Fusion

Incorporating information from multiple sources into the analytic calculus is called *fusion*. The analyst draws from police reports, investigative case files, public records, databases, and the news media. Publicly available information and sensitive law enforcement data merge in the fusion process to create a mosaic of intelligence that offers the analyst clues to interpret. For example, emergency room statistics might show a marked increase in the number of beating victims, suggesting the emergence of a gang as new members are "jumped in." A high incidence of small animal deaths in an area may be linked to noxious chemicals leaking into the environment, pointing to a possible drug production lab. Excessive utility consumption is another indicator of clandestine drug labs or marijuana grow rooms. Citizen complaints or police patrols might identify a new aggregation of drug users around a certain city block, hinting at the location of a drug house or distribution center. Taken together, disparate bits of data can point to an emerging *clica* foothold in an area, with ties to drug production and distribution.

The fusion process normally materializes in a collaborative center where multiple stakeholders join together to pool their data and analyze them in aggregate. The multiple organizations not only bring in their unique data streams but also offer their own organizational perspectives and analytical techniques. White-collar financial analysts are adept at dissecting fraud and money laundering, for example, while narcotics enforcement analysts can evaluate trends and shifts in drug production and distribution. Working together, they can cross-pollinate their analysis to discern new developments in gang activity. For example, the financial and narcotics analysts, together with customs officials, might uncover a new method the *maras* have developed to smuggle currency across borders, adapted from narco-trafficking techniques.

Establishing a standing task force is an approach that lends itself well to intelligence fusion, because the task force members develop a trusting, working relationship. The U.S. Department of Homeland Security has pushed states to establish fusion centers, primarily to prevent terrorism in the United States; to make the centers effective and relevant, however, Homeland Security has endorsed an "all-crimes" approach, making them the ideal vehicle for collaborative law enforcement. Fusion centers enable public service sector agencies from multiple jurisdictions to pool resources and information. Large centers, like the New York State Intelligence Center, allocate resources to analyze crime problems that smaller, individual jurisdictions are ill-equipped to tackle themselves.[13] The National Gang Intelligence Center (NGIC), a part of the U.S. Department of Justice, functions as a type of fusion center focused specifically on gangs. NGIC assists agencies at all jurisdictional levels by providing strategic analysis and information sharing on national and regional gangs.[14] In one instance, an NGIC intelligence analyst, who served part-time with the Wyoming National Guard, took a one-year assignment with the National Guard Counterdrug Program to build a gang intelligence apparatus in Cheyenne. Because of her background, she was able to apply her unique knowledge, analytical skills, and network contacts from NGIC to develop a successful program in Wyoming.[15]

Learning through Collaboration and Sharing

Effective gang mitigation efforts cut across multiple sectors of society. Public, private, national, regional, and local actors must work together, but in order to do so, they must operate from an integrated strategy founded on a common base of information. In military and government parlance, the term is *common operating picture*.

Various agencies must band together as a team and pool their information resources to build their common operating picture, if they are going to develop effective programs. This may present the greatest challenge in the countergang effort. Government agencies, often for budgetary reasons, are loath to share information so freely and openly even among themselves, much less with the private sector or with other governments. National-level agencies resist giving information to regional or local jurisdictions or even laterally to other national agencies. In some cases, knowledge is power, both real and political. Law enforcement organizations keep information on open investigations close to the chest to prevent compromise.

In the United States especially, some agencies do not exchange information because statute and culture have erected barriers to prevent any one agency from amassing too much data and thus too much power. For example, at the National Counterterrorism Center (NCTC), the CIA and FBI cells are held to age-old jurisdictional restrictions on sharing information: the FBI, which is responsible for domestic federal law enforcement, cannot pass active investigative case data to the CIA, which is forbidden to conduct domestic operations, and the CIA cannot share (noncriminal, non–law enforcement) intelligence information with the FBI. Each organization may hold a piece of the overall information jigsaw puzzle but is restricted from having the whole picture (thereby limiting its perceived power, since knowledge is power). Ironically, the legal and cultural barriers that hold fast for the FBI and the CIA do not apply to the other partner agencies in the NCTC, such as Customs, Treasury, or Homeland Security, which can see reports from both the FBI and CIA cells. U.S. law enforcement organizations enjoy greater leeway than national-level intelligence agencies in gathering information on citizens, because culturally and legally the United States does not endorse "spying" on its own people. In other cases, data in the private sector may be protected as a matter of privacy or proprietary interest, keeping it out of the hands of the police or intelligence personnel in all but the most compelling circumstances.

The *mara* problem in Central America owes much of its genesis to this culture of privacy and information protection. A considerable number of Central American immigrants served time in U.S. prisons for gang-related crimes in the 1980s and 1990s. Once their sentences were served, many of these gang members were deported back to Central America. U.S. immigration policy stipulated that officials could not disclose an individual's criminal history when deporting that person back to his country of origin. Critics have pointed out that this policy, put in effect to protect individual privacy, left Central American governments in the dark about the danger these individual deportees posed; once in-country, the new arrivals established *mara clicas* that took quick root and soon plagued the region. The Central American governments, caught unawares, did not anticipate the problems. The U.S. policy of withholding information not only hurt Central American societies but also injured U.S. relations with its neighbor governments, which squarely blamed the United States for this new criminal scourge.[16] (See further information on this issue in chapter 10.) While Central American governments deserve their fair share of criticism for the endemic corruption and inept policies that have allowed the *maras* to flourish, the fact remains that an atmosphere of openness and cooperation between all the hemisphere's governments, unfettered by finger-pointing, would go a long way to mitigate the *maras'* growth.

The transnational reach of the *maras* extends from the United States through Mexico and across Central America. Having learned from its immigration policy mistakes of the 1990s and early 2000s, combined with a new emphasis on terrorism prevention post-9/11, the United States is now trying to bolster information-sharing partnerships, both domestically and abroad. Regional governments throughout the Americas must leverage liaison relationships between their respective intelligence agencies, their diplomatic corps, and their law enforcement communities. The *maras* will continue to adapt and evolve, exploiting new markets and new criminal enterprises, taking over new territory, forging new business partnerships with drug cartels and organized crime syndicates, and altering their membership composition to survive in a changing environment. Effective innovations in one country or region will spread across the *mara* networks to other countries or territories. Authorities who observe such developments in their own jurisdictions can help their faraway partners and counterparts abroad get ahead of the trend by sharing what they have learned. A broad multisector, multijurisdictional, and multinational intelligence network can go a long way in curbing growth and adaptation in the *mara* enterprise.

The New Jersey Department of Corrections (NJDOC) established a collaborative gang intelligence project in 1997, wherein NJDOC tracked gang affiliation among prison inmates. NJDOC founded the Inter-Institutional Intelligence Committee to share intelligence on gangs and gang members with other agencies, thereby helping all constituents stay abreast of developing trends. NJDOC also works with the New Jersey State Parole Board to monitor identified gang members who are paroled from prison.[17] Because gangs tend to spread geographically and rarely confine their activities to a single jurisdiction, cross-jurisdictional data pooling helps police and analysts maintain a common "big picture" view. Massachusetts, for instance, began developing a state-wide database called MassGangs, that would provide access to gang data across all juris-dictions. Officers who arrested a suspected gang member traditionally had to contact individual police departments to track down any gang affilia-tion data on the suspect. With MassGangs, a suspected gang member's information would be readily accessible and comprehensive.[18] (Projected to go online in early 2009, MassGangs ultimately failed because police departments had insufficient funding to assign staff to enter gang infor-mation into the database.)

Collective information sharing and resource pooling help police, ana-lysts, and intelligence consumers maintain a strategic perspective while synchronizing their combined countergang efforts. Furthermore, a long-standing collaborative campaign is better suited to engage the *maras*, which require continuous mitigation efforts and the reevaluation of intelligence.

An Evolving Effort

The intelligence process must continue cyclically. As authorities apply pressure to a *mara*'s criminal operations and as prevention or suppression programs chip away at the organization itself, the gang will adapt. As the gang changes its methodology and its organizational makeup, the intelli-gence players must seek new indicators and new pressure points.

As documented in three country-specific chapters (Chapters 2–4), the main Central American *pandillas*, MS-13 and the 18th Street Gang, facing great pressure under aggressive eradication campaigns, have assumed a lower profile. Members' distinctive tattoos have made them prime targets for the police; what was once an intentional output to show gang affilia-tion and intimidate the community became an undesirable trait that drew unwanted attention from authorities. Some gangs, forced underground into a more covert existence, started to recruit from different segments of society, bringing in new members such as white-collar workers and professional women, who did not fit the standard profile and could blend in better with the larger society than the stereotypical young male thugs covered with tattoos.[19]

The new recruiting strategy presented an unintended benefit. The *maras* hoped to become more covert and less detectable by bringing in atypical newcomers, but the new members have also brought with them valuable business skills. The effort to expand the personnel base reinvigo-rated the organizations by opening avenues for new criminal enterprises.

The *maras'* well-educated rookies now teach white-collar crime skills to the veterans, enabling the gangs to extend their tendrils into more lucrative arenas like fraud and to enhance the profitability of their traditional criminal activities.[20]

A successful gang will adapt to external pressure and learn new ways to survive in its changing environment. Therefore those combating the *maras* must learn, too, and adjust their intelligence process to stay abreast—or, better yet, ahead of—the gangs' evolution.

CHAPTER 10

The Impact of U.S. Anti-gang Policies in Central America: Quo Vadis?

FLORINA CRISTIANA MATEI

Since the end of the Cold War, the United States has been supporting Latin America's development, democracy, and security through a series of diplomatic, economic, social, and security-related initiatives and programs.[1] Fighting gangs has been part of these endeavors since the early 1990s, when the U.S. government became aware of the challenges posed domestically by gangs and enacted numerous anti-gang initiatives, including deportations of Central American citizens. In the early 2000s, officials began to talk about the "significant security threat"[2] posed by gangs and gang-related crimes to both U.S. and Central American citizens and the rule of law, which led gradually to more U.S. agencies becoming engaged in both U.S. and regional anti-gang activities.[3] Central America has received even more focused attention from Washington since the mid-2000s. U.S. anti-gang policies and initiatives have emphasized prevention (avert and minimize gang activity and its negative consequences by discouraging young people from joining gangs); intervention (support, encourage, and respond to the needs of those who want to leave the gangs, including efforts to persuade gang members to abandon their gangs); and law enforcement (apprehension, detention, prosecution, incarceration, and deportation). This chapter looks at the United States' efforts to counter the gang problem in Central America. It first reviews the evolution of government involvement in fighting gangs and then evaluates the impact of said policies on the gang problem in the region.

U.S. Anti-Gang Approaches

The crossover effects of transnational gangs in Central America and the United States have been a mounting concern for governments and security agencies at the federal, state, and local levels. As FBI director Robert Mueller stated, "Criminal gangs and other illicit enterprises, operating in the U.S. and throughout the world, are of increasing concern for domestic . . . law enforcement and for the intelligence community."[4] In an effort to seek suitable solutions and advance effective approaches to Central America's gang problems, Washington has developed a host of anti-gang initiatives.

One of the early post–Cold War measures to deal with U.S. gangs was the implementation of deportation laws for non-U.S. citizens found guilty of a gang-related crime or determined to belong to a gang. The 1994 law known as Three Strikes and You're Out significantly expanded the mandatory prison sentences of recidivist criminals, which led to the imprisonment of thousands of Los Angeles gang members, including Central American–born individuals.[5] The Illegal Immigration Reform and Immigrant Responsibility Act (IIRIRA) and the Antiterrorism and Effective Death Penalty Act, both enacted in 1996, broadened the definition of "aggravated felony" to include violence, theft, commercial bribery, obstruction of justice, and gambling offenses (previously considered misdemeanors), thereby allowing deportation on any of these grounds.[6] The IIRIRA also applied the "aggravated felony" provision retroactively to gang members.[7] Notwithstanding blistering criticism on constitutional and human rights grounds, and ongoing legal and legislative disputes, these laws were implemented, and the number of annual deportations skyrocketed.[8]

The Executive Branch

Several U.S. federal agencies have supported Central America's anti-gang fight, through several different policies and programs. U.S. administration representatives have made several trips to Central American countries in recent years with the intent to identify common best-fitting solutions to current regional security issues and challenges, including gangs. A direct outcome has been the Mérida Initiative, a multiyear security assistance program to help Central America combat transnational organized crime. Launched by U.S. president George W. Bush in 2007, after an earlier meeting with Mexican president Felipe Calderón, in Mérida, Mexico, the Mérida Initiative enables the United States to provide resources, equipment, and training to Central American countries to support law enforcement, foster interagency and regional cooperation, assist security and judicial reforms, and contribute to the development of prosecutorial capacity, among other things.[9] A key component of the Mérida Initiative is the "U.S. Strategy to Combat Criminal Gangs from Central America and Mexico," developed in 2005–2006 by the U.S. Department of State and other federal agencies and launched in July 2007 at a joint security summit between the United States and the Central American Integration System (Sistema de la Integración Centroamericana, or SICA), a regional organization that focuses on security matters.[10] The strategy calls for a balanced and concerted approach ranging from effective law enforcement to youth crime prevention and intervention, not only on the domestic front but also cooperatively on the regional front. The concern is that without a coordinated regional policy, success in a specific area or country may simply shift the problem to adjacent areas or neighboring countries, given the gang members' peripatetic nature. This initiative involves Washington in five broad anti-gang endeavors: diplomacy, repatriation, law enforcement, capacity enhancement, and prevention.[11]

The U.S. Department of State's anti-gang initiatives have been part of a wider effort to curtail worldwide organized crime and violence, especially when related to drug trafficking. In 1978 the Department of State (DoS) created the Bureau of International Narcotics and Law Enforcement (INL) to develop policies and conduct programs on countering international crime and drug trafficking for countries affected by organized crime. In recent years INL has also become involved in Central America's fight against gangs by assisting the region's law enforcement agencies, through activities that include providing support for the anti-gang curriculum of the International Law Enforcement Academy (ILEA) in El Salvador; setting up a "Model Precinct" to enhance policing and police-community relations in Villanueva, Guatemala; helping to implement the International Narcotics Control and Law Enforcement (INCLE) program; and supporting rehabilitation and prevention programs.[12] Since 2008, INL has been in permanent contact with the governments of Central America through its regional gang adviser, who prepared a comprehensive gang assessment report on Honduras, El Salvador, and Guatemala and drafted an anti-gang work plan targeting investigative capacity, legal capacity, intelligence capacity, community policing, prevention, and prisons. The adviser has also become engaged in gang prevention activities, supported training and technical exchanges for law enforcement officers throughout Central America, taught an ILEA anti-gang course, and identified possible venues for future community policing programs in El Salvador and Honduras.[13] The DoS has also been tasked with the coordination and implementation of the Mérida Initiative in Central America. Through the initiative and INL's assistance to Mexico in setting up a Corrections Academy in Veracruz (operational since June 2009), in April 2009 the first class of Mexican federal correctional instructors graduated from the New Mexico Corrections Department's Training Academy in Santa Fe.[14]

The Department of Justice (DOJ) set up a number of agencies and task forces in 2005 to combat gangs, both within the United States and in cooperation with Central American states. Two of the Justice Department's first important steps in fighting gangs were the creation of the Federal Bureau of Investigation's MS-13 National Gang Task Force (NGTF) and the establishment of a National Gang Intelligence Center (NGIC), to assist law enforcement actions by coordinating information and intelligence.[15] The NGIC also organizes and shares information with Honduras, Guatemala, and El Salvador. The FBI established a liaison office in San Salvador to further coordinate information sharing and anti-gang efforts in the region.[16] In June 2005, on a fact-finding mission trip to Chiapas, Mexico, NGTF officers received 180 fingerprint records of gang members from Mexican law enforcement; after sharing and comparing the data with U.S. Immigration and Customs Enforcement (ICE) and U.S. Customs and Border Protection, the agencies learned that forty-six of the gang members whose fingerprints were obtained had already been identified in the United States.[17] Likewise, in September, during a one-day anti-gang operation in the United States, NGTF, in cooperation with 6,400 police officers, federal agents, and other officials from twelve U.S. states, Honduras, El Salvador, Guatemala, and southern Mexico apprehended more than 650 gang members.[18] Alongside the NGTF, the DOJ established an International Anti-Gang Task Force (IAGTF), featuring three operational working groups (Extradition and Mutual Legal Assistance, Law Enforcement Cooperation and Information Sharing, and Repatriation) to converge and coordinate the anti-gang efforts of federal agencies and their Central American counterparts.[19]

The FBI's most notable international anti-gang initiatives include Central American Fingerprint Exploitation (CAFE), Transnational Anti-Gang (TAG) units, the Central American Law Enforcement Exchange, the Central American Intelligence Program (CAIP), the Repatriation–Criminal History Information Program (CHIP), and an officer exchange program.

CAFE, an NGTF outgrowth, has been implemented by the FBI and INL since 2006 to ease the identification of and information sharing on gang members in Mexico, El Salvador, Guatemala, Belize, and Honduras, by incorporating Central American criminal biometric records into the FBI's Criminal Justice Information Services fingerprint databases, which can be searched by both U.S. and Central American law enforcement agencies. CAFE also provides training and equipment related to digital fingerprint identification and analysis. As of this writing, the CAFE database, called the Integrated Automated Fingerprint Identification System, has acquired over 72,000 gang members' fingerprints from the aforementioned countries.[20]

TAG units, initiated in El Salvador in 2007, are carefully chosen and trained police units that work reciprocally with FBI agents in San Salvador to investigate, deter, and contain gangs. The FBI office shares gang and crime intelligence that has been gathered in the United States with TAG units in El Salvador's national police (Policía Nacional Civil [PNC]), while the PNC collects information on gang members in El Salvador and channels it through the locally stationed FBI agents to the task force at FBI headquarters. From there this information is shared with the appropriate FBI field divisions. TAG's successful operations so far include the arrest of fifteen MS-13 members on charges that included arms trafficking, and the indictment of another twenty-six. With the Mérida funding for fiscal year 2009, TAG activities have been expanded into Mexico and Guatemala, and they will be brought to Honduras when the political situation permits.[21]

The Central American Law Enforcement Exchange, CAIP, and the Repatriation–Criminal History Information Program are joint initiatives (FBI-DoS, FBI-ICE, and FBI–Los Angeles civilian and law enforcement agencies, respectively) that bring together law enforcement and/or intelligence officers from the United States, Central America, and Canada (CAIP only) to train together and learn cooperative strategies, improve gang investigation and dismantlement practices, increase the effectiveness of intelligence sharing (especially the criminal histories of deported individuals), and lessen communication gaps.[22] The executive branch's Department of Homeland Security (DHS) has also been targeting gangs by increasing deportations and improving its collection of gang-related information on individuals. In February 2005, ICE launched Operation Community Shield, an anti-gang initiative that identifies violent street gangs; produces intelligence on their membership, associates, crimes, and migration patterns; arrests suspected gang members in the United States for possible prosecution and/or deportation; disrupts criminal activities and prosecutes gang members by tracing and seizing funding, weapons, and other assets; and coordinates anti-gang measures with Central

American and other foreign governments.[23] During Community Shield's first nine months, ICE processed 1,573 gang members, of whom 1,346 (85 percent) were charged with reentry after deportation (from Central America) and who had criminal charges against them.[24] Overall, from February 2005 to December 2009, ICE arrested at least 2,572 alleged MS-13 members within the United States.[25] DHS has also implemented an *Electronic* Travel Document System (*e*TD) to save and share personal information on deportees.[26]

The role of the U.S. Department of Defense in U.S. regional anti-gang activities is limited to administering the Mérida assistance package for Mexico through the Foreign Military Financing program, a maritime assistance package in Central America, and a proposed Regional Aircraft Modernization Program.[27] The latter two initiatives are intended to help recipient governments interdict and shut down transnational smuggling operations.

The U.S. Agency for International Development (USAID) has contributed to federal efforts to rein in gang activity since 2005, when it produced a study that assessed the transnational nature of gangs and the U.S. domestic anti-gang experience, as well as the gang situation in Central America.[28] This report was prompted by the "complex, multi-faceted, and transnational phenomenon" of the gangs and increasing concerns in Washington about their impact on U.S. national security. USAID has also funded the Regional Youth Alliance USAID-SICA, a regional anti-gang program cosponsored by SICA that began in 2008 and focuses on prevention and rehabilitation programs in Guatemala, Honduras, and El Salvador. This program assesses juvenile justice systems and reform endeavors, shapes and implements new policy responses, and helps coordinate Mérida Initiative–funded anti-gang programs.[29]

Aware of (and preoccupied with) the need to evaluate the effectiveness of domestic and international U.S. anti-gang efforts, the U.S. Congress began in 2005 to regularly summon representatives of both the executive branch and civil society to testify on security and stability risks in Central America and their impact on U.S. security. Congress also asked for analyses of U.S. and international policies in the region and urged leaders in other countries to find effective avenues for anti-gang cooperation.[30] Especially worth mentioning are the interest and involvement of several Congress members in particular, including Eliot Engel and Gregory W. Meeks (New York), Linda T. Sánchez and Elton Gallegly (California), Albio Sires, Donald M. Payne, and Christopher H. Smith (New Jersey), and Jo Ann Davis (Virginia), among others. The Congress has also been involved in the Mérida Initiative by appropriating the required funds and overseeing its implementation, as well as engaging in potential follow-up programs.

Quo Vadis: Are U.S. Anti-Gang Policies in Central America Working?

The preceding discussion showed that the U.S. government's response to gangs has evolved over three periods: (1) domestic policies in the 1990s, such as deportations, that affected gang development in Central America; (2) a definite (but not entirely explained) increase in attention to gangs in the early to mid-2000s; and (3) a more focused response by U.S. international policy makers beginning in the same period, exemplified by the explosion of initiatives outlined above. But how effective have all these approaches and policies been? Did Washington deliberate carefully enough before embarking on this plethora of programs to help Central American states fight gangs? Have U.S. initiatives done enough to arrest gang development in the region, or might they actually be promoting gang growth? Are deportations the main reason for the increase in gang violence in El Salvador and Honduras, and even the United States, as many researchers claim? Has the Mérida Initiative made any progress in the Central American fight against gangs?

Tremendous Will But Limited Impact

Critics argue that the United States has not invested sufficient thought, time, or resources in Central America as a whole, including toward fighting gangs. In fact, the United States has been increasingly involved in the region for the last two decades (an amount of time similar to what European nations and governmental organizations like the North Atlantic Treaty Organization and the European Union have invested in central and eastern Europe, whose security environment is more stable than that in Central America) and is likely to stay closely involved for the foreseeable future. But when it comes to sufficient thought and resources, the skeptics may have a point. U.S. policy makers do not seem to have thought carefully about consequences prior to developing and implementing certain anti-gang policies. First and foremost, Washington launched many anti-gang initiatives with Central American states before it had put things in order at home. Even today, after a few years of involvement in Central America, there is still broad disagreement within the U.S. government on which approach (e.g., prevention, law enforcement, military support) should prevail and which agency is the most appropriate to take the lead in fighting gangs (FBI, DoS, DHS, U.S. Southern Command, etc.). This lack of consensus has undermined interagency cooperation related to foreign assistance.

Furthermore, while the total amount of U.S. financial assistance for Central America is greater than that provided by other donors,[31] the entire amount of aid for Latin America (including Central America) has not increased much since the late 1990s, despite the constant renewal of funding for anti-drug programs. Thus, during the last decade (especially after 11 September 2001), funds for Latin America have remained fairly level (8.2 percent in 1998 and 10.8 percent in 2008 of overall foreign aid); the main beneficiaries of increased U.S. aid have been South Asia (from 4 percent in 1998 to about 17 percent in 2008) and Africa (from over 13 percent to almost 29 percent).[32] This lack of funding for Central America may be having a detrimental effect on anti-gang efforts there. The White House's 2011 foreign aid budget is reducing funding for Latin America as a whole by approximately 10 percent. Officials explain that the 10 percent cut for all of Latin America is because the purchase of helicopter and other heavy equipment for Mexico's Mérida Initiative investments were in the previous year's budget and therefore the program will enter a less expensive phase in 2011.[33] Skeptics, however, argue that Latin America has become "irrelevant" to the Obama administration in light of its preoccupation with the Persian Gulf region.[34] In addition, Washington's meager involvement in gang prevention and rehabilitation programs in Honduras, Guatemala, and El Salvador—mainly scattered efforts to strengthen school systems, departments of education, faculty, and a few specific youth violence prevention projects—have done little to alter the gang situation in the region.[35] The 2007 Mérida Initiative and the U.S. Strategy to Combat Criminal Gangs from Central America and Mexico, however, seem to represent a welcome change to U.S. policies, at least on paper, as they provide for a holistic and balanced approach (funds, law enforcement, deterrence, and rehabilitation) to the gang issue.

Another problem is that although no critic can deny the United States' willingness and interest in helping Central American states fight gangs, the impact of U.S. policies and initiatives on the evolution of the gang phenomenon in Central America is hard to quantify to date. On the one hand, diplomatic initiatives seem only to perpetuate meetings for the sake of more meetings. Whether or not they have affected gang evolution in the region in any way is hard to tell because there is not sufficient reliable evidence. On the other hand, although operational cooperation (including intelligence and information sharing) has had scattered success, and U.S. support for the professionalization of law enforcement in Central American countries has improved, it is too early to draw any conclusion on their effectiveness in denting the hemisphere's gang problem, again due to insufficient and unreliable information. Although the FBI and El Salvador's PNC praise recent improvements in the flow of information between the two countries[36] and TAG's success in hindering gang development, neither agency would provide the present author with actual data on deterrence.[37]

There are many other important questions that would need to be answered in order to draw realistic conclusions about the effectiveness of U.S. policy. For instance, how did these efforts affect the level of corruption among police officers? Are local governments continuing to professionalize their law enforcement agencies (for example, with incentives to fight corruption)? How have U.S. assistance and cooperation altered the criminal case buildup in Central American countries, if at all? Have they done anything to improve the weaknesses in the countries' prison systems, which are partly responsible for gang development in the region? What have they done to help gang prevention and rehabilitation? Has TAG influenced gang reduction in other countries, apart from El Salvador? These effects are not obvious.

U.S. Deportation Policies and Their (Lack of) Impact on Central America's Gang Problem

The sharp increase in deportations of MS-13 and 18th Street gang members from the United States, primarily to Honduras and El Salvador starting in the mid-1990s, propagated the belief throughout the region that the United States has inundated Central America with criminals who brought with them both a Los Angeles gang lifestyle and syndicate-like criminal techniques they learned in U.S. prisons. These U.S.-trained criminals are also said to be recruiting new members from among local youths, thus overwhelming law enforcement and escalating regional insecurity and instability. Critics from both the United States and Central America also contend that deportations have helped perpetuate a revolving door of gang members who move back and forth between north and south, bringing other illegal immigrants, including more gang members, to the

United States through Mexican smuggling routes, hence negatively affecting everyone's gang problems.[38] A direct proportionality between U.S. deportations and the growth of gang violence in Central America, however, is not as apparent as it may look from the above discussion.

The main reason for this inconclusiveness is a lack of reliable data on gang affiliation and violence (in particular related to deportees). A possible explanation (and yet another criticism of U.S. deportation policies) is that, up until 2007, U.S. agencies did not inform the receiving Central American governments about the criminal backgrounds of the deportees. At the other end (in what many critics consider to be a consequence of past failures to provide proper documentation on deportees), local Central American judicial and prison systems are unable to monitor deportees. At times, the Central American nations did not even know that the people being returned to their native countries were gang members. Much of the existing information on gangs is thus anecdotal, collected by researchers or the media from either gangsters themselves or law enforcement officers, neither of whom is always a credible source of information. Gang members would use the media to sell their story as either victims of U.S. policies or heroes of their countless successful illegal entries into the United States. By the same token, accounts by various law enforcement officials who claim that U.S. deportation policies have flooded Central America and the United States with gang violence also need to be more closely examined: how can these officials know the number of deported gang members if, first, they also blame the United States for not sharing evidence of gang membership; second, local governments have no idea how many deportees are coming back (besides not knowing the reasons for their deportation); and third, Central American law enforcement agencies have no indigenous database on gangs and gang violence, nor a proper methodology for identifying gangs and relating them to deportees?[39] Law enforcement officers may also deliberately inflate the seriousness of the gang problem to justify their raison d'être and to acquire more resources.

To complicate matters further, many accounts seem to conflate the presence of gangs with violence and deportees, without differentiating among the three. Just because violence increased in one country after receiving U.S. deportees, this does not automatically mean the increase is due to deportations or represents gang violence, nor does the illegal return of deportees to the United States directly link them to U.S. gang violence. And just because young people commit crimes in countries that have a gang problem, this does not mean that they must be gang members or deportees. According to a Congressional Research Service report of December 2009, despite the high numbers of deportees repatriated to Mexico, Honduras, Guatemala, and El Salvador—the four Latin American countries reporting the worst gang violence—the percentage of criminal deportees going to these countries was lower than that for other top receiving countries.[40] Arguably, if neither crime nor gang membership/affiliation are the main reasons for deportations from the United States, it follows that most deportees are not involved in any criminal or gang activities after repatriation. Likewise, it is plausible that the majority of deportees who try to get back into the United States want to start a new life there that does not necessarily involve crime or gang membership or affiliation; thus their only criminal activity is entering illegally, and not spreading violence.

While the literature and media reports are rife with anecdotal information about the correlation between gangs and deportees and tend to exaggerate the threat posed by gangs in Central America, there is not enough in-depth research on gang activities in the region to enable one to conclude that deportees from the United States are the main vectors for gang violence. A 2007 study conducted by the United Nations Office on Drugs and Crime questions the allegations that deportations and deportees are the main sources for the gang problem in Central America, arguing that while "there is no denying the effect gang culture from the United States has had on Central America's *maras* . . . more research is required to determine the extent to which deportees become involved in crime on their return."[41] The study further contends that even though Central American gangs "represent a source of criminality, they do not appear to be responsible for a particularly disproportionate share of the murders in the countries where they predominate."[42] For example, the former security minister of Honduras accused the *maras* of the majority of crimes in that country, without any evidence from the Honduran police; moreover, less than 5 percent of all crimes in Honduras are committed by individuals under eighteen years of age (as are most gang members). Also, while Salvadoran officials attribute 60 percent of the yearly murders in their country to gangs, there is no evidence to support these allegations; likewise, the regions in Guatemala that have the highest murder rates have an infinitesimal gang presence.[43] Officials typically make these claims largely for political reasons, which are examined at length in the chapters on El Salvador, Guatemala, and Honduras (Chapters 2–4) in this book.

The Mérida Initiative: Good Intentions, Yet to Be Realized

The Mérida Initiative, signed in 2007 and funded in 2008, has received a warm welcome across North and Central America. Many view the initiative as the "first big effort" by the United States to fight gangs in Mexico and Central America.[44] Yet, despite all its good intentions, the initiative has yet to accomplish its objectives.

To begin with, progress has been difficult and slow; the program is still in the initial phases of execution. The first problem has been an ongoing dispute among relevant agencies in Washington over the need for balancing security and law enforcement capabilities with funding for institution building. There is also disagreement over what would be the most suitable types and levels of security assistance for the region, an argument that actually resulted in the Congress approving a budget increase for prevention and economic and social development programs.[45] The second setback is the difficulty of tracing and accounting for Mérida funds, given that the DoS lacks a consolidated database, and each agency uses its own method to track funds.[46] Third is the delay in the availability and delivery of funds and programs. The DoS has been slow to submit the mandatory reports to Congress prior to the obligation of any Mérida funds, the program has run into the usual administrative and bureaucratic obstacles, and the initiative has suffered from an initial lack of institutional capacity within both the beneficiary governments and the responsible U.S. agencies.[47]

Not only do equipment and programs already obligated under Mérida have yet to be delivered, but the U.S. government is unable to anticipate when the majority of Mérida assistance will actually be available. So far, Mexico has been the beneficiary of the majority of assistance, having received approximately $100 million in equipment by March 2010.[48] The Mérida-recipient countries in Central America, by contrast, have received very little equipment and training to date.[49] And while a Congressional report finds that 42 percent of the training projects (e.g., law enforcement professionalization and continuing education, prison reform, prosecutorial capacity building, and human rights training) achieved "significant progress" in implementation by mid-November 2009,[50] the rest have been slow to show results. The fourth hurdle, one that is related to the previous issue, is weak interagency cooperation, due to persistent confusion, a general lack of coordination, and turf battles among the various U.S. agencies involved in the implementation of the initiative.[51] Since the initiative remains at an early stage of implementation, any effects on gang problems in the region are yet to be noticed.

Conclusion

This chapter has looked at the evolution of the United States' anti-gang involvement in Central America. It also has attempted to identify indicators of the U.S. impact on the evolution of gang activity in the region. Since the early 1990s, when concerns over gang violence and crime mounted in the United States, and especially during the 2000s, when Washington acknowledged the gang threat in several Central American countries, the United States has invested political, law enforcement, and financial capital in the regional fight against gangs. At a minimum the U.S. involvement has had sporadic success in a few locations in the region. Indeed, certain U.S. funding and assistance programs and initiatives (especially the 2007 Mérida Initiative and the Anti-Gang Strategy) that were aimed at strengthening the effectiveness of law enforcement agencies in Honduras, Guatemala, and El Salvador and consolidating democratic institutions in the region have provided governments with the theoretical and practical "democratic" tool kit to avert and counter gangs, while specific joint law enforcement operations have occasionally resulted in successful gang-related raids and imprisonments. But the overall effects on gang evolution in the region are fairly inconspicuous so far, mainly due to unreliable data. Likewise, with regard to deportations, although the United States has been excoriated for flooding Central America with gang members and gang-related crime and violence, it is virtually impossible to verify these allegations. At most, U.S. deportations may have slightly worsened the problem, but they are not the main reason Central American countries have a gang problem.

The Western Hemisphere's gang problem has been described as "long-term, and one for which there are no magic solutions."[52] Like other kinds of crime or natural disasters, it "can be reduced but never eliminated."[53] This is a truism for Central America, given the region's violent history, deeply ingrained official corruption, and chronic poverty. As is the case for combating crime or preparing for natural disasters, both of which require unremitting preparation and vigilance, fighting gangs is also an endless anticipative, strategic, and preparative process, aimed at minimizing to the degree possible the levels of violence, crime, and loss of life and property. The United States, as exemplified in the case of Los Angeles in this book, is a telling example. Despite devoting considerable resources toward preventing and hindering domestic gang expansion and gang-related crime and violence, U.S. domestic policies have succeeded in some states and counties, without eradicating the problem throughout the country. Thus, if the United States, which has strong and effective democratic institutions, has not been able to solve its own gang problem, how can it be expected to do so in Central America, a region plagued with ineffectual state institutions?

Arguably, U.S. anti-gang assistance for Honduras, Guatemala, and El Salvador will continue and, in line with the holistic approach recommended by many gang analysts and envisioned by the 2007 Mérida Initiative and the Anti-Gang Strategy, may possibly be more effective in minimizing the gang threat in Central America. But unless more accurate and reliable data and studies become available on gangs, violence, crime, and the control of deportees, and unless the countries receiving U.S. aid in the region become more engaged in the fight against gangs, it will still be difficult to prove or disprove the effectiveness of U.S. policies.

Conclusion: The Dilemma of Fighting Gangs in New Democracies

THOMAS BRUNEAU AND LUCÍA DAMMERT

The *maras* are still an elusive phenomenon in the Americas. Although youth violence is an increasing problem throughout the region, the MS-13 and 18th Street, whether in the United States or Central America, are substantially different from other street gangs in their levels of organization, violence, and adaptability. Although there is an increasing academic interest in this subject, most evidence is still unclear, and theories about their current activities, organizational structure, and number of members cannot be empirically contrasted. From neighborhood *clicas* to prison gangs and transnational smuggling operations, these gangs permeate Honduran, Salvadoran, and Guatemalan society to the degree that some believe they pose a threat to national security by undermining the ability of these states to govern, and to control their borders and even some barrios of their capitals. In several areas, such as the barrios of Tegucigalpa, and on public transportation in San Salvador and Guatemala City, *maras* have brought society to armed conflict as police and army units battle against gang members who are far more ruthless, and may even be better equipped, than they are. So far, no one has found an effective way to bring this phenomenon under control or to stem the flow of young people into the *maras'* ranks.

In the course of several research trips to Central America over the course of a decade, the authors were asked again and again to find an answer to the *maras* and their increasing contribution to the endemic violence and stunning homicide rates in El Salvador, Guatemala, and Honduras. That, however, was never the book's purpose, nor do the authors possess any unique insights that might lead to a solution. The dire gang situation in Los Angeles, California, where one of our coeditors was born, is humbling; even one of the wealthiest cities in one of the wealthiest U.S.

states cannot find a solution to the *mara* problem. And in Salinas, California, where there are an estimated 3,500 gang members, the record twenty-nine homicides in 2009 were all judged to be gang-related. If, however, policy makers in Central America and elsewhere are to have any hope of finding a solution or, more likely, some part of a solution to the challenge *maras* pose to Central American security, they must first develop an understanding of this very complex phenomenon that is based in fact, not emotions or political expedience. The tremendous amount that has been written in the popular media and some specialized journals on the *maras*, we believe, communicates little credible information. Even some scholarly venues for serious and objective analysis of this dynamic phenomenon have been overtaken by sensationalism on the one hand and a tendency to ideologically biased reporting on the other.

Paradoxically, the image of gang members as cruel and violent is not only portrayed in media and political discourses but also actively presented as such by gang members. The use of violence within the *mara* against its members at different points in the affiliation process, as well as the continuous fights among gangs for territorial control, has helped create a myth about the *marero*. Recent literature cited in this book has shown that although there is some truth in that perception, there are also many elements of fictional discourse in the portrayals of extreme use of violence.

Even in the United States, birthplace of the *maras*, where gang membership is now being handed down to the second and third generations, law enforcement experts like Al Valdez have something of a monopoly on gathering information about gangs and publishing analyses and policy recommendations. It is time for political scientists and scholars, such as the group gathered for this book, to build on the foundation laid by these frontline sources, by developing reliable empirical data and applying sound methodologies to its analysis. The goal of this book therefore has been to provide solid information and analysis that can serve as a baseline of knowledge about the *maras* and their effect on security in Central America.

While deportations of gang members from the United States to Central America have done much to spread the California *mara* lifestyle in the region, research for this book has made clear that street gangs were a well-established feature of the large cities of Central America long before the deportations began. When members of Mara Salvatrucha and the 18th Street Gang did begin to arrive, their extraordinarily violent lifestyle found fertile ground in the impoverished *barrios* of Central America's cities, where it took quick root. A revolving door of reentry and redeportation has since facilitated the establishment of transnational organizational structures and illicit business operations. With the *maras* now a hemisphere-wide and entrenched reality, the tendency of Central American governments to scapegoat the United States for their spread, and vice versa, serves only to distract from the serious discussion of cause and effect that must take place within each society.

Some authors in the United States have been quick to characterize the *maras* as insurgent organizations.[1] Again, by blowing up the image of these gangs into an international threat that requires an international military response, these societies are avoiding the hard work of dealing with the endemic poverty, violence, and vastly lucrative internal and external drug trade that nurture the *maras*—not to mention the fast-growing illegal immigration business built around weak government institutions, difficult borders, and a population that believes that migration to the United States will solve most of its problems.

While there is no evidence to link the *maras* to international terrorism, the issue of *maras* as a form of organized crime is somewhat less clear. The *maras*, and for that matter other street gangs in Central America, can be seen as a form of organized crime not because they are involved in drug trafficking—and some of them certainly are, even in Nicaragua—but first and foremost because they have been able to develop complex networks of protection rackets that allow them to survive as groups. Indeed, *maras* have evolved to become sophisticated and hierarchical organizations that carry out a variety of criminal activities. However, the key factor of these activities nowadays revolves around what is called *la renta*—namely, extortions. According to several sources, Central American gangs obtain most of their money by extorting the population. José Miguel Cruz, in his chapter, goes into some detail on this issue, and Bruneau, in his interviews in El Salvador and Honduras in March 2008 and July 2008, respectively, was informed by police authorities that this is indeed the case. *La renta* is the "bread and butter" of the gangs. *Maras* in El Salvador, Guatemala, and Honduras have been able to develop economies in which the members of the gang demand money from someone in return for protection against any threat or to avoid any harm perpetrated by the same members of the group.

In view of the security challenges posed by the *maras*, the issue is not whether anyone is doing anything but whether what they are doing entails a well-thought-out and effective use of scarce resources. Cris Matei details the enormous burst of anti-gang activity that took place within the executive branch of the U.S. government starting in about 2003, particularly with regard to controlling the movement of *mareros* between Central America and the United States. The FBI and the Department of Homeland Security created layers of task forces, investigative units, and joint training and operations programs, while Congress passed legislation regarding mandatory prison terms and the easing of restrictions on deportations. Currently, the Department of Defense, aside from the U.S. Navy's extensive drug interdiction program, administers the Mérida Initiative to boost law enforcement for Mexico, while USAID is limited to writing reports and making suggestions to the governments of Central America concerning prevention and rehabilitation. What Matei could not determine with any certainty was whether this enormous outpouring of money and effort is actually having any positive effect on the gang problem in Central America or in the United States. Indeed, follow-up communications with various agencies did not yield any hard data. In all cases there was at most a pro forma response. What Matei has been able to discover from investigation of the most recent policy statements is that the United States is increasing the quantity of resources, in terms of both funding and personnel, that are focused against the gang phenomenon. It remains all but impossible, however, to assess the impact of these expanding programs.

We have included a chapter in this volume on the use of intelligence in fighting against the gangs. Similar to our view that some objective knowledge is better than none in developing countergang strategies, we believe that better police and strategic intelligence is a basic requirement in formulating effective policies. There are already many bilateral and regional programs. Bilateral networking at the street level between agencies and departments is a good start, but the Americas need a multilateral mechanism for collating, analyzing, and disseminating gang-related intelligence. A Central American law enforcement intelligence center could serve as the hub for such international cooperation. The U.S. National Gang Intelligence Center, in tandem with the Department of Homeland Security, the Department of Justice, and the International Law Enforcement Academy (ILEA), could send a small contingent of advisers to help the Central American nations establish a regional, international gang intelligence fusion center. This center would combine attributes of the National Gang Intelligence Center, with its expertise in street gang intelligence analysis, and the DHS-sponsored state and local fusion centers (of which there are currently seventy-two in the United States) that assess all-crimes and all-hazards information in a regional, collaborative enterprise. A regional center would then orchestrate the strategic counter-gang intelligence effort. The United States and El Salvador already manage a baseline international training program. The International Training and Technical Assistance division of the U.S. Federal Law Enforcement Training Center has two ILEA campus programs at ILEA San Salvador, one in English and one in Spanish. This initiative could be further expanded. Considering the major infusion of resources, much more could be done to improve intelligence collection and fusion in the region to counter the gang phenomenon. Parallel to that process, police institutions in Central America could undergo a new phase of reforms centered on increasing transparency and accountability, limiting corruption, and consolidating police specialization. Regarding the consolidation of police specialization, an emphasis on strategic intelligence is key to increasing the effectiveness of policing strategies, especially those linked to investigative capabilities, since impunity of officials is alarmingly high in those countries.

The illegal drug trade within Latin America and between Latin America and the United States—involving mostly cocaine and marijuana and, increasingly, methamphetamine—has become a major funding stream for the Central American *maras*, some of which work in tandem with drug cartels to move the contraband along transit routes through Central America to Mexico and across the U.S. border. The *maras* also act as major distributors once the drugs are in the United States, controlling sales all the way down to the *clicas* at the street level. In the process, the *maras* enforce their own form of "market discipline," through the violent elimination of rivals and internal dissent. As some contributors to this book have pointed out, there is increasing evidence that the *maras* are branching out into arms and human smuggling as well. MS-13, the more pervasive of the two *maras*, has evolved to the point that some elements of it more closely resemble organized crime syndicates than street gangs. Methods used to combat the Mafia are not likely to be effective against MS-13, however, even within the United States, because unlike the Mafia, the gang also retains its relatively anarchical street base and symbiotic ties to prison gangs. Also, as Miguel Cruz points out in his overview chapter, *maras* respond to threats of violence or attacks by increasing group cohesion and strengthening their organization.

Maybe the only thing we can say with certainty about the gang problem in Central America is that broadly punitive *mano dura*–type policies do nothing to lessen the impact the *maras* are having on local, regional, or national security. The three case studies by Sonja Wolf, Elin Ranum,

and Joanna Mateo (Chapters 2–4) demonstrate clearly that these policies of rounding up young people indiscriminately and throwing them
into prison with hardened gang members not only failed to improve the
safety of citizens but actually helped the gangs organize and recruit. Two
other unintended effects came directly from these actions: youths who
had been treated so cavalierly by their government became alienated and
more susceptible to the enticements of *el vacil* (the gang lifestyle), while
the abysmal percentage of successful prosecutions that resulted from the
mass incarcerations only highlighted the underlying weaknesses of state
institutions.

Sonja Wolf lays much blame for El Salvador's burgeoning *maras* on the
government's tacit willingness to use extrajudicial means, such as armed
civilian militias, against the gangs and to violate its citizens' civil rights
when making mass arrests based on gang profiling. These are symptoms
of a pervasive culture of violence, which she analyzes extensively in Chapter 2, and official impunity that remains in the wake of Central America's
civil wars. As Mauricio Rubio forcefully maintains in Chapter 8, they
are also symptoms of weak and corrupt civil institutions controlled by
an elite class who use those institutions to maintain their own positions
of privilege. To make matters worse, once the Salvadoran government
came under fire for its harsh policies, it made a great show of passing
legislation that emphasized prevention and rehabilitation, but then failed
to adequately fund the programs or give them the political support they
needed to make a difference in the lives of the young people for whom
they ostensibly were intended. While many were hopeful of a new and
enlightened policy when the FMLN government of President Mauricio
Funes came into power in El Salvador in the spring of 2009, its policies
have been no more innovative or successful than the center-right ARENA
administrations. Indeed, El Salvador experienced a three-day stoppage
of public transportation in 2010 due to the *maras* and a subsequent mass
mobilization of the armed forces into the streets in support of the PNC.
Although El Salvador is the example being used here, these fundamental
problems of law and governance have played out in more or less the same
way in Honduras and Guatemala. Only Nicaragua, as has been described
at length by José Luis Rocha and José Miguel Cruz in chapters 5 and 7,
managed to avoid these traps by instituting demobilization and disarmament programs immediately after the end of its civil war and by eschewing
the *mano dura*.

The *maras* must be dealt with in terms of both supply and demand.
In other words, it is never going to be enough to combat them only with

the tools of law enforcement, which often leads to a spiral of escalating violence; policy makers must put at least as much effort into preventing youths from joining gangs in the first place, through education and employment, and helping those who want to leave the gang by assisting with their safety, rehabilitation, and reintegration into civil society. These kinds of solutions are time-consuming, difficult to set up, and very costly, and as several contributors noted, they do not garner the splashy headlines that politicians, police officials, and frightened citizens crave, but in the long run they are likely to be the most effective and resource-efficient means to undermine the strength of the gangs. It can be discouraging to note that even in the United States—with its enormous resources, strong independent judiciary, and embedded democratic values—resources for gang prevention and rehabilitation take a distant second place to law enforcement and imprisonment. The situation is far worse in Central American countries, where a history of violently repressive governments and long civil conflicts has left a legacy of trauma, fear, and the acceptance of extrajudicial means to solve civic problems.

Readers of this volume will have noted that every contributor, no matter where he or she has focused attention, comes back to the need to address the problem on the streets, at the level of the children and youths who find themselves trying to survive in violent, impoverished circumstances without access to any other tangible opportunities. This is almost as true in Los Angeles as it is in Tegucigalpa. There is no doubt that *maras* pose a serious threat to societies throughout North and Central America. The means to end that threat must come from across the range of civil society's actors and institutions.

Notes

Unless otherwise indicated, translations of quotations are by the author of that section or chapter.

Introduction

1. The 2008 homicide rates were assembled from data from various sources provided by José Miguel Cruz.

2. Charles Steward, "Member of Salvadoran Gang MS-13 Caught Here Last Week (Bee County, Texas)," *Bee-Picayune*, reprinted on *Free Republic* (blog), 3 July 2005, http://www.freerepublic.com/focus/f-news/1435817/posts.

3. John P. Sullivan, "Transnational Gangs: The Impact of Third Generation Gangs in Central America," *Air and Space Power Journal* (1 July 2008).

4. For short, well-documented reports on the gangs, see Clare Ribando Seelke, *Gangs in Central America* (Congressional Research Service [CRS] Report for Congress, RL341112, updated 11 January 2008); and Celinda Franco, *The MS-13 and 18th Street Gangs: Emerging Transnational Gang Threats?* (CRS Report for Congress, RL34233, updated 30 January 2008).

5. Franco, *MS-13 and 18th Street Gangs*, 4–6.

6. Sullivan, "Transnational Gangs."

7. The seven countries of Central America are, from north to south, Belize, Guatemala, Honduras, El Salvador, Nicaragua, Costa Rica, and Panama.

8. For one of the best analyses of "the great Central American wars" and their aftermath, see Ralph Lee Woodward, *Central America: A Nation Divided* (1976; New York: Oxford University Press, 1999).

9. By far the best book on this is Cynthia J. Arnson, ed., *Comparative Peace Processes in Latin America* (Palo Alto, CA: Stanford University Press, 1999).

10. Julissa Gomez-Granger, *Latin America and the Caribbean: Fact Sheet on Economic and Social Indicators*, CRS Report for Congress, RS22657, 2 March 2009.

11. United Nations Development Programme (UNDP), *UN Human Development Indices: A Statistical Update 2008*, http://hdr.undp.org/en/statistics/. The

full Human Development Reports going back to 1990 are available as PDF files at http://hdr.undp.org/en/reports/. Note that earlier reports used different criteria and a reverse ranking system that gave the least developed countries lower numbers, making multidecade comparisons difficult.

12. Theodore Leggett, *Crime and Development in Central America: Caught in the Crossfire* (United Nations Office on Drugs and Crime [UNODC], May 2007).

13. Ibid., 25.

14. Michael Shifter, "Latin America's Drug Problem," *Current History* 106, no. 697 (February 2007): 58–63.

15. Leggett, *Crime and Development in Central America*, 12.

16. Ibid.

17. Ibid., 29.

18. Ibid., 41.

19. Ibid., 34.

20. Heidrun Zinecker, *From Exodus to Exitus: Causes of Post-war Violence in El Salvador*, PRIF Reports, no. 80 (Frankfurt: Peace Research Institute Frankfurt, 2007).

21. Author's interview with Dr. Humberto Posada of the PNC, San Salvador, El Salvador, 9 July 2008.

22. These numbers are based on the author's interviews with academic experts, members of nongovernmental organizations (NGOs), and government officials in Tegucigalpa, Honduras, in August 2008, and San Salvador, El Salvador, in March 2009.

23. Douglas A. Kincaid, "Demilitarization and Security in El Salvador and Guatemala: Convergences of Success and Crisis," *Journal of Interamerican Studies and World Affairs* 42, no. 4 (Winter 2000): 39–58.

24. Ibid.

25. In the spring of 2010 the issue of age and incarceration was under political debate, and El Salvador's Congress raised the minimum age to fifteen years on 24 March. It remains to be approved or vetoed by President Mauricio Funes.

26. For a review of the various legislation, see Seelke, *Gangs in Central America*, 7–10.

27. In addition to various interviews over the years with PNC and military officers, I have benefited from an updated review with Colonel Osdiel Castro, of the Salvadoran Army, in San Salvador on 26 March 2009. Castro has worked extensively with the PNC in various parts of the country over several years.

28. Freddy Cuevas, "Ejército a las calles en Honduras," Associated Press, 5 March 2008.

29. Author's interviews with Dr. Humberto Posada, San Salvador, El Salvador, 24 March 2009. This situation arose from the assassination of three Salvadoran legislators in Guatemala on 21 February 2007 and the subsequent assassination, in a maximum-security prison in Guatemala, of the assassins. The lesson taken by outsiders was that there is total impunity for extrajudicial murders in Guatemala.

30. Author's interview with Ismael Rodríguez Batres, 27 March 2009.

31. Javier Monterroso Castillo, *Investigación criminal: Estudio comparativo y propuesta de un modelo de policía de investigación en Guatemala* (Guatemala City:

Instituto de Estudios Comparados en Ciencias Penales de Guatemala, 2007), 73, 158.

32. In addition to the sources cited for table 1.2, see Gustavo Sánchez Velásquez, *Maras, pandillas y desviación social* (Buenos Aires: Editora Dunken, 2008).

33. Author's meeting with U.S. government official in charge of security in Tegucigalpa, Honduras, 30 July 2008.

Chapter 1

1. Al Valdez, *Gangs: A Guide to Understanding Street Gangs* (San Clemente, CA: Law Tech Publishing, 2005).

2. John P. Sullivan, "Maras Morphing: Revisiting Third Generation Gangs," *Global Crime* 7, no. 3 (August–November 2006): 487–504.

3. Cheryl Maxson, "Gang Members on the Move," *Juvenile Justice Bulletin* (Office of Juvenile Justice and Delinquency Prevention, U.S. Department of Justice, Washington, DC), October 1998.

4. Viki L. Ruiz, "South by Southwest: Mexican Americans and Segregated Schooling, 1900–1950," *OAH Magazine of History* (Organization of American Historians) 15 (Winter 2001), http://www.oah.org/pubs/magazine/deseg/ruiz.html.

5. Al Valdez, "California's Most Violent Export," *Streetgangs.com*, 2000, http://www.streetgangs.com/topics/2002/18thexport.html.

6. Al Valdez, "Transnational Gangs," Center for Hemispheric Policy, University of Miami, Miami, 2008.

7. Ibid.

8. See, for example, Richard Valdemar, "Roots of Evil," *Police*, 10 April 2009, http://www.policemag.com/Blog/Gangs/Story/2009/04/Roots-of-Evil.aspx. There are many explanations for the name, but it seems to be based in Salvadoran slang: the *marabunta* is a fierce Central American species of ant; "*salva*" signifies El Salvador; and "*trucha*" means "truthful" or "alert." Charles Steward, "Member of Salvadoran Gang MS-13 Caught Here Last Week (Bee County, Texas)," *Bee-Picayune*, reprinted on *Free Republic* (blog), 3 July 2005, http://www.freerepublic.com/focus/f-news/1435817/posts.

9. Author's interview with Long Nguyen, Orange County district attorney investigator, Santa Ana, CA, June 2001; author's interview with Alex Sánchez, president of Homies Unidos, at symposium on Youth and Transnational Policy, University of California, Irvine, 8 February 2008.

10. Nguyen, interview, 2001.

11. Valdez, *Gangs: A Guide*.

12. Gang Reporting, Evaluation, and Tracking (GREAT), *Summary Report 1988: California* (GREAT, 1988), 2–8. GREAT was the early version of CalGang, the California gang database.

13. GREAT, *Summary Report 1991: California* (GREAT, 1991), 4–10.

14. "Crips," East Coast Gang Investigators Association website, www.gripe4rkids.org.

15. Rodney King is an African American man whose near-fatal beating in 1991 by several white L.A. police officers was captured on videotape by a by-

stander. The trial of four officers ended in acquittal for three by a jury that included no African Americans, sparking massive race riots in L.A. See Lou Cannon, *Official Negligence: How Rodney King and the Riots Changed Los Angeles and the LAPD* (Denver: Westview Press, 1999).

16. Author's interview with Richard Valdemar, sergeant (retired), Los Angeles County Sheriff's Department, Los Angeles, 1996.

17. Michael Montgomery, "Gangster Reveals Mexican Mafia Secrets," part 1, *All Things Considered*, National Public Radio, 6 September 2008.

18. "Mexican Mafia," *Drugs and Gangs Profile Bulletin* (National Drug Intelligence Center, U.S. Department of Justice), July 2003, 3.

19. Author's interview with Richard Valdemar, Fullerton, CA, July 1995.

20. Chris Blatchford, *The Black Hand: The Bloody Rise and Redemption of "Boxer" Enríquez, a Mexican Mob Killer* (New York: HarperCollins, 2008).

21. Valdemar, interview, 1996.

22. Tom Diaz, *No Boundaries: Transnational Latino Gangs and American Law Enforcement* (Ann Arbor: University of Michigan Press, 2009), 129–131.

23. Montgomery, "Gangster Reveals Mexican Mafia Secrets."

24. Ibid.

25. Author's interview with Wes McBride, president of California Gang Investigators Association, Huntington Beach, CA, February 1993.

26. Author's interview with Joe Guzman, sergeant (retired), Los Angeles County Sheriff's Department, Los Angeles, April 1992.

27. Nguyen, interview, 2001.

28. Chuck Schoville, *Sureños 2008: A Special Report* (Phoenix, AZ: Rocky Mountain Information Network, 2008).

29. "Markers" that investigators use to trace the origins and affiliations of Sureño and would-be Sureño cliques include types and colors of clothing; gang-specific hand signals, tattoos, and graffiti; and particular initiation practices. Celinda Franco, *The MS-13 and 18th Street Gangs: Emerging Transnational Gang Threats?* (Congressional Research Service [CRS] Report for Congress, RL34233, updated 30 January 2008), n. 12.

30. Federico Breve, "The Maras—A Menace to the Americas," *Military Review* (July–August 2007): 88–95.

31. Franco, *MS-13 and 18th Street Gangs*, 6.

32. Clair Ribando Seelke, *Gangs in Central America* (CRS Report for Congress, RL341112, updated 11 January 2008).

33. Author's interview with Wes McBride, president of California Gang Investigators Association, Anaheim, CA, 1996.

34. GREAT, *Summary Report 1995: California* (GREAT, 1995): 3–9.

35. Ibid.

36. Valdez, *Gangs: A Guide*, 113–120. See California Penal Code 186.20, known as the California Street Terrorism Enforcement and Prevention Act, passed in 1988, and subsequent legislation that further defined and expanded its provisions (http://www.gangtaskforce.org/gtf3.htm).

37. GREAT, *Summary Report 1997: California* (GREAT, 1997).

38. Salinas, California, with a population of 143,640 (as of 2008), is a prime example. Located near the Central California coast, this farming town, with its

deep, historically Mexican roots and a highly mobile seasonal farmworker population, is a nexus for the Norteño-Sureño rivalry. The county district attorney's office estimates there are more than 3,000 people "associated" with gangs in the area, and it documents more than 500 "gang-related incidents" a year, ranging from homicides, drive-by shootings, and robberies to police reports of gang-related conduct. Office of the District Attorney for Monterey County website, http://www.co.monterey.ca.us/da/gang.htm.

39. Blatchford, *Black Hand*, 149–161.
40. Ibid.
41. John Feere and Jessica Vaughan, *Taking Back the Streets: ICE and Local Law Enforcement Target Immigrant Gangs* (Washington, DC: Center for Immigration Studies, September 2008), 1–6, http://www.cis.org/ImmigrantGangs.
42. National Gang Intelligence Center, *National Gang Threat Assessment 2009*, product no. 2009-M0335-001 (Washington, DC: National Gang Intelligence Center, January 2009), 6.
43. Ibid., 10–11.
44. Valdez, *Gangs: A Guide*, 435–446.
45. David DeCastillo, Los Angeles Police Department gang officer, interview on Fox News special report, 12 June 2000.
46. Al Valdez, *Gangs across America* (San Clemente, CA: Law Tech Publishing, 2007), 469–484.
47. Ibid.
48. Ibid.
49. Franco, *MS-13 and 18th Street Gangs*, 4–6; John P. Sullivan, "Transnational Gangs: The Impact of Third Generation Gangs in Central America," *Air and Space Power Journal* (1 July 2008).
50. Sullivan, "Transnational Gangs," 5–6.
51. Franco, *MS-13 and 18th Street Gangs*, 7.
52. Edward DeVelasco and Al Valdez, remarks at anti-gang training, Kansas City, Mo., June 2006.
53. Valdez, "Transnational Gangs."
54. Franco, *MS-13 and 18th Street Gangs*, 4–6. Also see the FBI's website section on gangs: http://www.fbi.gov/about-us/investigate/vc_majorthefts/gangs.
55. Maxson, "Gang Members on the Move," 1–4.
56. National Drug Intelligence Center (NDIC), *National Street Gang Survey Report—1998* (Johnstown, PA: National Drug Intelligence Center, 1998).
57. Mary Jordan, "People Smuggling Now Big Business in Mexico," *Washington Post*, 17 May 2001.
58. Feere and Vaughan, *Taking Back the Streets*.
59. Ibid.
60. Herbert Covey, *Street Gangs throughout the World* (Springfield, IL: Charles C. Thomas, 2003).
61. Max Manwaring, *A Contemporary Challenge to State Sovereignty: Gangs and Other Illicit Transnational Criminal Organizations in Central America, El Salvador, Mexico, Jamaica, and Brazil* (Carlisle, PA: Strategic Studies Institute, U.S. Army War College, December 2007).
62. Sullivan, "Maras Morphing."

63. United Nations Office on Drugs and Crime (UNODC), "Executive Summary," in *World Drug Report 2007* (New York: UNODC, 2007), 7–21, http://www.unodc.org/unodc/en/data-and-analysis/WDR-2007.html.

64. National Drug Intelligence Center (NDIC), "Executive Summary," in *National Drug Threat Assessment 2007* (Johnston, PA: NDIC, October 2006), 1–4, 9–34.

65. National Alliance of Gang Investigators Associations, "Executive Summary," in *2005 National Gang Threat Assessment* (Washington, DC: U.S. Department of Justice, Bureau of Justice Assistance, 2005), v–vi. Also see the association's website at http://www.nagia.org.

66. Andrew Papachristos, "Gang World," *Foreign Policy* 147 (March–April 2005): 2–7.

67. Manwaring, *Contemporary Challenge*.

Chapter 2

1. "El país denuncia pandillas en la ONU," *El Diario de Hoy*, 26 September 2007.

2. "Ejército del bajo mundo," *El Diario de Hoy*, 22 August 2003.

3. "FARC está detrás de maras," *El Diario de Hoy*, 16 June 2004; "La MS y la 18 se disputan la venta de droga," *El Diario de Hoy*, 18 June 2004; "Sicarios y control de ventas de crack," *El Diario de Hoy*, 18 January 2005.

4. "Afinan plan para fichar a pandilleros deportados," *El Diario de Hoy*, 23 February 2005.

5. "Prometen capturar a descuartizadores," *El Diario de Hoy*, 8 May 2006.

6. "PNC sin estadísticas claras de pandillas," *La Prensa Gráfica*, 15 October 2007, http://archive.laprensa.com.sv/20071016/dpt15/noticias/15102007/895332.asp; "FGR: 'Homicidios son producto de pandillas,'" *La Prensa Gráfica*, 3 September 2008, http://archive.laprensa.com.sv/20080903/lodeldia/20080903/17764.asp.

7. The data in this section come from Sandra Argueta, Gisela Caminos, Margarita Mancía, and María de Los Ángeles Salgado, "Diagnóstico sobre los grupos llamados 'maras' en San Salvador: Factores psicosociales que prevalecen en los jóvenes que los integran" (bachelor's thesis, Universidad Centroamericana "José Simeón Cañas" de El Salvador, San Salvador, 1991).

8. Ibid., 195–198.

9. Marcela Smutt and Jenny Lissette E. Miranda, *El fenómeno de las pandillas en El Salvador* (San Salvador, El Salvador: United Nations Children's Fund [UNICEF] and Facultad Latinoamericana de Ciencias Sociales [FLACSO], 1998), 28–32.

10. Edgardo Amaya Cóbar, "Maras: Niñez, juventud y violencia; Breve caracterización del caso salvadoreño" (unpublished manuscript, 2004), 3–4.

11. "Los detienen hasta que matan," *El Diario de Hoy*, 3 August 2003.

12. Karen Molina and David Marroquín, "Maras obligan a iniciados que vayan a matar," *El Diario de Hoy*, 12 September 2007.

13. "Distribuyen fotos de fichados en la PNC," *La Prensa Gráfica*, 24 May 2006; "Pandilleros aumentan su operatividad en toda Centroamérica," *El Diario de Hoy*, 16 July 2009, http://www.elsalvador.com/mwedh/nota/nota_completa.asp ?idCat=6358&idArt=3831185.

14. The 2005 data are cited in José Miguel Cruz and Marlon Carranza, "Pandillas y políticas públicas: El caso de El Salvador," in Javier Moro, ed., *Juventudes, violencia y exclusión: Desafíos para las políticas públicas* (Guatemala City: MagnaTerra Editores, 2006), 163. The 2009 data were not publicly available at the time of this writing and were provided by the Ministry of Public Security and Justice upon the author's request.

15. Marlon Carranza, "Detención o muerte: Hacia dónde van los niños 'pandilleros' de El Salvador," in Luke Dowdney, ed., *Neither War nor Peace: International Comparisons of Children and Youth in Organised Armed Violence* (Rio de Janeiro: Viveiros de Castro Editora, 2005), 4, http://www.coav.org.br.

16. Jeannette Aguilar, *Pandillas juveniles transnacionales en Centroamérica, México y Estados Unidos: Diagnóstico de El Salvador* (San Salvador, El Salvador: Instituto Universitario de Opinión Pública [IUDOP], 2006, 12–13, http://www .wola.org/media/Gangs/diagnostico_salvador%281%29.pdf; Carranza, "Detención o muerte," 9; Jeannette Aguilar and Marlon Carranza, "Las maras y pandillas como actores ilegales de la región," talk prepared for the Informe Estado de la Región en Desarrollo Humano Sostenible 2008 (San Salvador, El Salvador: IUDOP, 2008), 7.

17. Aguilar, *Pandillas juveniles transnacionales*, 15.

18. Ibid., 18–19.

19. Jeannette Aguilar, "Los resultados contraproducentes de las políticas antipandillas," *ECA (Estudios Centroamericanos)*, no. 708 (2007): 879–880.

20. Ibid., 881.

21. Raúl Gutiérrez, "La herencia perversa del Gobierno Saca (II parte)," *Contrapunto*, 22 May 2009, http://www.contrapunto.com; U.S. Department of State, Bureau of Democracy, Human Rights, and Labor, *2008 Human Rights Report: El Salvador* (Washington, DC, 2009), http://www.state.gov/g/drl/rls/ hrrpt/2008/wha/119159.htm.

22. Aguilar, *Pandillas juveniles transnacionales*, 22–23; Aguilar and Carranza, "Maras y pandillas," 11.

23. Aguilar, "Los resultados contraproducentes," 884.

24. Aguilar and Carranza, "Maras y pandillas," 19, 21; Cruz and Carranza, "Pandillas y políticas públicas," 166–167.

25. Author's interview with Milton Vega, rehabilitation officer, CNSP, San Salvador, El Salvador, 7 April 2006.

26. James Diego Vigil, *A Rainbow of Gangs: Street Cultures in the Mega-City* (Austin: University of Texas Press, 2002), 132–136.

27. Ibid., 144–145.

28. Elana Zilberg, "Fools Banished from the Kingdom: Remapping Geographies of Gang Violence between the Americas (Los Angeles and San Salvador)," *American Quarterly* 56 (2004): 765–795.

29. Smutt and Miranda, *El fenómeno de las pandillas*, 36.

30. Donna DeCesare, "From Civil War to Gang War: The Tragedy of Edgar Bolaños," in Louis Kontos, David Brotherton, and Luis Barrios, eds., *Gangs and Society: Alternative Perspectives* (New York: Columbia University Press, 2003), 289; Smutt and Miranda, *El fenómeno de las pandillas*, 37.

31. José Miguel Cruz and Nelson Portillo Peña, *Solidaridad y violencia en las pandillas del gran San Salvador: Más allá de la vida loca* (San Salvador, El Salvador: UCA Editores, 1998), 199.

32. "Deportados," *El Diario de Hoy*, 22 February 2005; "EE.UU. triplica los envíos de deportados," *El Diario de Hoy*, 5 December 2007.

33. Cruz and Portillo, *Solidaridad y violencia en las pandillas*, 200.

34. Programa de las Naciones Unidas para el Desarrollo (PNUD), *Informe sobre desarrollo humano 2005: Una mirada al nuevo nosotros; El impacto de las migraciones* (San Salvador, El Salvador: PNUD, 2005), 316.

35. State Migration Office, cited in ibid., 317.

36. Cruz and Portillo, *Solidaridad y violencia en las pandillas*, 207–208; Smutt and Miranda, *El fenómeno de las pandillas*, 135–137.

37. Cruz and Portillo, *Solidaridad y violencia en las pandillas*, 223–224, 225–228, 231–232.

38. María Santacruz Giralt and Alberto Concha-Eastman, *Barrio adentro: La solidaridad violenta de las pandillas* (San Salvador, El Salvador: IUDOP and Organización Panamericana de Salud [OPS], 2001), 61, 125–126.

39. Ibid., 63–70, 112, 127.

40. IUDOP, *La violencia en El Salvador en los años noventa: Magnitud, costos y factores posibilitadores* (San Salvador, El Salvador: IUDOP, 1998), 11.

41. José Miguel Cruz, "El Salvador," in *La cara de la violencia urbana en América Central* (San José, Costa Rica: Fundación Arias para la Paz y el Progreso Humano, 2006), 110.

42. Gutiérrez, La herencia perversa del Gobierno Saca (II parte)"; "Funes recibe el país con 12.35 homicidios diarios," *La Prensa Gráfica*, 4 June 2009, http://www.laprensagrafica.com/el-salvador/judicial/37500—funes-recibe-el-pais-con-1235-homicidios-diarios.html.

43. "Centroamérica vive una 'guerra civil no declarada' según funcionario de OEA," *La Prensa Gráfica*, 24 June 2009, http://www.laprensagrafica.com.

44. See the IML's annual homicide statistics in Fabio Molina Vaquerano, *Defunciones por homicidios en El Salvador, 1999–2006* (San Salvador, El Salvador: Instituto de Medicina Legal, 2001–2007); and "Bajan homicidios en 2008," *La Prensa Gráfica*, 27 February 2009, http://www.laprensagrafica.com/index.php/el-salvador/judicial/20408.html.

45. José Miguel Cruz, "Los factores posibilitadores y las expresiones de la violencia en los noventa," *ECA (Estudios Centroamericanos)*, no. 588 (1997): 989.

46. "Violencia se ensaña con jóvenes y mujeres," *El Diario de Hoy*, 31 October 2005, http://www.elsalvador.com/noticias/2005/10/31/nacional/nac6.asp; "Asesinan a 13 personas a diario en el país," *El Diario de Hoy*, 16 June 2009, http://www.elsalvador.com/mwedh/nota/nota_completa.asp?idCat=6358&idArt=3738331; "Junio ha sido el mes más violento del año," *La Prensa Gráfica*, 6 July 2005, http://www.laprensagrafica.com.

47. Amaya Cóbar, "Maras," 5–7.

48. Molina Vaquerano, "Defunciones por homicidios"; "Solo 25% de homicidios atribuido a las pandillas," *La Prensa Gráfica*, 23 November 2007.

49. "El Salvador supera en tasa de homicidios a Colombia," *Diario Co Latino*, 13 February 2006, http://www.diariocolatino.com/es/20060213/nacionales/nacio nales_20060213_11248/.

50. Joint Group for the Investigation of Politically Motivated Illegal Armed Groups, *Report of the Joint Group for the Investigation of Politically Motivated Illegal Armed Groups in El Salvador* (San Salvador, El Salvador: 28 July 1994), transmitted with letter dated 11 August 1994 from the UN Secretary-General addressed to the President of the UN Security Council (S/1994/989), http://www.un.org, 24.

51. See the annual reports by the Fundación de Estudios para la Aplicación del Derecho (FESPAD), *Estado de la seguridad pública y la justicia penal en El Salvador, 2002–2005* (San Salvador, El Salvador: FESPAD, 2004–2005).

52. "'Viejo Lin' fue libre por 30 minutos," *El Diario de Hoy*, 23 May 2004, http://www.elsalvador.com/noticias/2004/05/23/nacional/nac4.asp; "Crean alianza contra las maras en C.A.," *El Diario de Hoy*, 5 April 2006, http://www .elsalvador.com/noticias/2006/04/05/nacional/nac15.asp.

53. Malcolm W. Klein, *The American Street Gang: Its Nature, Prevalence, and Control* (New York: Oxford University Press, 1995), 114; Malcolm W. Klein and Cheryl L. Maxson, *Street Gang Patterns and Policies* (New York: Oxford University Press, 2006), 81.

54. See the annual human rights reports by Tutela Legal, *La situación de los derechos humanos en El Salvador: Informe anual de Tutela Legal del Arzobispado de San Salvador 2006–2007* (San Salvador, El Salvador: Tutela Legal, 2006–2008).

55. FESPAD, *Estado de la seguridad pública, 2002–2003*, 117.

56. "Gobierno niega existencia de grupos de exterminio de pandilleros," *La Prensa Gráfica*, 19 August 2005, http://archive.laprensa.com.sv/20050819/lodel dia/08.asp.

57. Procuraduría para la Defensa de los Derechos Humanos (PDDH), *Violaciones a los derechos humanos por responsabilidad de la Policía Nacional Civil de El Salvador* (San Salvador, El Salvador: PDDH, 2007), 60–61.

58. Sidney Blanco Reyes and Francisco Díaz Rodríguez, *Deficiencias policiales, fiscales o judiciales en la investigación y juzgamiento causantes de impunidad* (San Salvador, El Salvador: PNUD, 2007), 18.

59. Ignacio Martín-Baró, in José Miguel Cruz, "Los factores asociados a las pandillas juveniles en Centroamérica," *ECA (Estudios Centroamericanos)*, no. 685–686 (2005): 1164.

60. Cruz, "Los factores asociados a las pandillas," 1159–1166; IUDOP, *La violencia en El Salvador*, 33–36.

61. Cruz, "Los factores asociados a las pandillas," 1164–1165; PNUD, *Armas de fuego y violencia* (San Salvador, El Salvador: PNUD, 2003), 133.

62. José Miguel Cruz and María Santacruz Giralt, *La victimización y la percepción de seguridad en El Salvador en 2004* (San Salvador, El Salvador: Ministerio de Gobernación and PNUD, 2005), 321.

63. Cruz, "El Salvador," 108, 135; PNUD, *Armas de fuego y violencia*, 47–48.

64. PNUD, *Armas de fuego y violencia*, 127.

65. IUDOP, *La violencia en El Salvador*, 39–40; PNUD, *Armas de fuego y violencia*, 60.

66. "Por el camino de la prevención," *La Prensa Gráfica*, 27 May 2009, http://www.laprensagrafica.com/el-salvador/social/35736-por-el-camino-de-la-prevencion.html; "La hora de los hornos," in "La vorágine de la violencia," special edition of *Raíces* (20 October 2008), http://www.raices.com.sv.

67. Mo Hume, *Armed Violence and Poverty in El Salvador* (Bradford, UK: Center for International Cooperation and Security, University of Bradford, 2004), 17, http://www.bradford.ac.uk/acad/cics/publications/AVPI/poverty/AVPI_El_Salvador.pdf; "La hora de los hornos."

68. John Booth, Christine Wade, and Thomas Walker, *Understanding Central America*, 5th ed. (Boulder, CO: Westview Press, 2010), 177.

69. Malcolm W. Klein, *Chasing After Street Gangs* (Upper Saddle River, NJ: Pearson, 2007), 52.

70. John Hagedorn, *A World of Gangs: Armed Young Men and Gangsta Culture* (Minneapolis: University of Minnesota Press, 2008), 37.

71. Dennis Rodgers, "Slum Wars of the 21st Century: Gangs, *Mano Dura* and the New Urban Geography of Conflict in Central America," *Development and Change* 40, no. 5 (2009): 969.

72. United Nations Office on Drugs and Crime (UNODC), *Crime and Development in Central America: Caught in the Crossfire* (Mexico City: UNODC, 2007), 38.

73. IUDOP, *La violencia en El Salvador*, 38.

74. Margaret Popkin, *Peace without Justice: Obstacles to Building the Rule of Law in El Salvador* (Philadelphia: Pennsylvania State University, 2000), 26–27.

75. Gino Costa, *La Policía Nacional Civil de El Salvador (1990–1997)* (San Salvador, El Salvador: UCA Editores, 1999), 134.

76. IUDOP, *La violencia en El Salvador*, 38.

77. Costa, *La Policía Nacional Civil*, 189.

78. José Miguel Cruz, "Violencia, inseguridad ciudadana y las maniobras de las élites: La dinámica de la reforma policial en El Salvador," in Lucía Dammert and John Bailey, eds., *Seguridad y reforma policial en las Américas: Experiencias y desafíos* (Mexico City: Siglo XXI Editores, 2005), 264; Costa, *La Policía Nacional Civil*, 204, 211.

79. Edgardo Amaya Cóbar, "Las políticas de seguridad en El Salvador 1992–2002," in Dammert and Bailey, *Seguridad y reforma policial en las Américas*, 222; Sonja Wolf, "The Politics of Gang Control: NGO Advocacy in Post-war El Salvador" (Ph.D. diss., Aberystwyth University, Wales, 2008), 63.

80. UNODC, *Crime and Development in Central America*, 12, 45.

81. PNUD, *El impacto de las drogas en la violencia* (San Salvador, El Salvador: PNUD, 2004), 41.

82. See "Detectan reunión entre cartel del Golfo y pandilla en El Salvador," *La Prensa Gráfica*, 7 December 2008, http://www.laprensagrafica.com/index.php/el-salvador/judicial/4769.html.

83. "DEA Says Mexican Drug Cartels Are Creeping South," Associated Press, 16 April 2009.

84. UNODC, *Crime and Development in Central America*, 17.

85. "Central America: An Emerging Role in the Drug Trade," *Stratfor*, 26 March 2009, http://www.stratfor.com/weekly/20090326_central_america_emerg ing_role_drug_trade.

86. José Miguel Cruz, Marlon Carranza, and María Santacruz Giralt, "El Salvador: Espacios públicos, confianza interpersonal y pandillas," in Equipo de Reflexión, Investigación y Comunicación (ERIC), Instituto de Encuestas y Sondeos de Opinión (IDESO), Instituto de Investigaciones Económicas y Sociales (IDIES), IUDOP, eds., *Maras y pandillas en Centroamérica: Pandillas y capital social*, vol. 2, *Pandillas y capital social* (San Salvador, El Salvador: UCA Editores, 2004).

87. PNUD, *Informe sobre desarrollo humano, El Salvador 2003: Desafíos y opciones en tiempos de globalización* (San Salvador, El Salvador: PNUD, 2003), 13–14.

88. Ibid., 35.

89. Cruz and Carranza, "Pandillas y políticas públicas," 134.

90. Equipo Regional de Monitoreo y Análisis de Derechos Humanos en Centroamérica, *Informe sobre Derechos Humanos y Conflictividad en Centroamérica 2008–2009* (Equipo Regional de Monitoreo y Análisis de Derechos Humanos en Centroamérica, 2009), 34.

91. "Cárceles al 224% de su capacidad," *La Prensa Gráfica*, 29 July 2007, http://www.laprensagrafica.com/lodeldia/20070729/13539.asp.

92. "Más cárcel como política de estado," *Políticas Públicas Hoy* (FESPAD), no. 26 (2007): 5.

93. IUDOP, "La delincuencia urbana: Encuesta exploratoria," *ECA (Estudios Centroamericanos)*, no. 534–535 (1993): 477.

94. Jeannette Aguilar and Lissette Miranda, "Entre la articulación y la competencia: Las respuestas de la sociedad civil organizada a las pandillas en El Salvador," in José Miguel Cruz, ed., *Maras y pandillas en Centroamérica*, vol. 4, *Las respuestas de la sociedad civil organizada* (San Salvador, El Salvador: UCA Editores, 2006), 94–118; Sonja Wolf, *Propuesta para la prevención de la violencia juvenil en El Salvador* (San Salvador, El Salvador: FESPAD Ediciones, 2007), 75–114.

95. "Barrerán a las maras," *El Diario de Hoy*, 24 July 2003; "El estado de excepción es la última alternativa," *El Diario de Hoy*, 24 July 2003.

96. "'Mano Dura' contra mareros," *La Prensa Gráfica*, 24 July 2003.

97. "Redadas arrancan en la penumbra," *El Diario de Hoy*, 25 July 2003; "Policía captura a 142 pandilleros," *La Prensa Gráfica*, 25 July 2003.

98. See Roxana Martel Trigueros, "Las maras salvadoreñas: Nuevas formas de espanto y control social," *ECA (Estudios Centroamericanos)*, no. 696 (2006): 957–979; Irene Vasilachis de Gialdino, "Representations of Young People Associated with Crime in El Salvador's Written Press," *Critical Discourse Studies* 4 (2007): 1–28.

99. Legislative Decree No. 158 of 9 October 2003, enacting the Ley Antimaras, D.O. No. 361, Ministerio de Gobernación, San Salvador, El Salvador, 10 October 2003.

100. For an analysis of the Ley Antimaras, see FESPAD, *Estado de la seguridad pública, 2002–2003*, 123–135.

101. "Análisis de la 'Ley Antimaras,'" *Proceso* (Instituto de Derechos Huma-

nos de la Universidad Centroamericana "José Simeón Cañas" de El Salvador) 24, no. 1062 (August 2008), http://www.uca.edu.sv/publica/proceso/proc1062.html; "Detenciones son 'ilegales,' dicen jueces," *La Prensa Gráfica*, 25 July 2003.

102. "Plan Mano Dura reduce delincuencia de pandillas," *La Prensa Gráfica*, 23 August 2003; "Oposición decide enviar al archivo Ley Antimaras," *La Prensa Gráfica*, 27 August 2003; "Foro dice 'no' a propuesta de ley," *La Prensa Gráfica*, 27 August 2003.

103. PDDH, *Demanda de inconstitucionalidad contra la Ley Antimaras* (San Salvador, El Salvador: PDDH, 2003), http://www.pddh.gob.sv. On the judges' position, see "Jueces: Ley no se puede aplicar," *La Prensa Gráfica*, 10 October 2003.

104. For a summary of the Court's ruling, see FESPAD, *Informe anual sobre justicia penal juvenil, El Salvador, 2004* (San Salvador, El Salvador: FESPAD Ediciones, 2004), 65–71.

105. Legislative Decree No. 305 of 1 April 2004, enacting the Ley para el Combate de las Actividades Delincuenciales de Grupos o Asociaciones Ilícitas Especiales, D.O. of 2 April 2004, Ministerio de Gobernación, San Salvador, El Salvador.

106. United Nations Convention on the Rights of the Child (UNCRC), 36th Session, "Consideration of Reports Submitted by States Parties under Article 44 of the Convention: Concluding Observations; El Salvador," CRC/C/15/Add.232 (New York: United Nations, 30 June 2004), 15.

107. FESPAD, *Estado de la seguridad pública y la justicia penal en El Salvador, 2004* (San Salvador, El Salvador: FESPAD Ediciones, 2005), 13.

108. "Los resultados de la política antidelincuencial: A un paso de la anomia," *Políticas Públicas Hoy* (FESPAD) 13 (October 2006): 2, http://www.fespad.org.sv.

109. On penal populism, see Julian V. Roberts, Loretta J. Stalans, David Indermaur, and Mike Hough, *Penal Populism and Public Opinion* (Oxford: Oxford University Press, 2003), 5, 66.

110. "Las elecciones municipales y legislativas del 16 de marzo de 2003," *ECA (Estudios Centroamericanos)*, no. 653–654 (2003): 178–184.

111. "Juicio político sobre las elecciones 2003," *ECA (Estudios Centroamericanos)*, no. 653–654 (2003): 169.

112. See IUDOP, "Las preferencias políticas en octubre de 2003: La mano dura de ARENA," *ECA (Estudios Centroamericanos)*, no. 660 (2003): 1075.

113. Ibid.; "Opinión pública a finales de 2003 y preferencias electorales: Encuesta de evaluación de fin de año," *ECA (Estudios Centroamericanos)*, no. 661–662 (2003): 1237.

114. IUDOP, "Las preferencias políticas," 1075.

115. "Los salvadoreños frente a las elecciones presidenciales de 2004," *Boletín de Prensa* (IUDOP) 18, no. 3 (October 2003): 2.

116. Ibid., 4–6.

117. IUDOP, "Las preferencias políticas," 1073.

118. See "ARENA a pescar votos con el plan antimaras," *La Prensa Gráfica*, 13 August 2003.

119. José Miguel Cruz, "Las elecciones presidenciales desde el comportamiento de la opinión pública," *ECA (Estudios Centroamericanos)*, no. 665–666 (2004): 266.

120. *País seguro: Plan de gobierno 2004–2009* (San Salvador, El Salvador: Gobierno de El Salvador, 2004), 8; http://www.servicios.gob.sv/descarga/PLAN_DE_GOBIERNO_2004-2009_PAIS_SEGURO.pdf.

121. Legislative Decree No. 393 of 28 July 2004, enacting reforms to the Penal Code, D.O. of 30 July 2004, Ministerio de Gobernación, San Salvador, El Salvador. See also "Se inicia la Súper Mano Dura," *El Diario de Hoy*, 31 August 2004, 2–3.

122. *País Seguro*, 40–41.

123. *Plan Nacional de Juventud 2005–2015* (San Salvador, El Salvador: Secretaría de la Juventud, 2005).

124. Ibid., 3; *Plan Nacional de Juventud 2005–2015: Ejes de Acción* (San Salvador, El Salvador, 2005), 47–48.

125. *Plan Nacional de Juventud 2005–2015*, 5.

126. On SJ promotional costs, see "Secretaría de la Juventud se promociona a un costo inexplicable," *El Faro*, 26 May 2008, http://www.elfaro.net; "Empresa desmiente a Secretaría de Juventud sobre artículos promocionales," *El Faro*, 9 June 2008, http://www.elfaro.net.

127. Author's interview with Anja Kramer, consultant for local economic development and employment, Gesellschaft für Technische Zusammenarbeit (GTZ), San Salvador, El Salvador, 27 February 2006; author's interviews with Xochitl Marchelli, human rights instructor, Academia Nacional de Seguridad Pública (ANSP), San Salvador, El Salvador, 4 May and 19 June 2006.

128. CNSP and European Union, "ProJóvenes de El Salvador," SLV/B7-3100/99/0133, Plan Operativo Anual, unpublished report (San Salvador, El Salvador: CNSP and European Union, 2005), 13.

129. "Gobierno y la Comisión Europea firman segunda parte de 'Pro Jóvenes,'" *La Página*, 18 August 2009, http://www.lapagina.com.sv/nacionales/15327/2009/08/18.

130. "Los salvadoreños evalúan la situación del país a finales de 2005 y opinan sobre las elecciones de 2006," *Boletín de Prensa* (IUDOP) 20, no. 3 (December 2005): 4.

131. El Salvador also adopted an anti–organized crime law with a view to applying it to gangs: Legislative Decree No. 190 of 20 December 2006, enacting the Ley Contra el Crimen Organizado y Delitos de Realización Compleja, D.O. 374 of 22 January 2007, Ministerio de Gobernación, San Salvador, El Salvador.

132. Wolf, "Politics of Gang Control," 93–98.

133. Aguilar, "Los resultados contraproducentes," 881.

134. Christian Poveda, filmmaker and director of the gang documentary *La vida loca*, conversation with author, Mexico City, 31 March 2009.

135. PNUD, *El impacto de las drogas*, 48.

136. Aguilar, "Los resultados contraproducentes," 879–880; José Miguel Cruz, "El barrio transnacional: Las maras centroamericanas como red," in Francis Pisani, Natalia Saltalamacchia, Arlene Tickner, and Nielan Barnes, eds., *Redes transnacionales en la cuenca de los huracanes: Un aporte a los studios interamericanos* (Mexico City: Instituto Tecnológico Autónomo de México [ITAM] and Miguel Ángel Porrúa, 2007), 367.

137. Aguilar, "Los resultados contraproducentes," 881–882; Cruz, "El barrio transnacional," 365–367.

138. Carranza, "Detención o muerte," 5; Demoscopía, *Maras y pandillas, comunidad y policía en Centroamérica: Hallazgos de un estudio integral* (San José, Costa Rica: Demoscopía, 2007), 16–19.

139. Aguilar, "Los resultados contraproducentes," 884.

140. Ibid., 887–888; Oscar Iraheta, "El setenta por ciento de las extorsiones son cometidas por maras," *El Diario de Hoy*, 19 August 2009, http://www.elsalvador.com/mwedh/nota/nota_completa.asp?idCat=6358&idArt=3930807.

141. Aguilar, *Pandillas juveniles transnacionales*, 40; Aguilar, "Los resultados contraproducentes," 884.

142. Klein, *Chasing After Street Gangs*, 38–39.

143. See "'Maras' no son principal causa de violencia, según la misma PNC," *El Faro*, 31 January 2005, http://www.elfaro.net/secciones/noticias/20050131/noticias3_20050131.asp.

144. "Libres 114 pandilleros e impunes 20 homicidios," *El Diario de Hoy*, 15 August 2009, http://www.elsalvador.com/mwedh/nota/nota_completa.asp?idCat=6358&idArt=3918774.

145. "La culpa de fiscales y policías," in "La vorágine de la violencia," special edition of *Raíces*, 20 October 2008, http://www.raices.com.sv.

146. Raúl Gutiérrez, "Entrevista a 'Puppet,' líder natural de la Pandilla 18," in "La vorágine de la violencia," special edition of *Raíces*, 20 October 2008, http://www.raices.com.sv.

147. Cruz and Portillo, *Solidaridad y violencia en las pandillas*, 204.

148. Christian Poveda, conversation with author, 1 April 2009.

149. Aguilar, *Pandillas juveniles transnacionales*, 29.

150. Ibid., 30.

151. Cruz, "El barrio transnacional," 363–364.

152. See Aguilar, *Pandillas juveniles transnacionales*, 46.

153. Cruz, "El barrio transnacional," 368.

154. Herbert C. Covey, *Street Gangs throughout the World* (Springfield, IL: Charles C. Thomas, 2003), 24.

155. Klein and Maxson, *Street Gang Patterns*, 186.

156. Covey, *Street Gangs throughout the World*, 24.

157. Klein, *American Street Gang*, 42; Klein and Maxson, *Street Gang Patterns*, 186.

158. Christian Poveda, conversation with author, 1 April 2009.

159. Aguilar, *Pandillas juveniles transnacionales*, 17.

160. Ibid., 18–19, 48.

161. United States Agency for International Development (USAID), *Central America and Mexico Gang Assessment* (Washington, DC: USAID, 2006), 46.

162. Klein, *American Street Gang*, 42; Klein and Maxson, *Street Gang Patterns*, 186.

163. Robert Franzese, Herbert Covey, and Scott Menard, eds., *Youth Gangs*, 3rd ed. (Springfield, IL: Charles C. Thomas, 2006), 28.

164. UNODC, *Crime and Development in Central America*, 63.

165. Christian Poveda, "Maras: La vida loca," *Le Monde Diplomatique—Mexico*, April 2009.

166. UNODC, *The Threat of Narco-Trafficking in the Americas* (Mexico City: UNODC, 2008), 19.

167. Poveda, "Maras," 18.

168. Carranza, "Detención o muerte," 14.

169. PNUD, *El impacto de las drogas*, 34–35.

170. "EE.UU. sentencia a ex diputado," *El Diario de Hoy*, 19 January 2006, http://www.elsalvador.com/noticias/2006/01/19/nacional/nac12.asp.

171. Demoscopía, *Maras y pandillas*, 90–92; Gutiérrez, "Entrevista a 'Puppet.'"

172. Cruz and Santacruz Giralt, *La victimización y la percepción*, 148–150.

173. "La prevención será el eje central en seguridad," *La Prensa Gráfica*, 2 June 2009.

Chapter 3

This chapter is based on research conducted in 2006 for the project "Transnational Youth Gangs," coordinated by the Instituto Universitario de Opinión Pública (IUDOP) and Instituto Tecnológico Autónomo de México (ITAM). For a more extended draft paper that describes the principal results of the study, see Elin Cecilie Ranum, "Pandillas juveniles transnacionales en Centroamérica, México y Estados Unidos," Diagnóstico Nacional Guatemala, Red Transnacional de Análisis sobre Maras, Centro de Estudios y Programas Interamericanos (ITAM and IUDOP, 2006), http://interamericanos.itam.mx/maras/docs/Diagnostico_Guatemala.pdf.

1. Lourdes Hum, Leslie Ramos, and Iván Monzón, "Respuestas de la sociedad civil al fenómeno de las maras y pandillas juveniles en Guatemala," in José Miguel Cruz, ed., *Maras y pandillas en Centroamérica*, vol. 4, *Las respuestas de la sociedad civil organizada* (San Salvador, El Salvador: UCA Editores, 2006).

2. Ibid.; Juan Merino, "Las maras en Guatemala," in Equipo de Reflexión, Investigación y Comunicación (ERIC), Instituto de Encuestas y Sondeos de Opinión (IDESO), Instituto de Investigaciones Económicos y Sociales (IDIES), and Instituto Universitario de Opinión Pública (IUDOP), eds., *Maras y pandillas en Centroamérica*, vol. 1 (Managua: UCA Editores, 2001).

3. The term "international gangs" should not be understood to mean an international organization in terms of structure, operations, and activities. Rather, such gangs are international because of their presence in several countries, particularly El Salvador, Guatemala, Honduras, and the United States.

4. U.S. Agency for International Development (USAID), Bureau for Latin American and Caribbean Affairs, Office of Regional Sustainable Development, *Central America and Mexico Gang Assessment* (Washington, DC: USAID, April 2006), http://www.usaid.gov/locations/latin_america_caribbean/democracy/gangs_cam.pdf.

5. Author's interview with police agent from the Anti-gang Unit of the National Civilian Police (Policía Nacional Civil), Guatemala City, June 2006. The agent asked to remain anonymous.

6. USAID, *Central America and Mexico Gang Assessment*.

7. Previous studies on gangs in El Salvador have noted some of these factors, which were also emphasized in interviews with representatives from civil society organizations and the judicial system. See Maria L. Santacruz Giralt, and Alberto Concha-Eastman, *Barrio adentro: La solidaridad violenta de las pandillas* (San Salvador, El Salvador: IUDOP, Organización Panamericana de Salud (OPS), and Homies Unidos, 2001); and Jeannette Aguilar and Lissette Miranda, "Entre la articulación y la competencia: Las respuestas de la sociedad civil organizada a las pandillas en El Salvador," in José Miguel Cruz, ed., *Maras y pandillas en Centroamérica*, vol. 4, *Las respuestas de la sociedad civil organizada* (San Salvador, El Salvador: UCA Editores, 2006), 94–118.

8. Numbers are from the PNC. See Ranum, "Pandillas juveniles transnacionales," for more details on the numbers of gangs, or *clicas*.

9. This chapter does not intend to determine factors that may explain these differences, which is an issue that requires further research before any conclusions are drawn.

10. Gangs in El Salvador and Honduras show similar patterns, and any reference to neighboring countries in this context refers to these two countries.

11. Hum, Ramos, and Monzón, "Respuestas de la sociedad civil"; José M. Cruz and Nelson Portillo Peña, *Solidaridad y violencia en las pandillas del gran San Salvador: Más allá de la vida loca* (San Salvador, El Salvador: UCA Editores, 1998); Marcela Smutt and Jenny Lissette E. Miranda, *El fenómeno de las pandillas en El Salvador* (San Salvador, El Salvador: United Nations Children's Fund [UNICEF] and Facultad Latinoamericana de Ciencias Sociales [FLACSO], 1998).

12. Some examples are the Capitols and Los Fives.

13. Merino, "Las maras en Guatemala."

14. Ibid.

15. Dennis Rodgers, "Youth Gangs and Violence in Latin America and the Caribbean: A Literature Survey" (Latin American and Caribbean Region Sustainable Development Working Paper 4, Urban Peace Program Series, World Bank, 1999).

16. Ibid.

17. I apply the term "Californian gangs" to the two gangs that originated in California—Mara Salvatrucha and the 18th Street Gang—as a way to distinguish them from the local gangs that originated in Guatemala. This distinction does not try to establish typological differences.

18. Note in particular the Salvadoran case, where literature has emphasized the importance of examining domestic factors. See Smutt and Miranda, *El fenómeno de las pandillas*; and Cruz and Portillo, *Solidaridad y violencia*.

19. Author's interviews with former gang members who experienced the transition from barrio gangs to MS and the 18th Street Gang, Guatemala City, 2006. Smutt and Miranda, in *El fenómeno de las pandillas*, have suggested a similar process in the Salvadoran case.

20. In several cases, the deported had few or no connections to Guatemala but their nationality; many had lived most of their lives in the United States, their Spanish was poor, their family was in the United States, and their social network in Guatemala was practically nonexistent. Thus their gang identity was one of the few factors on which they could build their new life.

21. The interactions among these conditions have been thoroughly analyzed by others, a task that is beyond the scope of this chapter. For such an analysis, and for information on the Pan American Health Organization model, see José Miguel Cruz and Marlon Carranza, "Pandillas y políticas públicas: El caso de El Salvador," in Javier Moro, ed., *Juventudes, violencia y exclusión: Desafíos para las políticas públicas* (Guatemala City: MagnaTerra Editores, 2006).

22. The only exception to elite or military rule after independence was the reform period between 1944 and 1954, under the popularly elected governments of Presidents Juan José Arévalo Bermejo (1945–1951) and Jacobo Árbenz Guzmán (1951–1954). In 1954 a U.S.-supported coup d'état reinstalled military rule.

23. For more on the impact of the war and the socialization of violence, see Charles Call, "Sustainable Development in Central America: The Challenges of Violence, Injustice and Insecurity" (Central America 2020 Working Paper 8, Institut für Iberoamerika-Kunde, Hamburg, 2000), http://ca2020.fiu.edu/Themes/Charles_Call/Call.pdf.

24. United Nations Development Programme (UNDP), *Human Development Report 2005: International Cooperation at a Crossroads; Aid, Trade and Security in an Unequal World* (New York: UNDP, 2005), http://hdr.undp.org/en/reports/global/hdr2005/.

25. PNUD, *Informe nacional de desarrollo humano, Guatemala 2007* (Guatemala City: PNUD, 2008).

26. UNDP, *Human Development Report 2005*.

27. PNUD, *Informe nacional de desarrollo humano*.

28. See "Anders Kompass: La población no se siente segura," *La Prensa Libre*, 2 January 2007; and United Nations Human Rights Council (UNHCR), *Los derechos civiles y políticos, en particular las cuestiones relacionadas con las desapariciones y ejecuciones sumarias: Informe del relator especial, Philip Alston, sobre las ejecuciones extrajudiciales, sumarias o arbitrarias; Misión a Guatemala 21 a 25 de agosto de 2006* (A/HRC/4/20/Add.2, UNHCR, 19 February 2007; English version available at http://www.universalhumanrightsindex.org/documents/841/1077/document/en/text.html).

29. See, for instance, "Dos grupos de exterminio operan en Guatemala," *El Faro*, 5 March 2007, http://www.elfaro.net/Secciones/noticias/20070305/noticias1_20070305.asp.

30. See, for instance, notes from the Guatemalan press: "Ex jefes de SAIA, por enfrentar juicio en Estados Unidos," *El Periódico*, 5 September 2006; and "Más policías corruptos," *La Prensa Libre*, 10 August 2006.

31. The army managed to get total control over important companies and enterprise sectors, such as telecommunications, the banking system, etc. See David Keen, "Demobilising Guatemala" (Crisis States Programme Working Paper 37, London School of Economics, 2003). For further comments on the relationship between the army and organized crime during the war, see Colletta A. Youngsters and Eileen Rosin, eds., *Drugs and Democracy in Latin America: The Impact of U.S. Policy* (Boulder, CO.: Lynne Rienner, 2005).

32. For a detailed report on some of these structures, see Susan C. Peacock and Adriana Beltrán, *Poderes ocultos: Grupos ilegales armados en la Guatemala post conflicto y las fuerzas detrás de ellos* (Washington, DC: Washington Office on Latin

America [WOLA], 2003; English version available athttp://www.wola.org/index
.php?option=com_content&task=viewp&id=48&Itemid=2). See also Juan Hernández Pico, *Terminar la guerra, traicionar la paz: Guatemala en las dos presidencias
de la paz; Arzú y Portillo (1996–2004)* (Guatemala City: FLACSO, 2005).

33. The Guatemalan army is still the main guarantor for both domestic and
external security. For more details on the problems regarding efforts to reduce
the military's formal power and the creation of the National Civilian Police, see
Iduvina Hernández, *Camino rocoso: Avances y desafíos de la reforma de inteligencia en
Guatemala* (Washington, DC: WOLA, 5 September 2005; available in English
and Spanish), http://www.wola.org; Hernández Pico, *Terminar la guerra*; Peacock and Beltrán, *Poderes ocultos*; Rachel Sieder, Megan Thomas, George Vickers, and Jack Spence, *Who Governs? Guatemala Five Years after the Peace Accords*
(Cambridge, MA: Hemisphere Initiative, 2002); Hugh Byrne, William Stanley,
and Rachel Garst, *Rescuing Police Reform: A Challenge for the New Guatemalan Government* (Washington, DC: WOLA, 2000); A. Douglas Kincaid, "Demilitarization and Security in El Salvador and Guatemala: Convergences of Success and
Crisis," *Journal of Interamerican Studies and World Affairs* 42, no. 4 (2000): 39–58;
and Jennifer Schirmer, "The Guatemalan Politico-Military Project: Legacies for
a Violent Peace?" *Latin American Perspectives* 26, no. 2 (March 1999): 92–107.

34. The weaknesses described in Sieder et al., *Who Governs?* persist. The complicated approval process for a law against organized crime, which finally passed
the Guatemalan Congress in 2006, and the much delayed approval of a legal
framework for the prisons system, are two examples of Congress's inefficiency.

35. Guillermo O'Donnell, "On the State, Democratization and Some Conceptual Problems: A Latin American View with Glances at Some Postcommunist
Countries," *World Development* 21, no. 8 (1993): 1355–1369.

36. See Peacock and Beltrán, *Poderes ocultos.*

37. Dinorah Azpuru, Juan Pablo Pira, and Mitchell A. Seligson, *La cultura
política y la democracia en Guatemala, 2004: VI Estudio a cerca de la cultura democrática de los guatemaltecos* (Guatemala City: ARO, Vanderbilt University, Asociación
de Investigación y Estudios Sociales [ASIES], and USAID, 2004).

38. UNDP, *Human Development Report 2005.*

39. Ibid.

40. Santacruz and Concha-Eastman, *Barrio adentro.*

41. Ibid.

42. Cruz and Portillo, *Solidaridad y violencia*; Santacruz and Concha-
Eastman, *Barrio adentro.* The survey was conducted by IUDOP in 2006 and was
a part of the study "Transnational Youth Gangs"; see Ranum, "Pandillas juveniles
transnacionales."

43. Several proposals were presented in Congress; none, however, passed the
legislative body.

44. Kristin Svendsen, "Detenciones y procesos legales por el delito de posesión para el consumo en Guatemala," *El Observador Judicial* (Instituto de Estudios Comparados de Ciencias Penales de Guatemala [ICCPG]) 8, no. 56 (May–
June 2005).

45. Author's interview with Gabriela Flores, ICCPG, Guatemala City, March
2006.

46. Author's interview with a minors' public defense lawyer, Guatemala City, June 2006.

47. Ibid.; author's interview with a former functionary of the judicial system, Guatemala City, March 2006.

48. In 2005 the police launched a plan dubbed Guatemala Segura (Safe Guatemala), in which 1,900 members of the armed forces were called to support civilian police agents. In contrast to Plan Escoba, Guatemala Segura was not an effort of mass detention of gang members and is hence not considered a crackdown plan. Estado de la Nación, *Decimecuarto informe sobre estado de la nación en desarrollo humano sostenible* (Fourteenth State of the Nation Report on Human Sustainable Development) (San José, Costa Rica: Estado de la Nación, 2008), http://www.estadonacion.or.cr/.

49. Author's interview with a police official from the anti-*mara* unit of the PNC, Guatemala City, June 2006.

50. Author's interview with a UNDP representative, Guatemala City, March 2006.

51. Author's interviews with representatives from civil society organizations working on gang issues and with former functionaries from the judicial system, Guatemala City, March, June, and September 2006.

52. The contact with other criminal actors, particularly those involved in organized crime, opened new opportunities for some gang members to engage in more sophisticated criminal activities. Although gang members may be involved in some organized crime activities, there are no indications of a formal relationship between gangs and organized crime. For more details, see Ranum, "Pandillas juveniles transnacionales."

53. Author's interviews (see note 51).

54. Author's interview with an active gang member detained in a juvenile justice center in Guatemala City, September 2006.

55. Author's interviews with representatives from civil society organizations working on gangs, Guatemala City, March, June, and September 2006; author's interview with a U.S. adviser to the PNC, Guatemala City, 2006.

56. Scott Decker, "Collective and Normative Features of Gang Violence," *Justice Quarterly* 13, no. 2 (1996): 243–264; Bruce A. Jacobs and Richard Wright, *Street Justice: Retaliation in the Criminal Underworld* (Cambridge: Cambridge University Press, 2006); John P. Sullivan, "Maras Morphing: Revisiting Third Generation Gangs," *Global Crime* 7, no. 3–4 (August–November 2006): 487–504.

57. Scott H. Decker, Tim Bynum, and Deborah Weisel, "A Tale of Two Cities: Gangs as Organized Crime Groups," *Justice Quarterly* 15, no. 3 (1998): 395–425; Sullivan, "Maras Morphing."

58. Ranum, "Pandillas juveniles transnacionales."

59. Guatemalan authorities have repeatedly attributed the majority of homicides to gang activity—e.g., author's interview with a senior officer of the PNC, 2006. See "Guatemala es el quinto país más violento de Latinoamérica," *El Periódico*, 27 June 2006.

60. For more details, see Ranum, "Pandillas juveniles transnacionales."

61. Theodore Leggett, *Crime and Development in Central America: Caught in the Crossfire* (United Nations Office on Drugs and Crime [UNODC], May 2007),

http://www.unodc.org/documents/data-and-analysis/Central-america-study-en
.pdf.

62. PNUD, *Informe estadístico de la violencia en Guatemala* (Guatemala City: Programa de Seguridad Ciudadana y Prevención de la Violencia del PNUD Guatemala, 2007).

63. PNUD, *Diversidad étnico-cultural: La ciudadanía en un estado plural; Informe nacional de desarrollo humano, Guatemala 2005* (Guatemala City: PNUD, 2005).

64. Author's interviews with representatives from the judicial system and civil society organizations working with gangs, Guatemala City, March, June, and September 2006.

65. Procurador de los Derechos Humanos (PDH), *Muertes violentas de niñez, adolescencia y jóvenes y propuestas para su prevención* (Guatemala City: PDH, 2004), http://www.pdh.org.gt/files/inf_especiales/MN2003.pdf.

66. UNHCR, *Los derechos civiles y políticos.*

67. It was during this administration that the above-mentioned scandal surrounding the PNC and the Ministry of Internal Affairs occurred. The incident forced the director of the PNC and the minister of internal affairs to resign. In the aftermath, several hundred police agents were dismissed from the PNC.

68. More than 500 cases of public lynching were reported in the period from 1996 to 2002. Carlos A. Mendoza, "Causas de linchamientos en Guatemala: ¿Barbarie o justicia popular?" (presentation at Universidad Centroamericana "José Simeón Cañas," San Salvador, El Salvador, 3 May 2006).

69. For more details on how gangs have been treated as a newly arising threat to national and hemispheric security, see Gaston Chiller and Laurie Freeman, *El nuevo concepto de seguridad hemisférica de la OEA: Una amenaza en potencia* (Washington, DC: WOLA, 2005).

Chapter 4

1. Data from World Bank, *Honduras Country Brief* (October 2008), http://www.worldbank.org.

2. "Gang Prevention in Honduras," Community Police presentation, Tegucigalpa, Honduras, March 2008.

3. Ibid. Also see Theodore Leggett, *Crime and Development in Central America: Caught in the Crossfire* (United Nations Office on Drugs and Crime [UNODC], May 2007), http://www.unodc.org/documents/data-and-analysis/Central-america-study-en.pdf; and "Annex 3: Honduras Profile," in U.S. Agency for International Development (USAID), Bureau for Latin American and Caribbean Affairs, Office of Regional Sustainable Development, *Central America and Mexico Gang Assessment* (Washington, DC: USAID, April 2006), http://www.usaid.gov/locations/latin_america_caribbean/democracy/gangs_cam.pdf. One study quotes a source that claims gang membership, including gang "sympathizers" and ex-gang members, to be as high as 100,000. See Hilda Caldera and Guillermo Jiménez, *Prevención de maras y pandillas: Realidad y desafíos* (Tegucigalpa, Honduras: Programa Nacional de Prevención, 2006).

4. Tomás Andino Mencía, *Las maras en la sombra: Ensayo de actualización del fenómeno pandillero en Honduras* (Universidad Centroamericana "Simeón Cañas," Instituto Universitario de Opinión Pública, September 2006), http://www.wola.org/media/Gangs/diagnostico_honduras.pdf, cited in *Transnational Study on Youth Gangs* (Washington Office on Latin America [WOLA], 30 March 2007).

5. Mark J. Ruhl, "Redefining Civil-Military Relations in Honduras," *Journal of Interamerican Studies and World Affairs* 38, no. 1 (Spring 1996): 33–66.

6. Ibid.

7. Charles T. Call, "Sustainable Development in Central America: The Challenges of Violence, Injustice and Insecurity" (Central America 2020 Working Paper 8, Institut für Iberoamerika-Kunde, Hamburg, 2000), http://ca2020.fiu.edu/Themes/Charles_Call/Call.pdf.

8. Ibid.

9. World Bank, *Honduras: Country Economic Memorandum/Poverty Assessment* (Report 13317-HO; World Bank, 17 November 1994). The report notes that "the percentage [of increase in urban poverty] may have been exaggerated by a methodological change in the classification of the data. Beginning in 1990, some rural clusters were reclassified as urban. Given the lack of documentation, these clusters cannot be identified and the degree of overestimation of urban poverty cannot be quantified." Yet the report does conclude that in 1993 the proportion of the urban poor population had increased.

10. See Cordula Strocka, "Youth Gangs in Latin America," *SAIS Review* 26, no. 2 (Summer–Fall 2006): 133–146.

11. Gustavo Sánchez Velázquez, *Maras, pandillas y desviación social* (Buenos Aires: Editorial Dunken, 2008).

12. Andino Mencía, *Las maras en la sombra*.

13. Testimony of Chris Swecker, assistant director, Criminal Investigation Division, Federal Bureau of Investigation, in *Gangs and Crime in Latin America: Hearing before the Subcommittee on the Western Hemisphere of the Committee on International Relations, U.S. House of Representatives*, 109th Cong., 1st sess., 20 April 2005.

14. Sánchez Velázquez, *Maras, pandillas y desviación social*.

15. WOLA, "Gangs in Honduras," in *Central American Gang-Related Asylum: A Resource Guide* (Washington, DC: WOLA, May 2008), 21–24, http://www.wola.org/media/Gangs/WOLA_Gang_Asylum_Guide.pdf.

16. "Shuttling between Nations, Latino Gangs Confound the Law," *New York Times*, 26 September 2004. For some, the illegal activity consisted of simply being in the United States without documentation.

17. Illegal Immigration Reform and Immigrant Responsibility Act of 1996, Public Law 104-208, 104th Cong., 2nd sess., 30 September 1996.

18. The numbers deported were 27,060 in 2006 and 29,737 in 2007. U.S. Department of Homeland Security, Office of Immigration Statistics, "Aliens Removed by Criminal Status and Region and Country of Nationality: Fiscal Years 1998–2007," table 37 in *2007 Yearbook of Immigration Statistics* (Washington, DC: U.S. Department of Homeland Security, Office of Immigration Statistics, 2008).

19. Andino Mencía, *Las maras en la sombra*.

20. Sánchez Velázquez, *Maras, pandillas y desviación social*.

21. Based on author's interviews with Honduran gang specialists. Also see WOLA, "Gangs in Honduras"; and Andino Mencía, *Las maras en la sombra*.

22. Observatorio Centroamericano sobre Violencia (OCAVI), "Tasas de homicidios dolosos en Centroamérica y República Dominicana por 100,000 habitantes (1999–2007)," OCAVI website, http://www.ocavi.com/docs_files/file_378 .pdf.

23. According to UNHCR Refworld, "The Code was promulgated by Decreto No. 73-1996 and published in the Diario Oficial la Gaceta No. 28.053 dated 5 September 1996." See UNHCR Refworld, http://www.unhcr.org/refworld/ docid/3dbe70415.html.

24. Andino Mencía, *Las maras en la sombra*.

25. Strocka, "Youth Gangs in Latin America." Also, research has shown that in countries such as Guatemala, El Salvador, and Honduras, as citizens' perceptions of insecurity increase, support for a break from democracy and rule of law also increases. See José Miguel Cruz, "The Impact of Violent Crime on the Political Culture of Latin America: The Special Case of Central America," in Mitchell A. Seligson, ed., *Challenges to Democracy in Latin America and the Caribbean: Evidence of the Americas Barometer 2006–2007* (Latin American Public Opinion Project, Vanderbilt University, March 2008), 219–249, http://www.vanderbilt .edu/lapop/.

26. Programa Estado de la Nación, "El dilema estratégico de la seguridad ciudadana y el estado democrático de derecho," in *Estado de la región en desarrollo humano sostenible, 2008: Un informe desde Centroamérica y para Centroamérica* (San José, Costa Rica: Programa Estado de la Nación, 2008).

27. The amended article is available at http://www.glin.gov/view.action ?glinID=91190.

28. OCAVI, "Tasas de homicidios dolosos."

29. Casa Alianza Honduras, *Análisis mensual sobre problemática de la niñez hondureña*, Report 2 (Tegucigalpa, Honduras: Casa Alianza Honduras, February 2006).

30. Petition 12.331 (Honduras) is a well-known case. Information on it can be found on the IACHR website, http://www.cidh.org/annualrep/2002eng/Hon duras.12331.htm#_ftnref5.

31. U.S. Department of State, Bureau of Democracy, Human Rights, and Labor, *Honduras*, 2006 and 2007 Country Reports on Human Rights Practices, http://www.state.gov/g/drl/rls/hrrpt/2006/78896.htm and http://www.state.gov/ g/drl/rls/hrrpt/2007/100644.htm. Also see Amnesty International, *Honduras: Zero Tolerance for Impunity; Extrajudicial Executions of Children and Youths since 1998*, AMR 37/001/2003 (Amnesty International, 25 February 2003), http://www .amnesty.org/en/library/info/AMR37/001/2003.

32. Author interviews with Honduran police officials.

33. Andino Mencía, *Las maras en la sombra*.

34. Programa Estado de la Nación, "El dilema estratégico."

35. Clare Ribando Seelke, "Anti-gang Efforts in Central America: Moving beyond *Mano Dura*?" (paper, *Maras*, Security and Development in Central America Task Force, Center for Hemispheric Policy, University of Miami, 10 April 2007).

36. Through the 2008 Mérida Initiative, the United States has pledged some $65 million to the entire Central American region, including Haiti and the Dominican Republic, for regional security initiatives. See the Mérida Initiative Portal, Mexico Institute, Woodrow Wilson International Center for Scholars, http://www.wilsoncenter.org/index.cfm?topic_id=5949&fuseaction=topics.item&news_id=407349.

37. European Commission, "Honduras: Country Strategy Paper, 2007–2013," 29 March 2007, http://ec.europa.eu/external_relations/honduras/csp/07_13_en.pdf.

38. Data are from 2006. See Programa Estado de la Nación, "El dilema estratégico."

Chapter 5

1. Ernesto Cardenal, *La revolución perdida: Memorias III* (Managua: Anamá, 2003), 291.

2. "Valoración pandillas," III Trimestre 2005 (Policía Nacional, Managua, 2005).

3. John M. Hagedorn, *A World of Gangs: Armed Young Men and Gangsta Culture* (Minneapolis: University of Minnesota Press, 2008), 7–10.

4. Deborah Levenson, *Por sí mismos: Un estudio preliminar de las "maras" en la ciudad de Guatemala*, Cuadernos de Investigación, no. 4 (Guatemala City: AVANCSO, 1988).

5. Dennis Rodgers, "Dying for It: Gangs, Violence, and Social Change in Urban Nicaragua" (Crisis States Programme Working Paper 35, London School of Economics, October 2003), 7, http://www.crisisstates.com/download/wp/wp35.pdf.

6. José Luis Rocha, "Pandillero: La mano que empuña el mortero," *Envío Digital*, no. 216 (March 2000): 17–25.

7. Rodgers, "Dying for It," 8.

8. Gonzalo Wielandt, *Hacia la construcción de lecciones del posconflicto en América Latina y el Caribe: Una mirada a la violencia juvenil en Centroamérica*, Comisión Económica para America Latina y el Caribe (CEPAL), Serie Políticas Sociales, no. 115 (Santiago, Chile: Naciones Unidas, 2005), 26.

9. Juan José Sosa and José Luis Rocha, "Las pandillas en Nicaragua," in Equipo de Reflexión, Investigación y Comunicación (ERIC), Instituto de Encuestas y Sondeos de Opinión (IDESO), Instituto de Investigaciones Económicas y Sociales (IDIES), and IUDOP, eds., *Maras y pandillas en Centroamérica*, vol. 1 (Managua: UCA Publicaciones, 2001), 339; Irene Agudelo, *El rápido tránsito: Imágenes de la adolescencia y la juventud en Nicaragua* (Managua: Sistema de las Naciones Unidas en Nicaragua [United Nations System, Nicaragua], 1999).

10. Programa de las Naciones Unidas para el Desarrollo (PNUD), *Diagnóstico de seguridad ciudadana en Nicaragua* (Managua: PNUD, 2002).

11. Policía Nacional, *Plan de prevención de las pandillas 1999*, internal report (Managua: Policía Nacional, 1999).

12. Dennis Rodgers, "Living in the Shadow of Death: Gangs, Violence and

Social Order in Urban Nicaragua, 1996–2002," *Journal of Latin American Studies* 38, no. 2 (May 2006): 267–292.

13. PNUD, *Diagnóstico de seguridad ciudadana en Nicaragua*.

14. United Nations Office on Drugs and Crime (UNODC), *Crime and Development in Central America: Caught in the Crossfire* (Mexico City: UNODC, 2007), 60.

15. Ministerio de Gobernación Policía Nacional de Nicaragua, "Atención y tratamiento a las pandillas: Un modelo preventivo en desarrollo" (PowerPoint presentation at Reunión de Ministros/as de Gobernación y/o Seguridad, Managua, 15 October 2007), http://www.ocavi.com/docs_files/file_669.pdf.

16. "Violencia juvenil" (PowerPoint presentation, Policía Nacional, Managua, 2003).

17. Hagedorn, *World of Gangs*, 31.

18. Levenson, *Por sí mismos*.

19. Sandra Argueta, "Diagnóstico de los grupos llamados 'maras' en San Salvador: Factores psicosociales que prevalecen en los jóvenes que los integran," *Revista de Psicología de El Salvador* 2, no. 43 (1992): 53–84.

20. Francisco Andrés Escobar, "Por mi madre vivo y por mi barrio muero: Una aproximación al fenómeno de las maras," *ECA (Estudios Centroamericanos)* 51, no. 570 (1996): 327–349.

21. National Alliance of Gang Investigators Associations (NAGIA), *2005 National Gang Threat Assessment* (Washington, DC: Bureau of Justice Assistance, U.S. Department of Justice, 2005), 8.

22. Alberto Martín, Ana Fernández, and Karla Villareal, "Difusión transnacional de identidades juveniles en la expansión de las maras centroamericanas," *Perfiles Latinoamericanos*, no. 30 (July–December 2007): 114.

23. These are my calculations, based on statistics from the U.S. Homeland Security Department. They do not include those deported from 1997 and considers Central Americans only from Guatemala, Honduras, El Salvador, and Nicaragua.

24. American Community Survey (U.S. Census Bureau, Washington, DC, 2004), http://factinder.census.gov.

25. Alejandro Portes and Alex Stepick, *City on the Edge: The Transformation of Miami* (Berkeley: University of California Press, 1993), 152–154.

26. José Miguel Cruz, "Factors Associated with Juvenile Gangs in Central America," in José Miguel Cruz, ed., *Street Gangs in Central America* (San Salvador, El Salvador: UCA Editores, 2007), 40.

27. Jorge Atilano González, *En busca de la fraternidad perdida: Micro-relatos de una juventud abandonada que busca su identidad* (Mexico City: Centro de Estudios Teológicos de la Compañía de Jesús, 2002), 55.

28. Ibid.

29. Edelberto Torres-Rivas, *La piel de Centroamérica* (San José, Costa Rica: Facultad Latinoamericana de Ciencias Sociales [FLACSO], 2007), 162; Edelberto Torres-Rivas, *Centroamérica: Entre revoluciones y democracia* (Bogotá: Consejo Latinoamericano de Ciencias Sociales [CLACSO] Coediciones, 2008), 125.

30. Torres-Rivas, *La piel de Centroamérica*, 139.

31. Juan Hernández Pico, *Terminar la guerra, traicionar la paz: Guatemala*

en las dos presidencias de la paz; Arzú y Portillo (1996–2004) (Guatemala City: FLACSO, 2005), 424.

32. David Close, *Los años con doña Violeta* (Managua: Lea Grupo Editorial, 2005), 149.

33. Wielandt, *Hacia la construcción de lecciones*, 13.

34. Antonio Lacayo, *La difícil transición nicaragüense en el gobierno con doña Violeta*, Serie Ciencias Humanas, no. 12, Colección cultural de Centroamérica, Colombia (Managua: Fundación Uno, 2005), 202.

35. Close, *Los años con doña Violeta*, 164; Richard L. Millett and Orlando J. Pérez, "New Threats and Old Dilemmas: Central America's Armed Forces in the 21st Century," *Journal of Political and Military Sociology* (Summer 2005), http://findarticles.com/p/articles/mi_qa3719/is_200507/ai_n14904111/.

36. Close, *Los años con doña Violeta*, 151.

37. Millett, "New Threats and Old Dilemmas."

38. Ibid.

39. Hernández Pico, *Terminar la guerra*, 433; Rachel Sieder, "Legal Globalization and Human Rights: Constructing the 'Rule of Law' in Post-conflict Guatemala," in P. Pitarch, S. Speed, and X. Leyva, eds., *Human Rights in the Maya Region: Global Politics, Moral Engagements, and Cultural Contentions* (Durham, NC: Duke University Press, 2008).

40. Adriana Beltrán, *The Captive State: Organized Crime and Human Rights in Latin America*, Washington Office on Latin America (WOLA) Special Report (Washington, DC: WOLA, October 2007); Peter Waldmann, *El estado anómico: Derecho, seguridad pública y vida cotidiana en América Latina* (Caracas: Nueva Sociedad, 2003), 111–138.

41. Roberto Cajina, *Transición política y reconversión militar en Nicaragua, 1990–1995* (Managua: Coordinadora Regional de Investigaciones Económicas y Sociales [CRIES], 1997).

42. Lacayo, *La difícil transición nicaragüense*, 203.

43. Close, *Los años con doña Violeta*, 156.

44. *Small Arms Survey 2007: Guns and the City* (Geneva: Graduate Institute of International Studies, 2007), http://www.smallarmssurvey.org/files/sas/publications/yearb2007.html.

45. Annekent Müller, "Concluye labor de función de armas," *Visión Policial: Revista de la Policía Nacional* 11, no. 75 (May–June 2008), 6.

46. *Small Arms Survey 2007*.

47. Observatorio Centroamericano sobre la Violencia (OCAVI), http://www.ocavi.com.

48. Ibid.

49. Ibid.

50. Zygmunt Bauman, *Tiempos líquidos: Vivir en una época de incertidumbre* (Barcelona: Tusquets Editores, 2008), 26–29.

51. Policía Nacional, *Plan de prevención*.

52. José Luis Rocha, "Mapping the Labyrinth from Within: The Political Economy of Nicaraguan Youth Policy Concerning Violence," *Bulletin of Latin American Research* 26, no. 4 (2007): 533–549.

53. Policía Nacional, Disposición no. 002/04.

54. Edwin Cordero, Hamyn Gurdián, and Carlos Emilio López, *Alcanzando un sueño* (Save the Children Suecia, Policía Nacional de Nicaragua, 2006), 78.

55. Author's interview with Hamyn Gurdián, Managua, 12 December 2005.

56. Cordero, Gurdián, and López, *Alcanzando un sueño*, 65.

57. Procuraduría para la Defensa de los Derechos Humanos (PDDH), *¿Cara o sol? Investigación socio-jurídica de adolescentes que se encuentran en privación de libertad en los departamentos de la policía a nivel nacional* (Managua: PDDH, 2002), 71.

58. Centro Nicaragüense de Derechos Humanos (CENIDH), *Informe sobre derechos humanos en Nicaragua, 2004–2005* (Managua: CENIDH, 2006), 33.

59. Richard Maclure and Melvin Sotelo, "Children's Rights as Residual Social Policy in Nicaragua: State Priorities and the Code of Childhood and Adolescence," *Third World Quarterly* 24, no. 4 (2003): 681.

60. CENIDH, *¿Dónde están los derechos?* (Managua: CENIDH, 2004), 31.

61. Ministerio de Gobernación Policía Nacional de Nicaragua, "Atención y tratamiento a las pandillas."

62. Ibid.

63. Rodgers, "Living in the Shadow of Death"; Rocha, "Mapping the Labyrinth from Within."

64. José Luis Rocha, "La Mara 18 tras las huellas de las pandillas políticas," *Envío*, no. 321 (2008): 26–31.

Chapter 6

1. On vigilantism, see Daniel Goldstein, *The Spectacular City: Violence and Performance in Urban Bolivia* (Durham, NC: Duke University Press, 2004).

2. On state links to organized crime, see Phil Williams, "Organizing Transnational Crime: Networks, Markets, and Hierarchies," in Phil Williams and Dimitri Vlassis, eds., *Combating Transnational Crime: Concepts, Activities, and Responses* (London: Frank Cass, 2001), 73; and Roy Godson, "The Political-Criminal Nexus and Global Security," in Roy Godson, ed., *Menace to Society: Political-Criminal Collaboration around the World* (New Brunswick, NJ: Transaction Publishers, 2003).

3. Ruth Berins Collier and David Collier, *Shaping the Political Arena: Critical Junctures, the Labor Movement, and Regime Dynamics in Latin America* (Princeton, NJ: Princeton University Press, 1991).

4. Laurie Gunst, *Born Fi' Dead: A Journey through the Jamaican Posse Underworld* (New York: Henry Holt, 1996); Amanda Sives, "Changing Patrons, from Politicians to Drug Dons: Clientelism in Downtown Kingston," *Latin American Perspectives* 29 (2002): 66–89. Also see Anthony Harriott, *Police and Crime Control in Jamaica: Problems of Reforming Ex-Colonial Constabularies* (Kingston, Jamaica: University of the West Indies Press, 2000).

5. Richard L. Millett, "Nicaragua: The Politics of Frustration," in Howard J. Wiarda and Harvey F. Kline, eds., *Latin American Politics and Development*, 6th ed. (Boulder, CO: Westview Press, 2007), 466–467. Former Sandinista leader Daniel Ortega was reelected to the presidency in 2006 for a five-year term.

6. Dwight Wilson, "Guatemala: A Second Decade of Spring?" in Wiarda and Kline, *Latin American Politics and Development*, 508–509.

7. On the genocide in Guatemala, see Jennifer Schirmer, "The Looting of Democratic Discourse by the Guatemalan Military: Implications for Human Rights," in Elizabeth Jelin and Eric Hershberg, eds., *Constructing Democracy: Human Rights, Citizenship, and Society in Latin America* (Boulder, CO: Westview Press, 1998), 86.

8. On lynchings in Guatemala, see Angelina Snodgrass Godoy, *Popular Injustice: Violence, Community, and the Law in Latin America* (Palo Alto, CA: Stanford University Press, 2006).

9. Stanley A. Pimentel, "The Nexus of Organized Crime and Politics in Mexico," in John Bailey and Roy Godson, eds., *Organized Crime and Democratic Governance: Mexico and the U.S.-Mexican Borderlands* (Pittsburgh: University of Pittsburgh Press, 2000); Leonardo Curzio, "Organized Crime and Political Campaign Finance in Mexico," in John Bailey and Roy Godson, eds., *Organized Crime and Democratic Governance: Mexico and the U.S.-Mexican Borderlands* (Pittsburgh: University of Pittsburgh Press, 2000).

10. Louise I. Shelley, "Transnational Organized Crime: The New Authoritarianism," in H. Richard Friman and Peter Andreas, eds., *The Illicit Global Economy and State Power* (Lanham, MD: Rowman and Littlefield, 1999), 44.

11. Paul Chevigny, *Edge of the Knife: Police Violence in the Americas* (New York: New Press, 1995), 234.

12. "La violencia en Medellín," *El Espectador*, 21 April 2009; "La violencia en Medellín: Un rompecabezas para armar," Agencia de Prensa IPC, 12 May 2009; Adrian Alsema, "Uribe Orders Militarization of Medellín Neighborhoods to Halt Gang Violence," *Colombia Reports*, 8 April 2009.

13. Enrique Desmond Arias, *Drugs and Democracy in Rio de Janeiro: Trafficking, Social Networks, and Public Security* (Chapel Hill: University of North Carolina Press, 2006).

14. See Chapter 3 in this volume.

15. Luiz Eduardo Soares, *Meu casaco de general: Quinhentos dias no Front da Segurança Pública* (São Paulo: Companhia das Letras, 2000), 34–35.

16. Rafael Ruiz, "Violencia tatuada," *El País*, 10 December 2006; Ana Arana, "How Street Gangs Took Central America," *Foreign Affairs* (May–June 2005): 98–110; Deborah Rebollo, "Photographer Documents Mara Salvatrucha in Prison," *La Plaza* (blog), *Los Angeles Times*, 30 October 2008, http://latimesblogs.latimes.com/laplaza/2008/10/the-intricate-1.html.

17. Francisco Alves Filho and Marcos Pernambuco, "No front inimigo," *Istoé* (São Paulo), 19 June 2002, 24–37; Jon Lee Anderson, "Gangland: Who Controls the Streets of Rio de Janeiro?" *New Yorker*, 5 October 2009, 47–57.

18. Matthew Price, "Inside Mexico's Most Dangerous City," BBC News, 23 March 2009, http://news.bbc.co.uk/2/hi/7959247.stm; Tom Bowman, "CIA and Pentagon Wonder: Could Mexico Implode?" National Public Radio, 27 February 2009, http://www.npr.org/templates/story/story.php?storyId=101215537.

Chapter 7

1. Ana Arana, "How the Street Gangs Took Central America," *Foreign Affairs*, May–June 2005, 98–110; José Miguel Cruz, "Factors Associated with Juvenile Gangs in Central America, in José Miguel Cruz, ed., *Street Gangs in Central America* (San Salvador, El Salvador: UCA Editores, 2007); U.S. Agency for International Development (USAID), Bureau for Latin American and Caribbean Affairs, Office of Regional Sustainable Development, *Central America and Mexico Gang Assessment* (Washington, DC: USAID, April 2006), http://www.usaid.gov/locations/latin_america_caribbean/democracy/gangs_cam.pdf.

2. Joan W. Moore, *Going Down to the Barrio: Homeboys and Homegirls in Change* (Philadelphia: Temple University Press, 1991).

3. Scott H. Decker and Barrik Van Winkle, *Life in the Gang: Family, Friends, and Violence* (Cambridge: Cambridge University Press, 1996); John Hagedorn, *A World of Gangs: Armed Young Men and Gansta Culture* (Minneapolis: University of Minnesota, 2008).

4. Enrique Desmond Arias, "The Dynamics of Criminal Governance: Networks and Social Order in Rio de Janeiro," *Journal of Latin American Studies* 38 (2006): 293–310.

5. María Santacruz Giralt and Elin Ranum, *"Seconds in the Air": Women Gang Members and Their Prisons* (San Salvador, El Salvador: UCA Editores, 2010); and José Miguel Cruz, "Central American *Maras*: From Youth Street Gangs to Transnational Protection Rackets," *Global Crime* 11, no. 4 (2010): 379–398.

6. Elin Cecilie Ranum, "Pandillas juveniles transnacionales en Centroamérica, México y Estados Unidos," Diagnóstico Nacional Guatemala, Red Transnacional de Análisis sobre Maras, Centro de Estudios y Programas Interamericanos (Instituto Técnologico Autónomo de México [ITAM] and Instituto Universitario de Opinión Pública [IUDOP], 2006), http://interamericanos.itam.mx/maras/docs/Diagnostico_Guatemala.pdf. See also chapter 3 of this volume.

7. See Programa de las Naciones Unidas para el Desarrollo (PNUD), *Informe sobre desarrollo humano para América Central 2009–2010* (San José, Costa Rica: PNUD, 2009).

8. Deborah Levenson, *On Their Own: A Preliminary Study of Youth Gangs in Guatemala City*, Cuadernos de Investigación, no. 4 (Guatemala City: AVANCSO, 1998).

9. See ibid.

10. IUDOP, "La delincuencia urbana: Encuesta exploratoria, *ECA (Estudios Centroamericanos)*, no. 534–535 (1993): 471–482.

11. Heidrun Zinecker, *From Exodus to Exitus: Causes of Post-war Violence in El Salvador*, PRIF Reports, no. 80 (Frankfurt: Peace Research Institute Frankfurt, 2007).

12. José Miguel Cruz, "Organized Civil Society and Gangs: Alternative Response by Central American Organizations," in Cruz, *Street Gangs in Central America*.

13. I am grateful to Tom Bruneau for suggesting this term.

14. José Luis Rocha, *Lanzando piedras, fumando piedras: Evolución de las pan-*

dillas en Nicaragua 1997–2006 (Managua: UCA Publicaciones, 2007). See also Rocha's chapter in this volume (Chapter 5).

15. USAID, *Central America and Mexico Gang Assessment*; José Miguel Cruz, ed., *Maras y pandillas en Centroamérica*, vol. 4, *Las respuestas de la sociedad civil organizada* (San Salvador, El Salvador: UCA Editores, 2006); Zinecker, *From Exodus to Exitus.*

16. Oscar Bonilla, "Las reformas al sector seguridad en América Latina y el impacto de las amenazas irregulares: El caso de El Salvador," in José Raúl Perales, ed., *Reforma de las fuerzas armadas en América Latina y el impacto de las amenazas irregulares* (Washington, DC: Woodrow Wilson International Center for Scholars, 2008), 15–23.

17. Rocha, *Lanzando piedras, fumando piedras.*

18. Francisco Bautista, "El papel de la policía ante la seguridad ciudadana y la violencia juvenil," paper read at the seminar "La responsabilidad penal juvenil desde las perspectiva de los derechos humanos," Guatemala City, 2004.

19. This cooperation is still going strong. The first Transnational Anti-Gang Center in the region opened in El Salvador in October 2007, and activities were expected to expand to Guatemala and Honduras by late 2009. The center in El Salvador operates with direct aid from the FBI in the form of agents and resources. See Clare Ribando Seelke, *Gangs in Central America* (Congressional Research Service [CRS] Report for Congress, 2009).

20. Bautista, "El papel de la policía."

21. Rocha, *Lanzando piedras, fumando piedras.*

22. Marlon Carranza, "Del asistencialismo a la incidencia y el cabildeo: Las diversas respuestas de la sociedad civil organizada al fenómeno de las pandillas en Honduras," in Cruz, *Maras y pandillas en Centroamérica*, vol. 4, *Las respuestas de la sociedad civil organizada*; Geoff Thale and Elsa Falkenburger, *Youth Gangs in Central America: Issues on Human Rights, Effective Policing, and Prevention*, WOLA Special Report (Washington, DC: WOLA, 2006).

23. Jeannette Aguilar and Lissette Miranda, "Entre la articulación y la competencia: Las respuestas de la sociedad civil organizada a las pandillas en El Salvador," in Cruz, *Maras y pandillas en Centroamérica*, vol. 4, *Las respuestas de la sociedad civil organizada*; Tomás Andino Mencía, *Las maras en la sombra: Ensayo de actualización del fenómeno pandillero en Honduras* (Universidad Centroamericana "Simeón Cañas," IUDOP, September 2006), http://www.wola.org/media/Gangs/diagnostico_honduras.pdf.

24. Aguilar and Miranda, "Entre la articulación y la competencia."

25. Andino, *Las maras en la sombra.*

26. In Guatemala these centers are known as *delitos de bagatela*. Ranum, "Pandillas juveniles transnacionales," 32.

27. Bautista, "El papel de la policía."

28. Rocha, *Lanzando piedras, fumando piedras.*

29. Coordinadora Juventud por Guatemala (CSG), *Informe de Auditoría Social a la Política Nacional de Prevención de la Violencia Juvenil y su ente rector la Comisión Nacional de Prevención de la Violencia y Promoción Integral de Valores de Convivencia (CONAPREPI)* (Guatemala City: CSG, 2007).

30. Andino, *Las maras en la sombra*.

31. Jeannette Aguilar, "La mano dura y las 'políticas' de seguridad," *ECA (Estudios Centroamericanos)*, no. 667 (2004): 439.

32. Sonja Wolf, "The Politics of Gang Control: NGO Advocacy in Post-war El Salvador" (Ph.D. diss., Aberystwyth University, Wales, 2008).

33. Emilio Goubaud and Frank LaRue, pers. comm., Guatemala City, October 2005.

34. For a discussion about the Nicaraguan police and its political relationship with the different administrations, see William Grigsby, "The National Police under Attack: The Clues behind the Crisis," *Envío Digital*, no. 265 (August 2003), http://www.envio.org.ni/articulo/2108; and William Grigsby, "The New National Police Chief Faces Colossal Challenges," *Envío Digital*, no. 301 (August 2006), http://www.envio.org.ni/articulo/3348.

35. Heidrun Zinecker, *Violence in a Homeostatic System: The Case of Honduras*, PRIF Reports, no. 83 (Frankfurt: Peace Research Institute Frankfurt, 2008).

36. Amparo María Marroquin Parducci, "Indiferencias y espantos: Relatos de jóvenes y pandillas en la prensa escrita de Guatemala, El Salvador, y Honduras," in G. Rey, ed., *Los relatos periodísticos del crimen* (Bogotá: Centro de Competencia en Comunicación, Fundación Friedrich Ebert, 2007); Roxana Martel Trigueros, "Las maras salvadoreñas: Nuevas formas de espanto y de control social," *ECA (Estudios Centroamericanos)*, no. 696 (2007): 957–979.

37. Fabio Molina Vaquerano, *Reconocimiento de defunciones por homicidios realizados por los (las) médicos(as) forenses del Instituto de Medicina Legal de El Salvador, año 2004 (Investigación y análisis epidemiológico de los homicidios)* (San Salvador, El Salvador: Instituto de Medicina Legal, Unidad de Estadísticas, 2005), 81; Roberto Masferrer, *Defunciones por homicidios, El Salvador 2005* (San Salvador, El Salvador: Instituto de Medicina Legal, Unidad de Estadísticas, 2006).

38. PNUD, *Informe sobre desarrollo humano, Honduras 2006: Hacia la expansión de la ciudadanía* (Tegucigalpa, Honduras: PNUD, 2006), 130.

39. Victor Meza, *Honduras: Hacia una política integral de seguridad ciudadana* (Tegucigalpa, Honduras: CEDOH, 2004).

40. Zinecker, *From Exodus to Exitus*.

41. Ibid., 25.

42. IUDOP, "Evaluación de la opinión pública sobre el gobierno de Francisco Flores," *ECA (Estudios Centroamericanos)*, no. 668 (2004): 606–616.

43. José Miguel Cruz and María Santacruz Giralt, *La victimización y la percepción de seguridad en El Salvador en 2004* (San Salvador, El Salvador: Ministerio de Gobernación and PNUD, 2005).

44. Consultoría Interdisciplinaria en Desarrollo (CID), *Estudio Opinión Pública: Honduras #61* (San José, Costa Rica: CID, 2006).

45. Cruz, "Organized Civil Society and Gangs."

46. Ibid.; Wolf, "Politics of Gang Control."

47. Nielan Barnes, "Transnational Youth Gangs in Central America, Mexico and the United States: Executive Summary," in Rafael Fernández de Castro, ed., *Pandillas juveniles transnacionales en Centroamérica, México y Estados Unidos* (Washington, DC: WOLA, 2007), http://www.wola.org/media/Gangs/executive_summary_gangs_study.pdf; Cruz, *Maras y pandillas en Centroamérica*, vol. 4, *Las res-*

puestas de la sociedad civil organizada; Demoscopía, *Maras y pandillas, comunidad y policía en Centroamérica: Hallazgos de un estudio integral* (San José, Costa Rica: Demoscopía, 2007); Thale and Falkenburger, *Youth Gangs in Central America.*

48. USAID, *Central America and Mexico Gang Assessment.*

49. Cruz, "Central American *Maras*"; José Miguel Cruz, "El barrio transnacional: Las maras centroamericanas como red," in Francis Pisani, Natalia Saltalamacchia, Arlene Tickner, and Nielan Barnes, eds., *Redes transnacionales en la cuenca de los huracanes: Un aporte a los studios interamericanos* (Mexico City: Instituto Tecnológico Autónomo de México [ITAM] and Miguel Angel Porrúa, 2007), 357–382.

50. Policía Nacional Civil de Guatemala, *Situación de maras en Guatemala* (San Salvador, El Salvador: Observatorio Centroamericano de la Violencia [OCAVI], 2007), http://www.ocavi.com/docs_files/file_424.pdf.

51. Oscar Iraheta, "El setenta por ciento de las extorsiones son cometidas por maras," *El Diario de Hoy*, 19 August 2009, http://www.elsalvador.com/mwedh/nota/nota_completa.asp?idCat=6358&idArt=3930807.

52. Charles Tilly, "War Making and State Making as Organized Crime," in P. Evans, D. Rueschemeyer, and T. Skocpol, eds., *Bringing the State Back* (Cambridge: Cambridge University Press, 1985).

53. USAID, *Central America and Mexico Gang Assessment.*

54. Rocha, *Lanzando piedras, fumando piedras*; Dennis Rodgers, "Living in the Shadow of Death: Gangs, Violence and Social Order in Urban Nicaragua, 1996–2002," *Journal of Latin American Studies* 38 (2006): 267–292.

55. Decker and Van Winkle, *Life in the Gang.*

56. Adriana Beltrán, *The Captive State: Organized Crime and Human Rights in Latin America*, WOLA Special Report (Washington, DC: WOLA, October 2007); Thale and Falkenburger, *Youth Gangs in Central America.*

57. Demoscopía, *Maras y pandillas.*

58. Beatriz Castillo, "Inspectoría presentará cargos en caso de exjefes policiales," *Diario Co Latino* (San Salvador, El Salvador), 2 February 2010; "Reaching the Untouchables: Guatemala and Organised Crime," *Economist*, 11 March 2010.

59. See U.S. Department of State, Bureau of Democracy, Human Rights, and Labor, *Honduras*, 2005 Country Reports on Human Rights Practices, 8 March 2006, http://www.state.gov/g/drl/rls/hrrpt/2005/61732.htm.

60. Tomás Andino and Guillermo Jiménez, "Violencia juvenil, maras y pandillas en Honduras." In POLJUVE, ed., *Informe para la discusión* (Tegucigalpa, Honduras: Interpeace, 2009).

61. See U.S. Department of State, Bureau of Democracy, Human Rights, and Labor, *Guatemala*, 2005 Country Reports on Human Rights Practices, 8 March 2006, http://www.state.gov/g/drl/rls/hrrpt/2005/61729.htm.

62. Amnesty International, *El Salvador: Open Letter on the Anti-maras Act*, *El Salvador*, AMR 29/009/2003 (Amnesty International, December 1, 2003), http://www.amnesty.org/en/library/info/AMR29/009/2003.

63. Aguilar and Miranda, "Entre la articulación y la competencia"; Gabriel Aguilera Peralta, "Las amenazas irregulares en la agenda de seguridad de Centroamérica," in José Raúl Perales, ed., *Reforma de las fuerzas armadas en América Latina y el impacto de las amenazas irregulares* (Washington, DC: Woodrow Wil-

son Center for International Scholars, 2008); Beltrán, *Captive State*; Thale and Falkenburger, *Youth Gangs in Central America*; Heidrun Zinecker, *Violence in Peace: Form and Causes of Postwar Violence in Guatemala*, PRIF Reports, no. 76 (Frankfurt: Peace Research Institute Frankfurt, 2006).

64. In 2001 both El Salvador and Honduras implemented a prison policy that separated gang members by their gang identity to reduce problems with violence inside the jails. In practice, this has led to certain jails being known as Mara Salvatrucha jails or Eighteenth jails. In Guatemala a similar measure was implemented later, in 2005, after a series of massacres committed by one gang against the other.

65. Cruz, "Central American *Maras*."

66. Grigsby, "New National Police Chief."

67. For an extensive account of these processes, see José Miguel Cruz, "Criminal Violence and Democratization in Central America: The Survival of the Violent State," *Latin American Politics and Society* (forthcoming, Winter 2011).

68. Ibid.

Chapter 8

Unless otherwise noted, all translations of quotations in this chapter are by Michael Solis.

1. All of the surveys were carried out through programs financed by the Banco Interamericano de Desarrollo (BID). For more details, see Mauricio Rubio, *De la pandilla a la mara: Pobreza, educación, mujeres y violencia juvenil* (Bogotá: Universidad Externado de Colombia, 2007), http://sites.google.com/site/mauriciorubiop/.

2. This section of this chapter is based on Terence Thornberry and Marvon Krohn, "The Self-Report Method for Measuring Delinquency and Crime," in D. Duffee, ed., *Measurement and Analysis of Crime and Justice*, vol. 4. (Washington, DC: U.S. National Institute of Justice, 2000), 33–83; and David Farrington, *What Has Been Learned from Self-Reports about Criminal Careers and the Causes of Offending?* Report for the Home Office (Institute of Criminology, University of Cambridge, 2003), http://www.homeoffice.gov.uk/rds/pdfs/farrington.pdf.

3. Josine Junger-Tas, J. G. Terlouw, and Malcolm Klein, *Delinquent Behavior among Young People in the Western World* (Amsterdam: Kugler, 1994).

4. María Victoria Llorente, Enrique Chaux, and Luz Magdalena Salas, *Violencia intrafamiliar y otros factores de riesgo de la violencia juvenil en Colombia*, Informe Final (Final Report) (Bogotá: Departamento Nacional de Planeación, División de Justicia y Seguridad [DNP-DJS], Centro de Estudios sobre Desarrollo Económico [CEDE], 2004).

5. All of the surveys were carried out through programs financed by BID. For more details, see Rubio, *De la pandilla a la mara*.

6. Statement by the chief of the Department of Communication, Office of Juvenile Issues, Nicaragua, on Univision/AFP, 27 June 2005.

7. Fernando Savater, "La montaña y Mahoma," *El País*, 16 August 2005.

8. Centro de Estudios de Guatemala (CEG), *Las maras . . . ¿Amenaza a la*

seguridad? Informe Especial (Guatemala City: CEG, 2005), http://www.ceg.org .gt/fotos/file/4 MARAS.pdf. Emphasis added.

9. See Rubio, *De la pandilla a la mara.*

10. Juan Merino, "Las maras en Guatemala," in Equipo de Reflexión, Investigación y Comunicación (ERIC), Instituto de Encuestas y Sondeos de Opinión (IDESO), Instituto de Investigaciones Económicas y Sociales (IDIES), and Instituto Universitario de Opinión Pública (IUDOP), eds., *Maras y pandillas en Centroamérica,* vol. 1 (Managua: UCA Editores, 2001), 115.

11. Simona Gonçalves de Assis, "Situación de la violencia juvenil en Río de Janeiro," in Organización Panamericana de la Salud/Organización Mundial de la Salud (OPS/OMS-ASDI-BID), *Taller sobre la violencia de los adolescentes y las pandillas (maras) juveniles* (San Salvador, El Salvador, 7–9 May 1997), 51–58, http://www.paho.org/Spanish/HPP/HPF/ADOL/taller.pdf; Alfredo Barbetta, "Situación de violencia juvenil en São Paulo," in OPS/OMS-ASDI-BID, *Taller sobre la violencia de los adolescentes,* 59–63.

12. Nicole Veash, "Children of Privileged Form Brazil Crime Gangs: 'Silver-Spoon' Bandits Target the Wealthy," *Boston Globe,* February 2002, cited in Herbert Covey, *Street Gangs throughout the World* (Springfield, Ill.: Charles C. Thomas, 2003).

13. Covey, *Street Gangs throughout the World.*

14. Manfred Liebel, "Pandillas y maras: Señas de identidad," *Envío Digital,* no. 244 (July 2002), http://www.envio.org.ni/articulo/1161.

15. Ramiro Martínez and Ricardo Falla, "Clases medias: Violentas y organizadas," *Envío Digital,* no. 171 (June 1996), http://www.envio.org.ni/articulo/223.

16. Rubio, *De la pandilla a la mara.*

17. On Colombia, see, for example, "La máquina de infiltración de las FARC es el Partido Comunista Clandestino Colombiano," *Semana,* 12 August 2006. On Mexico, see "La sierra de Sinaloa es el feudo del principal cártel de narcotraficantes en México: En los dominios del Chapo Guzmán," *El País,* 2 February 2007.

18. José Luis Rocha, "Pandillero: La mano que empuña el mortero," *Envío Digital,* no. 216 (March 2000), http://www.envio.org.ni/articulo/994.

19. Rafael Ramírez Heredia, *La mara* (Mexico City: Alfaguara, 2004), 200–206.

20. See Rubio, *De la pandilla a la mara,* chap. 2, sec. 6.

21. See, for example, María Jimena Duzán, "El Proceso 8000: Fernando; No te lleves el secreto," *El Tiempo,* 5 February 2007; and Mauricio Vargas, "Los niños bien," *Eltiempo.com* (blog), 23 February 2007.

22. Sergio González, *Huesos en el desierto* (Barcelona: Anagrama, 2002), 21.

23. This medieval practice gave a nobleman the right to lie with any bride from among the peasants beholden to him, on her wedding night.

24. María López Vigil, "Abuso sexual, incesto: Diez años tocando heridas," *Envío Digital,* no. 234 (September 2001), http://www.envio.org.ni/articulo/1103.

25. This refers to the Logit, whose independent variable is the report of having been raped. The Logit function is a discrete choice (logistic) regression. All of the coefficients are significant at the 99 percent level.

26. Results are statistically significant at 99 percent, 99 percent, and 95 percent, respectively.

27. Luis J. Rodríguez, *La vida loca: El testimonio de un pandillero en Los Ángeles* (New York: Simon and Schuster, 2005), 135. Emphasis added.

28. Rocha, "Pandillero."

29. Juan José Sosa and José Luis Rocha, "Las pandillas en Nicaragua," in ERIC, IDESO, IDIES, and IUDOP, *Maras y pandillas en Centroamérica* (Managua: UCA Publicaciones, 2001), 425.

30. "Maras: ¿Víctimas o delincuentes?" *La Prensa*, 2 November 2000.

31. Laura Etcharren, "Ñetas: Una mara, un color dentro del mundo de la globalización," 12 May 2006, http://lauraetcharren.blogspot.com/2006/05/etas.html (site discontinued).

32. Liebel, "Pandillas y maras." Translated from the Spanish by Mauricio Rubio.

33. This hypothesis is developed and contrasted with the findings of the survey carried out in Panama in Mauricio Rubio, *Pandillas, rumba y actividad sexual: Desmitificando la violencia juvenil* (Bogotá: Universidad Externado de Colombia, 2006); http://sites.google.com/site/mauriciorubiop/.

34. Quoted in Santiago Botello and Ángel Moya, *Reyes Latinos: Los códigos secretos de los Latin Kings en España* (Madrid: Temas de Hoy, 2005), 29, 73–74.

35. Antonio Jiménez Barca, "Yo soy un 'latin king,'" *El País*, 10 July 2005.

36. As in Rubio, *De la pandilla a la mara*.

37. Testimony of a soldier, in Margarita Carrera, "Persistencia del feminicidio en Guatemala," *Prensa Libre*, 17 June 2005.

38. Ibid.

39. "Contra el feminicidio en Guatemala," *Universia*, 21 November 2005, http://noticias.universia.es/vida-universitaria/noticia/2005/11/21/604824/contra-feminicidio-guatemala.html.

40. Amnesty International, *Guatemala: No Protection, No Justice; Killings of Women in Guatemala*, AMR 34/017/2005 (London: Amnesty International, June 2005), 15, http://www.amnesty.org/en/library/info/AMR34/017/2005/en.

Chapter 9

1. Thomas H. Carr (Washington/Baltimore High Intensity Drug Trafficking Area), "Information Brokering," lecture presented at the i2 National User Conference, Arlington, VA, 15 May 2008.

2. Mark M. Lowenthal, *Intelligence: From Secrets to Policy*, 3rd ed. (Washington, DC: CQ Press, 2006), 64.

3. Ibid., 65.

4. Tactic suggested by Major Alex Grynckewich, USAF, during a group discussion on terrorist financing at the Naval Postgraduate School, Monterey, CA, 5 June 2006.

5. Malcolm W. Klein and Cheryl L. Maxson, *Street Gang Patterns and Policies* (New York: Oxford University Press, 2006), 60–61.

6. Ibid., 59–60.

7. Marylin Peterson, *Intelligence-Led Policing: The New Intelligence Architec-

ture (Washington, DC: U.S. Department of Justice, Bureau of Justice Assistance, September 2005), 11.

8. Carl Peed, Ronald E. Wilson, and Nichole J. Scalisi, "Crime Mapping and Analysis," *Police Chief*, September 2008, 24.

9. José Miguel Cruz, ed., *Street Gangs in Central America* (San Salvador, El Salvador: UCA Editores, 2007), 82.

10. Ibid., 76, 78.

11. Ibid., 78.

12. Ibid., 83–85.

13. Peed, Wilson, and Scalisi, "Crime Mapping and Analysis," 28.

14. "CBP Announces Support for the National Gang Intelligence Center," http://www.cbp.gov/xp/cgov/newsroom/highlights/.

15. Christian Venhuizen, "Wyoming Army Guard Intel Cracks Gang Code," National Guard Bureau website, 18 June 2008, http://www.ng.mil/news/archives/2008/06/061808-gang-code.aspx.

16. Ana Arana, "How the Street Gangs Took Central America," in *Air War College Nonresident Studies Senior Leader Course*, book 4 (Maxwell AFB, Ala.: Air University Press, January 2006), 263, 268; reprinted from *Foreign Affairs*, May–June 2005, 98–110.

17. Peterson, *Intelligence-Led Policing*, 23.

18. Jay Atkinson, "Police Setting Up Database on Gangs," *Boston Globe*, 30 November 2008, http://www.boston.com/news/local/massachusetts/articles/2008/11/30/police_setting_up_database_on_gangs/.

19. "Gangs Ditch Tattoos, Go for College Look," Associated Press, 16 December 2007, http://www.msnbc.msn.com/id/22279005/.

20. Ibid.

Chapter 10

1. For example, during 2006–2009 the United States allocated approximately $7.45 billion for assistance to Latin America and the Caribbean, of which some $1.9 billion went to Central America for development and U.S. federal government programs such as International Military Education and Training, Foreign Military Financing, International Narcotics Control and Law Enforcement, and the International Law Enforcement Academy. In 2010, the request for Central America was $405 million. Connie Veillette, Clare Ribando, and Mark Sullivan, *U.S. Foreign Assistance to Latin America and the Caribbean*, Congressional Research Service (CRS) Report for Congress, RL32487, 28 March 2006; Connie Veillette, Clare Ribando, and Mark Sullivan, *U.S. Foreign Assistance to Latin America and the Caribbean: FY2006–FY2008*, CRS Report for Congress, RL34299, 28 December 2007; U.S. Office of Management and Budget, "Diplomatic and Consular Programs: Budget for Fiscal Year 2010" (Department of State and Other International Programs, Administration of Foreign Affairs), http://www.whitehouse.gov/omb/budget/fy2010/assets/sta.pdf; Melinda Brouwer, "President's FY 2009 Budget Increases Funding for State Department," *U.S. Diplomacy: The World Af-*

fairs Blog Network, Foreign Policy Association, 4 February 2008, http://diplomacy .foreignpolicyblogs.com/2008/02/05/bush-2009-budget-increases-funding-for- state-department/; Susan B. Epstein and Kennon H. Nakamura, *State, Foreign Operations, and Related Programs: FY2009 Appropriations*, CRS Report for Congress, RL34552, 3 April 2009.

2. Christy McCampbell, quoted in Eric Green, "US–Central American Cooperation Focuses on Fighting Gangs," *America.gov*, 24 July 2007, http://www .america.gov/st/washfile-english/2007/July/200707241205091xeneerg0.4201471 .html.

3. This increased scrutiny was especially noticeable in 2004, after Bush administration officials said they had received information on alleged meetings between an al-Qaeda suspect and gang leaders in El Salvador. Dennis Rodgers and Robert Muggah, "Gangs as Non-state Armed Groups: The Central American Case," *Contemporary Security Policy* 30, no. 2 (August 2009): 301–317.

4. Robert S. Mueller III (director, Federal Bureau of Investigation), "Priorities in the FBI's Criminal Programs," statement before the Senate Judiciary Committee on the Judiciary, 111th Cong., 2nd sess., 16 September 2009, http://www .fbi.gov/news/testimony/priorities-in-the-fbi2018s-criminal-programs.

5. Legislative Analyst's Office, "The Three Strikes and You're Out Law," Sacramento, CA, 22 February 1995, http://www.lao.ca.gov/analysis_1995/3strikes .html; Patrick Beary, "Globalization and Gangs: The Evolution of Central American," Illinois Wesleyan University Honors Projects, Paper 6 (2007), http:// digitalcommons.iwu.edu/intstu_honproj/6.

6. Freddy Funes, "Removal of Central American Gang Members: How Immigration Laws Fail to Reflect Global Reality," *University of Miami Law Review* 63, no. 301 (2008): 301–338.

7. Mary Helen Johnson, "National Policies and the Rise of Transnational Gangs," *Migration Information Source*, 1 April 2006, http://www.migra tioninformation.org/usfocus/print.cfm?ID=394.

8. For example, in the early 1990s the United States deported approximately 40,000 aliens per year, but after the passage of the above-mentioned laws, the number of deportees gradually increased by almost ten times (e.g., to 359,000 in 2008). Funes, "Removal of Central American Gang Members"; Beary, "Globalization and Gangs"; Kyung Jin Lee, "U.S. Deportations Double over the Last Ten Years," *Medill Reports* (Northwestern University, Chicago), 23 February 2010, http://news.medill.northwestern.edu/chicago/news.aspx?id=157904&print=1.

9. U.S. Department of State, Bureau of International Narcotics and Law Enforcement Affairs, "Merida Initiative: Myth vs. Fact," fact sheet, 23 June 2009, http://www.state.gov/p/inl/rls/fs/122395.htm; Colleen W. Cook, Rebecca G. Rush, and Clare Ribando Seelke, *Merida Initiative: Proposed U.S. Anticrime and Counterdrug Assistance for Mexico and Central America*, CRS Report for Congress, RS22837, 18 March 2008.

10. SICA's members are Panama, Belize, Honduras, Nicaragua, Guatemala, and El Salvador. U.S. Department of Justice, "Fact Sheet: Department of Justice Comprehensive Efforts to Fight Gang Violence," 24 June 2008, http://www.jus tice.gov/opa/pr/2008/June/08-ag-562.html; Bob Killebrew and Jennifer Bernal, *Crime Wars: Gangs, Cartels, and the U.S. National Security* (Washington, DC: Cen-

ter for a New American Security, September 2010), 3–77; Clare Ribando Seelke and Kristin M. Finklea, *U.S.-Mexican Security Cooperation: The Mérida Initiative and Beyond*, CRS Report for Congress, R41349, 16 August 2010.

11. Committee on Hemispheric Security, Permanent Council of the Organization of American States, "U.S. Strategy to Combat the Threat of Criminal Gangs from Central America and Mexico," paper presented at the Special Meeting on the Phenomenon of Criminal Gangs, 17 January 2008, www.scm.oas.org/doc_public/ENGLISH/HIST_08/CP19418E04.doc.

12. Clare Ribando Seelke, *Gangs in Central America*, CRS Report for Congress, RL341112, updated 11 January 2010; Connie Veillette, Clare Ribando, and Mark Sullivan, *U.S. Foreign Assistance to Latin America and the Caribbean*, CRS Report for Congress, RL32487, updated 3 January 2006.

13. Seelke, *Gangs in Central America*; Veillette, Ribando, and Sullivan, *U.S. Foreign Assistance*, RL32487, updated 3 January 2006. According to James W. Rose, Regional Gang Adviser, INL, U.S. Embassy, San Salvador, 1 April 2011, the Model Precincts in El Salvador and Honduras will be fully staffed and operational by May 2011.

14. Tia Bland, "Mexican Corrections Instructors Graduate from New Mexico Training Academy," media note, Bureau of Public Affairs, U.S. Department of State, 23 April 2009.

15. Mary Helen Johnson, "National Policies"; Ana Arana, "How Street Gangs Took Central America," *Foreign Affairs*, May–June 2005, 98–110.

16. Rodgers and Muggah, "Gangs as Non-state Armed Groups."

17. U.S. Agency for International Development (USAID), Bureau for Latin American and Caribbean Affairs, Office of Regional Sustainable Development, *Central America and Mexico Gang Assessment* (Washington, DC: USAID, April 2006), http://www.usaid.gov/locations/latin_america_caribbean/democracy/gangs_cam.pdf.

18. Ibid.; Seelke, *Gangs in Central America*.

19. USAID, *Central America and Mexico Gang Assessment*; Celinda Franco, *The MS-13 and 18th Street Gangs: Emerging Transnational Gang Threats?* CRS Report for Congress, RL34233, 22 January 2010.

20. Sources on CAFE: U.S. Federal Bureau of Investigation (FBI), "Going Global on Gangs: New Partnership Targets MS-13," announcement, 10 October 2007, http://www.fbi.gov/news/stories/2007/october/ms13tag_101007; Seelke, *Gangs in Central America*; John S. Pistole, "A United Front against Transnational Gangs," speech to second Los Angeles Summit on Transnational Gangs, Los Angeles, 3 March 2008, http://www.fbi.gov/news/speeches/a-united-front-against-transnational-gangs; FBI, "Fact Sheet: Department of Justice Efforts to Combat Mexican Drug Cartels," 2 April 2009, http://www.fbi.gov/news/pressrel/press-releases/fact-sheet-department-of-justice-efforts-to-combat-mexican-drug-cartels.

21. Sources on TAG: FBI, "Going Global on Gangs"; FBI, "Fact Sheet: Department of Justice"; Seelke, *Gangs in Central America*.

22. FBI, "United against MS-13: Our Central American Partnerships," announcement, 10 November 2009, http://www.fbi.gov/page2/nov09/calee_111009.html; FBI, "FBI Conducts Training for U.S. and Central American Law En-

forcement Partners," press release, 7 October 2009, http://www.fbi.gov/news/ pressrel/press-releases/fbi-conducts-training-for-u.s.-and-central-american- law-enforcement-partners; FBI, "United against MS-13," transcript, n.d., http:// www.fbi.gov/news/videos/mp4/callee.mp4/view; FBI, "Sharing Intelligence: To Fight Transnational Gangs," announcement, 11 July 2009, http://www.fbi.gov/ news/stories/2009/august/gangs_081109; Kenneth W. Kaiser (assistant direc- tor, FBI), Statement before the House Committee on Foreign Affairs, Subcom- mittee on the Western Hemisphere, 7 February 2008, http://www.fbi.gov/news/ testimony/combating-international-gangs-through-the-merida-initiative.

23. U.S. Immigration and Customs Enforcement (ICE), Operation Com- munity Shield, "Targeting Violent Transnational Street Gangs," http://www.ice .gov/pi/investigations/comshield/index.htm; Mary Helen Johnson, "National Policies"; Seelke, *Gangs in Central America*.

24. USAID, Bureau for Latin American and Caribbean Affairs, Office of Regional Sustainable Development, *Central America and Mexico Gang Assessment* (Washington, DC: USAID, April 2006).

25. Seelke, *Gangs in Central America*.

26. Robert B. Shiflett and Hugo Teufel III, "Privacy Impact Assessment for the *Electronic* Travel Document System (*e*TD)," 13 October 2006.

27. Clare Ribando Seelke and June S. Beittel, *Mérida Initiative for Mexico and Central America: Funding and Policy Issues*, CRS Report for Congress, R40135, 1 June 2009.

28. USAID, *Central America and Mexico Gang Assessment*.

29. Seelke, *Gangs in Central America*.

30. USAID, *Central America and Mexico Gang Assessment*; U.S. Congress, House of Representatives, *Deportees in Latin America and the Caribbean: Hearing and Briefing before the Subcommittee on the Western Hemisphere of the Committee of Foreign Affairs, House of Representatives*, 110th Cong., 1st sess., 24 July 2007.

31. EU funds for Central America average approximately $198 million yearly, while U.S. aid ranges from $200 up to $700 million. "EU–Central America: Con- clusion of New Political Dialogue and Co-operation Agreement," *Europa* (Euro- pean Union website), press release IP/03/1336, Brussels, 2 October 2003.

32. Curt Tarnoff and Marian Leonardo Lawson, *Foreign Aid: An Introduction to U.S. Programs and Policy*, CRS Report for Congress, R40213, 9 April 2009.

33. Andres Oppenheimer, "Commentary: Obama's Foreign Aid Budget Cuts Send Wrong Message to Latin America," McClatchy, 13 February 2010, http:// www.mcclatchydc.com/2010/02/13/84438/commentary-obamas-foreign-aid .html.

34. Ibid.

35. Geoff Thale, "International Assistance in Responding to Youth Gang Violence in CA," memorandum, 30 September 2005, Washington Office on Latin America (WOLA), Washington, DC, http://www1.american.edu/coun cils/americas/Documents/GangViolence/international_coop_memo.pdf; Seelke, *Gangs in Central America*.

36. Apart from the reason for deportation, the United States now provides a more thorough (yet still incomplete) criminal history and offers law enforcement

officials in receiving countries the opportunity to contact the FBI and request a complete criminal history check (including gang membership). Seelke, *Gangs in Central America*.

37. U.S. Department of Justice, "Twenty-six Members of MS-13 Indicted on Racketeering, Narcotics, Extortion and Firearms Charges," press release, 24 June 2008, http://www.justice.gov/opa/pr/2008/June/08-ag-564.html. According to an interview with James W. Rose, Regional Gang Adviser, INL, U.S. Embassy, San Salvador, 1 April 2011: Between the coming into office of President Funes in 2009 and today, cooperative programs between the U.S. and El Salvador were essentially put on hold.

38. Robert J. López, Rich Connell, and Chris Kraul, "Gang Uses Deportation to Its Advantage to Flourish in U.S.," *Los Angeles Times*, 30 October 2005, http://www.latimes.com/news/local/la-me-gang30oct30,1,5492282.story; Beary, "Globalization and Gangs."

39. Honduras authorities have no effective methods to keep track of gang members in the country. Thomas Bruneau, interview with author, Monterey, CA, 12 December 2009.

40. Seelke, *Gangs in Central America*.

41. United Nations Office of Drugs and Crime (UNODC), *Crime and Development in CA: Caught in the Crossfire* (Mexico City: UNODC, 2007).

42. For more information, see ibid.; and Clare Ribando Seelke, *El Salvador: Political, Economic, and Social Conditions and U.S. Relations*, CRS Report for Congress, RS21655, 21 January 2010.

43. UNODC, *Crime and Development*; Seelke, *El Salvador*.

44. Eric Green, "State's Negroponte Targets Illegal Drugs on Central American Trip: Mérida Initiative Would Help Mexico, CA Combat Trafficking," 12 June 2008, http://www.america.gov/st/democracy-english/2008/June/2008061212482 51xeneerg0.9950678.html.

45. Seelke and Beittel, *Mérida Initiative*; Seelke, *Gangs in Central America*.

46. Jess T. Ford, *Status of Funds for the Mérida Initiative*, GAO-10-253R (Washington, DC: Government Accountability Office, 3 December 2009).

47. Ibid.

48. Jess T. Ford, "Mérida Initiative: The United States Needs Better Performance Measures for Its Counternarcotics and Anticrime Support Efforts," testimony before the Subcommittee on the Hemisphere, Committee on Foreign Affairs, House of Representatives, GAO-10-913T (Washington, DC: Government Accountability Office, 21 July 2010); Seelke and Beittel, *Mérida Initiative*. It should also be noted that the Obama administration announced a new strategy called Beyond Mérida on 23 March 2010, which will continue Mérida assistance to Mexico after President Calderón's departure from office in 2012, in line with four pillars: disrupting the operational capacity of organized crime, institutionalizing the rule of law in Mexico, creating a "21st century border," and building strong and resilient communities. Seelke and Finklea, *U.S.-Mexican Security Cooperation*.

49. Ford, "Mérida Initiative; Seelke, *El Salvador*; Seelke and Beittel, *Mérida Initiative*; Steven S. Dudley, "Drug Trafficking Organizations in Central America: *Transportistas*, Mexican Cartels and *Maras*," Working Paper Series on

U.S.-Mexico Security Collaboration, Mexico Institute at the Woodrow Wilson Center, Washington, DC, and the Trans-Border Institute at the University of San Diego, May 2010.

50. Seelke and Beittel, *Mérida Initiative*, 21 January 2010. A more recent CRS report mentions significant progress in professionalizing the police by March 2010, yet without revealing a specific percentage. Seelke and Beittel, *Mérida Initiative*, 19 April 2010.

51. Seelke and Beittel, *Mérida Initiative*, 21 January 2010. Recognition of the challenges of implementing the Mérida Initiative has resulted in the creation of a new program. See Peter J. Meyer and Clare Ribando Seelke, *Central America Regional Security Initiative: Background and Policy Issues for Congress*, CRS Report for Congress, R41731, 30 March 2011.

52. Thale, "International Assistance."

53. Stephen C. Johnson (senior policy analyst for Latin America, Kathryn and Shelby Cullom Davis Institute for International Studies, Heritage Foundation), testimony, in *Gangs and Crime in Latin America: Hearing before the Subcommittee on the Western Hemisphere of the Committee on International Relations, House of Representatives*, 109th Cong., 1st sess, 20 April 2005.

Conclusion

1. For example, Max Manwaring, *A Contemporary Challenge to State Sovereignty: Gangs and Other Illicit Transnational Criminal Organizations in Central America, El Salvador, Mexico, Jamaica, and Brazil* (Carlisle, PA: Strategic Studies Institute, U.S. Army War College, December 2007).

Glossary

Many of the terms in this glossary—for example, "18th Street," *maras*, and *ladino*—are polemical, and not all researchers agree upon their meaning. In addition, some terms may have different meanings in different countries.

barrio Neighborhood, generally lower-class. "Barrio" is also sometimes used synonymously with "gang."

clica A local subgroup or cell of a gang.

concertación social Social accord or pact.

Contra Abbreviated Spanish term for counterrevolutionary forces in Nicaragua's civil war.

democradura A nominally democratic government under de facto military rule; e.g., Honduras in the 1980s.

18th Street Gang One of the more notoriously violent international gangs to come out of Los Angeles. Also known variously as Barrio 18, Calle Dieciocho, and 18th Street. Although its members reject the use of *mara* to refer to the 18th Street Gang, many people outside the gang refer to it as a *mara*.

Instituto Nicaragüense de la Juventud Nicaraguan Youth Institute.

jump in To be initiated into a gang, usually through a beating from gang members. For women, the *trencito*, a collective rape, is at times used as the initiation.

ladino A general term for a person of mixed European and Amerindian blood. Called mestizo in some parts of Latin America. A *ladino* can also be an indigenous person who no longer acts or dresses as an indigene.

La Eme Literally, "The M"; a nickname of the Mexican Mafia prison gang.

Ley Antimaras Anti-gang Law (El Salvador). Also used in Honduras to refer to modifications of the penal code regarding gang membership.

Mano Dura Literally, "Strong Hand" or "Strong Arm"; the name for repressive anti-gang policies that were implemented in Central America (specifically El Salvador) in the early 2000s.

mara A Salvadoran street slang term used long before MS-13 appeared in Los Angeles, now commonly used to refer to organized international gangs such as Mara Salvatrucha and the 18th Street Gang. In the Salvadoran—and Central

American—vernacular, the term commonly refers to any group of people and is widely used as a synonym of "folks." When Salvadoran gangs started hanging out together in Los Angeles as a distinctive group from other Hispanic gangs, they adopted the term *mara* to underline their own cultural roots.

Mara Salvatrucha   An international gang that originated in Los Angeles. Commonly known as MS or MS-13.

marero   Member of a *mara*.

pandilla   A general term for a street gang of youths.

pandillero   Member of a *pandilla*.

Plan Escoba   Operation Broom, in Guatemala.

Plan Mano Amiga   Friendly Hand Plan, in El Salvador.

Plan Mano Extendida   Extended Hand Plan, in El Salvador.

Procuraduría para la Defensa de los Derechos Humanos   Ombudsperson for the Defense of Human Rights (Nicaragua).

Secretaría de la Juventud   Youth Secretariat (El Salvador).

sicariato   Contract killing.

shot callers   A slang term for members of street or prison gangs who give the orders.

sur   South.

el vacil   The gang lifestyle. Comes from the verb *vacilar*, meaning "to cheat." As a noun, *el vacil* also means "hanging out"; generally the gangs use the term in this sense.

List of Acronyms

ARENA Alianza Republicana Nacionalista (Nationalist Republican Alliance, El Salvador)
ASIES Asociación de Investigación y Estudios Sociales
AVANCSO Guatemalan Association for the Advancement of Social Sciences
BID Banco Interamericano de Desarrollo
CAA counteractivity analysis
CAFE Central American Fingerprint Exploitation
CAIP Central American Intelligence Program
CEDE Centro de Estudios sobre Desarrollo Económico
CEPAL Comisión Económica para América Latina y el Caribe
CGA countergroup analysis
CHIP Repatriation–Criminal History Information Program
CIA Central Intelligence Agency (U.S.)
CID Consultoría Interdisciplinaria en Desarrollo
CNSP Consejo Nacional de Seguridad Pública (National Council of Public Security, El Salvador)
COBAMA Conocimientos Básicos en Maras (Basic Facts on Gangs, Honduras)
CONAPREPI Comisión Nacional de Prevención de la Violencia y Promoción Integral de Valores de Convivencia (National Council for Violence Prevention and the Promotion of Values and Coexistence, Guatemala)
COP crime-oriented policing
CRIES Coordinadora Regional de Investigaciones Económicas y Sociales
CRS Congressional Research Service
CSG Coordinadora Juventud por Guatemala
DHS Department of Homeland Security (U.S.)
DOD Department of Defense (U.S.)
DOJ Department of Justice (U.S.)
DOS Department of State (U.S.)
ELN National Liberation Army (Colombia)
EREM Educación para Resistir y Evitar las Maras (Education to Resist and Avoid Gangs, Honduras)

ERIC   Equipo de Reflexión, Investigación y Comunicación
FARC   Revolutionary Armed Forces of Colombia
FBI   Federal Bureau of Investigation (U.S.)
FGR   Fiscalía General de la República (Attorney General's Office, El Salvador)
FLACSO   Facultad Latinoamericana de Ciencias Sociales (Latin American Faculty of Social Sciences)
FMLN   Frente Farabundo Martí para la Liberación Nacional (Farabundo Martí National Liberation Front, El Salvador)
FSLN   Sandinista National Liberation Front (Nicaragua)
IACHR   Inter-American Commission on Human Rights
IAGTF   International Anti-Gang Task Force
ICCPG   Instituto de Estudios Comparados de Ciencias Penales de Guatemala
ICE   Immigration and Customs Enforcement (U.S.)
IDESO   Instituto de Encuestas y Sondeos de Opinión
IDIES   Instituto de Investigaciones Económicas y Sociales
IIRIRA   Illegal Immigration Reform and Immigrant Responsibility Act
ILEA   International Law Enforcement Academy
IML   Instituto de Medicina Legal (Forensic Institute, El Salvador)
INCLE   International Narcotics Control and Law Enforcement
INL   Bureau of International Narcotics and Law Enforcement (U.S.)
ITAM   Instituto Tecnológico Autónomo de México
IUDOP   Instituto Universitario de Opinión Pública
LAM   Ley Antimaras (Anti-gang Act, El Salvador)
LAPOP   Latin American Public Opinion Project
MS   Mara Salvatrucha
NAGIA   National Alliance of Gang Investigators Associations
NCTC   National Counterterrorism Center
NDIC   National Drug Intelligence Center
NGIC   National Gang Intelligence Center
NGO   nongovernmental organization
NGTF   National Gang Task Force
NJDOC   New Jersey Department of Corrections
OCAVI   Observatorio Centroamericano sobre la Violencia
OMS   Organización Mundial de la Salud
OPS   Organización Panamericana de Salud
PDDH   Procuraduría para la Defensa de los Derechos Humanos
PDH   Procurador de los Derechos Humanos (Human Rights Ombudsman's Office, Guatemala)
PNC   Policía Nacional Civil (National Civilian Police, El Salvador and Guatemala)
PNUD   Programa de las Naciones Unidas para el Desarrollo
SICA   Sistema de la Integración Centroamericana (Central American Integration System)
SJ   Secretaría de la Juventud (Youth Secretariat, El Salvador)
TAG   Transnational Anti-Gang
UNCRC   United Nations Convention on the Rights of the Child
UNDP   United Nations Development Programme

UNICEF   United Nations Children's Fund
UNO   National Opposition Union (Nicaragua)
UNODC   United Nations Office on Drugs and Crime
USAID   U.S. Agency for International Development
WOLA   Washington Office on Latin America
ZMVS   Municipal Zone Sula Valley (Honduras)

Bibliography

"Afinan plan para fichar a pandilleros deportados." *El Diario de Hoy*, 23 February 2005.

"Agentes del FBI iniciaron labor contra las pandillas." *El Diario de Hoy*, 26 August 2007.

Agudelo, Irene. *El rápido tránsito: Imágenes de la adolescencia y la juventud en Nicaragua*. Managua: Sistema de las Naciones Unidas en Nicaragua (United Nations System, Nicaragua), 1999.

Aguilar, Jeannette. "La mano dura y las 'políticas' de seguridad." *ECA (Estudios Centroamericanos)*, no. 667 (2004): 439–450.

———. *Pandillas juveniles transnacionales en Centroamérica, México y Estados Unidos: Diagnóstico de El Salvador*. San Salvador, El Salvador: Instituto Universitario de Opinión Pública (IUDOP), 2006. http://www.wola.org/media/Gangs/diagnostico_salvador%281%29.pdf.

———. "Los resultados contraproducentes de las políticas antipandillas." *ECA (Estudios Centroamericanos)*, no. 708 (2007): 879–880.

Aguilar, Jeannette, and Lissette Miranda. "Entre la articulación y la competencia: Las respuestas de la sociedad civil organizada a las pandillas en El Salvador." In José Miguel Cruz, ed., *Maras y pandillas en Centroamérica*, vol. 4, *Las respuestas de la sociedad civil organizada*, 94–118. San Salvador, El Salvador: UCA Editores, 2006.

Aguilera Peralta, Gabriel. "Las amenazas irregulares en la agenda de seguridad de Centroamérica." In José Raúl Perales, ed., *Reforma de las fuerzas armadas en América Latina y el impacto de las amenazas irregulares*, 5–14. Washington, DC: Woodrow Wilson Center for International Scholars, 2008.

Alsema, Adrian. "Uribe Orders Militarization Medellín Neighborhoods to Halt Gang Violence." *Colombia Reports*, 8 April 2009.

Amaya Cóbar, Edgardo. "Maras: Niñez, juventud y violencia; Breve caracterización del caso salvadoreño." Unpublished manuscript, 2004.

———. "Las políticas de seguridad en El Salvador 1992–2002." In Lucía Dammert and John Bailey, eds., *Seguridad y reforma policial en las Américas: Experiencias y desafíos*, 219–238. Mexico City: Siglo XXI Editores, 2005.

American Community Survey. U.S. Census Bureau, Washington, DC, 2004. http://factfinder.census.gov.

Amnesty International. *El Salvador: Open Letter on the Anti-Maras Act.* AMR 29/009/2003. Amnesty International, December 1, 2003. http://www.amnesty .org/en/library/info/AMR29/009/2003.

———. *Guatemala: No Protection, No Justice; Killings of Women in Guatemala.* AMR 34/017/2005. London: Amnesty International, June 2005. http://www .amnesty.org/en/library/info/AMR34/017/2005/en.

———. *Honduras: Zero Tolerance . . . for Impunity; Extrajudicial Executions of Children and Youths since 1998.* AMR 37/001/2003. Amnesty International, 25 February 2003. http://www.amnesty.org/en/library/info/AMR37/001/2003.

"Análisis de la 'Ley Antimaras.'" *Proceso* (Instituto de Derechos Humanos de la Universidad Centroamericana "José Simeón Cañas" de El Salvador) 24, no. 1062 (August 2008). http://www.uca.edu.sv/publica/proceso/proc1062.html.

"Anders Kompass: La población no se siente segura." *La Prensa Libre*, 2 January 2007.

Anderson, Jon Lee. "Gangland: Who Controls the Streets of Rio de Janeiro?" *New Yorker*, 5 October 2009, 47–57.

Andino, Tomás, and Guillermo Jiménez. "Violencia juvenil, maras y pandillas en Honduras." In POLJUVE, ed., *Informe para la discusión*. Tegucigalpa, Honduras: Interpeace, 2009.

Andino Mencía, Tomás. *Las maras en la sombra: Ensayo de actualización del fenómeno pandillero en Honduras*. Universidad Centroamericana "Simeón Cañas," Instituto Universitario de Opinión Pública, September 2006. http://www.wola .org/media/Gangs/diagnostico_honduras.pdf.

Arana, Ana. "How Street Gangs Took Central America." *Foreign Affairs*, May–June 2005, 98–110.

"ARENA a pescar votos con el plan antimaras." *La Prensa Gráfica*, 13 August 2003.

Argueta, Sandra. "Diagnóstico de los grupos llamados 'maras' en San Salvador: Factores psicosociales que prevalecen en los jóvenes que los integran." *Revista de Psicología de El Salvador* 2, no. 43 (1992): 53–84.

Argueta, Sandra, Gisela Caminos, Margarita Mancía, and María de Los Ángeles Salgado. "Diagnóstico sobre los grupos llamados 'maras' en San Salvador: Factores psicosociales que prevalecen en los jóvenes que los integran." Bachelor's thesis, Universidad Centroamericana, San Salvador, El Salvador, 1991.

Arias, Enrique Desmond. *Drugs and Democracy in Rio de Janeiro: Trafficking, Social Networks, and Public Security*. Chapel Hill: University of North Carolina Press, 2006.

———. "The Dynamics of Criminal Governance: Networks and Social Order in Rio de Janeiro." *Journal of Latin American Studies* 38 (2006): 293–310.

Arnson, Cynthia J., ed. *Comparative Peace Processes in Latin America*. Palo Alto, CA: Stanford University Press, 1999.

"Asesinan a 13 personas a diario en el país." *El Diario de Hoy*, 16 June 2009. http://www.elsalvador.com/mwedh/nota/nota_completa.asp?idCat=6358&idArt=3738331.

Assis, Simone Gonçalves de. "Situación de la violencia juvenil en Río de Janeiro." In Organización Panamericana de la Salud, Organización Mundial de la Salud

(OPS/OMS-ASDI-BID), *Taller sobre la violencia de los adolescentes y las pandillas (maras) juveniles*, 51–58. San Salvador, El Salvador, 7–9 May 1997. http://www .paho.org/Spanish/HPP/HPF/ADOL/taller.pdf.

Atkinson, Jay. "Police Setting Up Database on Gangs." *Boston Globe*, 30 November 2008. http://www.boston.com/news/local/massachusetts/articles/2008/11/30 /police_setting_up_database_on_gangs/.

Azpuru, Dinorah. *Political Culture of Democracy in Guatemala, 2008: The Impact of Governance*. Nashville, TN: Latin American Public Opinion Project (LAPOP), Vanderbilt University, November 2008.

Azpuru, Dinorah, Juan Pablo Pira, and Mitchell A. Seligson. *La cultura política y la democracia en Guatemala, 2004: VI Estudio a cerca de la cultura democrática de los guatemaltecos*. Guatemala City: ARO, Vanderbilt University, Asociación de Investigación y Estudios Sociales (ASIES), and USAID, 2004.

"Bajan homicidios en 2008." *La Prensa Gráfica*, 27 February 2009. http://www .laprensagrafica.com/index.php/el-salvador/judicial/20408.html.

Barbetta, Alfredo. "Situación de violencia juvenil en São Paulo." In Organización Panamericana de la Salud, Organización Mundial de la Salud (OPS/OMS-ASDI-BID), *Taller sobre la violencia de los adolescentes y las pandillas (maras) juveniles*, 59–63. San Salvador, El Salvador, 7–9 May 1997. http://www.paho.org /Spanish/HPP/HPF/ADOL/taller.pdf.

Barnes, Nielan. "Transnational Youth Gangs in Central America, Mexico and the United States: Executive Summary." In Rafael Fernández de Castro, ed., *Pandillas juveniles transnacionales en Centroamérica, México y Estados Unidos* 1–12. Washington, DC: Washington Office on Latin America (WOLA), 2007. http://www.wola.org/media/Gangs/executive_summary_gangs_study.pdf.

"Barrerán a las maras." *El Diario de Hoy*, 24 July 2003, 2–3.

Bauman, Zygmunt. *Tiempos líquidos: Vivir en una época de incertidumbre*. Barcelona: Tusquets Editores, 2008.

Bautista, Francisco. "El papel de la policía ante la seguridad ciudadana y la violencia juvenil." Paper read at the seminar "La responsabilidad penal juvenil desde las perspectiva de los derechos humanos," Guatemala City, 2004.

Beary, Patrick. "Globalization and Gangs: The Evolution of Central American." Illinois Wesleyan University Honors Projects, Paper 6 (2007). http://digital commons.iwu.edu/intstu_honproj/6.

Beltrán, Adriana. *The Captive State: Organized Crime and Human Rights in Latin America*. Washington Office on Latin America (WOLA) Special Report. Washington, DC: WOLA, October 2007.

Blanco Reyes, Sidney, and Francisco Díaz Rodríguez. *Deficiencias policiales, fiscales o judiciales en la investigación y juzgamiento causantes de impunidad*. San Salvador, El Salvador: Programa de las Naciones Unidas para el Desarrollo (PNUD), 2007.

Bland, Tia. "Mexican Corrections Instructors Graduate from New Mexico Training Academy." Media note, Bureau of Public Affairs, U.S. Department of State, 23 April 2009.

Blatchford, Chris. *The Black Hand: The Bloody Rise and Redemption of "Boxer" Enriquez, a Mexican Mob Killer*. New York: HarperCollins, 2008.

Bonilla, Oscar. "Las reformas al sector seguridad en América Latina y el impacto de las amenazas irregulares: El caso de El Salvador." In José Raúl Perales, ed.,

Reforma de las fuerzas armadas en América Latina y el impacto de las amenazas irregulares, 15–23. Washington, DC: Woodrow Wilson International Center for Scholars, 2008.

Booth, John, Christine Wade, and Thomas Walker. *Understanding Central America*. 5th ed. Boulder, CO: Westview Press, 2010.

Botello, Santiago, and Ángel Moya. *Reyes Latinos: Los códigos secretos de los Latin Kings en España*. Madrid: Temas de Hoy, 2005.

Bowman, Tom. "CIA and Pentagon Wonder: Could Mexico Implode?" National Public Radio, 27 February 2009. http://www.npr.org/templates/story/story.php?storyId=101215537.

Breve, Federico. "The Maras—A Menace to the Americas." *Military Review* (July–August 2007): 88–95.

Brouwer, Melinda. "President's FY 2009 Budget Increases Funding for State Department." *U.S. Diplomacy: The World Affairs Blog Network*, Foreign Policy Association, 4 February 2008. http://diplomacy.foreignpolicyblogs.com/2008/02/05/bush-2009-budget-increases-funding-for-state-department/.

Byrne, Hugh, William Stanley, and Rachel Garst. *Rescuing Police Reform: A Challenge for the New Guatemalan Government*. Washington, DC: Washington Office on Latin America (WOLA), 2000.

Cajina, Roberto. *Transición política y reconversión militar en Nicaragua, 1990–1995*. Managua: Coordinadora Regional de Investigaciones Económicas y Sociales (CRIES), 1997.

Caldera, Hilda, and Guillermo Jiménez. *Prevención de maras y pandillas: Realidad y desafíos*. Tegucigalpa, Honduras: Programa Nacional de Prevención, 2006.

California Street Terrorism Enforcement and Prevention Act. Enacted in 1988, followed by subsequent legislation to further define and expand its provisions. http://www.gangtaskforce.org/gtf3.htm.

Call, Charles. "Sustainable Development in Central America: The Challenges of Violence, Injustice and Insecurity." Central America 2020 Working Paper 8, Institut für Iberoamerika-Kunde, Hamburg, 2000. http://ca2020.fiu.edu/Themes/Charles_Call/Call.pdf.

Cannon, Lou. *Official Negligence: How Rodney King and the Riots Changed Los Angeles and the LAPD*. Oxford: Westview Press, 1999.

"Cárceles al 224% de su capacidad." *La Prensa Gráfica*, 29 July 2007. http://archive.laprensa.com.sv/20070729/lodeldia/20070729/13539.asp.

Cardenal, Ernesto. *La revolución perdida: Memorias III*. Managua: Anamá, 2003.

Carr, Thomas H. (Washington/Baltimore High Intensity Drug Trafficking Area). "Information Brokering." Lecture presented at the i2 National User Conference, Arlington, VA, 15 May 2008.

Carranza, Marlon. "Del asistencialismo a la incidencia y el cabildeo: Las diversas respuestas de la sociedad civil organizada al fenómeno de las pandillas en Honduras." In José Miguel Cruz, ed., *Maras y pandillas en Centroamérica*, vol. 4, Las respuestas de la sociedad civil organizada, 235–298. San Salvador, El Salvador: UCA Editores, 2006.

———. "Detention or Death: Where the "Pandillero" Kids of El Salvador Are Heading." In Luke Dowdney, ed., *Neither War nor Peace: International Compari-*

sons of Children and Youth in Organised Armed Violence, 212–231. Rio de Janeiro: Viveiros de Castro Editora, 2005. http://www.coav.org.br.

Carrera, Margarita. "Persistencia del feminicidio en Guatemala." *Prensa Libre*, 17 June 2005.

Casa Alianza Honduras. *Análisis mensual sobre problemática de la niñez hondureña.* Report 2. Tegucigalpa: Casa Alianza Honduras, February 2006.

Castillo, Beatriz. "Inspectoría presentará cargos en caso de exjefes policiales." *Diario Co Latino* (San Salvador, El Salvador), 2 February 2010.

Castillo, Javier Monterroso. *Investigación criminal: Estudio comparativo y propuesta de un modelo de policía de investigación en Guatemala.* Guatemala City: Instituto de Estudios Comparados en Ciencias Penales de Guatemala, 2007.

"Central America: An Emerging Role in the Drug Trade." *Stratfor*, 26 March 2009. http://www.stratfor.com/weekly/20090326_central_america_emerging_role_drug_trade.

"Centroamérica vive una 'guerra civil no declarada' según funcionario de OEA." *La Prensa Gráfica*, 24 June 2009. http://www.laprensagrafica.com.

Centro de Estudios de Guatemala (CEG). *Las maras . . . ¿Amenaza a la seguridad?* Informe Especial. Guatemala City: CEG, 2005.http://www.ceg.org.gt/fotos /file/4 MARAS.pdf.

Centro Nicaragüense de Derechos Humanos (CENIDH). *¿Dónde están los derechos?* Managua: CENIDH, 2004.

———. *Informe sobre derechos humanos en Nicaragua, 2004–2005.* Managua: CENIDH, 2006.

Chevigny, Paul. *Edge of the Knife: Police Violence in the Americas.* New York: New Press, 1995.

Chiller, Gaston, and Laurie Freeman. *El nuevo concepto de seguridad hemisférica de la OEA: Una amenaza en potencia.* Washington, DC: Washington Office on Latin America (WOLA), 2005.

Close, David. *Los años con doña Violeta.* Managua: Lea Grupo Editorial, 2005.

Collier, Ruth Berins, and David Collier. *Shaping the Political Arena: Critical Junctures, the Labor Movement, and Regime Dynamics in Latin America.* Princeton, NJ: Princeton University Press, 1991.

Committee on Hemispheric Security, Permanent Council of the Organization of American States. "U.S. Strategy to Combat the Threat of Criminal Gangs from Central America and Mexico." Paper presented at the Special Meeting on the Phenomenon of Criminal Gangs, 17 January 2008. http://www.scm.oas .org/doc_public/ENGLISH/HIST_08/CP19418E04.doc.

Consejo Nacional de Seguridad (CNSP) and European Union. "ProJóvenes de El Salvador." SLV/B7-3100/99/0133, Plan Operativo Anual, unpublished report. San Salvador, El Salvador: CNSP and European Union, 2005.

Consultoría Interdisciplinaria en Desarrollo (CID). *Estudio Opinión Pública: Honduras #61.* San José, Costa Rica: CID, 2006.

"Contra el feminicidio en Guatemala." *Universia*, 21 November 2005. http:// noticias.universia.es/vida-universitaria/noticia/2005/11/21/604824/contra-feminicidio-guatemala.html.

Cook, Colleen W., Rebecca G. Rush, and Clare Ribando Seelke. *Merida Initia-*

tive: Proposed U.S. Anticrime and Counterdrug Assistance for Mexico and Central America. Congressional Research Service (CRS) Report for Congress, RS22837, 18 March 2008.

Coordinadora Juventud por Guatemala (CSG). *Informe de auditoría social a la política nacional de prevención de la violencia juvenil y su ente rector la Comisión Nacional de Prevención de la Violencia y Promoción Integral de Valores de Convivencia (CONAPREPI).* Guatemala City: CSG, 2007.

Cordero, Edwin, Hamyn Gurdián, and Carlos Emilio López. *Alcanzando un sueño.* Save the Children Suecia, Policía Nacional de Nicaragua, 2006.

Córdova Macías, Ricardo, José Miguel Cruz, and Mitchell A. Seligson. *Political Culture of Democracy in El Salvador, 2008: The Impact of Governance.* San Salvador, El Salvador: LAPOP, August 2008.

Costa, Gino. *La Policía Nacional Civil de El Salvador (1990–1997).* San Salvador, El Salvador: UCA Editores, 1999.

Covey, Herbert. *Street Gangs throughout the World.* Springfield, IL: Charles C. Thomas, 2003.

"Crean alianza contra las maras en C.A." *El Diario de Hoy,* 5 April 2006, http://www.elsalvador.com/noticias/2006/04/05/nacional/nac15.asp.

"Crips." East Coast Gang Investigators Association website. http://www.gripe4rkids.org.

Cruz, José Miguel. "El barrio transnacional: Las maras centroamericanas como red." In Francis Pisani, Natalia Saltalamacchia, Arlene Tickner, and Nielan Barnes, eds., *Redes transnacionales en la cuenca de los huracanes: Un aporte a los studios interamericanos,* 357–381. Mexico City: Instituto Tecnológico Autónomo de México (ITAM) and Miguel Ángel Porrúa, 2007.

———. "Central American *Maras*: From Youth Gangs to Transnational Protection Rackets." *Global Crime* 11, no. 4 (2010): 379–398.

———. "Criminal Violence and Democratization in Central America: The Survival of the Violent State." *Latin American Politics and Society* (forthcoming, Winter 2011).

———. "Las elecciones presidenciales desde el comportamiento de la opinión pública." *ECA (Estudios Centroamericanos),* no. 665–666 (2004): 247–268.

———. "El Salvador." In *La cara de la violencia urbana en América Central.* San José, Costa Rica: Fundación Arias para la Paz y el Progreso Humano, 2006.

———. "Los factores asociados a las pandillas juveniles en Centroamérica." *ECA (Estudios Centroamericanos),* no. 685–686 (2005): 1164.

———. "Los factores posibilitadores y las expresiones de la violencia en los noventa." *ECA (Estudios Centroamericanos),* no. 588 (1997): 977–992.

———. "Factors Associated with Juvenile Gangs in Central America." In José Miguel Cruz, ed., *Street Gangs in Central America,* 13–65. San Salvador, El Salvador: UCA Editores, 2007.

———. "The Impact of Violent Crime on the Political Culture of Latin America: The Special Case of Central America." In Mitchell A. Seligson, ed., *Challenges to Democracy in Latin America and the Caribbean: Evidence of the Americas Barometer 2006–2007,* 219–249. Nashville, TN: Latin American Public Opinion Project (LAPOP), Vanderbilt University, March 2008. http://www.vanderbilt.edu/lapop/.

————, ed. *Maras y pandillas en Centroamérica*, vol. 4: *Las respuestas de la sociedad civil organizada*. San Salvador, El Salvador: UCA Editores, 2006.

————. "Organized Civil Society and Gangs: Alternative Responses by Central American Organizations." In José Miguel Cruz, ed., *Street Gangs in Central America*, 133–172. San Salvador, El Salvador: UCA Editores, 2007.

————, ed. *Street Gangs in Central America*. San Salvador, El Salvador: UCA Editores, 2007.

————. "Violencia, inseguridad ciudadana y las maniobras de las élites: La dinámica de la reforma policial en El Salvador." In Lucía Dammert and John Bailey, eds., *Seguridad y reforma policial en las Américas: Experiencias y desafíos*. Mexico City: Siglo XXI Editores, 2005.

Cruz, José Miguel, and Marlon Carranza. "Pandillas y políticas públicas: El caso de El Salvador." In Javier Moro, ed., *Juventudes, violencia y exclusión: Desafíos para las políticas públicas*, 133–176. Guatemala City: MagnaTerra Editores, 2006.

Cruz, José Miguel, Marlon Carranza, and María Santacruz Giralt. "El Salvador: Espacios públicos, confianza interpersonal y pandillas." In Equipo de Reflexión, Investigación y Comunicación (ERIC), Instituto de Encuestas y Sondeos de Opinión (IDESO), Instituto de Investigaciones Económicas y Sociales (IDIES), and Instituto Universitario de Opinión Pública (IUDOP), eds., *Maras y pandillas en Centroamérica*, vol. 2, *Pandillas y capital social*. San Salvador, El Salvador: UCA Editores, 2004.

Cruz, José Miguel, and Nelson Portillo Peña. *Solidaridad y violencia en las pandillas del gran San Salvador: Más allá de la vida loca*. San Salvador, El Salvador: UCA Editores, 1998.

Cruz, José Miguel, and María Santacruz Giralt. *La victimización y la percepción de seguridad en El Salvador en 2004*. San Salvador, El Salvador: Ministerio de Gobernación and Programa de las Naciones Unidas para el Desarrollo (PNUD), 2005.

Cuevas, Freddy. "Ejército a las calles en Honduras." Associated Press, 5 March 2008.

"La culpa de fiscales y policías." In "La vorágine de la violencia," special edition of *Raíces*, 20 October 2008. http://www.raices.com.sv.

Curzio, Leonardo. "Organized Crime and Political Campaign Finance in Mexico." In John Bailey and Roy Godson, eds., *Organized Crime and Democratic Governance: Mexico and the U.S.-Mexican Borderlands*, 83–102. Pittsburgh: University of Pittsburgh Press, 2000.

"DEA Says Mexican Drug Cartels Are Creeping South." Associated Press, 16 April 2009.

DeCastillo, David. Interview on Fox News special report, 12 June 2000.

DeCesare, Donna. "From Civil War to Gang War: The Tragedy of Edgar Bolaños." In Louis Kontos, David Brotherton, and Luis Barrios, eds., *Gangs and Society: Alternative Perspectives*, 287–313. New York: Columbia University Press, 2003.

Decker, Scott. "Collective and Normative Features of Gang Violence." *Justice Quarterly* 13, no. 2 (1996): 243–264.

Decker, Scott H., Tim Bynum, and Deborah Weisel. "A Tale of Two Cities: Gangs as Organized Crime Groups." *Justice Quarterly* 15, no. 3 (1998): 395–425.

Decker, Scott H., and Barrik Van Winkle. *Life in the Gang: Family, Friends, and Violence.* Cambridge: Cambridge University Press, 1996.

Demoscopía S.A. *Maras y pandillas, comunidad y policía en Centroamérica: Hallazgos de un estudio integral.* San José, Costa Rica: Demoscopía, 2007.

"Deportados." *El Diario de Hoy*, 22 February 2005.

"Detectan reunión entre cartel del Golfo y pandilla en El Salvador." *La Prensa Gráfica*, 7 December 2008. http://www.laprensagrafica.com/index.php/el-salvador/judicial/4769.html.

"Detenciones son 'ilegales,' dicen jueces." *La Prensa Gráfica*, 25 July 2003.

"Los detienen hasta que matan." *El Diario de Hoy*, 3 August 2003.

Diaz, Tom. *No Boundaries: Transnational Latino Gangs and American Law Enforcement.* Ann Arbor: University of Michigan Press, 2009.

"Distribuyen fotos de fichados en la PNC." *La Prensa Gráfica*, 24 May 2006.

"Dos grupos de exterminio operan en Guatemala." *El Faro*, 5 March 2007. http://www.elfaro.net/Secciones/noticias/20070305/noticias1_20070305.asp.

Dudley, Steven S. "Drug Trafficking Organizations in Central America: *Transportistas*, Mexican Cartels and *Maras.*" Working Paper Series on U.S.-Mexico Security Collaboration, Mexico Institute at the Woodrow Wilson Center, Washington, DC, and the Trans-Border Institute at the University of San Diego, May 2010.

Duzán, María Jimena. "El Proceso 8000: Fernando; No te lleves el secreto." *El Tiempo*, 5 February 2007.

"EE.UU. sentencia a ex diputado." *El Diario de Hoy*, 19 January 2006. http://www.elsalvador.com/noticias/2006/01/19/nacional/nac12.asp.

"EE.UU. triplica los envíos de deportados." *El Diario de Hoy*, 5 December 2007.

"Ejército del bajo mundo." *El Diario de Hoy*, 22 August 2003.

"Las elecciones municipales y legislativas del 16 de marzo de 2003." *ECA (Estudios Centroamericanos)*, no. 653–654 (2003): 178–184.

Embassy of the United States, San Salvador, El Salvador. "Authorities Commemorate First Anniversary of Transnational Anti Gang Unit." 25 September 2008. http://sansalvador.usembassy.gov/news/2008/09/25.html.

"Empresa desmiente a Secretaría de Juventud sobre artículos promocionales." *El Faro*, 9 June 2008. http://www.elfaro.net.

Epstein, Susan B., and Kennon H. Nakamura. *State, Foreign Operations, and Related Programs: FY2009 Appropriations.* Congressional Research Service (CRS) Report for Congress, RL34552, 3 April 2009.

Equipo Regional de Monitoreo y Análisis de Derechos Humanos en Centroamérica. *Informe sobre derechos humanos y conflictividad en Centroamérica 2008–2009.* Equipo Regional de Monitoreo y Análisis de Derechos Humanos en Centroamérica, 2009.

Escobar, Francisco Andrés. "Por mi madre vivo y por mi barrio muero: Una aproximación al fenómeno de las maras." *ECA (Estudios Centroamericanos)* 51, no. 570 (1996): 327–349.

"El estado de excepción es la última alternativa." *El Diario de Hoy*, 24 July 2003.

Estado de la Nación. *Decimecuarto informe estado de la nación en desarrollo humano sostenible* (Fourteenth State of the Nation Report on Human Sustainable De-

velopment). San José, Costa Rica: Estado de la Nación, 2008. http://www
.estadonacion.or.cr/.

Etcharren, Laura. "Ñetas: Una mara, un color dentro del mundo de la globalización." 12 May 2006. http://lauraetcharren.blogspot.com/2006/05/etas.html (site discontinued).

"EU–Central America: Conclusion of New Political Dialogue and Co-operation Agreement." *Europa* (European Union website), press release IP/03/1336, Brussels, 2 October 2003.

European Commission. "Honduras: Country Strategy Paper, 2007–2013." 29 March 2007. http://ec.europa.eu/external_relations/honduras/csp/07_13_en.pdf.

"Ex jefes de SAIA, por enfrentar juicio en Estados Unidos." *El Periódico*, 5 September 2006.

"FARC está detrás de maras." *El Diario de Hoy*, 16 June 2004.

Farrington, David. *What Has Been Learned from Self-Reports about Criminal Careers and the Causes of Offending?* Report for the Home Office, Institute of Criminology, University of Cambridge, 2003. http://www.homeoffice.gov.uk/rds/pdfs/farrington.pdf.

Feere, John, and Jessica Vaughan. *Taking Back the Streets: ICE and Local Law Enforcement Target Immigrant Gangs*. Washington, DC: Center for Immigration Studies, September 2008. http://www.cis.org/ImmigrantGangs.

"FGR: 'Homicidios son producto de pandillas.'" *La Prensa Gráfica*, 3 September 2008. http://archive.laprensa.com.sv/20080903/lodeldia/20080903/17764.asp.

Filho, Francisco Alves, and Marcos Pernambuco. "No front inimigo." *Isto é* (São Paulo), 19 June 2002.

Ford, Jess T. "Mérida Initiative: The United States Needs Better Performance Measures for Its Counternarcotics and Anticrime Support Efforts." Testimony before the Subcommittee on the Hemisphere, Committee on Foreign Affairs, House of Representatives. GAO-10-913T. Washington, DC: Government Accountability Office, 21 July 2010.

———. *Status of Funds for the Mérida Initiative*. GAO-10-253R. Washington, DC: Government Accountability Office, 3 December 2009.

"Foro dice 'no' a propuesta de ley." *La Prensa Gráfica*, 27 August 2003.

Franco, Celinda. *The MS-13 and 18th Street Gangs: Emerging Transnational Gang Threats?* Congressional Research Service (CRS) Report for Congress, RL34233, updated 30 January 2008.

Franzese, Robert, Herbert Covey, and Scott Menard, eds. *Youth Gangs*. 3rd ed. Springfield, IL: Charles C. Thomas, 2006.

Fundación de Estudios para la Aplicación del Derecho (FESPAD). *Estado de la seguridad pública, 2002–2003*. San Salvador, El Salvador: FESPAD, 2004.

———. *Estado de la seguridad pública y la justicia penal en El Salvador, 2002–2005*. San Salvador, El Salvador: FESPAD, 2004–2005.

———. *Estado de la seguridad pública y la justicia penal en El Salvador, 2004*. San Salvador, El Salvador: FESPAD Ediciones, 2005.

———. *Informe anual sobre justicia penal juvenil, El Salvador, 2004*. San Salvador, El Salvador: FESPAD Ediciones, 2004.

Funes, Freddy. "Removal of Central American Gang Members: How Immigration Laws Fail to Reflect Global Reality." *University of Miami Law Review* 63, no. 301 (2008): 301–338.

"Funes recibe el país con 12.35 homicidios diarios." *La Prensa Gráfica*, 4 June 2009. http://www.laprensagrafica.com/el-salvador/judicial/37500—funes-recibe-el-pais-con-1235-homicidios-diarios.html.

"Gang Prevention in Honduras." Community Police presentation, Tegucigalpa, Honduras, March 2008.

Gang Reporting, Evaluation, and Tracking (GREAT). *Summary Reports 1990–1997: California*. GREAT, 1990–1997.

"Gangs Ditch Tattoos, Go for College Look." Associated Press, 16 December 2007. http://www.msnbc.msn.com/id/22279005/.

"Gobierno niega existencia de grupos de exterminio de pandilleros." *La Prensa Gráfica*, 19 August 2005. http://archive.laprensa.com.sv/20050819/lodeldia/08 .asp.

"Gobierno y la Comisión Europea firman segunda parte de 'Pro Jóvenes.'" *La Página*, 18 August 2009. http://www.lapagina.com.sv/nacionales/15327/2009/08 /18/Gobierno-y-la-Comision-Europea-firman-segunda-parte-de-Pro-Jovenes.

Godoy, Angelina Snodgrass. *Popular Injustice: Violence, Community, and the Law in Latin America*. Palo Alto, CA: Stanford University Press, 2006.

Godson, Roy. "The Political-Criminal Nexus and Global Security." In Roy Godson, ed., *Menace to Society: Political-Criminal Collaboration around the World*, 1–26. New Brunswick, NJ: Transaction Publishers, 2003.

Goldstein, Daniel. *The Spectacular City: Violence and Performance in Urban Bolivia*. Durham, NC: Duke University Press, 2004.

Gomez-Granger, Julissa. *Latin America and the Caribbean: Fact Sheet on Economic and Social Indicators*. Congressional Research Service (CRS) Report for Congress, RS22657, 2 March 2009.

González, Jorge Atilano. *En busca de la fraternidad perdida: Micro-relatos de una juventud abandonada que busca su identidad*. Mexico City: Centro de Estudios Teológicos de la Compañía de Jesús, 2002.

González, Sergio. *Huesos en el desierto*. Barcelona: Anagrama, 2002.

Green, Eric. "State's Negroponte Targets Illegal Drugs on Central American Trip: Mérida Initiative Would Help Mexico, CA Combat Trafficking." *America. gov*, 12 June 2008. http://www.america.gov/st/democracy-english/2008/June /200806121248251xeneerg0.9950678.html.

———. "US–Central American Cooperation Focuses on Fighting Gangs." *America.gov*, 24 July 2007. http://www.america.gov/st/washfile-english/2007 /July/20070724120509 1xeneerg0.4201471.html.

Grigsby, William. "The National Police under Attack: The Clues behind the Crisis." *Envío Digital*, no. 265 (August 2003). http://www.envio.org.ni/arti culo/2108.

———. "The New National Police Chief Faces Colossal Challenges." *Envío Digital*, no. 301 (August 2006). http://www.envio.org.ni/articulo/3348.

"Guatemala es el quinto país más violento de Latinoamérica." *El Periódico*, 27 June 2006.

Gunst, Laurie. *Born Fi' Dead: A Journey through the Jamaican Posse Underworld.* New York: Henry Holt, 1996.

Gutiérrez, Raúl. "Entrevista a 'Puppet,' líder natural de la Pandilla 18." In "La vorágine de la violencia," special edition of *Raíces,* 20 October 2008. http://www.raices.com.sv.

———. "La herencia perversa del Gobierno Saca (II parte)." *Contrapunto,* 22 May 2009. http://www.contrapunto.com.

Hagedorn, John. *A World of Gangs: Armed Young Men and Gangsta Culture.* Minneapolis: University of Minnesota Press, 2008.

Harriott, Anthony. *Police and Crime Control in Jamaica: Problems of Reforming Ex-Colonial Constabularies.* Kingston, Jamaica: University of the West Indies Press, 2000.

"La herencia perversa del Gobierno Saca (II parte)." *Contrapunto,* 22 May 2009. http://www.contrapunto.com.

Hernández, Iduvina. *Camino rocoso: Avances y desafíos de la reforma de inteligencia en Guatemala.* Washington, DC: Washington Office on Latin America (WOLA), 5 September 2005. http://www.wola.org. Available in English and Spanish.

"La hora de los hornos." In "La vorágine de la violencia," special edition of *Raíces,* 20 October 2008. http://www.raices.com.sv.

Hum, Lourdes, Leslie Ramos, and Iván Monzón. "Respuestas de la sociedad civil al fenómeno de las maras y pandillas juveniles en Guatemala." In José Miguel Cruz, ed., *Maras y pandillas en Centroamérica,* vol. 4, *Las respuestas de la sociedad civil organizada,* 145–234. San Salvador, El Salvador: UCA Editores, 2006.

Hume, Mo. *Armed Violence and Poverty in El Salvador.* Bradford, UK: Center for International Cooperation and Security, University of Bradford, 2004, http://www.bradford.ac.uk/acad/cics/publications/AVPI/poverty/AVPI_El_Salvador.pdf.

Illegal Immigration Reform and Immigrant Responsibility Act of 1996. Public Law 104-208, 104th Cong., 2nd sess., 30 September 1996.

Instituto Universitario de Opinión Pública (IUDOP). "La delincuencia urbana: Encuesta exploratoria." *ECA (Estudios Centroamericanos),* no. 534–535 (1993): 471–482.

———. "Evaluación de la opinión pública sobre el gobierno de Francisco Flores." *ECA (Estudios Centroamericanos),* no. 667 (2004): 606–616.

———. "Opinión pública a finales de 2003 y preferencias electorales: Encuesta de evaluación de fin de año." *ECA (Estudios Centroamericanos),* no. 661–662 (2003): 1237.

———. "Las preferencias políticas en octubre de 2003: La mano dura de ARENA." *ECA (Estudios Centroamericanos),* no. 660 (2003): 1075.

———. *La violencia en El Salvador en los años noventa: Magnitud, costos y factores posibilitadores.* San Salvador, El Salvador: IUDOP, 1998.

Iraheta, Oscar. "El setenta por ciento de las extorsiones son cometidas por maras." *El Diario de Hoy,* 19 August 2009. http://www.elsalvador.com/mwedh/nota/nota_completa.asp?idCat=6358&idArt=3930807.

Jacobs, Bruce A., and Richard Wright. *Street Justice: Retaliation in the Criminal Underworld.* Cambridge: Cambridge University Press, 2006.

Jiménez Barca, Antonio. "Yo soy un 'latin king.'" *El País*, 10 July 2005.

Johnson, Mary Helen. "National Policies and the Rise of Transnational Gangs." *Migration Information Source*, 1 April 2006. http://www.migrationinformation.org/usfocus/print.cfm?ID=394.

Johnson, Stephen C. (senior policy analyst for Latin America, Kathryn and Shelby Cullom Davis Institute for International Studies, Heritage Foundation). Testimony. In *Gangs and Crime in Latin America: Hearing before the Subcommittee on the Western Hemisphere of the Committee on International Relations, House of Representatives*, 109th Cong., 1st sess, 20 April 2005.

Joint Group for the Investigation of Politically Motivated Illegal Armed Groups. *Report of the Joint Group for the Investigation of Politically Motivated Illegal Armed Groups in El Salvador*. S/1994/989. http://www.un.org.

Jordan, Mary. "People Smuggling Now Big Business in Mexico." *Washington Post*, 17 May 2001.

"Jueces: Ley no se puede aplicar." *La Prensa Gráfica*, 10 October 2003.

"Juicio político sobre las elecciones 2003." *ECA (Estudios Centroamericanos)*, no. 653–654 (2003): 169.

Junger-Tas, Josine, J. G. Terlouw, and Malcolm Klein. *Delinquent Behavior among Young People in the Western World*. Amsterdam: Kugler, 1994.

"Junio ha sido el mes más violento del año." *La Prensa Gráfica*, 6 July 2005. http://www.laprensagrafica.com.

Kaiser, Kenneth W. (assistant director, FBI). Statement before the House Committee on Foreign Affairs, Subcommittee on the Western Hemisphere, Washington, DC, 7 February 2008. http://www.fbi.gov/news/testimony/combating-international-gangs-through-the-merida-initiative.

Keen, David. "Demobilising Guatemala." Crisis States Programme Working Paper 37, London School of Economics, 2003.

Killebrew, Bob, and Jennifer Bernal. *Crime Wars: Gangs, Cartels, and the U.S. National Security*. Washington, DC: Center for a New American Security, 2010.

Kincaid, A. Douglas. "Demilitarization and Security in El Salvador and Guatemala: Convergences of Success and Crisis." *Journal of Interamerican Studies and World Affairs* 42, no. 4 (2000): 39–58.

Klein, Malcolm W. *The American Street Gang: Its Nature, Prevalence, and Control*. New York: Oxford University Press, 1995.

———. *Chasing After Street Gangs*. Upper Saddle River, NJ: Pearson, 2007.

Klein, Malcolm W., and Cheryl L. Maxson. *Street Gang Patterns and Policies*. New York: Oxford University Press, 2006.

Lacayo, Antonio. *La difícil transición nicaragüense en el gobierno con doña Violeta*. Serie Ciencias Humanas, no. 12, Colección Cultural de Centroamérica, Colombia. Managua: Fundación Uno, 2005.

Lee, Kyung Jin. "U.S. Deportations Double over the Last Ten Years." *Medill Reports* (Northwestern University, Chicago), 23 February 2010. http://news.medill.northwestern.edu/chicago/news.aspx?id=157904&print=1.

Leggett, Theodore. *Crime and Development in Central America: Caught in the Crossfire*. United Nations Office on Drugs and Crime (UNODC), May 2007. http://www.unodc.org/documents/data-and-analysis/Central-america-study-en.pdf.

Legislative Analyst's Office. "The Three Strikes and You're Out Law." Sacramento, CA, 22 February 1995. http://www.lao.ca.gov/analysis_1995/3strikes .html.

Legislative Decree No. 158 of 9 October 2003, enacting the Ley Antimaras. D.O. No. 361, Ministerio de Gobernación, San Salvador, El Salvador, 10 October 2003.

Legislative Decree No. 190 of 20 December 2006, enacting the Ley Contra el Crimen Organizado y Delitos de Realización Compleja. D.O. No. 374 of 22 January 2007, Ministerio de Gobernación, San Salvador, El Salvador.

Legislative Decree No. 305 of 1 April 2004, enacting the Ley para el Combate de las Actividades Delincuenciales de Grupos o Asociaciones Ilícitas Especiales. D.O. of 2 April 2004, Ministerio de Gobernación, San Salvador, El Salvador.

Legislative Decree No. 393 of 28 July 2004, enacting reforms to the Penal Code. D.O. of 30 July 2004, Ministerio de Gobernación, San Salvador, El Salvador.

Levenson, Deborah. *On Their Own: A Preliminary Study of Youth Gangs in Guatemala City*. Cuadernos de Investigación, no. 4. Guatemala City: AVANCSO, 1998.

———. *Por sí mismos: Un estudio preliminar de las "maras" en la ciudad de Guatemala*. Cuadernos de Investigación, no. 4. Guatemala City: AVANCSO, 1988.

"Libres 114 pandilleros e impunes 20 homicidios." *El Diario de Hoy*, 15 August 2009. http://www.elsalvador.com/mwedh/nota/nota_completa.asp?idCat=63 58&idArt=3918774.

Liebel, Manfred. "Pandillas y maras: Señas de identidad." *Envío Digital*, no. 244 (July 2002). http://www.envio.org.ni/articulo/1161.

Llorente, María Victoria, Enrique Chaux, and Luz Magdalena Salas. *Violencia intrafamiliar y otros factores de riesgo de la violencia juvenil en Colombia*. Informe Final (Final Report). Bogotá: Departamento Nacional de Planeación, División de Justicia y Seguridad (DNP-DJS), Centro de Estudios sobre Desarrollo Económico (CEDE), 2004.

Lopez, Robert J., Rich Connell, and Chris Kraul. "Gang Uses Deportation to Its Advantage to Flourish in U.S." *Los Angeles Times*, 30 October 2005. http:// www.latimes.com/news/local/la-me-gang30oct30,1,5492282.story.

López Vigil, María. "Abuso sexual, incesto: Diez años tocando heridas." *Envío Digital*, no. 234 (September 2001). http://www.envio.org.ni/articulo/1103.

Lowenthal, Mark M. *Intelligence: From Secrets to Policy*. 3rd ed. Washington, DC: CQ Press, 2006.

Maclure, Richard, and Melvin Sotelo. "Children's Rights as Residual Social Policy in Nicaragua: State Priorities and the Code of Childhood and Adolescence." *Third World Quarterly* 24, no. 4 (2003): 681.

"'Mano Dura' contra mareros." *La Prensa Gráfica*, 24 July 2003.

Manwaring, Max. *A Contemporary Challenge to State Sovereignty: Gangs and Other Illicit Transnational Criminal Organizations in Central America, El Salvador, Mexico, Jamaica, and Brazil*. Carlisle, PA: Strategic Studies Institute, U.S. Army War College, December 2007.

"La máquina de infiltración de las FARC es el Partido Comunista Clandestino Colombiano." *Semana*, 12 August 2006.

"'Maras' no son principal causa de violencia, según la misma PNC." *El Faro*, 31 January 2005. http://www.elfaro.net/secciones/noticias/20050131/noticias 3_20050131.asp.

"Maras: ¿Víctimas o delincuentes?" *La Prensa*, 2 November 2000.

Marroquín Parducci, Amparo María. "Indiferencias y espantos: Relatos de jóvenes y pandillas en la prensa escrita de Guatemala, El Salvador, y Honduras." In G. Rey, ed., *Los relatos periodísticos del crimen*, 55–91. Bogotá: Centro de Competencia en Comunicación, Fundación Friedrich Ebert, 2007.

Martel Trigueros, Roxana. "Las maras salvadoreñas: Nuevas formas de espanto y control social." *ECA (Estudios Centroamericanos)*, no. 696 (2006): 957–979.

Martín, Alberto, Ana Fernández, and Karla Villareal. "Difusión transnacional de identidades juveniles en la expansión de las maras centroamericanas." *Perfiles Latinoamericanos*, no. 30 (July–December 2007): 114.

Martínez, Ramiro, and Ricardo Falla. "Clases medias: Violentas y organizadas." *Envío Digital*, no. 171 (June 1996). http://www.envio.org.ni/articulo/223.

"Más cárcel como política de estado." *Políticas Públicas Hoy* (FESPAD), no. 26 (2007): 5.

Masferrer, Roberto. *Defunciones por homicidios, El Salvador 2005*. San Salvador, El Salvador: Instituto de Medicina Legal, Unidad de Estadísticas, 2006.

"Más policías corruptos." *La Prensa Libre*, 10 August 2006.

Maxson, Cheryl. "Gang Members on the Move." *Juvenile Justice Bulletin* (Office of Juvenile Justice and Delinquency Prevention, U.S. Department of Justice, Washington, DC), October 1998.

McKay, Jim. "Law Enforcement Database Tracks Gang Members Statewide." *Government Technology*, 22 June 2009. http://www.govtech.com/gt/692043.

Mendoza, Carlos A. "Causas de linchamientos en Guatemala: ¿Barbarie o justicia popular?" Presentation at Universidad Centroamericana "José Simeón Cañas," San Salvador, El Salvador, 3 May 2006.

Mérida Initiative Portal. Mexico Institute, Woodrow Wilson International Center for Scholars. http://www.wilsoncenter.org/index.cfm?topic_id=5949 &fuseaction=topics.item&news_id=407349.

Merino, Juan. "Las maras en Guatemala." In Equipo de Reflexión, Investigación y Comunicación (ERIC), Instituto de Encuestas y Sondeos de Opinión (IDESO), Instituto de Investigaciones Económicas y Sociales (IDIES), and Instituto Universitario de Opinión Pública (IUDOP), eds., *Maras y pandillas en Centroamérica*, vol. 1, 109–217. Managua: UCA Editores, 2001.

"Mexican Mafia." *Drugs and Gangs Profile Bulletin* (National Drug Intelligence Center, U.S. Department of Justice), July 2003, 3.

Meyer, Peter J., and Clare Ribando Seelke. *Central America Regional Security Initiative: Background and Policy Issues for Congress*. Congressional Research Service (CRS) Report for Congress, R41731, 30 March 2011.

Meza, Victor. *Honduras: Hacia una política integral de seguridad ciudadana*. Tegucigalpa, Honduras: CEDOH, 2004.

Millett, Richard L. "Nicaragua: The Politics of Frustration." In Howard J. Wiarda and Harvey F. Kline, eds., *Latin American Politics and Development*, 6th ed., 456–469. Boulder, CO: Westview Press, 2007.

Millett, Richard L., and Orlando J. Pérez. "New Threats and Old Dilemmas: Central America's Armed Forces in the 21st Century," *Journal of Political and Military Sociology* (Summer 2005). http://findarticles.com/p/articles/mi_qa3719 /is_200507/ai_n14904111/.

Ministerio de Gobernación Policía Nacional de Nicaragua. "Atención y tratamiento a las pandillas: Un modelo preventivo en desarrollo." PowerPoint presentation at Reunión de Ministros/as de Gobernación y/o Seguridad, Managua, 15 October 2007. http://www.ocavi.com/docs_files/file_669.pdf.

Molina, Karen, and David Marroquín. "Maras obligan a iniciados que vayan a matar." *El Diario de Hoy*, 12 September 2007.

Molina Vaquerano, Fabio. *Defunciones por homicidios en El Salvador, 1999–2006*. San Salvador, El Salvador: Instituto de Medicina Legal, 2001–2007.

———. *Reconocimiento de defunciones por homicidios realizados por los (las) médicos(as) forenses del Instituto de Medicina Legal de El Salvador, año 2004 (Investigación y análisis epidemiológico de los homicidios)*. San Salvador, El Salvador: Instituto de Medicina Legal, Unidad de Estadísticas, 2005.

Montgomery, Michael. "Gangster Reveals Mexican Mafia Secrets." Part 1. *All Things Considered*, National Public Radio, 6 September 2008.

Moore, Joan W. *Going Down to the Barrio: Homeboys and Homegirls in Change*. Philadelphia: Temple University Press, 1991.

"La MS y la 18 se disputan la venta de droga." *El Diario de Hoy*, 18 June 2004.

Mueller, Robert S., III (director, Federal Bureau of Investigation). "Priorities in the FBI's Criminal Programs." Statement before the Senate Judiciary Committee, 111th Cong., 2nd sess., 16 September 2009. http://www.fbi.gov/news /testimony/priorities-in-the-fbi2018s-criminal-programs.

Müller, Annekent. "Concluye labor de función de armas." *Visión Policial: Revista de la Policía Nacional* 11, no. 75 (May–June 2008): 6.

National Alliance of Gang Investigators Associations (NAGIA). *2005 National Gang Threat Assessment*. Washington, DC: U.S. Department of Justice, Bureau of Justice Assistance, 2005.

National Drug Intelligence Center (NDIC). "Executive Summary." In *National Drug Threat Assessment 2007*. Johnstown, PA: National Drug Intelligence Center, October 2006.

———. *National Street Gang Survey Report—1998*. Johnstown, PA: National Drug Intelligence Center, 1998.

National Gang Intelligence Center. *National Gang Threat Assessment 2009*. Product no. 2009-M0335-001. Washington, DC: National Gang Intelligence Center, January 2009.

Observatorio Centroamericano sobre Violencia (OCAVI). "Tasas de homicidios dolosos en Centroamérica y República Dominicana por 100,000 habitantes (1999–2007)." OCAVI website. http://www.ocavi.com/docs_files/file_378.pdf.

O'Donnell, Guillermo. "On the State, Democratization and Some Conceptual Problems: A Latin American View with Glances at Some Postcommunist Countries." *World Development* 21, no. 8 (1993): 1355–1369.

Office of the District Attorney for Monterey County website. http://www.co .monterey.ca.us/da/gang.htm.

"Oposición decide enviar al archivo Ley Antimaras." *La Prensa Gráfica*, 27 August 2003.

Oppenheimer, Andres. "Commentary: Obama's Foreign Aid Budget Cuts Send Wrong Message to Latin America." McClatchy, 13 February 2010. http://www.mcclatchydc.com/2010/02/13/84438/commentary-obamas-foreign-aid.html.

"El país denuncia pandillas en la ONU." *El Diario de Hoy*, 26 September 2007.

País seguro: Plan de gobierno 2004–2009. San Salvador, El Salvador: Gobierno de El Salvador (GOES), 2004. http://www.servicios.gob.sv/descarga/PLAN_DE_GOBIERNO_2004–2009_PAIS_SEGURO.pdf.

"Pandilleros aumentan su operatividad en toda Centroamérica." *El Diario de Hoy*, 16 July 2009. http://www.elsalvador.com/mwedh/nota/nota_completa.asp?idCat=6358&idArt=3831185.

Papachristos, Andrew. "Gang World." *Foreign Policy* 147 (March–April 2005): 2–7.

Peacock, Susan C., and Adriana Beltrán. *Poderes ocultos: Grupos ilegales armados en la Guatemala post conflicto y las fuerzas detrás de ellos*. Washington, DC: Washington Office on Latin America (WOLA), 2003. English version available at http://www.wola.org/index.php?option=com_content&task=viewp&id=48&Itemid=2.

Peed, Carl, Ronald E. Wilson, and Nichole J. Scalisi. "Crime Mapping and Analysis." *Police Chief*, September 2008, 24.

Pérez, Orlando J. *Political Culture of Democracy in Nicaragua, 2008: The Impact of Governance*. Nashville, TN: Vanderbilt University, LAPOP, October 2008.

Peterson, Marylin. *Intelligence-Led Policing: The New Intelligence Architecture*. Washington, DC: U.S. Department of Justice, Bureau of Justice Assistance, September 2005.

Pico, Juan Hernández. *Terminar la guerra, traicionar la paz: Guatemala en las dos presidencias de la paz; Arzú y Portillo (1996–2004)*. Guatemala City: FLACSO, 2005.

Pimentel, Stanley A. "The Nexus of Organized Crime and Politics in Mexico." In John Bailey and Roy Godson, eds., *Organized Crime and Democratic Governance: Mexico and the U.S.-Mexican Borderlands*, 33–58. Pittsburgh: University of Pittsburgh Press, 2000.

Pistole, John S. "A United Front against Translational Gangs." Speech to second Los Angeles IACP Summit on Transnational Gangs, Los Angeles, 3 March 2008. http://www.fbi.gov/news/speeches/a-united-front-against-transnational-gangs.

"Plan Mano Dura reduce delincuencia de pandillas." *La Prensa Gráfica*, 23 August 2003.

Plan Nacional de Juventud 2005–2015. San Salvador, El Salvador: Secretaría de la Juventud, 2005.

Plan Nacional de Juventud 2005–2015: Ejes de Acción. San Salvador, El Salvador: Secretaría de la Juventud, 2005.

"PNC sin estadísticas claras de pandillas." *La Prensa Gráfica*, 15 October 2007. http://archive.laprensa.com.sv/20071016/dpt15/noticias/15102007/895332.asp.

"Policía captura a 142 pandilleros." *La Prensa Gráfica*, 25 July 2003.

Policía Nacional. *Plan de prevención de las pandillas 1999*. Internal report. Managua: Policía Nacional, 1999.

Policía Nacional Civil de Guatemala. *Situación de maras en Guatemala*. San Salvador, El Salvador: Observatorio Centroamericano de la Violencia (OCAVI), 2007. http://www.ocavi.com/docs_files/file_424.pdf.

Popkin, Margaret. *Peace without Justice: Obstacles to Building the Rule of Law in El Salvador*. Philadelphia: Pennsylvania State University Press, 2000.

"Por el camino de la prevención." *La Prensa Gráfica*, 27 May 2009. http://www.laprensagrafica.com/el-salvador/social/35736-por-el-camino-de-la-prevencion.html.

Portes, Alejandro, and Alex Stepick. *City on the Edge: The Transformation of Miami*. Berkeley: University of California Press, 1993.

Poveda, Christian. "Maras: La vida loca." *Le Monde Diplomatique—Mexico*, April 2009.

"La prevención será el eje central en seguridad." *La Prensa Gráfica*, 2 June 2009.

Price, Matthew. "Inside Mexico's Most Dangerous City." BBC News, 23 March 2009. http://news.bbc.co.uk/2/hi/7959247.stm.

Procurador de los Derechos Humanos (PDH). *Muertes violentas de niñez, adolescencia y jóvenes y propuestas para su prevención*. Guatemala City: PDH, 2004. http://www.pdh.org.gt.

Procuraduría para la Defensa de los Derechos Humanos (PDDH). *¿Cara o sol? Investigación socio-jurídica de adolescentes que se encuentran en privación de libertad en los departamentos de la policía a nivel nacional*. Managua: PDDH, 2002.

———. *Demanda de inconstitucionalidad contra la Ley Antimaras*. San Salvador, El Salvador: PDDH, 2003. http://www.pddh.gob.sv.

———. *Violaciones a los derechos humanos por responsabilidad de la Policía Nacional Civil de El Salvador*. San Salvador, El Salvador: PDDH, 2007.

Programa de las Naciones Unidas para el Desarrollo (PNUD). *Armas de fuego y violencia*. San Salvador, El Salvador: PNUD, 2003.

———. *Diagnóstico de seguridad ciudadana en Nicaragua*. Managua: PNUD, 2002.

———. *Diversidad étnico-cultural: La ciudadanía en un estado plural; Informe nacional de desarrollo humano, Guatemala 2005*. Guatemala City: PNUD, 2005.

———. *El impacto de las drogas en la violencia*. San Salvador, El Salvador: PNUD, 2004.

———. *Informe estadístico de la violencia en Guatemala*. Guatemala City: Programa de Seguridad Ciudadana y Prevención de la Violencia del PNUD Guatemala, 2007.

———. *Informe nacional de desarrollo humano, Guatemala 2007*. Guatemala City: PNUD, 2008.

———. *Informe sobre desarrollo humano, El Salvador 2003: Desafíos y opciones en tiempos de globalización*. San Salvador, El Salvador: PNUD, 2003.

———. *Informe sobre desarrollo humano, Honduras 2006: Hacia la expansión de la ciudadanía*. Tegucigalpa, Honduras: PNUD, 2006.

———. *Informe sobre desarrollo humano para América Central 2009–2010*. San José, Costa Rica: PNUD, 2009.

———. *Informe sobre desarrollo humano 2005: Una mirada al nuevo nosotros; El impacto de las migraciones*. San Salvador, El Salvador: PNUD, 2005.

Programa Estado de la Nación. "El dilema estratégico de la seguridad ciudadana y el estado democrático de derecho." In *Estado de la región en desarrollo humano sostenible, 2008: Un informe desde Centroamérica y para Centroamérica*, 467–523. San José, Costa Rica: Programa Estado de la Nación, 2008.

"Prometen capturar a descuartizadores." *El Diario de Hoy*, 8 May 2006.

Ramírez Heredia, Rafael. *La mara*. Mexico City: Alfaguara, 2004.

Ranum, Elin Cecilie. "Pandillas juveniles transnacionales en Centroamérica, México y Estados Unidos." Diagnóstico Nacional Guatemala, Red Transnacional de Análisis sobre Maras, Centro de Estudios y Programas Interamericanos. Instituto Tecnológico Autónomo de México (ITAM) and Instituto Universitario de Opinión Pública (IUDOP), 2006. http://interamericanos.itam.mx /maras/docs/Diagnostico_Guatemala.pdf.

"Reaching the Untouchables: Guatemala and Organised Crime." *Economist*, 11 March 2010.

Rebollo, Deborah. "Photographer Documents Mara Salvatrucha in Prison." *La Plaza* (blog), *Los Angeles Times*, 30 October 2008. http://latimesblogs.latimes .com/laplaza/2008/10/the-intricate-1.html.

"Redadas arrancan en la penumbra." *El Diario de Hoy*, 25 July 2003.

"Los resultados de la política antidelincuencial: A un paso de la anomia." *Políticas Públicas Hoy* (FESPAD) 13 (October 2006). http://www.fespad.org.sv.

Roberts, Julian V., Loretta J. Stalans, David Indermaur, and Mike Hough. *Penal Populism and Public Opinion*. Oxford: Oxford University Press, 2003.

Rocha, José Luis. *Lanzando piedras, fumando piedras: Evolución de las pandillas en Nicaragua 1997–2006*. Managua: UCA Publicaciones, 2007.

———. "Mapping the Labyrinth from Within: The Political Economy of Nicaraguan Youth Policy Concerning Violence." *Bulletin of Latin American Research* 26, no. 4 (2007): 533–549.

———. "La Mara 18 tras las huellas de las pandillas políticas." *Envío*, no. 321 (2008): 26–31.

———. "Pandillero: La mano que empuña el mortero." *Envío Digital*, no. 216 (March 2000): 17–25. http://www.envio.org.ni/articulo/994.

Rodgers, Dennis. "Dying for It: Gangs, Violence, and Social Change in Urban Nicaragua." Crisis States Programme Working Paper 35, London School of Economics, October 2003. http://www.crisisstates.com/download/wp/wp35 .pdf.

———. "Living in the Shadow of Death: Gangs, Violence and Social Order in Urban Nicaragua, 1996–2002." *Journal of Latin American Studies* 38, no. 2 (May 2006): 267–292.

———. "Slum Wars of the 21st Century: Gangs, *Mano Dura* and the New Urban Geography of Conflict in Central America." *Development and Change* 40, no. 5 (2009): 969.

———. "Youth Gangs and Violence in Latin America and the Caribbean: A Literature Survey." Latin American and Caribbean Region Sustainable Development Working Paper 4, Urban Peace Program Series. World Bank, 1999.

Rodgers, Dennis, and Robert Muggah. "Gangs as Non-state Armed Groups: The Central American Case." *Contemporary Security Policy* 30, no. 2 (August 2009): 301–317.

Rodríguez, Luis J. *La vida loca: El testimonio de un pandillero en Los Ángeles*. New York: Simon and Schuster, 2005.

Rubio, Mauricio. *De la pandilla a la mara: Pobreza, educación, mujeres y violencia juvenil*. Bogotá: Universidad Externado de Colombia, 2007. http://sites .google.com/site/mauriciorubiop/.

——. *Pandillas, rumba y actividad sexual: Desmitificando la violencia juvenil*. Bogotá: Universidad Externado de Colombia, 2006. http://sites.google.com /site/mauriciorubiop/.

Ruhl, Mark J. "Redefining Civil-Military Relations in Honduras." *Journal of Interamerican Studies and World Affairs* 38, no. 1 (Spring 1996): 33–66.

Ruiz, Rafael. "Violencia tatuada." *El País*, 10 December 2006.

Ruiz, Viki L. "South by Southwest: Mexican Americans and Segregated Schooling, 1900–1950." *OAH Magazine of History* (Organization of American Historians) 15 (Winter 2001). http://www.oah.org/pubs/magazine/deseg/ruiz.html.

"Los salvadoreños evalúan la situación del país a finales de 2005 y opinan sobre las elecciones de 2006." *Boletín de Prensa* (IUDOP) 20, no. 3 (December 2005): 4.

"Los salvadoreños frente a las elecciones presidenciales de 2004." *Boletín de Prensa* (IUDOP) 18, no. 3 (October 2003): 2.

"El Salvador supera en tasa de homicidios a Colombia." *Diario Co Latino*, 13 February 2006. http://www.diariocolatino.com/es/20060213/nacionales/na cionales_20060213_11248/.

Santacruz Giralt, María L., and Alberto Concha-Eastman. *Barrio adentro: La solidaridad violenta de las pandillas*. San Salvador, El Salvador: Instituto Universitario de Opinión Pública (IUDOP), Organización Panamericana de Salud (OPS), and Homies Unidos, 2001.

Santacruz Giralt, María L., and Elin Ranum. *"Seconds in the Air": Women Gang Members and Their Prison*. San Salvador, El Salvador: UCA Editores, 2010.

Savater, Fernando. "La montaña y Mahoma." *El País*, 16 August 2005.

Schirmer, Jennifer. "The Guatemalan Politico-Military Project: Legacies for a Violent Peace?" *Latin American Perspectives* 26, no. 2 (March 1999): 92–107.

——. "The Looting of Democratic Discourse by the Guatemalan Military: Implications for Human Rights." In Elizabeth Jelin and Eric Hershberg, eds., *Constructing Democracy: Human Rights, Citizenship, and Society in Latin America*, 85–100. Boulder, CO: Westview Press, 1998.

Schoville, Chuck. *Sureños 2008: A Special Report*. Phoenix, AZ: Rocky Mountain Information Network, 2008.

"Secretaría de la Juventud se promociona a un costo inexplicable." *El Faro*, 26 May 2008. http://www.elfaro.net.

Seelke, Clare Ribando. "Anti-gang Efforts in Central America: Moving beyond *Mano Dura*?" Paper. *Maras*, Security and Development in Central America Task Force, Center for Hemispheric Policy, University of Miami, 10 April 2007.

——. *El Salvador: Political, Economic, and Social Conditions and U.S. Relations*. Congressional Research Service (CRS) Report for Congress, RS21655, 21 January 2010.

——. *Gangs in Central America*. Congressional Research Service (CRS) Report for Congress, RL341112, updated 11 January 2008.

——. *Gangs in Central America*. Congressional Research Service (CRS) Report for Congress, RL3411, updated 3 January 2011.

Seelke, Clare Ribando, and June S. Beittel. *Mérida Initiative for Mexico and Central America: Funding and Policy Issues.* Congressional Research Service (CRS) Report, R40135, 21 January, 19 April, and 1 June 2009.

Seelke, Clare Ribando, and Kristin M. Finklea. *U.S.-Mexican Security Cooperation: The Mérida Initiative and Beyond.* Congressional Research Service (CRS) Report for Congress, R41349, 16 August 2010.

"Se inicia la Súper Mano Dura." *El Diario de Hoy,* 31 August 2004.

"El setenta por ciento de las extorsiones son cometidas por maras." *El Diario de Hoy,* 19 August 2009. http://www.elsalvador.com/mwedh/nota/nota_com pleta.asp?idCat=6358&idArt=3930807.

Shelley, Louise I. "Transnational Organized Crime: The New Authoritarianism." In H. Richard Friman and Peter Andreas, eds., *The Illicit Global Economy and State Power,* 25–61. Lanham, MD: Rowman and Littlefield, 1999.

Shiflett, Robert B., and Hugo Teufel III. "Privacy Impact Assessment for the *Electronic* Travel Document System (*e*TD)." U.S. Department of Homeland Security, 13 October 2006.

Shifter, Michael. "Latin America's Drug Problem." *Current History* 106, no. 697 (February 2007): 58–63.

"Shuttling between Nations, Latino Gangs Confound the Law." *New York Times,* 26 September 2004.

"Sicarios y control de ventas de crack." *El Diario de Hoy,* 18 January 2005.

Sieder, Rachel. "Legal Globalization and Human Rights: Constructing the 'Rule of Law' in Post-conflict Guatemala." In P. Pitarch, S. Speed, and X. Leyva, eds., *Human Rights in the Maya Region: Global Politics, Moral Engagements, and Cultural Contentions,* 67–91. Durham, NC: Duke University Press, 2008.

Sieder, Rachel, Megan Thomas, George Vickers, and Jack Spence. *Who Governs? Guatemala Five Years after the Peace Accords.* Cambridge, MA: Hemisphere Initiatives, 2002.

"La sierra de Sinaloa es el feudo del principal cártel de narcotraficantes en México: En los dominios del Chapo Guzmán." *El País,* 2 February 2007.

Sives, Amanda. "Changing Patrons, from Politicians to Drug Dons: Clientelism in Downtown Kingston." *Latin American Perspectives* 29 (2002): 66–89.

Small Arms Survey 2007: Guns and the City. Geneva: Graduate Institute of International Studies, 2007. http://www.smallarmssurvey.org/files/sas/publications /yearb2007.html.

Smutt, Marcela, and Jenny Lissette E. Miranda. *El fenómeno de las pandillas en El Salvador.* San Salvador, El Salvador: United Nations Children's Fund (UNICEF) and Facultad Latinoamericana de Ciencias Sociales (FLACSO), 1998.

Soares, Luiz Eduardo. *Meu casaco de general: Quinhentos dias no Front da Segurança Pública.* São Paulo: Companhia das Letras, 2000.

"Solo 25% de homicidios atribuido a las pandillas." *La Prensa Gráfica,* 23 November 2007.

Sosa, Juan José, and José Luis Rocha. "Las pandillas en Nicaragua." In Equipo de Reflexión, Investigación y Comunicación (ERIC), Instituto de Encuestas y Sondeos de Opinión (IDESO), Instituto de Investigaciones Económicas y Sociales (IDIES), and Instituto Universitario de Opinión Pública (IUDOP), eds., *Maras y pandillas en Centroamérica*, vol. 1, 335–430. Managua: UCA Publicaciones, 2001.

Steward, Charles. "Member of Salvadoran Gang MS-13 Caught Here Last Week (Bee County, Texas)." *Bee-Picayune*, reprinted at *Free Republic* (blog), 3 July 2005. http://www.freerepublic.com/focus/f-news/1435817/posts.

Strocka, Cordula. "Youth Gangs in Latin America." *SAIS Review* 26, no. 2 (Summer–Fall 2006): 133–146.

Sullivan, John P. "Maras Morphing: Revisiting Third Generation Gangs." *Global Crime* 7, no. 3–4 (August–November 2006): 487–504.

———. "Transnational Gangs: The Impact of Third Generation Gangs in Central America." *Air and Space Power Journal* (1 July 2008).

Svendsen, Kristin. "Detenciones y procesos legales por el delito de posesión para el consumo en Guatemala." *El Observador Judicial* (Instituto de Estudios Comparados de Ciencias Penales de Guatemala [ICCPG]) 8, no. 56 (May–June 2005).

Swecker, Chris. Testimony. In *Gangs and Crime in Latin America: Hearing before the Subcommittee on the Western Hemisphere of the Committee on International Relations, U.S. House of Representatives*, 109th Cong., 1st sess., 20 April 2005.

Tarnoff, Curt, and Marian Leonardo Lawson. *Foreign Aid: An Introduction to U.S. Programs and Policy*. Congressional Research Service (CRS) Report for Congress, R40213, 9 April 2009.

Thale, Geoff. "International Assistance in Responding to Youth Gang Violence in CA." Memorandum. Washington Office on Latin America (WOLA), Washington, DC, 30 September 2005. http://www1.american.edu/councils/ameri cas/Documents/GangViolence/international_coop_memo.pdf.

Thale, Geoff, and Elsa Falkenburger. *Youth Gangs in Central America: Issues on Human Rights, Effective Policing, and Prevention*. Washington Office on Latin America (WOLA) Special Report. Washington, DC: WOLA, 2006.

Thornberry, Terence, and Marvon Krohn. "The Self-Report Method for Measuring Delinquency and Crime." In D. Duffee, ed., *Measurement and Analysis of Crime and Justice*, vol. 4, 33–83. Washington, DC: U.S. National Institute of Justice, 2000.

Tilly, Charles. "War Making and State Making as Organized Crime." In P. Evans, D. Rueschemeyer, and T. Skocpol, eds., *Bringing the State Back*, 169–187. Cambridge: Cambridge University Press, 1985.

Torres-Rivas, Edelberto. *Centroamérica: Entre revoluciones y democracia*. Bogotá: Consejo Latinoamericano de Ciencias Sociales (CLACSO) Coediciones, 2008.

———. *La piel de Centroamérica*. San José, Costa Rica: Facultad Latinoamericana de Ciencias Sociales (FLACSO), 2007.

Tutela Legal. *La situación de los derechos humanos en El Salvador: Informe anual de Tutela Legal del Arzobispado de San Salvador 2006–2007*. San Salvador, El Salvador: Tutela Legal, 2006–2008.

United Nations, Comisión Económica para América Latina y el Caribe (CEPAL). *Anuario Estadístico de América Latina y el Caribe, 2009*. CEPAL, 2010. http://www.eclac.org.

United Nations Convention on the Rights of the Child (UNCRC), 36th Session.

"Consideration of Reports Submitted by States Parties under Article 44 of the Convention: Concluding Observations; El Salvador." CRC/C/15/Add.232. New York: United Nations, 30 June 2004.

United Nations Development Programme (UNDP). *Human Development Report 2005: International Cooperation at a Crossroads; Aid, Trade and Security in an Unequal World.* New York: UNDP, 2005. http://hdr.undp.org/en/reports/global /hdr2005/.

———. *UN Human Development Indices: A Statistical Update 2008.* http://hdr .undp.org/en/statistics/.

United Nations Human Rights Council (UNHCR). *Los derechos civiles y políticos, en particular las cuestiones relacionadas con las desapariciones y ejecuciones sumarias: Informe del relator especial, Philip Alston, sobre las ejecuciones extrajudiciales, sumarias o arbitrarias; Misión a Guatemala 21 a 25 de agosto de 2006.* A/HRC/4/20 /Add.2. UNHCR, 19 February 2007. English version available at http://www .universalhumanrightsindex.org/documents/841/1077/document/en/text .html.

United Nations Office on Drugs and Crime (UNODC). *Crime and Development in Central America: Caught in the Crossfire.* Mexico City: UNODC, 2007.

———. "Executive Summary." In *World Drug Report 2007*, 7–21. New York: UNODC, 2007. http://www.unodc.org/unodc/en/data-and-analysis/WDR-2007.html.

———. *The Threat of Narco-Trafficking in the Americas.* Mexico City: UNODC, 2008.

U.S. Agency for International Development (USAID), Bureau for Latin American and Caribbean Affairs, Office of Regional Sustainable Development. *Central America and Mexico Gang Assessment.* Washington, DC: USAID, April 2006. http://www.usaid.gov/locations/latin_america_caribbean/democracy /gangs_cam.pdf.

U.S. Congress. House of Representatives. *Deportees in Latin America and the Caribbean: Hearing and Briefing before the Subcommittee on the Western Hemisphere of the Committee of Foreign Affairs, House of Representatives*, 110th Cong., 1st sess., 24 July 2007.

U.S. Department of Homeland Security, Office of Immigration Statistics. "Aliens Removed by Criminal Status and Region and Country of Nationality: Fiscal Years 1998–2007." Table 37 in *2007 Yearbook of Immigration Statistics.* Washington, DC: U.S. Department of Homeland Security, Office of Immigration Statistics, 2008.

U.S. Department of Justice. "Fact Sheet: Department of Justice Comprehensive Efforts to Fight Gang Violence." 24 June 2008. http://www.justice.gov/opa /pr/2008/June/08-ag-562.html.

———. "Twenty-six Members of MS-13 Indicted on Racketeering, Narcotics, Extortion and Firearms Charges." Press release, 24 June 2008. http://www .justice.gov/opa/pr/2008/June/08-ag-564.html.

U.S. Department of State, Bureau of Democracy, Human Rights, and Labor. *Guatemala.* 2005 Country Reports on Human Rights Practices, 8 March 2006, http://www.state.gov/g/drl/rls/hrrpt/2005/61729.htm.

————. *Honduras*. 2005 Country Reports on Human Rights Practices, 8 March 2006. http://www.state.gov/g/drl/rls/hrrpt/2005/61732.htm.

————. *Honduras*. 2006 Country Reports on Human Rights Practices, 6 March 2007. http://www.state.gov/g/drl/rls/hrrpt/2006/78896.htm.

————. *Honduras*. 2007 Country Reports on Human Rights Practices, 11 March 2008. http://www.state.gov/g/drl/rls/hrrpt/2007/100644.htm.

————. *2008 Human Rights Report: El Salvador*. Washington, DC, 2009. http://www.state.gov/g/drl/rls/hrrpt/2008/wha/119159.htm.

U.S. Department of State, Bureau of International Narcotics and Law Enforcement Affairs. "Merida Initiative: Myth vs. Fact." Fact sheet, 23 June 2009. http://www.state.gov/p/inl/rls/fs/122395.htm.

U.S. Federal Bureau of Investigation (FBI). "Fact Sheet: Department of Justice Efforts to Combat Mexican Drug Cartels." 2 April 2009. http://www.fbi.gov/news/pressrel/press-releases/fact-sheet-department-of-justice-efforts-to-combat-mexican-drug-cartels.

————. "FBI Conducts Training for U.S. and Central American Law Enforcement Partners." Press release, 7 October 2009. http://www.fbi.gov/news/pressrel/press-releases/fbi-conducts-training-for-u.s.-and-central-american-law-enforcement-partners.

————. "Going Global on Gangs: New Partnership Targets MS-13." Announcement, 10 October 2007. http://www.fbi.gov/news/stories/2007/october/ms13tag_101007.

————. "Sharing Intelligence: To Fight Transnational Gangs." Announcement, 11 July 2009. http://www.fbi.gov/news/stories/2009/august/gangs_081109.

————. "United against MS-13." Transcript, n.d. http://www.fbi.gov/news/videos/mp4/callee.mp4/view.

————. "United against MS-13: Our Central American Partnerships." Announcement, 10 November 2009. http://www.fbi.gov/page2/nov09/calee_111009.html.

U.S. Immigration and Customs Enforcement (ICE), Operation Community Shield. "Targeting Violent Transnational Street Gangs." http://www.ice.gov/pi/investigations/comshield/index.htm.

U.S. Office of Management and Budget. "Diplomatic and Consular Programs: Budget for Fiscal Year 2010" (Department of State and Other International Programs, Administration of Foreign Affairs). http://www.whitehouse.gov/omb/budget/fy2010/assets/sta.pdf.

Valdemar, Richard. "Roots of Evil." *Police*, 10 April 2009. http://www.policemag.com/Blog/Gangs/Story/2009/04/Roots-of-Evil.aspx.

Valdez, Al. "California's Most Violent Export." *Streetgangs.com*, 2000. http://www.streetgangs.com/topics/2002/18thexport.html.

————. *Gangs across America*. San Clemente, CA: Law Tech Publishing, 2007.

————. *Gangs: A Guide to Understanding Street Gangs*. San Clemente, CA: Law Tech Publishing, 2005.

————. "Transnational Gangs." Center for Hemispheric Policy, University of Miami, Miami, 2008.

Vargas, Mauricio. "Los niños bien." *Eltiempo.com* (blog), 23 February 2007.

Vasilachis de Gialdino, Irene. "Representations of Young People Associated with Crime in El Salvador's Written Press." *Critical Discourse Studies* 4 (2007): 1–28.

Veash, Nicole. "Children of Privileged Form Brazil Crime Gangs: 'Silver-Spoon' Bandits Target the Wealthy." *Boston Globe*, February 2002. Cited in Covey, *Street Gangs throughout the World*.

Veillette, Connie, Clare Ribando, and Mark Sullivan. *U.S. Foreign Assistance to Latin America and the Caribbean*. Congressional Research Service (CRS) Report for Congress, RL32487, 3 January 2006.

———. *U.S. Foreign Assistance to Latin America and the Caribbean*. Congressional Research Service (CRS) Report, RL32487, 28 March 2006.

———. *U.S. Foreign Assistance to Latin America and the Caribbean: FY2006–FY2008*. Congressional Research Service (CRS) Report, RL34299, 28 December 2007.

Velásquez, Gustavo Sánchez. *Maras, pandillas y desviación social*. Buenos Aires: Editora Dunken, 2008.

Venhuizen, Christian. "Wyoming Army Guard Intel Cracks Gang Code." National Guard Bureau website, 18 June 2008. http://www.ng.mil/news /archives/2008/06/061808-gang-code.aspx.

"'Viejo Lin' fue libre por 30 minutos." *El Diario de Hoy*, 23 May 2004, http://www .elsalvador.com/noticias/2004/05/23/nacional/nac4.asp.

Vigil, James Diego. *A Rainbow of Gangs: Street Cultures in the Mega-City*. Austin: University of Texas Press, 2002.

"La violencia en Medellín." *El Espectador*, 21 April 2009.

"La violencia en Medellín: Un rompecabezas para armar." Agencia de Prensa IPC, 12 May 2009.

"Violencia se ensaña con jóvenes y mujeres." *El Diario de Hoy*, 31 October 2005. http://www.elsalvador.com/noticias/2005/10/31/nacional/nac6.asp.

Waldmann, Peter. *El estado anómico: Derecho, seguridad pública y vida cotidiana en América Latina*. Caracas: Nueva Sociedad, 2003.

Washington Office on Latin America (WOLA). "Gangs in Honduras." In *Central American Gang-Related Asylum: A Resource Guide*, 21–24. Washington, DC: WOLA, May 2008. http://www.wola.org/media/Gangs/WOLA_Gang_ Asylum_Guide.pdf.

Wielandt, Gonzalo. *Hacia la construcción de lecciones del posconflicto en América Latina y el Caribe: Una mirada a la violencia juvenil en Centroamérica*. Comisión Económica para América Latina y el Caribe (CEPAL), Serie Políticas Sociales, no. 115. Santiago, Chile: Naciones Unidas, 2005.

Williams, Phil. "Organizing Transnational Crime: Networks, Markets, and Hierarchies." In Phil Williams and Dimitri Vlassis, eds., *Combating Transnational Crime: Concepts, Activities, and Responses*, 57–88. London: Frank Cass, 2001.

Wilson, Dwight. "Guatemala: A Second Decade of Spring?" In Howard J. Wiarda and Harvey F. Kline, eds., *Latin American Politics and Development*. Boulder, CO: Westview Press, 2007.

Wolf, Sonja. "The Politics of Gang Control: NGO Advocacy in Post-war El Salvador." Ph.D. diss., Aberystwyth University, Wales, 2008.

———. *Propuesta para la prevención de la violencia juvenil en El Salvador*. San Salvador, El Salvador: FESPAD Ediciones, 2007.

Woodward, Ralph Lee. *Central America: A Nation Divided*. 1976; New York: Oxford University Press, 1999.

World Bank. *Honduras Country Brief*. October 2008. http://www.worldbank.org.

———. *Honduras: Country Economic Memorandum/Poverty Assessment*. Report 13317-HO. Washington, DC: World Bank, 17 November 1994.

Youngsters, Colletta A., and Eileen Rosin, eds. *Drugs and Democracy in Latin America: The Impact of U.S. Policy*. Boulder, CO: Lynne Rienner, 2005.

Zilberg, Elana. "Fools Banished from the Kingdom: Remapping Geographies of Gang Violence between the Americas (Los Angeles and San Salvador)." *American Quarterly* 56 (2004): 765–795.

Zinecker, Heidrun. *From Exodus to Exitus: Causes of Post-war Violence in El Salvador*. PRIF Reports, no. 80. Frankfurt: Peace Research Institute Frankfurt, 2007.

———. *Violence in a Homeostatic System: The Case of Honduras*. PRIF Reports, no. 83. Frankfurt: Peace Research Institute Frankfurt, 2008.

———. *Violence in Peace: Form and Causes of Postwar Violence in Guatemala*. PRIF Reports, no. 76. Frankfurt: Peace Research Institute Frankfurt, 2006.

About the Contributors

Editors

THOMAS BRUNEAU is Distinguished Professor of National Security
Affairs at the Naval Postgraduate School, Monterey, California. He
joined the department in 1987 after having taught in the Department
of Political Science at McGill University. After becoming the chair-
man of the Department of National Security Affairs in 1989, he continued in that position until 1995. In November 2000 he became the
director of the Center for Civil-Military Relations, a position he held
until December 2004. Between 1998 and 2001 he served as rapporteur
of the Defense Policy Board that provides the Secretary of Defense
with independent advice on questions of national security and defense
policy. Bruneau has four recently published books. He is coeditor, with
Scott D. Tollefson, of *Who Guards the Guardians and How: Democratic
Civil-Military Relations* (Austin: University of Texas Press, 2006). His
second book, also published by University of Texas Press, is *Reforming Intelligence: Obstacles to Democratic Control and Effectiveness*, coedited
with Commander Steven C. Boraz. His next coedited book, with Harold
Trinkunas, *Global Politics of Defense Reform*, was published by Palgrave
Macmillan in February 2008. His most recent book, *Patriots for Profit:
Contractors and the Military in U.S. National Security*, was published by
Stanford University Press in mid-2011.

LUCÍA DAMMERT was the director of the Security and Citizenship
Program, Latin American Faculty of Social Sciences (FLACSO)—
Chile. She currently works with the Global Consortium on Security
Transformation. She holds a PhD in sociology from the University of

Leiden, Netherlands, a master's degree in urban and regional planning, a specialization certificate in Latin American Studies from the University of Pittsburgh, and a bachelor's degree in sociology from the National University of Cuyo, Argentina. She has worked as a researcher for the Center of Studies on Citizen Security of the University of Chile; Georgetown University; the Woodrow Wilson International Center for Scholars; and the National University of General San Martín, Buenos Aires. She has also been an adviser for several international organizations (such as the Public Security Department of the Organization of American States), national public bodies (Citizen Security Division of the Chilean Ministry of Interior; the Metropolitan Region City Council, Santiago, Chile), and foreign organizations (Public Security Secretariat, Mexico; citizen security consultant for Interior Ministry of Argentina). She has also worked as an adviser for the URB-AL Programme (European Commission) on Citizen Security.

ELIZABETH SKINNER is think tank coordinator and editor in the Strategic Issues and Engagement branch of NATO Allied Command Transformation, Norfolk, Virginia. At the direction of the Supreme Allied Command Transformation (SACT), she works with a team of experts and analysts to prepare reports for publication both within and outside the alliance. Her most recent project is ACT's 2011 report on NATO engagement in the global commons. Prior to coming to ACT, she spent twelve years working as an editor and publications manager, both as a freelancer and in the National Security Affairs Department of the Naval Postgraduate School, Monterey, California. She received her bachelor's degree in Russian studies from the University of California, Santa Cruz, and her master's degree in international policy studies from the Monterey Institute of International Studies.

Authors

ENRIQUE DESMOND ARIAS is an associate professor of political science at the John Jay College of Criminal Justice and a member of the faculty of the Doctoral Program in Criminal Justice at the City University of New York Graduate Center. He is the author of *Drugs and Democracy in Rio de Janeiro: Trafficking, Social Networks, and Public Security* (Chapel Hill: University of North Carolina Press, 2006), as well as articles in the *Journal of Latin American Studies*, *Qualitative Sociology*, *Latin American Politics and Society*, and *Comparative Politics*.

JOSÉ MIGUEL CRUZ is a visiting assistant professor at the Department of Politics and International Relations, Florida International University. He has been director of the University Institute of Public Opinion at the Central American University (IUDOP-UCA) in San Salvador and has conducted several research projects on Central American gangs since 1996.

CLIFFORD GYVES is a special agent with the Air Force Office of Special Investigations (AFOSI), currently serving as the liaison to the National Guard Bureau in the National Capitol Region. Lieutenant Colonel Gyves has master's degrees in East Asian studies and homeland security and defense, with specialized training and work experience in criminal and fraud investigations, counterintelligence, and antiterrorism. Over the course of his career, he has served in Latin America, Korea, and Afghanistan and has taught AFOSI students at the Federal Law Enforcement Training Center. He is currently authoring a book on adapting intelligence methodologies for domestic law enforcement application to antiterrorism. His publications include "Algerian Groupe Salafiste de la Predication et le Combat (Salafi Group for Call and Combat, GSPC): An Operational Analysis" (with Major Chris Wyckoff, USAF), *Strategic Insights* 5, no. 8 (November 2006); and "What Is a Terrorist Network?" in *Proceedings of the Second Annual International Conference on Networking and Electronic Commerce (NAEC) Research* (October 2006).

FLORINA CRISTIANA MATEI is a lecturer at the Center for Civil-Military Relations (CCMR) at the Naval Postgraduate School (NPS), Monterey, California. She joined the center in 2003 after having worked for the Romanian Ministry of Defense as a civilian subject matter expert. She has researched, published, and lectured on a wide range of issues concerning democratization of civil-military relations (including security sector reform, defense institution building, private security contractors, and reforming intelligence in a democracy), as well as countering/combating terrorism and organized crime, for CCMR's resident and nonresident programs and international conferences, as well as in support of NPS National Security Affairs master's courses. She holds a master's degree in international security affairs and civil-military relations from the NPS (2001) and a bachelor's degree in physics (nuclear interactions and elementary particles) from the University of Bucharest, Romania (1996). Her most recent publications include "Toward a New Conceptualization of Civil-Military Relations" (with Thomas Bruneau), in *Democratization*, 2008; "National Security Councils: Their Potential Functions in Democratic Civil-Military Relations" (with Thomas Bruneau and Sak Sakoda), in *Defense and Security Analysis*, 2009; and "Romania's Transition to Democracy: The Role of the Press in Intelligence Reform," in *Reforming Intelligence: Obstacles to Democratic Control and Effectiveness* (University of Texas Press, 2007).

JOANNA MATEO serves as the human rights analyst with the Human Rights Division at the U.S. Southern Command in Miami, Florida. Previously she was the senior policy analyst with the Western Hemisphere Security Analysis Center, a partnership between Florida International University and the U.S. Southern Command. She also served as the associate editor of *World Link* in London, England, the international politics and business magazine of the World Economic Forum. She has conducted extensive research and policy analysis and has authored and contributed to numerous articles on politics and security and development issues in Latin America. She holds a master's degree from the Johns Hopkins University School of Advanced International Studies and was a Fulbright Scholar to Argentina.

ELIN CECILIE RANUM carried out the research for her chapter in this volume when she worked as a researcher at the Institute of Public Opinion at the Central American University "José Simeón Cañas" in San Salvador (IUDOP-UCA). As the former director of the Central American Coalition for the Prevention of Youth Violence and an associate expert at the United Nations Office on Drugs and Crime in Mexico, she has several years of experience with youth gangs, crime, violence, and public security issues in Central America. She holds a master's degree in Latin American studies from the Institute of Latin American Studies of the University of London. She is currently working as program coordinator for Central America in the Development Fund, a Norwegian nongovernmental organization.

JOSÉ LUIS ROCHA is a senior researcher at the Central American University (UCA) in Managua, Nicaragua, and an associate researcher with the Brooks World Poverty Institute at the University of Manchester. His work focuses on issues relating to youth gangs, local government, disaster prevention and management, the coffee industry, and migration. He is a member of the editorial committees of the academic journals *Envío* and *Encuentro* and is also the research coordinator of the Central American Jesuit Service for Migrants. His publications include the bilingual Spanish/English books *Central Americans Redefining the Borders/ Centroamericanos redefiniendo las fronteras* (Envío, 2008) and *Una región desgarrada: Dinámicas migratorias en Centroamérica/A Region Torn Apart: The Dynamics of Migration in Central America* (San José, Costa Rica: Lara Segura, 2006); "Understanding the Logic of Nicaraguan Juvenile Justice," in *Youth Violence in Latin America: Gangs and Juvenile Justice in Perspective* (New York: Palgrave Macmillan, 2009); "Mapping the Labyrinth from Within: The Political Economy of Nicaraguan Youth Policy Concerning Violence," *Bulletin of Latin American Research* 27, no. 4 (2007): 533–549; and (with Ian Christoplos) "Disaster Mitigation and Preparedness on the Nicaraguan Post-Mitch Agenda," *Disasters* 25, no. 3 (2001): 240–250. His most recent works on youth gangs are *Lanzando piedras, fumando piedras: Evolución de las pandillas en Nicaragua 1997–2006* (Managua: UCA Publicaciones, 2007); and (with Dennis Rodgers) *Gangs of Central America* (Managua: Envío-UCA, 2008).

MAURICIO RUBIO is a doctoral candidate in economics at Harvard University and holds a DEA in sociology at Universidad Complutense de Madrid. His current affiliation is with Universidad Externado de Colombia. As a consultant for the Inter-American Development Bank he coordinated the application of self-report surveys among gang members and a control group of students in Honduras, Nicaragua, Panama, and the Dominican Republic. Reflecting his research interests, his publications include "Ni puta ni trabajadora sexual: Prostituta," *Borradores de Método* 51 (2008); "Palomas y sankis: Prostitución adolescente en Republica Dominicana," Documento de Trabajo 25, Facultad de Economía, Universidad Externado de Colombia (2008); and *De la pandilla y la mara: Pobreza, educación, mujeres y violencia juvenil* (Bogotá: Universidad Externado de Colombia, 2007).

AL VALDEZ is currently a professor at the University of California, Irvine, after retiring in April 2006 from the Orange County District Attorney's Office, where he was the Gang Unit supervisor. He has over twenty-eight years of law enforcement experience, with special emphasis on narcotic and gang investigations, undercover field operations, and multiagency task forces and prosecutions. He has written more than eighty articles and published seven books on gang histories, customs and practices, and related issues. His latest book, the fifth edition of *Gangs: A Guide to Understanding Street Gangs*, was released in August 2009 by Law Tech Publishing, San Clemente, California.

SONJA WOLF is a postdoctoral researcher at the National Autonomous University of Mexico, where she studies street gangs and drug trafficking in Mexico and Central America. Previously she was a research fellow at Mexico City's ITAM, where she explored the transnational dimension of Central American street gangs. She has published in the *Journal of Latin American Studies*, *Foreign Affairs Latinoamérica*, and the *Latin American Research Review* and is currently preparing a research monograph on street gangs and gang control in El Salvador. She holds a PhD in international politics from Aberystwyth University, where she completed a dissertation on El Salvador's Mano Dura gang policies and NGO strategies aimed at advocating alternative forms of gang control.

Index

military groups in, 131, 170; self-report survey in, 162
common operating picture, 192
Congress, U.S., 202–203, 208, 214
Contra war, 54, 90, 110, 125, 259
COP. *See* crime-oriented policing (COP)
corruption: in Brazil, 128–129; and criminal justice generally, 9; in El Salvador, 55, 56, 153–154; and gang activities, 128–130; in Guatemala, 17, 130, 153–154; in Honduras, 17, 153–154; in Mexico, 128–129; in Nicaragua, 116, 129–130, 133, 154; police corruption, 17, 55, 56, 68, 69, 129–130, 133, 153–154
Costa Rica, 6, 7, 13, 108, 113
counteractivity analysis (CAA), 187–188
countergroup analysis (CGA), 187–191
crack cocaine, 27, 40, 45, 50, 67
crime: aggravated felony defined, 198; demographic, social, and economic vulnerabilities to, 9; and displacement and deportation, 9–10, 13–14, 43, 49, 206–207, 209, 234n20, 256n36; in El Salvador, 11–12, 43, 48–53, 64, 140; by female gang members, 32; in Guatemala, 77–78, 83–86, 133–134; in Honduras, 88, 94, 95–97, 148, 207; and limited capacity for criminal justice, 9; in Los Angeles, 3, 28, 30, 32, 39, 41; by *maras* generally, 11–12, 23, 37, 183–184; media on, 37; in Nicaragua, 133–134, 152; and popular fear in Central America, 133–135; and poverty, 8, 9; and transnational gangs, 36–41; UN report on Central America's vulnerability to, 7–10; by upper-class gang members, 167–172, 179. *See also* drug trade; extortion; homicides; human trafficking; rape; robberies; violence
crime-oriented policing (COP), 190
criminal justice system: in Central

America generally, 9; in Colombia, 172; and corruption generally, 9; in El Salvador, 16, 17–18, 64–65; in Guatemala, 18, 79–80, 111–112, 144; in Honduras, 18, 96–101, 144; in Nicaragua, 144; and police corruption, 17, 55, 56, 68, 69, 129–130, 133, 153–154. *See also* police; prisons and prisoners
Cristiani, Alfredo, 56, 149
Cruz, José Miguel, 2, 11, 16, 137–157, 190, 213, 215, 216, 293
Customs and Border Protection, U.S., 200

Dammert, Lucía, 211–217, 291–292
death squads, 55, 90, 130
Defense Department, U.S., 202, 214
democradura, 259
democratic consolidation in Central America, 6–10, 109–110
deportation by United States: and boomerang effect, 38–39, 205–206; and crime in Central America, 9–10, 13–14, 43, 49, 206–207, 209, 212; criminal history of deportees, 206, 256n36; to El Salvador, 14, 38, 43, 48, 48–49, 108, 109, 205–207; of gang members to Central America, 30, 82, 205–207, 234n20; and globalization of violent urban gang culture generally, 23, 24, 42; to Guatemala, 74, 127; to Honduras, 14, 93–96, 103, 205–207; and *maras* in Central America, 9–10, 13–14, 23, 139, 205–207, 209, 212; media on, 206, 207; of Nicaraguans, 108–109; statistics on, 14, 30, 38, 108, 109, 254n8; and Three Strikes and You're Out law, 198
dress code, 44, 47, 63, 98, 99, 106, 143
Drug Enforcement Agency, U.S., 11, 39, 142
drug trade: in Central America generally, 8, 11–12, 95–96; and cocaine, 3, 40, 56, 67, 68, 77, 95, 106, 107, 135, 215; in Colombia, 57, 67, 123;

213, 215; in Nicaragua, 133–134; and protection rackets, 152; and state power, 123
Ortega, Daniel, 130, 244n5

palabrero (leader), 63
Panama, 7, 37, 113, 162–172, 252n33, 254n10
pandillas (street gangs): characteristics of, 3, 113–114, 164; and citizens' perceptions of insecurity, 164–166; compared with *maras*, 164; definition of, 1, 2, 260; elite membership of, 167–172, 179; in El Salvador, 45; in Honduras, 88, 96, 109; in Nicaragua, 1, 13, 106–107, 113–120, 125–126, 129–130, 164
pandillero, 260
Plan Escoba (Operation Broom), 16, 79–80, 132, 146, 237n48, 260
Plan Guardian, 17
police: in Brazil, 128–129; corruption among, 17, 55, 56, 68, 69, 129–130, 133; crime-oriented policing (COP), 190; and death squads, 55, 130; and drug trade, 129; in El Salvador, 11–12, 15–18, 43, 45–46, 52, 55–56, 64, 65, 68, 69, 143, 147–150, 153–155, 199, 201, 216; extralegal violence against gangs ("social cleansing") by, 13, 83–85, 98, 117, 130, 153–155; in Guatemala, 17, 72, 73, 76, 79–80, 83–85, 130, 135, 147, 149, 150, 153–155, 199, 237n48, 238n67; in Honduras, 16, 17, 18, 89, 91, 96–98, 101, 149, 150, 153–155; joint police-military anti-gang squads, 17, 58, 98; in Mexico, 128; in Nicaragua, 13, 106–107, 114–119, 129–132, 135, 141, 142, 144–145, 147, 149, 150, 154; torture by, 55; training of, 100, 199, 200, 208, 214–215, 253n1, 258n50; trust in, 149, 150
Portillo, Alfonso, 146, 147
poverty: in Central America, 7, 8, 9, 11, 75, 87, 92, 93, 99, 102, 209; in Los Angeles, 93; violence and

crime associated with, 8, 9, 92, 171–172
prisons and prisoners: and drug cartels, 23, 24; in El Salvador, 18, 46–47, 57, 220n25, 250n64; gang organization and recruitment in prisons, 155–156, 216; gangs in prisons generally, 34; in Guatemala, 12, 79–82, 144, 235n34, 250n64; in Honduras, 16, 98, 101, 143–144, 154, 250n64; and Mano Dura (Strong Hand) policies, 153, 155; Mexican Mafia prison gang, 3, 24, 27–30, 32, 33; in Nicaragua, 12, 118, 144; policies on gang members in prison, 250n64; sentences for gang members, 16, 18, 31–32; in United States, 198, 214; violence in prisons, 81–82, 98, 151, 154

Ranum, Elin Cecilie, 5, 12, 14, 16, 71–86, 126, 130, 132, 139, 215–216, 294
rape, 3, 36, 54, 56, 172–179, 259
Reagan, Ronald, 13, 48, 127
rehabilitation programs. *See* gang prevention and rehabilitation
renta, la. See extortion
Repatriation-Criminal History Information Program (CHIP), 200, 201
robberies, 44, 45, 48, 50, 55, 56, 64, 83, 84, 88, 96
Rocha Gómez, José Luis, 5, 13–14, 105–120, 125, 129, 141, 142, 144–145, 216, 294–295
Rubio, Mauricio, 2, 4, 5, 12, 15, 159–179, 216, 252n33, 295

Saca, Elias Antonio, 15, 59, 60–61, 148, 149
Salinas, Calif., 212, 222–223n38
Salvadoran immigrants, 25–26, 33, 48, 92, 108
Sandinista National Liberation Front (FSLN), 6, 13, 105, 110, 112, 115, 119, 125–126, 127, 130
Santacruz Giralt, Maria L., 78

Secretaría de la Juventud (El Salvador), 260
security: citizen security, 14–15, 106, 115, 116; citizens' perceptions of insecurity in Central America, 53, 59, 60, 69, 83, 97, 99–100, 135, 164–166, 240n25; national security, 14–15, 106; phases of security policies in El Salvador, 140–141; public security, 14–15
self-report surveys, 5, 160–169
sexing-in initiation rite, 35, 175
sexualized violence. *See* rape
shot callers (gang elites), 35, 260
SICA, 199, 202, 254n10
sicariato and *sicarios* (contract killing), 18, 43, 260
Skinner, Elizabeth, 292
social class: of gang members, 44, 167–172, 179; and rape, 172–176
"social cleansing": in El Salvador, 52, 111, 154–155, 216; in Guatemala, 9, 76, 84, 85, 117, 130, 154–155; in Honduras, 9, 98–99, 154–155; by police, 13, 83–85, 98, 112, 130, 153–155; and upper-class adolescents, 169–170
social network analysis, 5, 187–191
soldado (one who executes assigned missions), 63
Somoza, Anastasio, 54, 105, 125, 126
State Department, U.S., 87, 154, 199–200, 208
state power: and Central American *maras*, 123–138; and criminal structures in Latin America, 124–127; and policy choices in propagating *maras*, 131–133; popular fear and crime in Central America, 133–135. *See also specific countries*
street gangs. *See pandillas* (street gangs)
Strong Hand policies. *See* Mano Dura (Strong Hand)
sur (south), 29–30, 260
Sureños, 27–30, 32, 189, 222n29, 223n38. *See also* Mexican Mafia; MS-13 (Mara Salvatrucha)

"tags" and "taggers," 31, 33
TAG units, 200, 201, 205
tattoos, 29–30, 44, 47, 63, 95, 98, 99, 105, 134, 143, 146–147, 195
terrorism and terrorism prevention, 1, 4, 159, 167, 192, 193, 194, 213
testigos criteriados (offender as witness in different case), 64–65
Three Strikes and You're Out law, 198
transeros (drug dealers), 67–68
Transnational Anti-Gang Center, 247n19
Transnational Anti-Gang (TAG) units, 200, 201, 205
"Transnational Youth Gangs" survey (2006), 78, 80, 82, 85
trencito (gang rape), 3, 175, 259
turf-oriented gangs, 33, 36

United Nations: Committee on the Rights of the Child, 59; crime vulnerability report by, 7–10; on deportees and gang problem in Central America, 207; Development Programme of, 83, 148; on drug trade, 40, 57; Human Development Reports by, 7, 75–76; on Ley Antimaras (Anti-gang Law, or LAM), 59; Office on Drugs and Crime, 83, 207; on organized crime in El Salvador, 52; on "social cleansing" in Guatemala, 84–85; *World Drug Report* by, 39–40
United States: anti-gang policies of, in Central America, 197–210, 213–214; Central American policies of, 90–92, 197–210; foreign aid by, 204; gang intelligence projects in, 194–195; gang prevention and rehabilitation in, 217; Guatemalan immigrants in, 108, 126–127; Honduran immigrants in, 92–96, 108; illegal drug use in, 40, 56, 77, 78; immigration policies of, 30, 38, 48–49, 93–95, 126–127, 194, 205–207; Nicaraguan immigrants in, 108–109, 127; Salvadoran im-